M000234852

GAME CHANGER

How **Strategic Pricing** Shapes Businesses, Markets, and Society

Jean-Manuel Izaret & Arnab Sinha
Global Leaders of the BCG Pricing Practice

Published by John Wiley & Sons, Inc., Hoboken, New Jersey.
Published simultaneously in Canada.

For general information on our other products and services or for technical support, please contact our Customer Care Department within the United States at (800) 762-2974, outside the United States at (317) 572-3993 or fax (317) 572-4002.

Wiley also publishes its books in a variety of electronic formats. Some content that appears in print may not be available in electronic formats. For more information about Wiley products, visit our web site at www.wiley.com.

Library of Congress Cataloging-in-Publication Data

Names: Izaret, Jean-Manuel, author. | Sinha, Arnab, author.
Title: Game changer : how strategic pricing shapes businesses,
  markets, and society / Jean-Manuel Izaret, Arnab Sinha.
Description: First edition. | Hoboken, New Jersey : Wiley, [2024] |
  Includes index.
Identifiers: LCCN 2023025590 (print) | LCCN 2023025591 (ebook) | ISBN
  9781394190584 (cloth) | ISBN 9781394190607 (adobe pdf) | ISBN
  9781394190591 (epub)
Subjects: LCSH: Pricing. | Strategic planning. | Consumer behavior. | Game
  theory.
Classification: LCC HF5416.5 .I943 2024 (print) | LCC HF5416.5 (ebook) |
  DDC 658.8/16—dc23/eng/20230721
LC record available at https://lccn.loc.gov/2023025590
LC ebook record available at https://lccn.loc.gov/2023025591

Cover Design: BCG BrightHouse
Author Photos: Elijah Ellis & Lauren Janney

SKY10054242_082923

To our parents (Christiane, Pierre, Rita, and Tuhin), for the intellectual curiosity and rigor they fostered and the sense of collective responsibility and empathy they exemplified.

To our families (Christine, Axel, Ernest, Varsha, Arjun, and Saahil), for the joy and pride they bring us every day and for their tolerance for the enormous space the book took in our lives.

Contents

INTRODUCTION

Changing the Pricing Conversation

Companies, governments, and individuals make countless price decisions every day, because every commercial transaction involves a price. The collective sum of the value they exchange represents not only the size of the world economy – estimated at roughly $100 trillion per year – but also all of the decisions about how that "pie" gets divvied up.[1] Prices are the numerical shorthand that allows the transacting parties to make quick, easy comparisons to other transactions and gives them trust and confidence that the money exchanged represents a fair trade.

That's why business executives and economists acknowledge that prices play a critical role in markets and society. But the current conversation around pricing – as expressed in economics textbooks, anecdotal "war stories," political discourse, and the backs of cocktail napkins – makes it easy to believe that pricing is nothing more than a technical, tactical, and, for most people, boring game based on four premises:

1. **Zero sum:** Think of your price as a position on a slider bar of fixed length. The more you charge, the less the other party gets, and vice versa.

2. **Value extraction:** Given a zero-sum scenario, sellers have a natural and strong incentive to extract the maximum value, and buyers strive to strike the best bargains. Neither party wants to leave money on the table.

3. **Static:** Demand, customer needs, willingness to pay, capacity, and competition are all given. Markets set prices, whether guided by

Adam Smith's invisible hand or other interpretations of collective action. Your only incentive is to act and react to earn what you can within those constraints.

4. **Numbers:** The goal for every seller is always to find the "right" price. This elusive quest for the perfect number focuses an organization's energy on analytical methods, each more sophisticated than the last. But no number is ever "right" for more than a few microseconds, because every factor is always in flux.

We think that this game and its underlying premises are myopic. It is important for business leaders to step back and look at two things: the choices they make before they set prices and the real-life consequences their prices have on businesses, markets, and societal outcomes. This strategic perspective about pricing expands the degrees of freedom that business leaders can use to reshape their pricing models and enhance their competitive advantages. Customers, in turn, can do much more than simply evaluate whether the prices they pay are cheap or expensive, relative to the value they receive. They can pay attention to the seller's pricing structure and decide whether it aligns with how they derive value.

Our mission with *Game Changer: How Strategic Pricing Shapes Businesses, Markets, and Society* is to change the game of pricing, literally and figuratively. We will expose the dangerous flaws behind the prevailing pricing "game," because there is too much at stake to let misperceptions about pricing persist. But our larger and more important mission is to show you, step by step, how the right pricing strategy can change the entire trajectory of your business, your industry, and, in many cases, society as well.

To change the conversation around pricing, let's start by refuting the flawed premises behind the current game of pricing. When you read the four new perspectives below, notice how the incentives and tradeoffs have changed. Notice how they create new opportunities and open more degrees of freedom for you to pursue them.

1. **Collaborative growth, not zero sum:** Before wondering about your position on that zero-sum slider bar, you need to decide what variable calibrates it. Prices are expressed as an amount per unit, but the choice of unit can incentivize buyers and sellers to work collaboratively as opposed to against each other. The standard pricing unit in the music industry, for example, was per album or per song, until streaming services led a shift to pricing per person per month. This shift reversed a long decline in industry revenues. The International

Federation of the Phonographic Industry (IFPI) reported that global recorded music revenues grew for the eighth consecutive year in 2022 to $26.2 billion – a level not seen in absolute dollar terms since 1999 – after having bottomed out at $13.1 billion in 2014. Streaming – a revenue source that barely existed at all 15 years ago – accounted for two-thirds of overall revenue,[2] and revenue from physical formats such as vinyl grew as well. Consumers were willing to listen to more music and spend more on this category, but the old pricing unit had been constraining volume and overall market size. Pricing is your means to create and align incentives, grow your market, and escape the high–low constraints of a zero-sum mentality.

2. **Value sharing, not value extraction:** When you view pricing as a way to share value rather than extract it, you foster a sense of fairness and give customers incentives to try and then reuse your offerings. By balancing how and when to share value, you also create opportunities to scale your business massively and quickly and then retain or upsell loyal customers over the course of a long relationship, not a transactional one. The question *"How much money should we leave on the table?"* is no longer heretical. It becomes an essential strategic question for every business leader.

3. **Dynamic, not static:** Demand, customer needs, willingness to pay, capacity, and competition are fluid and dynamic, not given. This helps explain why startups can successfully innovate and change markets by introducing new pricing models. Google reshaped the advertising industry by using auctions to sell advertising inventory. Salesforce.com revolutionized the software sector and created growth opportunities for its customers by selling software as a service. Uber created a new mobility business by charging by the ride rather than flat rates for the mile and minute.

4. **Strategy, not numbers:** No matter how many data scientists or advanced algorithms you deploy in the quest for optimal prices, the numbers aren't helpful unless you have the right pricing models in place. A pricing model is the manifestation of your pricing strategy, a set of choices that aligns incentives across your entire business, both in the market and within your organization. These choices include defining the offer itself, the pricing basis, and how to determine and adjust prices as market conditions change. Business leaders need to make all of these choices before they ever set a price.

This new way to talk about pricing – eagerly, comfortably, and, above all, strategically – is long overdue. It takes pricing out of your company's boiler room and places it in the boardroom, where it belongs. It allows pricing to inform and determine corporate strategy, rather than serve it, because it motivates vision and structure, not the myopic quest for better price points.

No matter how future markets around the world evolve, pricing will remain the common business challenge that every executive and manager must address. Every commercial transaction involves an exchange of value, and the amounts of money involved – for better or worse – are the direct results of strategic pricing decisions the seller makes long before the transaction takes place.

We define a pricing strategy as a business leader's conscious decisions on how to shape their market by determining the amount of money available, how that money flows, and to whom. It reflects the company's philosophy on how to acquire, retain, and satisfy customers by sharing value with them fairly. How much a company can share depends on the characteristics of their market and how they choose to play in that market with their competitive advantages. How much value a business leader wants to share depends on the company's short- and long-term objectives. The choices of sharing method and model reflect how they want to use the pricing agency at their disposal.

Those decisions will shape not only your own business, but your market and society as well. In the following three examples, none of the business leaders or companies could have made their choices within the constraints of zero-sum, value extraction, static, and number mentalities. We found in our work with thousands of companies that this strategic perspective can add points of margin and growth to almost any business. In our work with social ventures the impact can multiply their reach. The strategic view of pricing we introduce in this book is what makes their changes possible.

How pricing strategy shapes a business

Imagine that you are planning a large function such as a wedding or a graduation party. Several caterers offer you quotes, and you choose the one that best fits your plans and budget.

But how do caterers arrive at their prices? Most use the "cost-plus" method, the world's oldest and still most widely used way to set a price.[3] They sum up their costs – for food and drink, preparation, delivery, and service – and then add their desired profit margin.

Judgment then comes into play, because the caterers want to avoid the high–low anxiety of zero-sum pricing. Strong demand may boost their confidence to nudge prices higher, while weak demand may lead them to cut prices to get cash to cover themselves and their fixed costs. Ultimately, they settle on a price that represents the safest compromise.

How can the caterers escape this anxiety? It may sound paradoxical, but an experienced caterer in the western US named Mark escaped it by focusing on upside opportunities in ways that are *less risky* for his business over time than making safe compromises. Instead of being everything to everybody at whatever price he can negotiate, he formulated a pricing strategy by making conscious choices about how to shape demand, share value, and design his prices.

He started by rethinking how he creates value to meet his customers' needs. That is an easy statement to make, but it's little more than pricing pixie dust without a way to apply it. The caterer's customers want the best fit to the venue, the menu, the desired level of refinement in food preparation, and the nature and length of service. Each of these requirements will vary significantly across different types of customers. Some customers will have fixed budgets, while others can afford to spend more, perhaps because they will ask attendees to participate financially in the event.

Based on what he learned, Mark decided how to use these variations to his own advantage. What imbalances will allow him to play to his strengths, by aligning what he does best with the customers who want that kind of service? Knowing that allowed him to craft a few packages with different options, with a fixed price per either event or person. That fixed price – which can include some allowance for changes within a similar range of menu items or service level – offered more certainty to customers with a fixed budget and avoided the hassle of change orders.

Academics, consultants, and other observers often refer to this approach as "value-based pricing." But that phrase grossly oversimplifies what Mark could now accomplish. His new pricing strategy went far beyond the numbers. It changed every aspect of his business, from procurement to marketing to sales to staffing. It also changed the level of ambition he could pursue. Catering is a business with few barriers to entry, so margins can be thin. A value-based pricing approach increased the predictability and stability of his business, both on the volume side (thanks to higher win rates) and on the profitability side.

How pricing strategy shapes an industry

Carriers in the cellular service industry face frequent "innovate or die" challenges. Over the past few decades, they have survived the transition from analog to digital, the launch of the iPhone, and the successive introduction of next-generation technologies from (so far) 2G to 5G.

To encourage customers to join their networks, carriers once subsidized the adoption of new mobile devices in exchange for the predictable revenue stream of a contract, typically lasting two years. But this stability – and the carriers' profits – came under threat when global spending on phone subsidies ballooned by an estimated 40% to $48.5 billion per year between 2009 and 2011, thanks to the introduction of more expensive smartphones.[4,5]

The prevailing pricing model also posed a threat to carriers' profits. Churn rates spiked for customer cohorts reaching the end of their two-year contracts, because customers had strong incentives to shop around for another subsidized device. Why should they keep paying the same monthly amount when they had already amortized the cost of a device that was likely obsolete anyway? Churn substantially reduced customer lifetime value and forced carriers to increase their already high levels of spending on new customer acquisition.

These dynamics changed in June 2012, when Verizon reshaped the market by changing the pricing model from uniform individual plans to plans that bundled devices, minutes, messages, and data allowance under one household account with one bill.[6] The "Share Everything Plan" gave customers a strong incentive to stay with the same carrier, because the hassle of coordinating among family members would outweigh the benefits of switching.

AT&T launched a similar bundle in August 2012.[7] Sprint and T-Mobile initially resisted, but eventually launched their own shared data plans in 2014.[8] One year after introduction, their average monthly churn rates for postpaid contracts decreased by 64 basis points and 19 basis points, respectively.[9,10]

The extent and impact of bundling in the telecommunications industry goes well beyond family plans for cellular service. In Europe, mobile and fixed-line offerings started converging under one bill in the early 2010s. Spain's Telefónica saw the penetration of its fixed-mobile bundle increase from 16% in 2013 to 48% in 2017, and its churn rates fall by half.[11,12] Average revenue per user (ARPU) for the bundle rose by around 25% between 2014 and 2017, suggesting that the sharing of value under the new model benefited both Telefónica and its customers.

How pricing strategy shapes society

Tipping incentivizes good service, because it allows customers to show their gratitude to the individuals who served them. The practice has existed in many countries for several centuries, but it is not universal.[13] It is impolite to tip service workers in Japan, for example, because of the implicit assumption that the server lacks the means to survive without the tip. In the United States, however, service workers in hospitality, foodservice, and other sectors rely on tips to make a living.

Tipping may seem like a benign and convenient two-part pricing structure. The customer pays for the service – such as the meal, the repair, or the valet parking – and then adds an incremental amount for the server, who has an incentive to perform their job well. That tipped amount is usually either a percentage of the service charge (say, 15%) or a flat amount, such as a $20 cash tip for a mechanic who provided roadside assistance.

By using this two-part structure, the seller shifts some of the responsibility for labor costs from themselves to the customers. This shift shapes society, because it leaves vulnerable groups susceptible to mistreatment and lower incomes, which in turn magnifies the effects of existing class biases. All else being equal, customers tend to tip service workers differently on the basis of race, sex, or other characteristics protected under labor laws.[14]

Male customers often get away with harassing female service workers, who are caught in the dilemma of either saying nothing or reporting the harassment and possibly forfeiting extra tips, which represent a significant portion of their salary.[15] The *Washington Post* reported in 2016 that the restaurant industry generates five times the average number of sexual harassment claims per worker.[16] Only 7% of American women work in restaurants, but 37% of all sexual harassment complaints to the Equal Employment Opportunity Commission come from this industry.[17] Tipping also has implications along racial lines. Studies show that this structural bias is so pervasive in American society that even Black customers tip white service workers more on average for the same level of service.[18]

Recent evidence from the United States shows that changing this pricing model could start to reshape society. Seven states – Alaska, California, Minnesota, Montana, Nevada, Oregon, and Washington – have passed laws to raise minimum cash wages for tipped workers to the state's full minimum wage, while 15 states still keep it at the US federal minimum of $2.13 per hour.[19] Those seven states show consistently higher restaurant sales per capita and tipped worker job growth than the others.[20]

It's time to change the game of pricing

As we said earlier, one of our primary objectives with this book is to change the game of pricing, literally and figuratively. That takes us beyond refuting the four premises that underpin the generally accepted version of how the game of pricing works. *Game Changer: How Strategic Pricing Shapes Businesses, Markets, and Society* replaces that game with seven distinct pricing games that, in aggregate, cover nearly every challenge and opportunity a business leader will encounter.

These games and their distinct natures are not arbitrary or gimmicky choices, nor are they mere byproducts of what we and our colleagues have experienced over the past few decades. They are, in fact, the logical outcomes of a thought process that integrates familiar pricing inputs, frameworks, and methods in a systematic way.

This process culminates in the Strategic Pricing Hexagon, a proven empirical framework we have designed to help executives make strategic choices about pricing with greater speed, confidence, efficiency, and impact.

The locations of the seven games within the Strategy Hex, as we will refer to it throughout the book, are not coincidental. They arise from intersections and interactions across information sources (cost, competition, and customer value), economic frameworks (elasticity, differentiation, game theory, and supply and demand), and specific market characteristics. Each game is subject to six well-defined market forces, and each game has a function within an organization that serves as its natural leader for strategic pricing decisions.

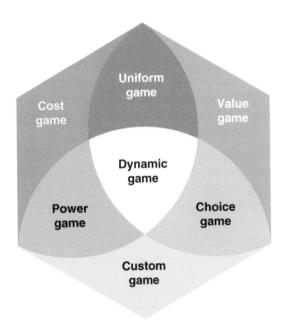

FIGURE I.1 The Strategic Pricing Hexagon

By synthesizing all this information, the Strategy Hex becomes a decision support tool that enables any business leader to formulate a clear pricing strategy and shape their business and markets with authority. It is a logical, common-sense guide to help you identify the imbalances in your market, assess the resulting opportunities and risks, and then frame your options based on your pricing strategy and your pricing agency. It also prevents you from acting on incomplete information, falling prey to the misconceptions about how pricing works, or applying frameworks or techniques that are ineffective or inefficient for a particular game.

For a variety of reasons – from university training to corporate legacy to experience – you might easily and intuitively imagine that your company is playing one of the three games at the top of the Hex.

- **Value: Aligning prices of unique solutions with customer value**
  Think breakthrough or highly differentiated products. Companies succeed when they express their differentiation convincingly and match it with a pricing model that reinforces the value. Companies in the high-tech, luxury goods, and pharmaceuticals sectors tend to choose the Value Game.

- **Uniform: Optimizing the same price for all customers**

  Crack open an Economics 101 textbook and at some point, you'll see the hallmarks of the Uniform Game: companies offering one transparent price to all customers. Sellers weigh the tradeoffs between volume and margin to optimize their own uniform price and maximize profits. Retailers and many consumer goods companies choose to play the Uniform Game.

- **Cost: Driving efficiency to set prices in commoditized markets**

  Cost-plus is common in markets with a high proportion of variable costs and several small suppliers competing for the business of very large customers. A seller needs a pricing model that incentivizes customers to work with them toward the shared goal of optimal efficiency. Tailoring their offers in a cost-effective way is paramount. Many industrial suppliers and distributors play the Cost Game very well.

But these three games apply, in aggregate, only to a minority of the challenges that confront business leaders. That brings us to the four games in the middle and lower half of the Strategy Hex.

- **Power: Negotiating high-stakes deals in concentrated markets**

  The stakes are high in markets where a small number of sellers with highly standardized offerings negotiate with a small number of customers. Losing even one major deal can wreck a seller's business. Customers, meanwhile, can suffer when they give a seller an exclusive deal and that seller suddenly faces supply constraints and cannot deliver. In the Power Game, it is vital for sellers to understand the very fine advantages they might have versus each competitor at each customer. Their pricing model must enable them to keep prices in harmony within this delicate balance of power.

- **Custom: Customizing offers and discounts to beat competitors**

  Think of an industry with a handful of suppliers selling to hundreds or thousands of customers. The core offerings of each competitor are usually comparable, but the negotiated terms, conditions, and supplemental offerings can make each deal unique. In that sense, the Custom Game is the polar opposite of the Uniform Game. Individual customer discounts form the primary tool for price differentiation.

- **Choice: Shaping customer behavior with segmented offers**

  When a few companies in a market offer a variety of products or services at a wide range of prices, how those prices compare to each other matters far more than the individual prices themselves. The way that the offers are presented – factually and emotionally – influences how customers choose, which means that behavioral biases drive outcomes much more than the precision of price points do. A well-structured lineup of offerings incentivizes returning customers to upgrade progressively and choose higher-margin options.

- **Dynamic: Managing floating prices based on real-time dynamics**

    Pricing can become dynamic when demand fluctuates, capacity is fixed, marginal costs are low, and competitive prices constantly shift over time. Airlines were the first ones to price dynamically, but this approach has spread to hotels, sports teams, e-commerce retail, and many more sectors. Technology is critical, because it enables a company first to collect all the inputs at high frequency and second to process them and determine prices for every customer at any point in time. Some companies have begun to apply artificial intelligence together with human judgment to make initial attempts to play this game, but in many industries the evolution of the Dynamic Game remains in its early stages.

One consequence of the Strategy Hex is that there are no standard off-the-shelf pricing strategies that you can quickly cut and paste to your own situation. To assume that pricing strategies or pricing methods are universally applicable and fungible is tantamount to saying that playing golf, basketball, soccer, and baseball all demand the same skills and fitness, simply because each sport involves a ball.

Deciding which of the seven games you will play is one essential part of defining your pricing strategy. The following section introduces the full step-by-step process.

Define your own pricing strategy

Our book offers you a structured and powerful way to craft a well-founded pricing strategy with speed, confidence, efficiency, and impact. The process builds on three questions:

1. **How do you create and share value?**
2. **What pricing game do you want to play?**
3. **What pricing model best fits your value creation strategy?**

Answering each question, in turn, depends on your answers to a block of more detailed questions.

Question 1: How do you create and share value?

Your answer to this first fundamental question derives from your answers to these three questions:

1a. What do you do to create **measurable value** for your customers?

1b. What are your main **drivers of value** and the **limitations** to value creation?

1c. How well do your **differentiation and growth objectives** justify how you share value with your customers?

Our foundations for pricing strategy begin with the premise that pricing is about value sharing in a repeated game – which describes virtually all markets – rather than maximizing one's own outcome by extracting value from a zero-sum game. We also assert that business leaders themselves set the rules and guidelines for shaping demand and sharing value.

We are not referring to value sharing in the sense of what Michael Porter and Mark Kramer defined over a decade ago. They referred to "shared value" as "creating economic value in a way that also creates value for society by addressing its needs and challenges."[21] While we address the important societal impact of pricing in Part IV, our definition of shared value is narrower and more precise. We focus on the voluntary exchanges between buyers and sellers, regardless of how large or small the impact on society may be.

Question 2: What pricing game do you want to play?

Your initial answer to the second fundamental question – what game do you want to play? – derives from your answers to these three questions:

2a. Which game aligns best with the **characteristics of your market**?

2b. Which game aligns best with your current **pricing approach**?

2c. Which game aligns best with the **market forces** and your **competitive advantages**?

We feel confident that your answers will evolve over the course of our book. Here are the seven games again in summary form:

The Seven Games in the Strategic Pricing Hexagon

Value Game: Aligning prices of unique solutions with customer value

Uniform Game: Optimizing the same price for all customers

Cost Game: Driving efficiency to set prices in commoditized markets

Power Game: Negotiating high-stakes deals in concentrated markets

Custom Game: Customizing offers and discounts to beat competitors

Choice Game: Shaping customer behavior with segmented offers

Dynamic Game: Managing floating prices based on real-time dynamics

Question 3: What pricing model best fits your value creation strategy?

Your answer to this third fundamental question derives from your answers to these three questions:

3a. What should your **pricing architecture** be (i.e., pricing basis, offer structure, and pricing mechanism)?

3b. What should drive your **price variation** (e.g., geography, channel, and time)?

3c. What **price adjustment** levers should you use (i.e., customer programs, transaction incentives, and fees and functional discounts)?

Figure I.2 – which we will use throughout the book – provides an organized view of these questions. The pricing architecture assembles all the decisions that leaders need to make before they can even set a price: the unit to express the price, the offer that people get when they pay the price, and the way the number is determined. Once a company can set a price, it needs to decide what will make that price vary, whether over time, by location, by store, by customer, or other factors. Finally, in markets where companies first anchor their prices around a number – a list

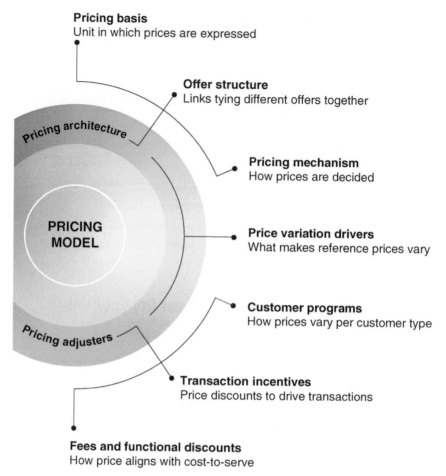

Pricing basis
Unit in which prices are expressed

Offer structure
Links tying different offers together

Pricing architecture

Pricing mechanism
How prices are decided

PRICING MODEL

Price variation drivers
What makes reference prices vary

Customer programs
How prices vary per customer type

Pricing adjusters

Transaction incentives
Price discounts to drive transactions

Fees and functional discounts
How price aligns with cost-to-serve

FIGURE I.2   The elements of a pricing model

price or reference price – they adjust those prices, sometimes by very small amounts and sometimes by much larger amounts. We refer to the means they use to make these changes as price adjusters and classify them by the purpose they serve. All these pricing model decisions have one point in common: implicitly or explicitly, they come before a buyer and a seller agree on any price. These decisions provide the strategic frame for the price.

* * *

Preview of what you'll find in the book . . .

Part I introduces the logical building blocks of the Strategy Hex – information sources, economic frameworks, market characteristics, and market forces – and then shows how typical functions within any organization, such as marketing, sales, and finance, fit to each game. Part I concludes with guidance on how to use the Hex to understand and exercise your pricing agency. By the end of Part I, you should already be able to answer the second fundamental question for defining your pricing strategy: What game do you want to play?

Part II devotes one full chapter to each of the seven games. By the end of Part II, you should have a complete basis for understanding each game and how you can win yours. You should also be able to answer the third fundamental question for defining your pricing strategy: What pricing model best fits your value creation strategy?

But we do not stop there.

Part III brings the Strategy Hex to life by showing you how to play the games when market-shaping events occur. How do you bring an innovation to market? How do you make a transition to an "as a service" pricing model? Your choice of which game to play is not permanent. Companies change their games or defend their positions as their businesses and markets evolve.

Part IV shows that pricing strategies have social consequences. Think, for example, about how you would define a "fair price." You may be surprised to read how your definition stands up to scrutiny. At the same time, pricing strategy can address social problems that people normally don't view as pricing challenges, such as how a nonprofit can achieve a greater impact or how societies can reduce net emissions of CO_2.

. . . and some shortcuts as you start reading

This book's structure should allow you to navigate toward the parts and chapters that align with your strongest interests. As with most business books, you will probably not read the chapters in this book sequentially. But we do have some specific recommendations to guide your reading plan.

In Part I, Chapters 1 and 2 cover very familiar ground for people with a basic economics background. But we advise all readers to read Chapter 3 carefully. It explains what makes the games so different from each other. Understanding the rationale behind how market characteristics define the games is foundational for all the arguments we make in the book. Chapter 3 should also enable you to identify the one or two games that best fit your market situation. Chapters 4 through 6 develop a more nuanced understanding of the games. You can read them sequentially or skim them and come back later as needed, say, if you are wondering why we connect different organization functions, market trends, or pricing levers to their natural positions in the Hex.

If you have an appetite for targeted reading, skip straight to the chapters in Parts II and III that you find most intriguing. Part III chapters should be easy to navigate, depending on what is happening in your market. We hope that chapters focused on adjacent games will be instructive as well, highlighting opportunities for strategic moves or risks of market shifts.

Unique among pricing books, this one is not only for people who need to set pricing strategies and prices. It is also for all those interested in understanding how our modern free-market societies are shaped by the way commercial transactions are structured. Chapters 20 and 21 cover age-old questions such as the fairness of prices and how value is shared or distributed between buyers and sellers. They provide a more detailed logic behind some of our more provocative claims about the ethical case for price differentiation or the importance for businesses to share value.

Chapters 22 to 25 address specific societal challenges where strategic pricing approaches can help contribute to solutions. They include the challenges to provide broad or universal access to drugs or education, how to shape demand in order to scale sustainable, environment-friendly products, and solutions on how to disincentivize CO_2 emissions.

Finally, we suspect that this is going to be a book worth keeping in your library for frequent reference. We hope you will find many connections between the real world and the games that will trigger diving into the relevant chapter. No matter how you use this book, though, we welcome feedback and reactions to the ideas we present.

Now let's answer Question 1

To help with the active reading of this book, we will have some brief exercises to help you translate the ideas of the book into practical real-world consequences. If you are working in a business or a nonprofit organization, we assume that you can articulate your answers to Question 1 in a few sentences. If you are a student, pick a business you are familiar with. This is the starting point of your journey.

Question 1: How do you create and share value?

1a. What do you do to create **measurable value** for your customers?

1b. What are the main **drivers of value** and the **limitations** to value creation?

1c. How well do your **differentiation and growth objectives** justify how you share value with your customers?

Try to keep your answers simple and pragmatic, perhaps no longer than what you could scribble on a small sheet of paper. The most challenging part of the question is probably the one about value sharing. Please keep that piece of paper handy and see how your answers evolve as you proceed through the book.

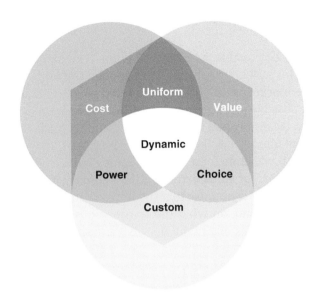

PART I

Rethinking Pricing Strategically

The impacts of strategic pricing decisions can reshape a business, an industry, or society, as our stories in the Introduction demonstrated.

Sometimes, though, the right pricing strategy can reshape all three at the same time, with consequences that last for decades.

Think back to the Model T, the automobile that Ford Motor Company founder Henry Ford launched in the early 1900s. Ford receives credit for standardizing the product ("Any customer can have a car painted any color that he wants so long as it's black"), for mass production with the modern assembly line, and even for labor policies with the minimum wage of $5 per day for an eight-hour workday.[1,2]

You might be surprised, however, to learn that these breakthroughs in design, manufacturing, and labor management all resulted directly from one common motivation: Ford's pricing strategy.

Ford wanted to manufacture a product that even his own factory workers could afford. But that goal clashed with the prevailing pricing strategies of carmakers at the time, such as Ford's former employer, the Detroit Automotive Company. "The whole thought was to make to order and to get the largest price possible for each car," wrote Ford about Detroit's pricing strategy in his autobiography.[3] Detroit applied the same philosophy to the sale of aftermarket parts. "It was considered good business to sell parts at the highest possible price on the theory that, since the man had already bought the car, he simply had to have the part and would be willing to pay for it," Ford explained.[4]

He realized it was time for a pricing strategy built around growth and value sharing instead of value extraction in a zero-sum game. He started his own company on the premise that the industry needed to "throw overboard the idea of pricing on what the traffic will bear and instead go to the common-sense basis of pricing on what it costs to manufacture and then reducing the cost of manufacture."[5] In Ford's view, the manufacturer should then share the value of those lower costs with customers "at once" in the form of lower prices.[6] But he also realized that "I never could produce a thoroughly good motor car that might be sold at a low price under the existing cut-and-try manufacturing methods."[7] So he designed and launched the Model T, a car that was easy to manufacture and maintain.

The implementation of Ford's pricing strategy succeeded beyond belief and would shape the automotive market, its supporting ecosystems, and societies around the world for decades to come. By 1921, this "Swiss Army Knife of automobiles" accounted for 57% of the world's car production and remained the best-selling car of the twentieth century until the Volkswagen Beetle surpassed it in 1972.[8,9,10]

Changing the conversation around pricing – and changing the game – also means changing the way people talk about business success stories. The unparalleled growth of the automotive industry – and personal mobility in general – is as much a history of strategic pricing model innovations as it is about innovations in technology, manufacturing, or organization. Beyond the Model T, many strategic pricing innovations have shaped and reshaped the auto industry over the past century:

- **Taxicabs:** In 1915, an Austrian immigrant named John Hertz founded the Yellow Cab Company in Chicago to offer temporary mobility as a service. In the 1920s and 1930s, regulation of the taxicab service codified this service with a pricing model of fixed rates per mile and minute.[11,12]

- **Car rentals:** In 1918, a Chicago entrepreneur named Walter Jacobs offered access to automobiles under a temporary, time-based pricing model when he began to rent a fleet of 12 Model Ts.[13] He sold his company a few years later to the very same John Hertz, whose last name eventually became synonymous with car rentals.

- **Financing:** General Motors pioneered automotive financing in 1919 when it established General Motors Acceptance Corporation (GMAC). This innovation created a pay-per-month pricing basis that enabled more customers to acquire their own cars. Prior to that, car buyers needed to either pay cash or secure bank loans to buy a vehicle.[14]

- **Cars by segment:** In the 1920s, General Motors identified subsegments within the mass market for cars and began to advertise "a car for every purse and purpose."[15] This tiered pricing model diversified and targeted the kinds of cars that people could buy, while encouraging trade-ups within the range as people's incomes and situations changed.

- **Leasing:** In the 1990s, leasing became "an innovative way for auto makers to put customers in mainly high-end vehicles with relatively low monthly payments at a time when new-vehicle prices were rising faster than personal income."[16] This usage-based pricing model provided greater access to new vehicles by shortening the purchase cycle.

- **Mobility:** More than a century after the revolutionary pricing model behind the Model T, yet another new pricing model for mobility emerged. Uber and other ride-sharing apps created a new marketplace for rides at prices set dynamically depending on destination, time of day, and the availability of drivers.

You will note that our range of strategic pricing decisions is very broad. The composition and communication of the offer, for example, are also strategic pricing decisions, because they are intimately linked to how a company designs its prices and how customers perceive the pricing models as well as the price they pay.

The origins of strategic pricing decisions

The Strategic Pricing Hexagon integrates several elements – business intelligence, economic frameworks, market characteristics, market forces, and organizational authority – into a tool that enables you to make impactful strategic pricing decisions more efficiently and confidently.

1
Information sources driving price variations

2
Economic framework used to set prices based on how sources of information are combined

3
Strategic pricing games deter- mined by market characteristics where economic framework is most relevant

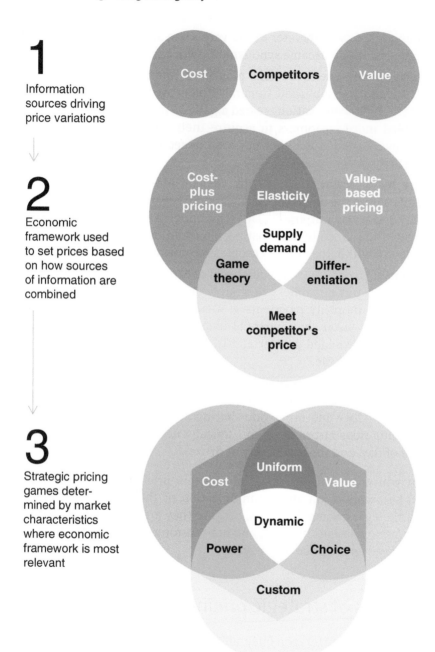

FIGURE PI.1 The layers of the Strategic Pricing Hexagon

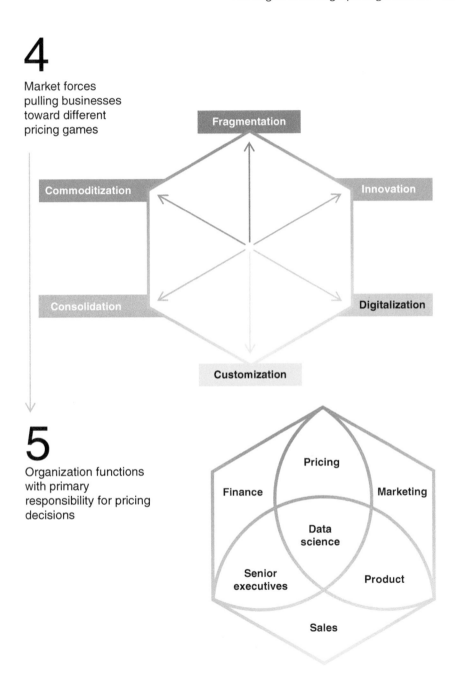

4

Market forces
pulling businesses
toward different
pricing games

5

Organization functions
with primary
responsibility for pricing
decisions

FIGURE PI.1 (*Continued*)

The seven games in the Strategy Hex arise organically from the logical combinations of these elements, as shown in the two figures on the facing pages. We realize these two figures present a lot of information to absorb, but we wanted to reveal the entire inner workings of the Strategy Hex before we devote a separate chapter to each individual layer.

Figure PI.1 illustrates the internal consistency and the logic that fully define the seven games in the Strategy Hex. Each of the five foundational layers – which correspond to the first five chapters of Part I – builds successively on the preceding layers.

- **Information sources (Layer 1):** Cost, competition, and value are three fundamental inputs to the development of any business strategy. These three information sources are also the three primary drivers of price variation.

- **Economic frameworks (Layer 2):** Each of the seven possible combinations of the information sources in Layer 1 provides the inputs for an economic framework for designing and setting prices. The application of price elasticity, for example, depends on cost and value. Chapter 2 covers traditional microeconomics, elasticity, differentiation, game theory, and supply and demand.

- **Market characteristics (Layer 3):** None of the frameworks in Layer 2 is universally applicable. Each is well suited to certain combinations of market characteristics – such as the level of concentration among buyers and sellers and the diversity of customer needs – but ill-suited to others. This is the critical layer, where the natures of the seven games start to emerge more clearly.

- **Market forces (Layer 4):** Six strong forces affect the state and the stability of the underlying three layers. Their combined push and pull can cause a market to shift toward a different part of the Strategy Hex. Business leaders can harness these forces to help their companies reshape their business and their market. Chapter 4 will explore the impact and power of these six forces: innovation, commoditization, customization, digitalization, fragmentation, and concentration.

- **Governance (Layer 5):** Pricing decisions are often hotly debated by the many functions within organizations. Chapter 5 describes how a company's game and position in the Strategy Hex influences how sales, marketing, finance, and other functions should work together to make strategic pricing decisions.

Part I concludes with Chapter 6, which defines the strategic pricing decisions and describes how they depend on the seven pricing games.

CHAPTER 1

Three Information Sources

C osts, competition, and value are ways to categorize the business and market information most commonly used as inputs to pricing decisions. These three inputs, shown in Figure 1.1, form the foundation of the Strategy Hex at its deepest basic level.

Most companies currently use one or two of these inputs as the basis for price setting, often directly in a formulaic way. Each is the primary input for a classic pricing method that generates a number from that narrow perspective: cost-plus pricing, pricing relative to the competition, or value-based pricing. But those price methods have inherent limitations that go beyond the fact that they keep companies trapped in the "numbers game" we described in the Introduction.

Perhaps the most fundamental limitation is that there is no standard, off-the-shelf definition for defining costs, competitors, or value that applies universally to any business. Nor is any of them an immutable given that lies beyond the influence of business leaders. This often explains why many companies struggle to establish a single source of truth for their decision making.

Listed below are the high-level definitions we will use consistently throughout the book. The precise definitions for any company and any offering are the conscious choice of its business leaders.

- **Costs:** Companies incur several direct and indirect costs, but throughout the book we focus primarily on the direct costs – variable and fixed – that are usually measured explicitly as "dollars-out." The indirect costs include marginal, opportunity, sunk, and societal costs.

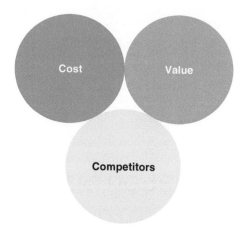

FIGURE 1.1 Three information sources used to make pricing decisions

- **Value:** This input represents the difference between the perceived utility that a buyer or user derives from a product or service and the amount of money they paid for it. Classical economics claims that rational customers seek to maximize this difference, or surplus, regardless of whether they are buying a candy bar, a car, or a shipment of chemicals. Behavioral and emotional factors can alter perceived utility and prompt a customer to forgo the purchase of an objectively superior product.
- **Competitors:** A competitor is anyone with the means, motive, and opportunity to take a current or potential customer away from you. Customers also become direct competitors when they develop a do-it-yourself (DIY) solution.

More important from a strategic standpoint, however, is not what your costs are down to the penny, but rather what your cost drivers are. The same applies to your competition and also to the amount of value you deliver. The drivers of competition matter more than the competitor, and the drivers of value matter more than its exact quantification.

The drivers matter more than the amounts

Cost, competitors, and value are never constant. Their magnitudes depend on several sources of variance that can be strong enough to create imbalances in a market. These, in turn, affect the way that a leadership team decides which pricing game to play and how to play it. The specific drivers of variation, whose intensity varies from market to market, are:

- **Location:** Costs, competitors, and value for an identical offering can vary across regional, national, and local borders, even from neighborhood to neighborhood. The price for a single-serve beverage is a classic example. Within a radius of a few blocks, its price can vary by an order of magnitude.

- **Time:** The available value to share can vary by season, month, and time of day, and even from minute to minute for a perishable product. A heated seat in an automobile is much less valuable in summer. An umbrella in Las Vegas is worthless except on the rare occasions when a downpour hits. But fluctuations of cost, competitors, and value are not always so obvious or predictable. Time also applies to the time horizon for a company's objectives: How do you plan to trade off value today versus value tomorrow? How does this factor into your decisions on how much money to leave on the table?

- **Customer segment:** The wider the variation in customers' needs and willingness to pay, the more it makes sense to cluster them and customize offerings, communication, and prices. Technological advancements now make it possible to customize these at an individual level. For some business-to-business (B2B) markets with opaque and complex negotiations, each customer is already its own segment. Leaders often need to decide how and why to share value with some customers and not others.

- **Occasion:** The reason or the impetus for a transaction can increase or decrease costs, competition, and value available as well. Ordering a missing ingredient for a dinner at the last minute is worth more to a consumer than buying the same amount of the same thing during a routine shopping trip. B2B customers will value a product delivered just in time differently than one delivered to a warehouse in bulk for future use.

- **Supply and capacity:** The management and utilization of capacity can affect the costs of meeting demand, the availability of alternatives, and how customers value them. Luxury goods producers artificially constrain capacity to preserve scarcity, whereas airlines, hotels, and sports teams adjust capacity to respond to fluctuations in demand. Finally, unexpected shocks that lead to supply chain disruptions can create acute imbalances between supply and demand.

- **Volume:** Offering lower unit prices for higher volumes is a nearly universal practice, based on the presumption of lower unit costs. This occurs when consumers buy multiple units at a big-box club retailer or an industrial purchaser buys goods in bulk. The ability to offer higher volumes consistently or the ability to enforce scarcity can also change whom a company competes against.
- **Channel/source/pathway:** How a customer accesses information about an offering and then transacts also influences costs, competition, and value. The simplest distinction is the online and offline sales channels for many B2B and business-to-consumer (B2C) products.

In many situations, every one of these drivers plays a role in defining both the value available to share and the fair way to share it. For simplicity's sake, let's look at something as seemingly generic as a men's haircut. The average price of a men's haircut in the United States is $28, but the prices can range from $10 to $100.[1] The price of a haircut in preparation for a special occasion such as a wedding could run even higher. Based on the seven drivers of variance we mentioned above, we are confident that we could find a haircut available in the United States at every price point between $10 and $100, inclusive of tip, with each providing a different margin to the supplier. Haircuts are a service, but we could also do a similar exercise with the ranges of prices of physical products with national distribution (gasoline, beer) and regionally or locally produced products such as cupcakes.

A strategic view of costs

For close to a century, costs and sales volumes were the only forms of data that business leaders could know with a high degree of confidence. They would invest in cost measurement and cost reduction, because cost reductions had immediately visible and measurable impacts on profit. It was only natural, then, for them to use cost data as the basis for pricing decisions. But how strong should a leader's confidence be in what they view as "costs"?

Imagine that you are planning a two-day trip of business meetings to a remote city with no local public transportation system. You know when and where you are flying, but still need to decide between renting a car and using local taxicabs for transportation in the city. What factors will drive your decision?

- **The case for car rental:** You will keep the car for two days, but it will sit idle when you aren't driving. You will have to pay for fuel, but you will have no costs for a driver, because you drive yourself and can choose when you leave and what routes you take. Your only other costs for driving are potentially the opportunity cost of your time, if you had used it to work while you are in the car.
- **The case for taxis:** You will use the car only during transit times, which make up only a small part of your two days. You incur no costs for fuel, but you will have the additional cost of the cabbie.

Without knowing any specific prices for either option, your main tradeoff will be between the cost of the rental car while you are not driving compared to the cost of the cabbie. The greater the amount of transit time – because you have to go to many places or drive very far – the greater the likelihood that the rental car will be the better option. But if you have one meeting close to your hotel and the hotel is near the airport, cabs would be the better option.

In the context of these two offers, let's look at what it costs to provide them (see Figure 1.2). The cost structures and cost drivers for the car rental and the cab companies are similar. What distinguishes the two businesses are the choices of which costs are variable and which are fixed. For the cab company, the variable costs are the fuel and the cabbie, and the respective cost drivers are distance and transit time. For the rental car company, the variable cost is the car, and the cost driver is how long someone has the car in their possession. It is thus no coincidence that cabs have a dual pricing basis – transit distance and time – while the pricing basis of the rental car is per day.

This illustrates the connection between a pricing basis and how a company looks at its cost structure. Strategically, the natural choice for a pricing basis is the set of variables that drive various cost components. The choice is easy when these variables are all highly correlated. But the choice gets more complicated when the variables pull in different directions. For the car rental company, there is not necessarily a perfect correlation between how long someone rents a car and how much fuel they consume. Getting the customer to pay for the fuel separately is a good solution. In the case of the taxicab, the two variable cost drivers – transit time and distance – also lack a strong correlation, but the cab companies manage this with a different pricing formula. In most cities, the main pricing basis is the distance, but if the cab gets stuck in traffic, a secondary pricing basis – price per minute – applies and is added to the fare.

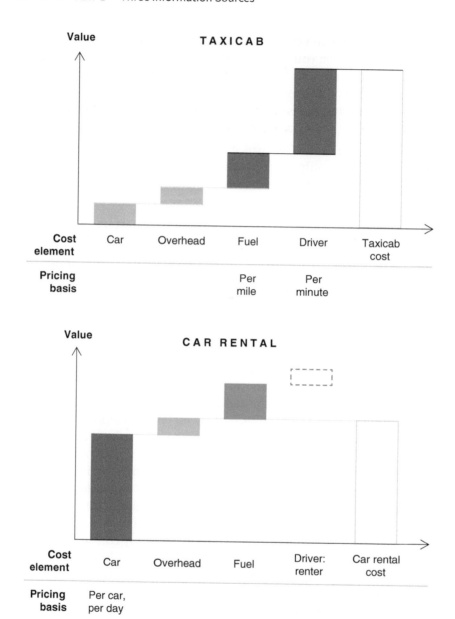

FIGURE 1.2 Renting a car versus taking a taxi from the seller's perspective

A strategic look at your cost structure can inspire ideas for new pricing models. Think of airlines, which have two main variable cost drivers: the number of passengers and the distance flown. But other cost drivers, such as the number of luggage pieces or the number of meals, are not perfectly correlated with the number of passengers. Some passengers travel without luggage, and some do not want to eat the airline food. It made sense, then, from a cost perspective, when airlines decided to unbundle luggage and food from the airline ticket and create separate fees for each. We explore the other perspectives of that change in Chapter 9.

A strategic view of value

Like costs, value is not a constant, but rather is strongly influenced by all the sources of variation. The value of a haircut, for example, differs by gender, age, occasion, purpose (e.g., professional, desire to feel better and more confident), and many other factors.

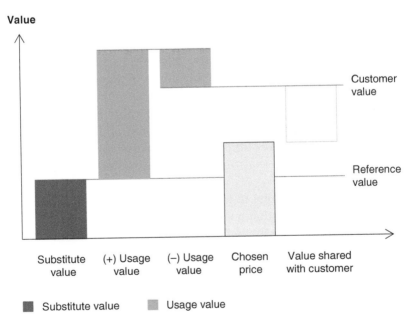

FIGURE 1.3   The value ladder

We look at value as the sum of two components: substitute and usage value. Substitute value reflects the value of the next best competitive alternative (NBCA). It sets a reference value for customers. In a market with homogenous customer needs where competitors offer similar products, the value will tend to cluster around this reference value. In markets with greater differentiation – i.e., greater separation between the means customers can use to solve their problems – the usage value comes into play.

Usage value accounts for relative value differences, both positive and negative, to that next best alternative. The net usage value is the sum of all of your offering's relative differences (positive and negative) to your closest competitor or NBCA. Usage in a broad sense includes both the functional usage of a product or service as well as the emotional benefits of owning or using the product or having purchased the service. Functional value includes utilitarian benefits such as convenience, speed, reliability, risk mitigation, incremental income, and direct cost savings, each measurable and quantifiable in terms of time, money, or capacity. Emotional value derives from the customer's intangible, subjective benefits, such as fun, exclusivity, prestige, self-esteem, recognition, respect, and a sense of connection or belonging.

Substitute and usage value have slightly different natures, even though both are expressed in the same monetary currency. In practice, the substitute value is a "hard" version of the currency, because customers and competitors can observe the price of substitutes in the marketplace. Usage value is a softer currency because it requires quantifying functional usage and emotional benefits. Of course, emotional value is hard to quantify, because it is highly subjective, but even functional value requires assumptions. If a new product saves time, the seller needs to quantify the amount of time, but the value of that time can vary considerably depending on who the buyer is.

The ratio of usage value to substitute value, therefore, has profound implications. Companies that have a large proportion of usage value have more value to share and usually have more degrees of freedom on how to share it. But because the value is simultaneously harder to quantify and partially subjective, they will need to spend more time and energy communicating that value and making the case for their differentiation.

Value – and the fair way to share it – changes depending on that ratio as well. If total value is solely driven by substitute value – such as a lower price for a product with many substitutes – the customer can reliably calculate their savings, independent of their characteristics or the context of usage. But when usage value accounts for most or all of the value, customers may feel they have a right to a higher proportion of that value, because of its uncertainty and because deriving that value usually depends on who they are and how they act.

Value can also change significantly over time, as the course of the relationship between company and customer evolves. The feeling of sunk costs, greater emotional attachment, and perceived product performance all enhance the perception of value. Their absence at the beginning of the customer relationship tends to make customers more price sensitive, which means they are more responsive even to small price changes. Even slightly lower prices can encourage disproportionately greater adoption, while slightly higher prices can discourage it.

Perceptions of value at the individual level validate the old cliché that "one man's trash is another man's treasure." In 2005, a man from Montreal named Kyle MacDonald took advantage of those kinds of imbalances to turn a red paper clip into a house in western Canada through a series of 14 barter exchanges. In each case, the exchanging parties felt they had achieved a fair surplus.[2,3] Inspired by MacDonald, a woman in San Francisco did something similar in 2020. She parlayed a bobby pin into a bicycle food truck, with trades along the way involving Nike shoes, a skateboard, and Apple hardware.[4]

Those transactions happened without the exchange of money, but they illustrate a fundamental point about value. There is always a distribution of value across all the forms of variation. The challenge lies in figuring out what these distributions look like and where the best sharing opportunities exist.

A strategic view of competition

Market definition is a fundamental task that helps a business leader understand who their current and future competitors are. The late Coca-Cola CEO Roberto Goizueta gets the credit for switching the definition in the market for carbonated soft drinks (CSDs) from that narrow definition to the much broader "share of stomach." When Goizueta introduced the idea, Coca-Cola had a share of just 3% of the average fluid intake per day.[5] Suddenly, Coca-Cola's competitors included water, milk, juice, and coffee, rather than being limited to other CSDs.

The same logic could apply to alcoholic beverages. The "direct" competitors for a beer company are other beer companies, and the competition in that narrow definition can be particularly intense on certain occasions, such as the week before a major holiday or during sports events such as the Super Bowl or soccer's World Cup. Over the medium term, however, the bigger competitive threats for many beer companies may be wine and spirits rather than their direct competitors.

The "share of stomach" idea pioneered many ways of defining competition, which now include share of wallet and even share of mind. All of these definitions can have consequences for how a company defines its added value, shapes the demand for it, and shares value. The value you create is always defined in relation to a competitive alternative, as the value ladder in Figure 1.3 showed. The more differentiation opportunities you have, the easier it is to shape a market. The challenge is harder in crowded markets with similar offers.

More generous sharing of value with customers can improve customer acquisition, accelerate transaction frequency, and help a company generate higher volumes to create scale and lower manufacturing costs. Less generous levels of sharing can signal exclusivity, improve margin, and reposition a company in a different competitive set with different customer segments. That happens, for example, when a company transforms a mass market product or service into a premium one.

Once companies have defined their competitive field, they need to analyze what differentiates them from their chosen competition. We refer to these differences as imbalances. A competitive advantage in pricing is an imbalance you can use in your favor to create more value and increase penetration, share, or profits.

We consider three levels of imbalances. The first ones are input imbalances, which are the most fundamental. Imbalances are relative to competitors, which means that input imbalances derive from the other two information sources: costs and value.

- **Costs:** These include structural imbalances such as the one between the rental car and taxicab substitutes, or imbalances in invested capital and its efficiency.
- **Value:** Some offers can create more value over time and across segments than competitors' offers can.

These imbalances are fundamental, because they explain some but not all of the imbalances at the next levels.

The second level is imbalances in market characteristics, and again, we have two comparisons with competitors:

- **Customer base:** Imbalances result because competitors focus on different customer segments. Some, for example, may have a higher share in the fragmented part of the market with small customers, or a higher share of larger customers.
- **Offer structure:** Beyond differences in value, offers can differ in terms of structure. Companies can also have gaps in their portfolios, or overweight one part of the portfolio, such as offering a broader lineup of high-end products.

As mentioned, these imbalances can result from input imbalances. Shares of different customer segments can arise from differences in value propositions for these segments, or from legacy decisions to prioritize some segments over others.

The third level of imbalances involves how companies go to market:

- **Sales channel:** Companies can serve the same segments, but through different channels, such as overweighting online sales or establishing direct relationships with many of their customers.
- **Pricing model:** Every component of the pricing model could vary from one competitor to another. These differences will be more impactful if they reinforce other imbalances.

Imbalances in inputs or market characteristics are not the only causes of go-to-market imbalances. Tesla, for example, decided to sell directly to consumers, which was a deliberate departure from the established practice of automotive original equipment manufacturers (OEMs) to go through a dealer network, even at the high end of the market. We explore this in more detail in Chapter 17.

A company selling durable goods, for example, could bundle its warranty and advertise it as included in the normal price, if there is a value imbalance in its favor, stemming from higher reliability. But sometimes companies differentiate their pricing models uncoupled from any imbalances. Such moves are unlikely to result in long-term sustainable advantage. Rolls Royce coined the phrase "Power-by-the-Hour" in 1962 when it started to offer a complete jet engine and parts replacement service at a fixed rate per flying hour, rather than charging a large up-front price for an engine. As Rolls Royce explained, this pricing mechanism "aligned the interests of the manufacturer and operator, who only paid for engines that performed well."[6] Such models also help the manufacturers extend credit during times when airlines need to limit the amount of debt they can take on to pay for equipment.

Purely from a pricing-model perspective, Power by the Hour was a brilliant move. However, competitors such as General Electric followed and adopted a similar pricing mechanism.[7] Even though Power by the Hour was celebrated in pricing books and articles, it did not create a long-term sustainable advantage for Rolls Royce. GE was able to take advantage of the model because it had GE Capital, a cheap source of financing for airlines. Capitalizing on this cost and value imbalance helped GE increase its share of the market in the ensuing decades.

As we said earlier, a potential competitor is anyone with the means, motive, and opportunity to take a current or potential customer away from you. The long-term success of a pricing strategy therefore depends heavily on a company's ability to understand the incentives of its competitors and to interpret their intent. What is their mix of goals – short, medium, and long term – and how do they differ from other companies'? What incentives do they offer their sales teams and channels? Some companies have the publicly stated goal of increasing their market share disproportionately to the market's overall growth. Whom will they steal share from? An intense price war can result if several companies in a market pursue that same strategy, and over time each can undermine its own long-term ability to serve customers.

Finally, it is important to know what pricing game you are playing. When we apply the Strategy Hex in Part III to several strategic business challenges, we will show that companies sometimes face competitors in different games than their own. The leaders of those companies have decided to play a different game as the best way to meet their strategic objectives.

The conflicting answers from pricing methods

Let's revisit the information sources shown in Figure 1.1. As we mentioned, some companies make the direct leap from one or more of these core inputs to price setting. This presents many fundamental problems, but the most immediately obvious one is that the price numbers derived from each input can be vastly different.

Relying solely on the information sources in isolation is not sufficient to escape the constraints of zero-sum thinking, value extraction, the static market, and the numbers game. Even within those limitations, there is no clear answer.

Imagine that Mark, the caterer from the Introduction, notices that many of his customers love the homemade cupcakes he sometimes prepares for desserts. He decides to start a side business by opening a single storefront to sell the cupcakes. Now he needs to decide what to charge for them. Figure 1.4 shows what each input from information source suggests for a price to charge per cupcake.

If he uses the cost-plus method to come up with a price, he reaches the result shown in the first row of Figure 1.4. Variable costs for flour, sugar, other flavorings, and packaging materials total $1.00. Fixed costs total $25,000. If he wants to make a gross margin of 50%, he can use the cost-plus methodology and set a price of $2.00 per cupcake.

When he looks directly at the competition, he notices that potential customers could buy roughly similar cupcakes at three other locations in the neighborhood. Figure 1.4 shows those prices. Being new to the neighborhood as a cupcake seller, he decides that if he were to price on the basis of competition, he should temper his gross margin expectations in the short term and charge a price equal to the lowest competitor's price.

Then comes the lens of value. To gain some initial insights into value, he conducts two experiments. First, he uses the "pay-what-you-want"

Input	Amount	Methodology	Price per cupcake
Costs	$1.00 variable $25,000 fixed	Cost-plus with a 50% target gross margin	$2.00
Competition	Three nearby stores: two charge $1.75, one charges $1.99	Price to competition: defaulting to the lowest price because the business is new	$1.75
Customer Value	Monday test: $2.30 (average) Saturday test: $2.03 (average) Interviews: $2.47	Estimated customer value using different test methods	From $2 to $2.50

FIGURE 1.4   Cupcake prices using different standard pricing methods

method to set prices. Customers can take cupcakes and pay whatever they feel is appropriate. To account for potential differences in occasion, those trials took place once on a Monday morning and once on a Saturday morning.

For the second experiment, Mark contacts a local college professor to see if some students would do some pricing research as part of a class project. The students interviewed around 50 people who said they had eaten a cupcake at least once in the last three months. Besides general questions on likes and dislikes, the students also ask the interviewees to cite four different prices for one of Mark's cupcakes: a price they would consider to be too cheap, a price that would indicate good value, one that would make the cupcakes seem expensive, and one that would make them seem too expensive.[8] The third row of Figure 1.4 shows the results of those trials.

Together with the information in the other two rows, the results leave Mark totally confused. Not only did the three methods lead to conflicting results, but one of the methods (value-based pricing) yielded conflicting results on its own. The best Mark could do with this information would be to make an informed and uncomfortable guess, with similar anxieties to the ones he used to experience in his catering business: What is the "right" price?

As he did with his catering business, Mark realizes he can't answer that question with one input, one standard process, or one basic approach to make a pricing decision. He needs not only a different thought process, but also an entirely different question: What is the right pricing strategy?

Key takeaways

Before deciding on specific prices, a critical pricing decision is about what should drive price variations. There are three main sources of information that drive price variation: costs, value, and competitor actions.

- Costs are the traditional driver of prices because companies need to ensure a minimum level of profitability to be viable.
- Value drivers are the next common source of variation for pricing, and their importance increases when an offer is so differentiated that who benefits from it is more important than what competitors offer.

- Competitor offers and their prices are the last fundamental drivers of price variations when their offers are very comparable. Competitors can drive price variation when their presence depends, for instance, on geographic locations or when their prices vary, for instance, over time.

- Costs, value, and competitor prices all vary for different reasons in different circumstances. Understanding the combined effects of these variations and how to take advantage of them is the essence of strategic pricing.

CHAPTER 2

Four Economic Frameworks

B usiness leaders often confuse pricing methods with pricing strategies, so it is important for us to distinguish sharply between the two. Pricing methods yield a price number as a finite output. These outputs can vary significantly, depending on the information sources used, as the cupcake entrepreneur learned at the end of Chapter 1.

Pricing strategies demand that leaders look beyond prices – beyond the numbers – to take the entirety of their current and future market situations into consideration, rather than focusing narrowly on one input or one method to the exclusion of other information. Pricing strategies express intentions and offer guidance and direction. They are subjective and require astute judgment.

The next step in going beyond prices and developing a pricing strategy is to look at the combinations of the three information sources. Cost, competition, and value can generate important and more powerful insights in combination than in isolation. The intersections we show in Figure 2.1 show the four natural overlaps that result in practical frameworks backed by large bodies of economic theory.

The frameworks at the respective overlaps – elasticity, differentiation, game theory, and supply and demand – form Layer 2 of the Strategy Hex. Each of these frameworks can either facilitate or hinder strategic pricing decisions, depending on how business leaders apply them. Figure 2.1 also shows the three pricing methods we described in the previous chapter – cost-plus, pricing to competition, and value-based pricing – with each

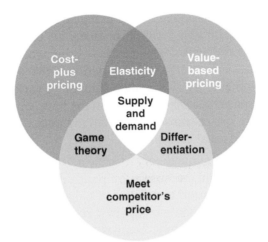

FIGURE 2.1 Venn diagram of information sources forming four economic frameworks

anchored to its primary information source. Below we elaborate on the four frameworks at the intersections.

- **Price elasticity:** The elasticity framework lies at the intersection of cost and value, because cost and willingness to pay are the two inputs necessary to calculate an optimal price based on elasticity. Price elasticity provides a numerical answer to questions such as *"What will happen if we raise prices by 5%?"* or *"How much of a price cut would we need to boost volumes by 10%?"* because it captures the presumptive cause-and-effect relationship between prices and volumes. Changes in price alter a buyer's perceived value derived from an offering. Incorporating cost information allows a leadership team to understand the financial consequences of those price changes.

- **Price differentiation:** This framework lies at the intersection of competition and value, because a company can differentiate prices relative to competitors and relative to its own products. This framework combines insights from the economic theories of price discrimination and behavioral science. Price discrimination refers to selling the same offer to different customers at different price points, either directly (first-degree price discrimination) or through discounts (second- and third-degree discrimination). We think this perspective is too restrictive from a practical standpoint. That is why our definition of differentiation is broader: the combination of price discrimination and behavioral science. In other words, differentiation means price variation and product variation. Behavioral science studies how customers choose among a company's various offers. It has highlighted numerous biases that humans have when making such choices. These biases transcend and often contradict the numerical rationality of classical economics.

- **Game theory:** The game theory framework lies at the intersection of costs and competition, because a company only needs costs and competitor price information to define optimal prices in that framework. It applies primarily when a company's prices depend on the pricing behavior of a few individual competitors whose offerings all have very similar value. In such circumstances, the game theory framework helps leaders make better-informed unilateral moves, because they understand the effects those moves will have on competitors and on their own company.

- **Supply and demand:** This framework lies at the intersection of all three sources of information. The market's supply curve is, by definition, based on the costs, capacities, and prices of every competitor. The demand curve, meanwhile, is a function of either the aggregated willingness to pay of individuals or the value they derive. This framework tends to apply very well when costs, competition, and value have multiple significant and simultaneous drivers, with time usually the most important one.

Let's now look at each framework individually.

The role of elasticity

Price elasticity of demand is a dimensionless number defined as the percentage change in volume divided by the percentage change in price. Following that mathematical definition strictly, the elasticity is negative, because higher prices generally lead to lower volumes and lower prices to higher volumes. In practice, it is more intuitive to consider the absolute value and refer to the elasticity as a positive number. This avoids confusion when talking about a high or low elasticity.

Thus, if a company increases prices on a specific offering by 5% and experiences a 10% decline in volume, that offering has a price elasticity of 2. Conversely, if a company assumes or observes an elasticity of 2 in its industry, it would need a 5% price cut to induce a 10% increase in volumes. The higher the elasticity number, the more elastic the offering is.

These situations resemble the stylized problems you might see in an economics textbook, when a large number of suppliers with similar offers sell to a large number of customers with similar needs. The calculus is simple in that context and makes price elasticity an insightful number. If a company changes prices by a small amount, up or down, how much of that large, anonymized mass of customers will it gain or lose? It is easier to infer a cause-and-effect relationship between price and volume changes because there are usually no other factors or variance (e.g., rapid growth, product differentiation, diverse customer needs) to mess up the attribution.

The elegance of the elasticity framework lies in the simple formula – known as the Lerner Rule – that defines the profit-maximizing price point as a function of elasticity. Assuming a constant elasticity across all price ranges, a company can achieve its optimal price when its unit gross margin is the inverse of the elasticity. If the constant elasticity is 5, the profit-maximizing unit margin is 20%. A markup of 25% on variable costs will thus yield the optimal gross margin. In other words, a company can determine its profit-optimal price point with the knowledge of only two numbers: a product's variable cost and its elasticity. Figure 2.2 describes how buyers and sellers share value in such a situation. The uniform pricing model means that all customers pay the same price. The demand curve describes how value varies as a function of the cumulative units that customers are willing to buy. The surplus is the aggregate value distributed to customers, while the total margin is the value retained by the seller. We can see that the two surface areas in this example are similar, indicating a roughly equal sharing of value between buyers and the seller.

Such a framework may seem like it would have broad application with far-reaching implications, but it has several limitations.

The further a market's situation differs from the textbook examples – with their supply and demand equilibrium, perfect competition, one fixed price, and attributable price response – the less indicative or relevant the elasticity framework becomes. The dependence on a uniform price is a particular weakness in those situations.

The elasticity framework generally doesn't help when a small number of known suppliers sells to a small number of known customers, because the demand curve becomes very lumpy. Nor does it help when

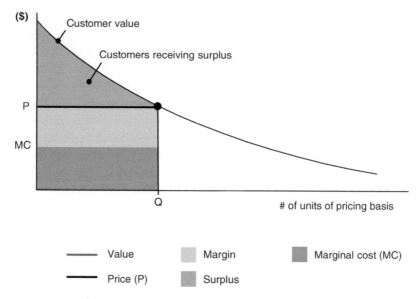

FIGURE 2.2   Uniform pricing model value distribution

slight variations in terms, conditions, and ancillary services make a negotiated deal with a buyer special, if not unique. This includes markets that
feature a multitude of price points and companies that use price models
that make individual offers harder to compare. It also includes markets in
which marginal costs have declined to near zero.[1]

Some estimated elasticities are less than 1, at which point the Lerner
Rule breaks down. In practice, such elasticities mean a company could
increase prices substantially until they reach a point on the demand
curve with an elasticity higher than 1. Such low elasticity estimates happen quite frequently, but many companies decide not to raise prices. This
means they are choosing to share a significant proportion of value with
their customers. It is also an indication that the elasticity framework alone
is insufficient to make strategic pricing decisions. Companies need to sup-
plement it with other approaches and considerations.

The role of differentiation

This framework is especially helpful for companies that use available data
on customers – their demographics, their behavior, their needs – to create

offers that are unique to the segment and have a segment-specific price. The proliferation of granular reliable data on willingness to pay is making this feasible for the first time for many companies on a large scale, at the segment level or even the individual customer level.

Companies can measure their relative value more precisely and calibrate how they want to share that value with customers (positive differential) or offset a value gap (negative differential). We refer to this as competitive discrimination when high levels of substitute value compel a company to design differentiated combinations of offerings and prices that target specific segments. Companies often employ techniques from behavioral science – including the compromise effect, decoys, and anchoring – to help guide customers through the range of offerings and help them self-select.

Price discrimination can also serve as a force for social good, such as when it provides people access to goods and services they could otherwise not afford. Airlines practice a form of price discrimination known as yield management. They use different fare classes and restrictions to capitalize on the higher willingness to pay from business customers, while offering lower prices to many consumers who could otherwise not afford to visit friends and family or travel abroad. This is a proportional form of value sharing, as the experience in business class or first class – both before, during, and after the flight – is usually far superior to what a coach or economy traveler enjoys. Over the past 30 years, this practice has driven the enormous growth of long-distance travel while maintaining a very competitive market with relatively low margins and levels of return. In other words, price discrimination has clearly expanded access to air travel without the rampant gouging or profiteering some people fear.

But like all four frameworks, price differentiation has weaknesses as well as limits to its applicability. The main barriers to applying price differentiation are market forces and psychology. Differentiation can be unprofitable when competitors do not adopt a similar strategy. Customers might also react negatively if they perceive it as discrimination, which has become a virtual synonym for racism and prejudice.

In addition, legal issues can arise, because it is possible to abuse competitive differentiation. Eugene Zelek, an expert lawyer on pricing, notes that the Robinson-Patman Act of 1936 (RPA) prohibits price discrimination on products sold to B2B customers that compete with each other, unless costs-to-serve or competitive quotes justify the price differences.[2] These exceptions are so pervasive, however, that prices for B2B products vary widely in practice. Many forms of B2B price discrimination are in fact legal. The RPA, for example, does not apply to B2B services. This gives businesses even more degrees of freedom for price discrimination.

Most B2C price discrimination is permitted by law, except for protected consumer categories and certain industries. Banks, for example, may vary interest rates based on the credit risk of consumers, but they must ensure that their algorithms do not have an explicit or implicit bias against certain races or protected categories. The same applies to insurance companies.

Even cases of positive discrimination, such as some university admissions policies, leave mixed feelings. But, as we discuss in greater detail in Chapters 20 and 21, perceptions of fairness can be paradoxical.[3] Most people consider a fair price to be a price others pay for a good or service, implying an expectation of uniform prices. But at the same time, research by the BCG Henderson Institute (BHI) has revealed that most people also consider giving a lower price to certain groups – such as seniors, students, or low-wage earners – to be fair.

The role of game theory

Game theory lies at the intersection of competition and cost. Imagine that you have one major competitor who decides to cut prices on their best-selling product by 5%. How do you respond to that move? The classic Prisoner's Dilemma model offers a simple way to frame the options, as Figure 2.3 shows. Let's say that in the status quo, you and your competitor each have a 50% share of a stable market and earn the same profit because you have a similar cost structure. We assume for simplicity's sake that you and your competitor each sell 10 units to half of the 20 customers in the market, i.e., 100 units total.

After your competitor cuts its price (move 1 in Figure 2.3), their profit increases so they have a clear interest in doing so. This is because the volume increase (20%) brings them more profit than the price decrease. This happens at your expense, as your volume and profits decline. The temptation for many business leaders is to counter the price cut in full, shown as move 2 in Figure 2.3. Your action restores the volumes and market shares to their equilibrium and increases your profit so it is in your interest to do so. However, the profits for both parties have eroded. This is the typical result of the Prisoner's Dilemma where both parties, following their self-interest, will lower their profits.

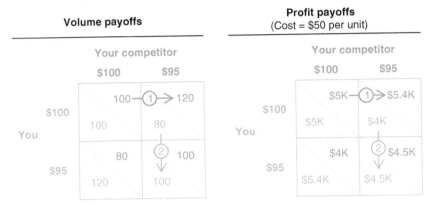

FIGURE 2.3 Duopoly equilibrium upset by a competitor cutting prices by 5%

Eventually these games will settle at a Nash equilibrium, a combination of strategic choices where no individual player can improve their payoff unilaterally. These equilibria often have significantly lower payoffs for all players than other combinations. This tendency for prices to work their way downward in a market is a hallmark of applied game theory.

Companies can avoid this fate by creating asymmetries that work to their advantage. The situation shown in Figure 2.3 depends on symmetry – similar market shares, similar cost structures, similar customers. Asymmetries or imbalances, repeated games, and careful coordination across accounts can help break the cycle and help you achieve a better outcome by skewing the Nash equilibrium to your advantage. Sources of asymmetries and imbalance include:

- **Costs:** This means you can sell the same product at a lower cost due to differences in production, distribution, or some other element of the business. A cost advantage allows you to bid lower and still maintain a profit.
- **Offerings:** Better quality or performance due to a difference in one or more product features or specifications can provide an advantage.
- **Customer relationships:** This reflects a customer preference for one supplier over another and is often called a brand or loyalty effect. In Figure 2.3, imagine that you had lost only one customer after your competitor's price cut rather than two customers, thanks to your longstanding relationships. That alone would have been enough to make your competitor worse off than you after their price cut.

Repetitions of a base game across multiple products and customers is called a repeated game. Whether in a simulation or a real market, the knowledge that competitors will play the game over and over alters their behavior. Game theorists have devised and tested various strategies in repeated games and have recognized that tit for tat – which calls for responses that imitate the other player's last move – is often a successful strategy, but there is no universal winning strategy.[4]

Game theory provides useful frameworks when market concentration is high, and sellers can track the outcomes of negotiations. Problems arise when there is the appearance of collusion, even when it is logically clear that the competitors are acting independently in line with their interests. A leadership team can influence its own company's costs, offerings, and customer relationships, but influencing competitors or coordinating with them is illegal. Pricing moves must be unilateral, which means you make them with the intention that your competitor does not respond. But there is a difference between doing something illegal and paying no attention to what one's competitors are doing. A company can still act unilaterally while informed and conscious of its role in the market, the equilibrium points, and how a market will develop given certain strategic choices.

The role of supply and demand

The phrase "supply and demand" dates to the 1700s, but the modern understanding of it reflects work by British economist Alfred Marshall in the late 1800s.[5] This framework builds on the idea that a market-clearing or market equilibrium price exists at the point where a demand curve and a supply curve intersect.

The demand curve slopes downward, because a given offer becomes less attractive as its price rises, and vice versa. At the same time, the supply curve slopes upward, indicating that production – even in costlier forms – becomes more attractive to more competitors as prices rise, and vice versa. The point at which these two curves intersect is the market equilibrium price, as illustrated in Figure 2.4.

The true power of the supply–demand framework emerges when we move from the aggregated supply and demand market views down to the individual transactions that comprise these curves.

Imagine that you have just wrapped up a productive day of meetings at the Philadelphia convention center. You check your airline app and see

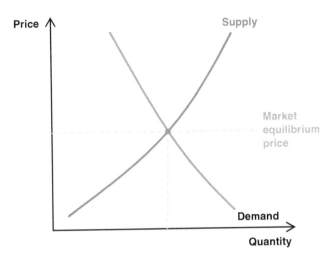

FIGURE 2.4   Supply–demand curve

that your flight to San Francisco, scheduled for 7 p.m., is still on time – miraculously and unexpectedly – despite thunderstorms all day.

The bad news is that it is already 5:30 p.m. You are running late, crossing your fingers that you can get a taxi to the airport right away.

Your hopes fade when you see at least 30 people ahead of you in the queue for cabs. Then you notice a sign at the entrance to the queue: "Flat Rate between the Airport and the Center City Zone. $32 per one way trip for one (1) passenger."

Let's first talk about the $32. Someone must have looked at the aggregate demand for airport rides in Philadelphia over many days, months, and years and created a demand curve like the one shown in Figure 2.4. They also looked at the supply of rides and arrived at the equilibrium price of $32. This may correctly represent what the average person would pay for a ride to the airport. But you are not the "average" person right now. You are late and you cannot wait for 30 people to get their cabs ahead of you.

You are experiencing, in real time, the failure of the aggregate supply–demand curve.

Then you open your favorite rideshare app, where you experience, also in real time, the power of individualized supply–demand matching. An SUV to the airport with zero wait time is available for $75. This is more than double the average fare, but because you are currently at the far left of the demand curve in Figure 2.4, you go for it. And it all ends well – a productive day and a flight that gets you home on time.

Sophisticated algorithms and robust data, often AI-driven, make it possible to disaggregate demand down to individuals at a specific moment. For the ride to the airport, an algorithm looks across context (rain, traffic), urgency (wait time), and special requests, and then configures an offer that fulfills that unique need.

The proliferation of granular data and the growing sophistication of AI algorithms are making aggregate supply–demand matching and average prices obsolete, because companies can now set prices at an individual transaction level. This transaction-by-transaction build-up provides the economic framework of the Dynamic Game.

Key takeaways

There are seven analytical approaches to set prices, as shown in the Venn diagram of Figure 2.1:

- The four main economic frameworks used to define prices combine the three sources of information (cost, competition, value) in different ways:
  - Price elasticity uses value and cost information.
  - Price differentiation uses value and competitive information.
  - Game theory uses cost and competitive information.
  - The supply–demand framework uses all three sources.
- Many companies make their pricing decisions based on only one type of information: either costs, comparison to their competitors, or value.
- Each approach has strengths and weaknesses, implying that none has universal relevance for a company's strategic pricing decisions.

The relevance of each pricing approach depends on the market characteristics, which we explore next.

CHAPTER 3

Seven Games in the Strategic Pricing Hexagon

T he previous two chapters introduced the three information sources – cost, competition, and value – and showed how their combinations naturally yield four basic economic frameworks for pricing. These frameworks complement the conventional price-setting approaches that rely solely on one of the information sources.

In Chapter 2 we highlighted some of the strengths and limitations of those economic frameworks, without providing specific and systematic guidance on which framework a business should select to help make faster, more confident, and more effective pricing decisions. The central question to developing that guidance is: Under what market conditions or characteristics are these frameworks most helpful?

There are natural links – but not strict deterministic ones – between the economic frameworks and market characteristics that lead directly to the seven strategic pricing games, which form the uppermost layer of the Strategy Hex (Figure 3.1).

Market characteristics are the strongest indicators that a particular pricing approach or economic framework fits a particular game. These characteristics include the concentration of buyers and sellers, the diversity of customer needs, and the variety and differentiation of offers. The cost structure of the offers can also play a role. The matrix in Figure 3.2 summarizes these market characteristics and matches them to each of the seven games.

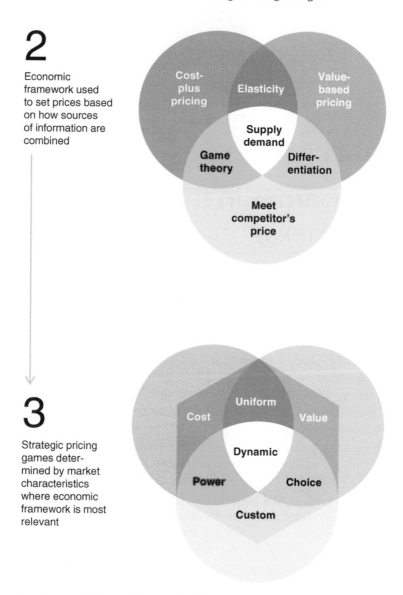

2

Economic framework used to set prices based on how sources of information are combined

3

Strategic pricing games determined by market characteristics where economic framework is most relevant

FIGURE 3.1 How the Venn diagram of information sources transforms into the Hex

Framework	Buyers	Sellers	Offers	Game
Value-based pricing	Fragmented customer base	Clear leader	Unique-differentiated offers with far superior value proposition	**Value**
Elasticity	Broad base of buyers with similar needs	Fragmented competitors of similar sizes	Narrowly differentiated	**Uniform**
Cost-plus pricing	Major buyers with specific needs	Extremely fragmented with no clear leader	Commoditized offers with high proportion of variable costs	**Cost**
Game theory	Concentrated, sophisticated buyers with similar needs	Concentrated competitors with similar market share	Technical standards limiting differentiation	**Power**
Price to competition	Broad customer base of very different sizes	Highly concentrated sellers competing for most deals	Offers customized from a large set of options	**Custom**
Differen-tiation	Fragmented customer base with diverse needs	Concentrated, often with clear leader	Broad offer lineup often with low marginal cost	**Choice**
Supply demand	Many buyers with different and fluctuating needs	Can be concentrated, but not necessarily	Perishable inventory or unpredictable and fluctuating demand	**Dynamic**

FIGURE 3.2   Summary of the market characteristics where an economic framework is most relevant

- **Buyers:** Customers can vary by their sheer numbers, but they can also differ by the volumes they buy and their individual needs. The latter two factors can show very large variance within a market. Some markets will have millions or even tens of millions of customers with relatively homogeneous needs, while other equally large markets can have such a diversity of customer needs that a "segment of one" can make sense. Customized offers that address a segment of one can lead to "fewer product shortage and quality issues, better service levels, lower costs and resource requirements, [and] greater supply chain robustness and agility."[1]

- **Sellers:** Seller concentration can vary from low to high. A fragmented market tends to have several competitors with small market shares. A concentrated market has a small number of sellers, often no more than four, but the power dynamics can vary considerably depending on whether one or two of those companies have high shares or whether the market shares are more evenly distributed. In some markets a quasi-monopoly situation can exist when a company has patent protection or offers a product or service with exceptionally high perceived value.

- **Offers:** The offers in a given market usually vary according to their complexity and their degree of differentiation. These two aspects do not necessarily correlate. Advanced or complex machinery, for example, can still show a high degree of standardization across suppliers, who need to find subtle forms of differentiation or compete on cost and efficiency. We often witness imbalances between the range of offers and the diversity of customer needs, but these imbalances often work in favor of companies. The needs of buyers of cutting-edge biopharmaceuticals or luxury goods may differ significantly, but many leading companies in those industries offer little or no product variation.

The next logical step is to combine the insights from Figure 3.1 and Figure 3.2 to observe how strongly the different information sources and economic frameworks associate with the seven pricing games.

Rationales for connecting market characteristics and pricing approaches

There is an intuitive connection between market characteristics and pricing approaches. Many keen pricing practitioners and market observers have made some of these connections. For instance, pricing to value is much easier to implement if a company is a leader in its market with a very differentiated value proposition.

We now describe the full reasoning behind Figure 3.2, which connects every one of the seven positions in the Venn diagram to the three main market characteristics and highlights the most critical ones. We build this connection by asking which combinations of market characteristics are the best fit to the seven pricing approaches. This way, observing the market characteristics enables leaders to determine which of the seven pricing approaches they should choose.

We start with the Value Game, then move counterclockwise around the Strategy Hex.

Value Game

A value-based pricing approach is most helpful when an offering's usage value – economically and emotionally – is much larger than its substitute value, and the buyers are so numerous and fragmented that no individual customer or group holds significant purchasing power. The seller's value proposition is either unique or so differentiated that buyers have few alternatives. Such markets tend to have very few sellers, and in extreme situations, one seller holds a quasi-monopoly position in lucrative niches thanks to patent protection or a far superior value proposition. If the buying side were concentrated instead of numerous and fragmented, they could offset the value-based approach by using their purchasing power to avoid being locked into a limited or unique set of offers. But that is not the case.

This is the essence of the Value Game.

Many biopharmaceutical companies and luxury goods manufacturers play the Value Game, but it is by no means limited to those sectors. Some companies – whether startups or incumbents – launch innovative products that can give them a foothold in the Value Game. Companies can also move from other games to the Value Game by recognizing and harnessing the forces we describe in Chapter 4.

Apple also plays the Value Game. When Apple launched the iPod and iPhone, each was an unbeatable product in its respective category (MP3 player and smartphone). Each had premium functional specifications, albeit not best-in-class for the iPhone. In such situations, other sellers become irrelevant unless they figure out how to catch up with the market leader. Nokia responded slowly to the iPhone and went from a 38% market share in 2007 (based on revenue) to a complete market exit in

2014.[2] Samsung, in contrast, released high-quality smartphones with sleek designs and intuitive interfaces and achieved 20% market share by the early 2020s. But the iPhone's unique combination of functional and emotional features still leaves Apple with approximately 40% of the market.[3]

Customers who valued design and ease of use simply had no alternative when the iPod and iPhone launched. This fragmented customer base gave Apple almost unconstrained freedom to decide how much value to share with the customers and to set prices accordingly. The annual sales of the iPod peaked at almost 55 million units in 2008[4] and annual worldwide smartphone shipments would reach 1.46 billion units in 2017,[5] with virtually all devices being purchased by individuals.

Chapter 7 goes into greater detail on how Apple succeeded in the Value Game.

Uniform Game

The elasticity framework is the best approach for making efficient and confident pricing decisions when a company's market has certain characteristics. First, to gain a sample size that makes estimates and statistics accurate, the markets must have a very large number of buyers. Second, these buyers have relatively homogenous needs, and the offers of numerous sellers are very comparable. These characteristics rule out the application of game theory as a primary framework, because it is impossible to monitor the prices of every single competitor. In addition, sellers are usually of similar sizes. If there were a clear leader, game theory would start to apply, because the leader's price moves would affect all competitors' pricing decisions. These characteristics also rule out price discrimination, because the buyers' needs and sellers' offers are too homogeneous.

This is the essence of the Uniform Game.

It resembles the domain of the proverbial widget maker in an economic textbook: countless anonymous customers with homogeneous needs served by suppliers with similar cost structures and similar standardized products sold at transparent and uniform prices. Consumer packaged goods companies and retailers tend to play the Uniform Game. One example is Nona Lim, a maker of convenient healthy Asian-inspired soups and broths.

Her company's soups are positioned at the high end of the market with a focus on taste, nutrition, and quality ingredients. Her products put her at the nexus of several rapidly growing and attractive consumer categories that have retained or regained their momentum after the Covid-19 pandemic.[6] Heading into 2020, the Whole Foods grocery chain listed "Out-of-the-Box, Into-the-Fridge Snacking" as one of its top 10 food trends and specifically recommended Nona Lim's drinkable soups as one way to "try the trend."[7]

Her retail partners give her access to millions of customers. Whole Foods, for example, operates over 500 stores in North America and the United Kingdom.[8] One of their locations on the north side of Chicago experiences just under 140,000 visits per month from around 70,000 customers, all of them essentially anonymous to Nona.[9]

These characteristics, at first glance, may make Nona Lim seem like a potential player in the Value Game. But other market characteristics make the Uniform Game a better fit for Nona Lim than the Value Game. On the supplier side, the soup category is so fragmented that even the iconic Campbell Soup Company claims that "the number of competitors cannot be reliably estimated."[10] Similarly, the forms of products and their packaging are fragmented, ranging from dry instant soup to canned soup all the way to prepared soups in the deli section of grocery stores. This makes market definition a critically important exercise.

Narrowly speaking, Nona Lim's products compete against the products adjacent to hers on the store shelf. More broadly, her Heat&Sip soup cups compete against coffee and other beverages, because they are "pretty much designed for modern millennials who always have a smartphone in one hand."[11] Her differentiation, however, is not so large that she can define her own category.

Chapter 8 takes a more detailed look at how Nona Lim succeeds in the Uniform Game.

Cost Game

Many businesses use a cost-plus approach to set prices, even though that approach is only warranted when certain market characteristics apply. This tends to be the case when a fragmented base of sellers competes for the business of a much larger buyer in a commoditized market. That buyer, in turn, can switch between sellers easily because they have little or no meaningful differentiation. This is particularly the case when the buyers have very different needs that will drive large cost differences to serve them. The customer base tends to be concentrated, the supplier base fragmented, and the offers commoditized with a high proportion of variable costs.

This is the essence of the Cost Game.

Companies playing the Cost Game know their individual customers well. Think of an automotive supplier in a fragmented supply chain. It sells its products to a small number of systems suppliers – perhaps only one – which in turn sells their finished products directly to automotive OEMs. Fixed contracts or bidding processes set the terms of transactions, including prices, and govern the relationships between the suppliers and customers. Customers have significant buying power in these markets, and some of these markets are monopsonies.

The challenge for suppliers is to write and control their own margin equation. Their upside in terms of prices is minimal, which means their profits and in many cases their viability hinges on their ability to manage costs. The more efficiently they can produce their offers, the greater their degrees of freedom and pricing agency become.

Let's look at the challenges faced by a company we will refer to as Wrightway, a major European construction company. Wrightway competes in a field with fragmented competitors and concentrated customers. Its competitors include national players as well as smaller regional and local players. But all of these sellers compete for just one customer: the government.

The roadwork projects that Wrightway delivers are standardized and largely undifferentiated. They require the same raw materials (e.g., asphalt, concrete), equipment, and engineering expertise, such as earthwork, excavation, and drainage. Projects are often defined with so much standardization that the government can choose a seller primarily based on price, because the final product is likely to be the same, regardless of seller. Thus, the pricing mechanism in the Cost Game tends to be a simple markup of underlying costs.

However, costs are highly variable and can differ by supplier and by project. For example, construction companies will have different round-trip travel costs, and projects will have different search costs, based on terrain and access. The magnitude of differences can be very large, with the cost of Wrightway's projects ranging from less than €50,000 to several million euros.

Chapter 9 shows how Wrightway separated itself from others in a market driven by cost efficiency.

Power Game

Game theory is the main framework for pricing decisions when two market characteristics exist simultaneously: a market is concentrated on both the buyer and seller sides, and offers show limited differentiation, because buyers impose technical standards that only a few sophisticated sellers can fulfill. Because of these standards, offers are very comparable and sellers make significant investments to analyze subtle differences across every deal with every buyer. These dynamics create a delicate balance of power between buyers and sellers and also between sellers. The stakes are high, because the win or loss of any individual customer relationship can have a material effect on a supplier and can potentially reshape the entire market.

This is the essence of the Power Game.

Game theory becomes less relevant when either of those market characteristics does not apply. If sellers or buyers are fragmented, it becomes difficult, if not impossible, for any seller to track what each other seller is doing or to perform the necessary analyses on every deal with every buyer. If the offer from one seller is highly differentiated, it renders the value propositions of other competitors, and, consequently, the moves of other competitors, less relevant for decision-making at the company with the far superior value proposition.

Success in the Power Game depends on a leadership team's ability to understand and manage fine points of equilibrium in the market. This characterized the market for hard-disk drives (HDDs) in the early 2000s. HDD manufacturers had only a handful of direct customers, even though hundreds of millions of consumers worldwide used their products. Seagate derived roughly two-thirds of its revenue in the early 2000s from global computer manufacturers such as Compaq and Hewlett-Packard (which merged in 2002) as well as Dell and IBM.[12] One of its primary competitors, Western Digital, earned at least half of its revenue every year from the same top-tier computer makers.[13] Dell alone accounted for 20% of Western Digital's revenue in its 2003 fiscal year.[14]

The supply side of the HDD market showed even greater concentration than the demand side. In 2003, four manufacturers – Western Digital, Seagate, Maxtor, and Hitachi Global Storage Technologies – accounted for approximately 85% of the total market.[15]

HDDs were "highly substitutable due to the industry mandate of technical form, fit and function standards" and therefore seemed like commodities, even though they are very sophisticated products requiring advanced engineering capabilities to design and manufacture.[16] Each manufacturer offered a wide range of standard products, which varied by several performance factors but primarily by capacity, speed, and type of interface. In 2001, an HDD with a capacity of 80 gigabytes (GB) represented "the upper limit of demand for PC buyers,"[17] and cost around $4 per GB.[18] In 2004, the largest HDD that Seagate offered had a capacity of 200 GB[19] and cost around $0.60 per GB,[20] but the bulk of its sales came from products with less than 100 GB of storage capacity.

Compare that to the early 2020s, when the storage capacities of standard HDDs varied by a factor of 125. Smaller or older machines capacities used HDDs with capacities of 16, 32, or 64 GB, while machines for users who play games or store high-resolution files had hard drives with 1 or 2 terabytes of storage, and cost around $0.02 per GB.[21,22]

Chapter 10 shows the Power Game approaches that HDD manufacturers used to maintain the equilibrium in the market.

Custom Game

Pricing to competition is the approach when several market characteristics prevent a convergence toward large customer segments, common price structures, and similar product configurations. First, these markets tend to have few sellers but a large, fragmented base of buyers. This makes the consistent tracking and benchmarking of competitors feasible, but also means that the stakes with any specific customer tend to be lower, unlike the Power Game. The number of customers can range from dozens or hundreds for a manufacturer of industrial goods to millions for an automotive OEM.

A specific competitor's prices also serve as the primary input for pricing decisions in profitable markets (i.e., ones with predictably positive margins) where there is only slight differentiation across competitors. This minimizes the direct roles of costs and value as inputs into pricing decisions. Core offers may be undifferentiated among competitors, but the addition of a wide variety of product options, and the ability to adjust terms and conditions along numerous dimensions, make each transaction unique. This lack of standardization precludes the creation of bundles, packages, or other segment-specific offers with transparent prices, because there is always a risk that a competitor will offer the option combination the customer needs for the discounted bundle price.

This is the essence of the Custom Game.

Discount management is vitally important in the Custom Game, because discounts form the primary tool for price differentiation. But determining discounts can seem chaotic, because the transactions are subject to all the drivers of variance we mentioned in Chapter 1. When a customer buys, why they buy, in which channel, and where they are located can all influence the level of discounts and the outcomes of negotiations.

Daimler Trucks North America (DTNA) faced the challenges of this chaos acutely during the Great Recession of 2008–2009. DTNA's potential customer base was diverse, comprising hundreds of thousands of commercial customers, from individual owner-operators to logistics companies or retailers with large fleets, such as Fedex (more than 30,000 trucks) and Walmart (10,000 trucks).[23,24]

Four major manufacturers made up the highly concentrated supplier side: DTNA, Navistar, Volvo, and Paccar, although Paccar's two major brands – Kenworth and Peterbilt – operated independently. In 2008, Daimler was the market leader in Class 8 trucks, with 25.4% market share.[25] It was also the North American leader in several other vehicle categories, including school buses.[26]

The range of products also typified the Custom Game. If you recall ever driving past a truck dealership along the highway, you may have had the impression that Class 8 trucks such as semis all look similar. That impression is deceiving, because there are more than 100 types of medium- and heavy-duty trucks, including long-haul semis, utility and trash trucks, dump trucks and cement mixers, fire trucks, and box trucks of all shapes and sizes.

In fact, it can take more than 200 features to define an individual truck, depending on numerous criteria, including the nature of the job and the needs of the customer. Trucks come with options from the fundamentals (engine, axles, transmissions) to customized interior amenities. Local regulations and constraints splinter the taxonomy of trucks even further, as designs and product options need to take into account aspects such as climate and the weight limits for bridges.

Chapter 11 shows how DTNA managed this chaotic environment successfully.

Choice Game

Price differentiation is the best economic framework for pricing decisions when a market has a broad customer base with diverse needs. This allows competitors to differentiate themselves more consistently than they can in the Custom Game, because it is easier for them to develop offers for specific customer segments. In that sense, differentiation means differentiation both from competition and across the offers of a particular seller. Behavioral science plays an important role as a means to help steer customers to the offer that is best for them among a broad lineup of available choices.

These markets tend to have only a small number of competitors, because sellers need sufficient scale to serve such a diverse set of customers. Price differentiation is especially important when offers have limited or no marginal costs. Otherwise, competition tends to drive down prices close to marginal costs, limiting overall revenues and ability to invest in improved offers.

There is less need for price differentiation if customer needs are homogenous, and less need for a diverse range of offers in a market comprising very few customers. Likewise, when a large number of sellers compete, they tend to concentrate on specific segments with specific needs. In that case, the price elasticity framework (with uniform pricing) becomes the optimal framework within each segment.

This is the essence of the Choice Game.

Companies in the Choice Game design offers to match the needs of certain clusters or segments of customers, and usually offer a wide range of options to differentiate themselves across multiple segments. Software companies are common examples of Choice Game players, but companies in sectors as diverse as quick service restaurants (QSRs) and specialty restaurants – such as Starbucks – also play the Choice Game successfully.

Starbucks CEO Howard Schultz consciously designed the Starbucks coffee house business as an immersive experience for taste-driven consumers as opposed to convenience-driven consumers. In a 1986 memo, he wrote that "we will offer superior coffee and related products" and be "genuinely interested in educating our customers."[27] He was also trying to emulate the experience of sitting at the terrasse of a café in Italy with an espresso.

Subsegments within those taste-driven consumers began to emerge, ranging from the customers seeking the very best coffee beans to those intrigued by fancy coffee-based drinks with Italian names, enjoyed in a communal atmosphere, which Starbucks called the Third Place. Over time, Starbucks created such a structured yet differentiated lineup to serve the growing number of subsegments within the premium coffee category. In 1995, it launched the frappuccino to cater to customers who favored creamy, flavorful, iced coffees and were willing to pay a small premium. In 1997, it introduced nondairy milks and sugar-free syrups as add-ons to existing drinks.[28] It also began to serve convenience-driven consumers as well.

Coffee's marginal cost is also low compared to the retail price. In 1991, the year before its IPO, Starbucks enjoyed a healthy 50% gross margin.[29] In sectors such as software, marginal costs are negligible. This combination of high value and negligible marginal costs helped the enterprise software company Citrix, for example, earn gross margins of 80.6% in 2022, down from 84.6% in 2021.[30]

Customers in the Choice Game usually have a limited set of suppliers to choose from. In the coffee category, national QSR chains such as McDonald's and Dunkin' Donuts serve regular brewed coffee and now offer espresso-based drinks, as do independent premium coffeeshops. But on-the-go coffee drinkers usually find their options defined by their commuting route or whatever they have available within a walk or short drive from their home.

Chapter 12 describes how Starbucks thrives in the Choice Game.

Dynamic Game

Some companies are in markets where they have no choice but to understand and manage the full complexity of the supply–demand framework. This requires them to incorporate all information sources and multiple pricing approaches simultaneously into their pricing decisions.

This can arise when companies have adjustable capacity, perishable inventory of relatively undifferentiated products, or constantly fluctuating demand from a broad base of customers. The drivers of variance that we described in Chapter 1 – location, time, customer segment, occasion, supply and capacity, volume, and channel – all affect marginal costs, customer value, and willingness to pay. Because competitors face similar pressures, they may vary their prices significantly and thus contribute to high price volatility.

This is the essence of the Dynamic Game.

The primitive version of the Dynamic Game is the farmer's market or the bazaar, but those transactions in many cases are not parts of repeated games. In the contemporary Dynamic Game, companies generally need to assume that they are playing a repeated game and that customer relationships matter. The yield management programs of airlines were among the first examples. Over decades, airlines have honed their ability to react to the complex ebbs and flows within their markets as well as to external shocks, which can range from localized events (e.g., an airport closure) to global events with unforeseeable consequences (e.g., the Covid-19 pandemic). Nowadays their advanced algorithms attempt to take strategic, behavioral, and financial inputs into account simultaneously, accompanied by human judgment.

At first glance it would seem obvious to equate the Dynamic Game with the concept of dynamic pricing. But there is a fundamental difference between companies that use dynamic pricing and companies that are playing the Dynamic Game. When a petrochemical wholesaler squeezes out an extra 100 to 250 basis points of margin by using artificial intelligence (AI) to model their market complexity, they are using dynamic pricing to play the Cost Game better.[31] When an automotive OEM makes its dealer incentive programs 10% more cost effective by gaining a better understanding of market dynamics at the local level, they are attempting to play a better version of the Custom Game.[32]

The players of the Dynamic Game actively shape the underlying dynamism within their markets by influencing customer access, adjusting their range of options, and improving efficiency. Each player makes an ongoing commitment to become smarter, faster, and fairer with the way they share value, as they gain a richer and more reliable understanding of the factors that drive buying behavior. They find themselves in a continuous loop of self-optimization, using all the inputs and economic frameworks simultaneously with a growing level of complexity. Whenever they think they have mastered the game, it's time to change the game.

Markets in the Dynamic Game can be quite concentrated, because playing the game effectively requires scale. Implementation demands a high level of experience and maturity. Buyers in the Dynamic Game are typically fragmented but tend to see the offers of the various competitors as undifferentiated.

Chapter 13 shows examples of how companies are winning the Dynamic Game.

What pricing game are you playing?

The second fundamental question to developing a pricing strategy is: What pricing game do you want to play?

You should now be well equipped to answer the first two questions, which will together determine what game you're playing now. As a reminder, the two questions are:

2a. Which game aligns best with the **characteristics of your market**?

2b. Which game aligns best with your **current pricing approach**?

A discrepancy in those answers indicates that you have an opportunity to better align your pricing approach with your market. Let's say you sell a consumer product through a large number of retailer partners and are the fifth-strongest competitor among a group of more than 10 brands. Your market characteristics clearly indicate that you are in the Uniform Game.

Figure 3.3 summarizes the concentration or fragmentation of buyers and sellers in a market, their relative strengths within a market, and the complexity and structure of the offers in that market. You'll notice that the offers in the Uniform and Cost Games have few defining dimensions, the first one with uniform coloring of each face and the other one with no color differentiation, indicating a high degree of commoditization. The offers in the Power and Custom Games are more complex. The offer in the Power Game shows a complex pattern that illustrates the technical sophistication imposed by buyers. The nature of the offers in the Choice and Value Games have a much different structure. The first one reflects the portfolio consistency of a good-better-best lineup as well as the stair steps of the migration paths from one offer to the next. The diamond serves as a symbol of the unique nature of the offer. Finally, the Dynamic Game's offer has no rigid form, because companies adjust their offers in response to supply and demand.

The triangles represent the sellers, and the circles represent the buyers. You'll notice that the number of each varies by game (reflecting concentration or fragmentation) and their relative size varies within a given game. The Power Game has the highest concentration on both sides and the smallest deviations among buyers and sellers in terms of size and

△ Sellers   ▢ Offers   ○ Buyers

FIGURE 3.3 Offer, seller, and buyer characteristics by game

strength. At the other extreme, the Uniform Game has numerous competitors of similar size selling to markets that are usually very large, with customers who have similar value perceptions and similar buying power.

The market characteristics shown in Figure 3.2 are ranges, not absolutes. Similarly, the size and distribution of the buyers and sellers in Figure 3.3 are illustrative. Therefore, you may find that more than one game describes your situation. A startup, for example, may enter a very fragmented market with a breakthrough product that they plan to sell in retail stores with a uniform pricing model. The market they enter typifies the Uniform Game, but their product is so superior that they might want to play a Value Game. In this case, they have a current position and an ideal position. Their go-to-market and pricing strategy will need to determine how they can anchor themselves in the Value Game and avoid being dragged into the more homogeneous Uniform Game. They may need to avoid traditional retailers and find another channel.

This means that the Hex is not like a game board with only seven positions. It is more like a map, and you may find yourself in a market that leaves you on the boundary between two games or at a nexus where multiple games intersect. You may also choose to operate your business as a pure play in one game or find that your portfolio of businesses or products requires you to play multiple games.

The last question to decide which game or combination of games you want to play is:

2c. Which game aligns best with the **market forces** and your **competitive advantages**?

This depends on the market forces and your competitive advantages or imbalances vis-à-vis your competitors. We study six market forces in the next chapter.

Key takeaways

The seven economic frameworks defined by the Venn diagram of information sources are the most relevant to define prices, but their application depends on market characteristics: buyer and seller fragmentation or concentration, diversity of customer needs, and differentiation of offers.

- The combination of these characteristics determines the seven games displayed in the Strategic Pricing Hexagon.
- The organization of the games in the Strategy Hex with the underlying Venn diagram is a reminder of which sources of information are most critical to making pricing decisions.
- The organization also means that some information sources and economic frameworks are less well suited for a particular game. For example:
    - Elasticity is a core framework for the Uniform Game, but it is significantly less important for business leaders playing the Power, Custom, or Choice Games.

- ○ Cost as an information source is less important in the Custom, Choice, and Value Games, but more important in the Power Game and of paramount importance in the Cost Game.
- ○ Game theory is less relevant in the Value Game because the leading solution is far superior to competitor alternatives.
- Each game has a unique set of rules and dynamics that companies should understand to develop successful long-term strategies.
- Most markets fit very well to one of the games, but some may fit to more than one game. This is not a flaw, but rather an opportunity for leaders to decide which game to play, based on their competitive advantages.

CHAPTER 4

Six Market Forces

Companies occupy different positions within the fields of the seven pricing games in the Strategy Hex. But none of these positions is permanent, nor are they necessarily stable, because of the influence of the six forces shown in Figure 4.1.

The presence of these forces creates imbalances in markets and compels business leaders to decide whether they want to accelerate the underlying trends, resist them, or let them play out. These are often strategic decisions, because they can require significant investments in technology, geographic expansion, product development, marketing, and production assets. They also reinforce the tight link between corporate strategy and pricing strategy.

Regardless of whether they are initiated by a competitor, another external agent, or the company itself, these forces will invariably drive a leadership team's decisions on whether to continue to play a particular game or how to play the current game better.

Think of these forces as vectors acting on the position of a company within its game. If intense enough, these forces can alter the underlying characteristics of a market to such an extent that the market becomes a better fit to another game. They can change the number of buyers and sellers, influence customer needs, and reduce or increase the complexity and differentiation of offerings.

The six market forces manifest themselves in many different forms. Their strong active presence does not rob executives of their agency, nor

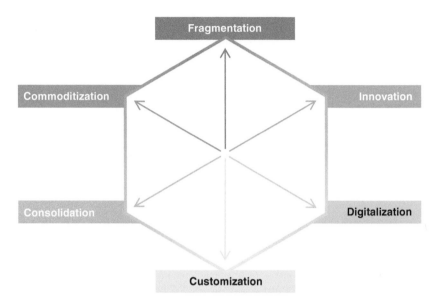

FIGURE 4.1   The six forces that influence a company's position in the Hex

does it prescribe what they should do. They usually expand and clarify the leadership team's options. Leaders need to determine how much pressure each force exerts and what imbalances they create, and then assess their degrees of freedom to harness those forces to their advantage.

The chapters in Part III show how the forces can alter market characteristics enough to create a temporary or permanent imbalance that a company can use to its advantage. Where a company ends up – and, to some extent, where it starts – results from conscious decisions that the leadership teams make after weighing their available options, which usually turn out to be more extensive and more nuanced than they imagined.

Let's look at each force individually and how it can influence a company's position and a leader's decisions. We'll go counterclockwise around the Strategy Hex, starting with fragmentation.

Fragmentation

Fragmentation pressures a company's position toward the top of the Strategy Hex. As the number of competitors increases, it is harder to keep track of what each competitor is doing and simpler to adopt a uniform pricing approach with elasticity as the primary pricing framework.

With a large number of competitors, prices tend to converge around a common point as each player mitigates the ever-present risk that one player lowers their prices and starts to attract customers. The likelihood is also high that competitors emulate the incremental innovations or offer variations of others. The differences in value delivered by various competitors therefore tend to diminish. Small price differences can still exist, reflecting potential slight value differences, but these differences tend to freeze, with all competitor prices moving up and down simultaneously.

Fragmentation can also affect the demand side when the number of customers increases by an order of magnitude. This happens in high-growth markets over time or when high-end offers go down market. Luxury goods, for example, can become mass consumption items if their exclusivity cachet disappears. If many competitors enter the market simultaneously, elasticity replaces value-based pricing as the primary framework.

Another consequence of market fragmentation is price transparency. With many competitors serving many customers, it is harder for any advantageous or disadvantageous transaction to stay a secret for a long time. If someone brags about a great deal they got, then friends talk to each other about it, and social media spreads the information. This all plays toward uniform pricing.

As with all six forces, business leaders have the opportunity to resist, accept, or accelerate the trends. The way to counter the effects of fragmentation is to create a scale advantage or increase differentiation, e.g., through innovation.

Commoditization

Market commoditization pressures a company to move toward the upper left of the Hex, where cost competitiveness becomes a driving force of pricing decisions. Commoditization means offers have less and less value differentiation. Cost advantage thus becomes the only sustainable source of price advantage, because at some point, competitors can no longer match the lower prices of the cost leader without endangering their own margins.

The entry of a low-cost supplier can draw an entire market toward the Cost Game. This is often an aggressive move by a competitor, who may want to diminish others' competitive advantages or undercut their prices. Even companies in the Value Game are not immune to the potential effects of commoditization, despite their strong or protected value propositions. In the technology sector, many startups develop cheaper good-enough solutions that can change underlying market conditions. They can threaten the position of incumbents by offering simple products without bells and whistles, simplifying the pricing model by eliminating high discounts, and converting new customer segments.

Like each of the six forces, commoditization is the direct consequence of certain decisions that business leaders make. The increasing technological obsolescence of a company's or an industry's products can shift it toward the Cost Game. This may have resulted from underinvestment in a product or platform or from saturation of a given customer group. It may also result from a conscious decision to phase out offerings that have reached technological maturity or the end of their life cycle. The pursuit of industry standardization can also lead to commoditization.

Companies are almost always better off financially if they resist the force of commoditization. The exception is when they have a significant cost advantage that competitors cannot replicate in the short term. Those situations are rare, though, in mature markets where competitors often have similar cost structures. Resisting commoditization often means identifying the intensity of other trends so that the balance of pressure on a company's position works in its favor. Put another way, companies could innovate their way out of a commoditization threat or look for another way to create advantageous imbalances.

Consolidation

Consolidation is any change that increases the concentration on the supplier or customer side. It can swiftly reshape a market, especially when it reduces the number of suppliers and alters the balance of power.

Directionally, it forces a company toward the bottom left of the Strategy Hex, where the Power Game is located. If a company switches to the Power Game, it will need to embrace game theory as its critical pricing framework. This makes adverse Nash equilibria more likely.

Consolidation can take many forms. It includes mergers and acquisitions, but the same effects can occur through reductions of capacity through plant closures, market exits (by choice or by bankruptcy), or *force majeure* (war, asset seizure, regime change) that takes a company's capacity offline for an indefinite period.

In B2B markets, the combination of two customers can create a risk for a supplier because it creates price transparency and exposes how consistent or inconsistent a supplier's prices have been. This risk is especially high in the Custom Game, where terms and conditions in any given deal are often unique to a customer. Consolidation also creates scale and may give buyers enough future leverage to alter a seller's position in its current game.

Customization

Customization exerts pressure on a company to move downward in the Strategy Hex. It refers to the tailoring or slight modification of a core offering to meet the needs of an individual customer.

Customization can encompass a set of product options, supplemental services ranging from slight product alterations, more extensive support, or co-development and co-selling activities. In B2B markets, these slight modifications can also include terms and conditions, special discounts, rebates, bonuses, free goods, and surcharges.

Meeting bespoke customer requirements can generate higher loyalty and value. This means that firms should look for ways to accelerate this trend when the economics are feasible. A strong trend toward customization does not necessarily create the conditions for the Custom Game. When it exerts a strong force on companies in the Value Game, it can create the market characteristics better suited for the Choice Game. This occurs, for example, when a company flanks a competitor's successful, high-value, high-margin product with tailored offerings that appeal to distinct subsegments.

Digitalization

Digitalization confers the data-driven ability for companies to create customer experiences and prices that are unique to a customer. It draws companies to the lower right in the Strategy Hex.

By enabling companies to offer valuable data-driven services at negligible marginal costs, digitalization has already transformed several industries by deprioritizing or eliminating physical products or channels. Classic examples of transformed industries include music, television, movies, news, software, shopping, personal financial services, and personal transportation, which has led to the steep decline or elimination of newspapers, physical media, shopping malls, bank branches, and taxi cabs. The effects of digitalization have been so pervasive on the fates of businesses and the lives of consumers that it is becoming harder and harder to imagine the world prior to the commercial internet, when the fax machine and the overnight FedEx envelope set the standards for rapid communication.

Digitalization will remain a powerful transformative force. Advanced analytics and artificial intelligence allow companies that traditionally sell physical supplies to measure the performance and outcomes that their products create. In other words, they can gain a precise and customer-specific understanding of their usage value. This creates opportunities for innovative pricing models based on consumption, usage, or outcomes.

The transformative power of "digital natives" has been swift and unprecedented. Within three decades or less, Amazon, Google, Uber, Apple's smartphone division, Facebook, and Tesla have gone from market shares of zero to market leadership positions. Amazon, Google (Alphabet), Tesla, Apple, and Microsoft had also exceeded a market capitalization on $1 trillion, as of December 2021.[1]

Innovation

This force pressures companies toward the top right of the Strategy Hex. In its strongest form, it can allow a company to move from the left side of the Hex to the right side, where they can focus on defining and managing the value ladder instead of focusing on margin.

Innovations create more value to share with customers and therefore give companies more options on how much to share and how to share it. They can range from incremental improvements to existing products all the way to game-changing products or services that have a sharp, significant effect on existing market players and their value propositions. The development and launch of the iPod and iPhone, for example, show how innovation can transform markets that had characteristics of a Choice Game (mobile phones, cameras, gaming devices) into a Value Game. Through its own innovations, Samsung has eliminated Apple's quasi-monopoly position, but preserved the market for smartphones as a Value Game played by a small number of companies.

The literal game-changing innovations come about when companies identify unmet needs, respond to a stratification of customer needs, or witness a fundamental shift in their cost structure such as the negligible marginal costs arising from digitalization. Companies can also repurpose existing technologies or platforms. Finally, business model innovations can also reshape markets. We describe briefly in Chapter 15 how Salesforce.com accomplished that shift.

* * *

So far, we have presented the structural layers of the Strategy Hex, the nature of the seven pricing games that arise logically within it, and the forces that influence the stability and viability of a company's position within its chosen game. But these structures and insights are still not sufficient for a company to determine its pricing strategy. Leaders also need to choose the right pricing model, a challenge we explore in Chapter 6.

But before we get to that chapter, we will look at the impact that the positions and forces in the Strategy Hex have on a company's organization and its governance structure. Who holds pricing authority in terms of strategy and implementation?

Key takeaways

Markets constantly evolve due to a number of forces. Six of these forces have a major influence on the nature of a market and the position of a company within the Hex: fragmentation, commoditization, consolidation, customization, digitalization, and innovation.

- Companies need to be aware of how these forces can change the game they are playing, so that they can adapt their pricing model and strategy.
    - Digitalization tends to lower marginal costs and allow a broader set of offers and thus push companies toward the Choice Game.

- o Alternatively, competitors catching up with your offers can drag you into a Cost Game, which carries the risk of lower margins if your company does not have or cannot achieve a cost advantage through scale or efficiencies.
- Companies can also initiate and take advantage of these forces to change the game they are playing.
  - o Innovation offers opportunities for companies to move to the Value Game if they achieve enough differentiation.

CHAPTER 5

What the Hex? The Political Angles of Pricing Decisions

T he definition of pricing strategy – a leader's conscious decisions on how to shape their market by determining the amount of money available, how that money flows, and to whom – makes pricing inherently political. The person or people who can direct those flows of money within a firm and a market wield enviable power.

That power creates either a struggle or a vacuum within nearly every company, regardless of sector or size: How does the firm keep sales, marketing, finance, and other functional teams aligned around a common strategic objective? Put more precisely: What governance model will ensure that these teams work in harmony to manage and, ideally, maximize the value the company creates and shares?

Figure 5.1 shows how each executive or functional area within an organization has a natural fit to one of the seven pricing games. The positions in Figure 5.1 indicate which functions should have the leadership role, because their main responsibility is to manage the most critical trade-offs in that game. But there is also broad consensus that pricing is a team sport. Pricing decisions require cross-functional input and insights, which means that other functions always have important roles and obligations. They provide necessary insights and information and serve as checks and balances on the function with the primary responsibility.

FIGURE 5.1 The natural fit between organizational functions and the seven pricing games

Each major organizational function has a logical and natural fit to one of the games in the Strategy Hex. Marketing's expertise lies in value, because it gets into the mind of the customers and knows what they want. Sales can claim the richest and deepest view of competitor behaviors, because salespeople get closest to customers and know what everyone in the market is doing. Finance is ideally positioned to ensure that margins don't plummet, because they have the greatest expertise in costs and the most detailed information on them. We refer to them as major functions in a pricing context, because each has its own lens on the market, manifested in the three information sources we described in Chapter 1. This obligates each of these functions to use these lenses to bring the most refined credible arguments into the decision-making process on pricing.

But beyond these major functions, other functional areas have relevant information and expertise that enables them to influence or even lead pricing decisions. The product team – also known as the R&D function or design team – is in charge of developing offers that meet customer needs at competitive price points.

We have found it important to distinguish between the pricing team and the data science teams. Almost every organization now has a pricing team that performs analyses and manages the pricing process. These pricing teams may have different names – such as revenue management or revenue growth management – depending on the industry or company. We highlight the role of data science in the Dynamic Game, though, because the pricing teams in the Dynamic Game need to have stronger and deeper analytics capabilities.

Finally, the C-suite has the full top-line and bottom-line perspective and often maintains senior relationships with the largest customers.

In light of this wide range of expertise and insights, no function should truly "own" pricing or monopolize the decision making. Nonetheless, attempts to claim exclusive ownership of this cross-functional and strategic set of decisions explain why pricing is one of the most politically charged activities in any company. Owning pricing eventually translates into dominating the pricing conversation. When one party tries to force their own theories, anecdotes, experience, and incentives to the forefront of the pricing process, it minimizes or undermines the contributions that other functions can make to improve pricing and help the company achieve its objectives.

That is why we use the term *leadership* instead of *ownership*. Our goal is to prepare your organization to have pricing discussions that bring all relevant parties to the table and equip them with the best possible data, insights, and perspectives. This allows them to resolve uncomfortable tradeoffs in a logical and balanced way and thus avoid conflicts.

Asymmetric incentives can cause tension when people make decisions around price points. Short-term incentives based on revenue or volume, for example, could mean that sales, marketing, and product teams benefit from lower prices, while incentives based on profit metrics could mean that finance benefits from higher prices. The incentives for the pricing and data science teams will depend on where they report. Senior executives in theory have a more balanced set of incentives and therefore less asymmetry, but they could have a bias toward lower prices if they view their pricing agency as limited – i.e., they see the firm as a price taker.

The functions shown in Figure 5.1 occupy different levels within an organization. The leaders of the three major functions – sales, marketing, and finance – usually report directly to the CEO or the head of a business unit. Pricing or data science teams tend to report one level down, but exactly which function they should report to depends on the game and the perspective of the potential lead function. We think that the hierarchical reporting line between pricing or data science, the three major functions, and the C-suite should follow the path with the strongest strategic orientation. The more immersed a functional area is in its own biases, the greater the risk that pricing loses its strategic orientation if it reports to that function.

Pricing authority and leadership in the seven pricing games

Pricing is political, but if it is also a team sport, the whole should be greater than the sum of its parts. The nature of each pricing game – together with their underlying information sources and economic frameworks – offers guidance on how to structure that team, from leadership roles to supporting roles. Companies positioned on the right side of the Hex should be managing a value equation based on the value ladder, while the companies on the left side of the Hex focus on managing a traditional margin equation based on prices, costs, and elasticities.

Let's look at the natural guidance for each game, starting again with the Value Game and working counterclockwise around the Hex.

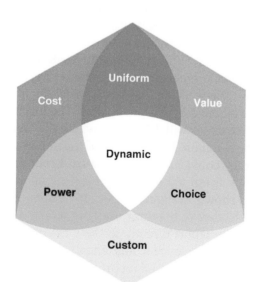

FIGURE 5.2 The Strategic Pricing Hexagon (the Hex)

Value Game

The marketing organization takes a natural leadership role. Broadly speaking, the marketing function is in charge of understanding customers: what they want, what they need, and how best to communicate with them. We assume that companies choosing to play this game have a far superior value proposition. But customers are not necessarily aware of that superiority, especially in the case of a new offer. In such circumstances, the ability to create, communicate, and reinforce a superior value proposition is essential to open up degrees of freedom and set a value-based pricing methodology.

Once marketing anchors that superior value proposition, sales represents and reinforces it in a disciplined way. This requires broad training, such as on how to respond to customer questions about competitive comparisons by reframing them as discussions about customer benefits.

Finance plays its traditional role of ensuring that the organization meets its financial targets by monitoring and tracking sales and identifying areas for improvement. Finance also scrutinizes return on investment (ROI) to ensure that returns are sufficient to fund the product team's development of the innovations that will allow the company to continue playing and winning the Value Game.

The role of the pricing team here is to quantify the value and ensure consistency of prices across channels and geography, to avoid undermining the value proposition.

Senior leadership serves two important roles. It provides marketing and sales the explicit backing – and therefore the backbone – to price higher and maintain the integrity of those prices. Steve Jobs and Michael Bloomberg played a critical role in encouraging their teams at Apple and Bloomberg to embrace the strength of their value proposition and anchor customer perception of that value. Senior leaders also serve as important checks on the company's pricing approach by calling out any moves that may undermine the brand's value proposition. In 2002, Porsche offered a seemingly trivial discount of $500 on its Boxster model to Porsche Club of America members without seeking corporate approval. CEO Wendelin Wiedeking intervened and stopped the program, saying that discounts – even small ones – could tarnish the brand.[1]

Uniform Game

The leadership role falls to a dedicated pricing team, which optimizes the uniform prices that all customers see. This team is often called revenue management to convey its broader responsibilities, which can range from strategic pricing, offer management, and growth all the way to tactical pricing implementation, including measuring price elasticities, identifying optimal prices, and managing downstream promotions and discounts. The challenge falls to the pricing team, because profits in the Uniform Game are very sensitive to price levels. Prices that are suboptimal by even a few percentage points can reduce profits by a multiple of that amount. Most companies in the modern Uniform Game sell their offerings in multiple channels. This makes omnichannel consistency very important, because high price sensitivity can make it easy for a company to cannibalize too much of its business.

The pricing team must conduct its work in close coordination with sales, which controls the relationship with customers and channel partners, monitors competitor activity, and can provide early warnings when changes appear in the market. Joint demand forecasting and capacity planning are critical and require a single source of truth, due to the high cost of oversupply and missing demand.

The economic framework within the Uniform Game is elasticity, which is at the intersection of the cost and value information sources. This means finance and marketing have natural roles to play as well. Finance is critical to evaluating product cost, production cost, and cost-to-serve accurately and precisely. It also ensures that the company's realized balance between market share and margin is consistent with the business objectives. But in a counterintuitive twist, finance should not institute artificial average margin rules that would encourage or require the margins of all products to land within the same target range or corridor, because such ranges often ignore the high variability of price elasticities. We have found that price elasticities in the Uniform Game tend to vary by a factor of 5 across products, channels, and geographies. Optimal margins will also vary proportionally, meaning that margins can range from 10% to 50%, for instance. Artificially narrowing that range around an average margin robs the company of the degrees of freedom it needs to set and implement optimal prices.

Pricing advisors and consultants often advocate that companies should have a chief pricing officer (CPO) who reports directly to the CEO.

In the Uniform Game and the Dynamic Game, we agree and think a CPO can play an effective role within a senior executive team, because of the highly sensitive link between price points and profits.

Marketing needs to support demand through communication aimed at influencing the level of price elasticity. Strong messages about the brand can reduce price sensitivity, while price-driven messages can increase it. Senior management sets the overall direction for the pricing strategy, but this also needs to reflect the nature of the Uniform Game and the company's position within it.

Cost Game

The finance organization takes a natural leadership role and exercises control over the approval of most deal structures. Efficiency and cost management are paramount, because the company needs to hit key price points profitably by eliminating unnecessary costs and looking for ways to consolidate or streamline activities. Finance also ensures that the markup – the "plus" in the cost-plus pricing method – is aligned with the company's pricing strategy and fixed-cost structure. The pricing team should report to the finance function and execute all these activities. It establishes price corridors for each offer, and the sales team operates within these corridors when quoting prices to customers or bidding on projects. Sales plays a more limited role in pricing in the Cost Game, because margins tend to be thin and tightly controlled.

Marketing plays an important role in establishing the company's perceived value as a collaborator or a trustworthy long-term partner. The executive team in this game should stay focused on the strategic aspects of pricing. Do we have the right pricing architecture? Can we make some costs variable and align our fee structure? Can we incentivize our customers to implement mutual cost savings? But in general, they should stay out of the final decision-making process for large deals, because they are prone to grant unnecessary incremental discounts.

Power Game

Senior leadership plays the leadership role in pricing decisions, even tactical ones, because the negotiations in the Power Game tend to take place at the senior-executive level on both sides, and because these negotiations require full internal coordination and discipline. The stakes are so high that the loss of any deal can materially harm a company. These losses often result from actions – such as excessive price concessions – that upset the fine equilibria that enable a company to play the Power Game over the long term.

Because the results of any individual deal will affect other deals, companies playing the Power Game need an incentive structure that encourages sales and marketing to serve the greater good and maintain those market equilibria. Sales incentives, for example, should not focus exclusively on revenue or volume metrics.

The central economic framework for the Power Game is game theory, which sits at the intersection of the cost and competitive information sources. The deal-by-deal analytics and reporting from finance are critical, as is the role of cost management. Small cost advantages can create an imbalance that can change a market equilibrium in a company's favor.

Sales provides competitive intelligence, but its most important role is to build and maintain strong relationships. These can lead to a level of commercial co-dependence, as the buyer and seller participate in joint business planning and look for opportunities to customize products.

The pricing team can report to finance or sales, depending on whether the CFO or head of sales has the stronger strategic mindset. The team's role is critical to frame senior negotiations by making the consequences of every pricing decision fully transparent. They create scenarios that analyze implications across the client portfolio and across time. Enforcing the implementation of all negotiated clauses is also important to ensure that what is planned turns into reality.

Marketing plays a similar role as in the Cost Game by establishing the company's perceived value as a collaborator or a trustworthy long-term partner.

The role of the product team is, not surprisingly, focused on developing great products as fast and efficiently as possible, ideally faster and better than competitors. In markets with high levels of innovation, that role can extend deeply into pricing decisions. This would also be the case if the product team develops a product that is more differentiated than usual. In these circumstances, they need to quantify and communicate the benefits of their new product clearly to other functions and to senior leadership. Otherwise, the natural momentum of the organization will lead it to market and price the product as an incremental innovation, and the company will not be able to counter the efforts of customer purchasing departments to force this innovation into its existing comparable standards. If the value proposition of the new product is sufficiently high, senior executives could consider choosing to shift from the Power Game to the Value Game, which would also entail a full rewiring of existing processes to take full advantage of the new product's strengths.

Custom Game

The sales function has the natural leadership role, because a company needs to customize deals and prices to win against competition and respond in a timely manner. But at the same time, this game may have the most intricate system of personal checks and balances of any of the seven games. Successful negotiations in the Custom Game depend primarily on two factors. First, salespeople need to customize the price and the offer simultaneously, rather than concede on price for a fixed offer until the customer is satisfied. Second, the company needs to establish a pricing structure that absorbs most of the effects of price variation, rather than giving salespeople full discretion to make ad-hoc adjustments. Let's look at each separately.

Salespeople need to customize the offer to match customer needs, and then anchor the conversation on benefits and value, not price. Their assessment of competitive alternatives allows them to determine a price range that could win the deal, and then they negotiate a final deal – a combination of customized offer and price – that the customer could refuse but won't.[2] The pricing team supports sales with analytics that provide reliable data on the outcomes of similar deals as well as a clear logic for how to present price options to customers.

This is one essential part of a rigorous process intended to foster consistency of pricing outcomes, independent of the specific individuals involved. It requires skills, training, and experience across the entire sales force, to preserve the integrity of the price–value equation and to prevent a rogue salesperson from setting a bad precedent or risking a price war with an unnecessarily low price. Finally, it requires an efficient escalation process and a price structure with well-calibrated discretion so that negotiations can proceed without unnecessary delays.

That pricing structure and its supporting systems – built together with the finance team – generate target prices for individual deals that discourage salespeople from chasing business at artificially low prices.

The incentives and discount discretion with centralized logic should empower salespeople to have more confidence when they quote a price, because they believe in the underlying story and understand how the system built the price from the ground up. Finance also plays an important role in tracking discount process consistency across channels, deal sizes, and other meaningful sources of price variation.

Senior leaders often need to initiate this process of checks and balances, because the Custom Game is prone to a battle for pricing "ownership," primarily between sales and finance. To break this impasse, it is often practical to have a deal desk embedded within the sales organization, while the finance organization oversees a small pricing team that controls structural pricing decisions and policies.

The product and marketing teams contribute within their traditional boundaries. The product team needs to ensure that adapting and customizing offers is not only feasible, but also easy, all without creating too much complexity. Marketing needs to aggregate data on customer needs and competition, and also frame and communicate the advantages of the company's solutions.

Choice Game

The product organization plays the ideal leadership role. Maintaining the right product portfolio and architecture – often a mix of physical products, services, and customer experiences – is more important in this game than the precise price of any individual offering. What matters instead are the interrelationships between features, benefits, and prices. They should make it easy for customers to trade up or down across the right segment-specific offerings, depending on their needs and circumstances.

To illustrate the critical role that the product function plays in pricing, consider the tricky decisions on how to migrate features down the product portfolio. These migrations can strengthen the whole portfolio if corresponding innovations simultaneously bring new, differentiated features at the high end. They may also be necessary if competitors make a similar move first. Such feature migrations are implicit pricing decisions, because they change the benefits that customers get for the same price. If a feature was the primary reason why customers bought a particular offer in the portfolio, its migration downward could also compel customers to trade down, with detrimental effects on profits.

Sales and marketing also play critical roles in guiding customers to the right offering. The marketing team influences customer behavior up front in the purchase process, while the sales team guides potential customers to the most suitable offering while also encouraging them to upgrade or explore additional offers.

The finance team provides a check through cost control and management to ensure that the portfolio delivers long-term profitability and ROI. Profit margins tend to be high in the Choice Game, because many products and services in the portfolio have little or no marginal costs. Research and development costs, however, can be high. Together with product management, finance can help the company build an enduring advantage by gaining scale and driving marginal costs down. That, in turn, enables the company to invest in automation and digitalization to further stretch their cost advantage.

The pricing team works very closely with the product team to translate features and benefits into prices and ensure consistent implementation. One of their main responsibilities is to design and optimize the pricing architecture, especially the pricing basis. When offerings are fully digital products, such as software or data services, product teams have complete degrees of freedom to pick a pricing basis and discount structure that best fits a particular offer.

One inherent risk within the Choice Game is isolated optimization, which occurs when individual product teams create unmanageable complexity by doing what is best for their own offering without regard to the rest of the portfolio. The pricing team needs to anticipate these issues and propose a framework and architecture that will optimally serve all customer segments. The pricing team also plays a tactical role by tightly controlling price adjustments such as promotions and discounts. For example, they should manage approval processes carefully, so that price concessions do not accumulate.

Organizations playing the Choice Game often struggle with where this pricing team should report. Finance makes sense from a controlling perspective, while marketing makes sense because it can influence pricing structure decisions. Sales makes sense because of the need to observe and adapt quickly to slight shifts in market conditions. As with the Power Game, we don't think there is a perfect universal answer. We have seen all three options implemented effectively, as long as the leader of the "host" function takes a strong strategic, cross-functional view about what is best for the portfolio as a whole.

Dynamic Game

The data science team – the counterpart to the pricing team in other games – is the natural fit for the pricing leadership. Companies in the Dynamic Game need robust and reliable algorithms to guide the large volume of automated pricing decisions they make on a daily basis, often by customers in real time. This team carries broad responsibility for all dynamic pricing decisions. Data science will tend to feel like a natural fit for tactical pricing decisions, but it is important that they also feel responsible for coordinating strategic pricing decisions. We highlight the role of data science in this game more than in any other game because the required sophistication of pricing analytics is at least an order of magnitude more advanced.

Data science, in this context, is a broad collective term used in the same way that we use pricing as a broad collective term that comprises a number of decisions, from the offer design to the specifics of the pricing model. Naming conventions for the data science team vary from industry to industry and company to company. Some organizations call the function "revenue management," for example, because the team's purview includes inventory management in addition to tactical pricing decisions.

Of course, "human intervention" also plays a critical role, both within the data science team and beyond it. In the Dynamic Game, marketing has a special role beyond understanding customers and developing effective communications and outreach programs. It also needs to be attuned to customer perceptions and sensitivities around pricing fairness. Consumers tend to be upset when they learn that others have paid less than they have. Companies must be ready to explain the logic of their pricing transparently and have solid rationales to help customers understand the differences. We explore the issue of fairness in more detail in Part IV.

Finance performs marginal cost calculations and controls the financial performance across the various parts of the business. Sales often manages relationships with partners that can generate incremental revenues, such as hotel chains and rental car agencies in the case of airlines. To maximize the benefits of such relationships, sales needs to coordinate well with the data science team to personalize offers and pricing at the customer level. In B2B markets, sales often provides a last look and final adjustment – within the bounds of their allowed discretion – before quoting a price.

The role of senior leadership in the Dynamic Game is to help the data science teams think "outside the black box" and look for ways to alter their models instead of optimizing them. Data science teams and their PhDs tend to overinvest in fine-tuning existing models rather than developing completely new approaches. The airlines, for example, made such a change when they tapped unbundling as a source of new profits after a couple of decades of deep investments in yield management models. This is another illustration of the role of senior leaders in keeping pricing conversations on a strategic plane instead of losing focus on a myopic pursuit of optimal price points.

Key takeaways

Pricing governance may not be as sexy as pricing strategy, dynamic pricing, or anything connected to AI, but you can't play any pricing game for long without it. We envision approaches to pricing governance that maximize value for the company and the customers. These governance structures help companies leave behind the confines of the traditional pricing beliefs – zero-sum, value extraction, static, and numbers – and treat pricing games as an inspiration and determinant for corporate strategy.

- The governance model determines how you manage and distribute business intelligence and pricing authority within your organization.
- The right governance model depends on what game you are playing and what tools and capabilities you have at your disposal.
- The lead function in any pricing game is the one that manages the most critical tradeoffs.
- The other functions provide necessary checks and balances on that leadership role, because pricing is inherently cross-functional.
- The role of the pricing team – and where it should report in the broader organization – differs by game, which is one of the fundamental reasons why there is so much debate about these decisions.

CHAPTER 6

What's Next? The Design of Pricing Models

A company's entire revenue is the outcome of its pricing decisions. This makes pricing strategy indispensable. A leadership team's decisions on how to share value with customers not only determines the financial performance of a company and its ecosystem, but also affects the medium- and long-term shape of markets: Who gains customers, who is best positioned to serve them and retain them, who stays in the market, and who leaves?

A company's pricing strategy also influences a company's decisions on where to invest, whether in innovation, capacity expansion, market communication, or mergers and acquisitions. It is not something that a leader should select from an à la carte menu or accessorize with a trendy approach. The impulse or idea to "add a subscription" or "go dynamic" may sound appealing, but it needs to emerge organically from the Strategy Hex, not the loudest voice in the room, the insistence of the data scientists, or the success of a company in another sector.

Let's now focus on the third question for the development of a pricing strategy: What pricing model best fits your value creation strategy?

Exploring price models does not mean that we will dive into the mathematical mechanics that go into the precise determination of the price points. Instead, we will stay on the strategic plane – above the numbers – and help you understand the overall extent of your pricing agency and how to act on it.

The organization of Figure 6.1 reflects the three questions that we defined to help you decide on the best pricing model for your game. A pricing model is a function of the answers to these questions:

3a. What should your **pricing architecture** be (i.e., pricing basis, offer structure, and pricing mechanism)?

3b. What should drive your **price variation** (e.g., geography, channel, and time)?

3c. What **price adjustment** levers should you use (i.e., customer programs, transaction incentives, and fees and functional discounts)?

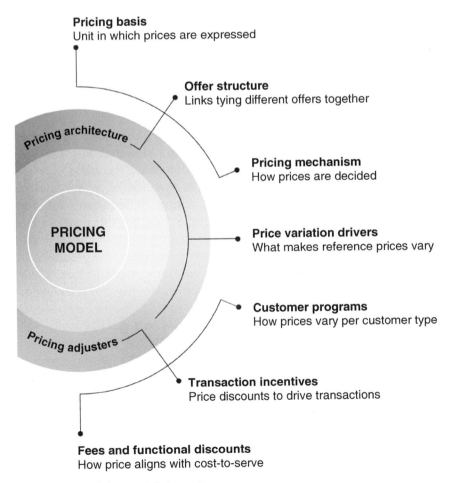

Pricing basis
Unit in which prices are expressed

Offer structure
Links tying different offers together

Pricing architecture

Pricing mechanism
How prices are decided

PRICING MODEL

Price variation drivers
What makes reference prices vary

Customer programs
How prices vary per customer type

Pricing adjusters

Transaction incentives
Price discounts to drive transactions

Fees and functional discounts
How price aligns with cost-to-serve

FIGURE 6.1   Pricing model elements

Figure 6.1 shows the specific areas where leaders have opportunities to exercise their pricing agency. We make a clear distinction between pricing architecture and pricing adjusters, with price variation serving as the bridge between the two. The architecture decisions have a much greater impact on how much value the company shares – and how it shares it – than the adjuster levers do.

Why each of these pricing model decisions matters

Price is much more than a number and also much more than a mere product attribute or a marketing lever. Above all, it is a strategic lever. A price can't even exist until senior leaders have made decisions on their pricing architecture: price mechanism, pricing basis, and offer structure. Problems arise when companies make these decisions by default or make them consciously but then never reevaluate them. In the latter case, they end up treating those decisions as immutable givens, even if market characteristics and company objectives have evolved far beyond where they stood when someone made those original decisions. That tacit acceptance of prevailing price models contributes to the impression that business leaders have little agency and few degrees of freedom when it comes to pricing.

The architecture decisions require the attention of senior leaders, because those decisions will have far-reaching consequences for how much revenue and profit a company generates, how large its market share will be, and how long it can maintain and sustain those positions. Sometimes a company's review of its architecture decisions will reinforce its choice of pricing game and offer insights into how it can win or at least play the game better. In other cases, companies identify and seize opportunities to change their decisions, change their pricing game, and reshape their markets, often with the outcome of more robust growth.

Most companies, however, unfortunately take the architecture decisions for granted and instead devote their resources to the adjuster decisions shown in Figure 6.1. These decisions – involving programs, incentives, fees, and functional discounts – allow a company to adjust prices flexibly as market conditions warrant. They can also have a significant impact on a company's performance and ultimately on its market position, which is why senior leaders should be involved or at least have input into these decisions as well.

Bridging the gap between the pricing architecture and pricing adjuster decisions is price variation, which can take many forms. Understanding price variation starts with a trip back to the information sources we described in Chapter 1. Should prices vary over time because customer value is changing fundamentally, or should they change because of costs? Supply and demand imbalances can also lead to price variation, although we emphasize once again that such imbalances are one input into a leader's decision-making, not a foregone conclusion that renders decision-making moot. Prices can also vary by channel, geography, or segment. The decisions in Figure 6.1 are shown from top to bottom by the magnitude of price variations they can drive.

Price variation is a blessing because it helps expose differences in willingness to pay across customer contexts or across other circumstances. But it can become a curse when customers notice price differences that do not seem justified and thus violate their perceptions of fairness. To transform these blessings and curses into one powerful asset, companies need to look for opportunities to anchor these price variations within their architecture decisions rather than trying to stretch the adjuster levers beyond their limits.

The success of Google's AdWords platform exemplifies how a company can seize such opportunities. When Google launched its first advertising program in early 2000, advertisers placed text-based ads called sponsored links and paid based on the number of times their ads were displayed on users' search results pages.[1] By the end of the year, however, Google had made a bold decision that would align its offer much better with advertisers' willingness to pay for leads.

It decided to change its pricing mechanism to an auction system called AdWords, an online self-service program that enabled advertisers to create text-based ads, bid on the keywords that would trigger the display of their ads, and set daily spending budgets.[2] The advertising quickly accounted for the vast majority of Google's revenues, which grew at a compound annual growth rate (CAGR) of 94% between 2002 and 2008.

Google's architecture strategic decisions reshaped an entire market. Its success is one of many examples of how strategic conversations and decisions are really pricing conversations and decisions.

Making decisions on pricing architecture

Let's now take a closer look at the three architecture decisions that enable a price to exist.

Main pricing basis

Imagine that someone offers tutoring services to high school students. Using the capacity dimension shown in Figure 6.2, they could charge students *per hour* for their work. The longer the session lasts, the more money they earn. Alternatively, they could charge *per session*, which puts them in the middle of the Hex. Regardless of how long the session lasts, they receive the same amount of money. Finally, they could move to the right side of the Hex and charge *per grade improvement*, which is an outcome-based dimension. They only make money if the student's grades improve, regardless of how many sessions they offer or how long they last.

These examples show how the choice of a pricing unit or pricing basis can change the essence of a business. The pricing basis has three components – the dimension, the unit quantity, and time – but the most interesting component is the dimension, which arrays itself on the horizontal axis of the Hex as shown in Figure 6.2. The range for the dimension is from capacity on the left (linked to costs as the information source) to outcomes and performance on the right (linked to value as the information source).

On the left side of the Hex, the dimension links to capacity, defined in units of product or labor. In the middle of the Hex, the dimension is linked to usage, which is typical of a service such as a haircut or a meal, where the seller uses labor and assets. The number of users is a dimension

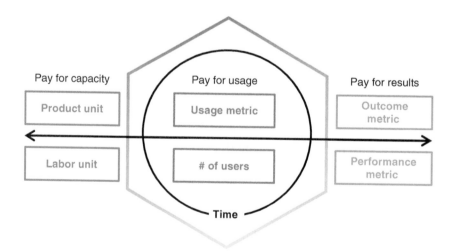

FIGURE 6.2 Dimensions of the main pricing basis

that tends to correlate with a usage metric, particularly when heavy users and light users pay different amounts. On the right side of the Hex, the dimension links to performance or outcomes. Each of these options exists for the same offering, which means that the seller must choose their position. The unit quantity then comes into play once the seller establishes the dimension. It is the term that follows the "per" in a price expression, as we initially explained in Chapter 1.

Offer structure

The offer structure refers to how the different elements of an offer – and different offers in a portfolio – all relate to each other. The structures we highlight below are not tightly bound to any game in the Hex, although some may fit better to one game than another, as shown in Figure 6.3.

- **Good-better-best:** When customers have choices, they self-select in predictable ways. In the good-better-best lineup, the majority of customers tends to choose the middle option.[3] This lineup is well suited to the Choice Game.

FIGURE 6.3   Some offer structures fit better to certain games

- **Razor-and-blades:**[4] This model establishes a link between two parts of an offering, a reusable one purchased once (razor) and a depletable one purchased repeatedly (blades). Home printers that need ink or toner have this offer structure. The blades are usually exclusively tied to a company's razor, which allows the supplier to align the price with the value that customers derive from the razor-and-blades combination. Many B2B companies use this structure, especially for proprietary parts for capital equipment. This structure allows a company to move from the Cost, Uniform, or Custom Game toward the Value Game.

- **Flavors:** When the diversity of needs and price points is relatively narrow, a company can increase demand by developing products that share a similar positioning but have one slight variation or "flavor." This variation will appeal strongly to one specific subsegment rather than the broader market.

- **Bundling:** Bundling allows companies to incentivize customers to buy several products or services together as one unit. They commonly group high-margin offers with more commoditized ones. Sellers in almost any game will use bundles, but they are least effective in the Cost Game, where margins are similar across offers and sellers are more indifferent to which offer a customer buys. They are also ineffective in the Custom Game, because of the extreme heterogeneity of offers.

- **Base plus options:** In this structure, a core product comes with an array of options that the customer can buy to enhance or customize it. This structure is common in the Custom Game, where it offers latitude for companies to adapt their offering to customers' diverse needs without adding too much operational complexity.

- **Scaled differentiation:** Similar to good-better-best, each offer in the portfolio differs in terms of quality and price. But in this case, the separation between each offer is a function of a measurable, quantitative performance parameter, such as power or storage capacity. This occurs often in situations where buyers are very concentrated and try to strengthen their negotiation power by imposing standards that make it easier to compare offers from different suppliers. If suppliers are concentrated as well, they will tend to limit the number of choices in order to gain efficiencies of scale. Buyers tend to accept this, because they also benefit from scale.

FIGURE 6.4   Pricing mechanisms along vertical and horizontal axes in the Hex

Price mechanism

Five pricing mechanisms have logical positions within the Strategy Hex, as shown in Figure 6.4.

Three of them move a company along a vertical axis through the Hex:

- **Fixed price:** The seller sets a price that applies to all customers, who can either accept the price or look for an alternative. This use of this mechanism shifts a company toward the top of the Hex.
- **Negotiated price:** Buyers and sellers jointly determine the price through negotiations. This mechanism shifts a company toward the bottom of the Hex.
- **Market (algorithmic) prices:** This means prices are set automatically with little or no human intervention. Examples include market supply–demand mechanisms in financial markets or algorithms in the yield management systems of airlines. In both situations, these mechanisms pull a market or company toward the center of the Hex. The algorithm's prices tend to be individualized by customer and vary over time.

The other two mechanisms move a company along a horizontal axis through the Hex.

- **Auctions:** Buyers decide what they are willing to pay and make an offer. The resolution of an auction can have several forms, including the Vickrey form, under which the highest bidder pays the price offered by the second-highest bidder.
- **Bids:** Sellers submit their prices, and the buyer decides which price to accept. A reverse auction, for example, has sellers underbid each other until one seller remains. Bid mechanisms make sense in situations where cost variation is highly uncertain and hard for the buyer to forecast.

By making these architecture decisions, a seller consciously determines how they will share value, how they will manage the drivers of price variation to their advantage, and how they will shape demand for their offering. This applies equally to a Fortune 500 firm as it does to a private individual or to a small business such as the caterer in the Introduction.

Making decisions on pricing adjusters

Pricing adjusters are also powerful ways for a seller to exercise pricing agency. These decisions usually don't have the same fundamental impact as the architecture decisions, but still make significant contributions to a company's success. Each type is closely associated with one of the three information sources (cost, competition, and value) and exerts a force in the direction of the corresponding Hex corners.

Customer programs

Customer programs are value-driven incentives to drive buying behavior over a specified period. They can enhance customer lifetime value because they provide the seller with the levers to manage it. In the best cases, customer loyalty is so high that it endures even when competitors replicate the programs. As we see in Figure 6.5, customer programs are associated with customer value and exert a force toward the Value Game. Sometimes, customers pay a price – often called a program fee – to

FIGURE 6.5   Customer programs are associated with long-term customer value

participate. The function of these fees is different from fees and functional discounts, however, as the latter are linked to specific transactions and designed to cover costs. Program fees, in contrast, represent a longer-term mutual commitment between buyers and sellers.

Customers in long-term relationships with their suppliers usually derive more value over time because they move down the experience curve. In other words, they learn how to take advantage of their supplier's value propositions while minimizing transaction costs. This creates a tension that the seller must decide how to resolve. They have an interest in finding mechanisms to claim a fair share of the higher value or cross-sell higher-margin offerings. But at the same time, they need to avoid overshooting and trying to claim too large a share of that value.

How much money should the company leave on the table? That is a delicate balance. Every company should have a perspective on how to answer that question. The following programs have similar objectives, but their implementation depends on what game in the Strategy Hex the seller is playing.

- **Membership programs:** The customer pays a fee to acquire benefits like the right to buy products or services at a lower price than non-members. Stores such as Costco and Sam's Club use these two-part pricing models. Membership fees often account for the bulk of the seller's profits, because the revenue from product sales is often calibrated to cover cost of goods and operating expenses.

- **Loyalty programs:** These entitle customers to future discounts or at-cost prices for products and services, once they have met specific thresholds for revenue, volume, or purchase frequency. These have been particularly effective for airlines, hotel chains, and retailers playing the Dynamic Game.

- **Rebates:** These promise partial reimbursement for purchases once the customer fulfills preestablished conditions, such as buying a certain mix of products. Rebates help align the economic interest of both parties, because they are only paid after the buyer meets the conditions. Players in the Power Game use rebates to discourage cherry picking, which occurs when a customer buys only selected products rather than a mix.

- **Volume discounts:** Very common in B2B industries, these incentivize a buyer to increase their aggregate volume beyond a certain threshold in a specified period, such as a quarter or a year.

- **Enterprise license agreements (ELAs):** An ELA defines a long-term value exchange between the buyer and seller by codifying a buyer's long-term commitment to purchase across several product lines and over an extended period. ELAs are common in the software sector.

Transaction incentives

Transaction incentives are price reductions designed to trigger an immediate "here and now" purchase. They are conditional discounts, which means that they do not have the permanence or universality of an outright price decrease. They can have a powerful short-term impact because they are connected to higher elasticities and therefore can generate a lot of volume. The main issue is that that volume does not always come from new customers. It can come from your competitors or from pulling your own volume forward, which is in most cases counterproductive.

Pulling volume from competitors, while attractive at first, can turn into a zero-sum game if competitors match the incentives quickly. As a result, their repeated aggressive use can trigger a price war. Unless one company has a vastly superior cost position, however, all sellers tend to lose price wars, which reduce margins without necessarily generating additional volume or sustainable advantage.

As shown in Figure 6.6, transaction incentives exert a downward force in the Hex. Companies must monitor these incentives carefully, both in terms of their magnitude and the size of customer population they apply to. Extensive use of these incentives is beneficial over the long term only when they are aligned with a significant competitive advantage.

All these incentives have different characteristics and we positioned them based on where they are most effective. Some industries use different names for these tactics, but the quick overview describes how they generally work.

Promotions and limited time offers (LTOs) are temporary price reductions aimed at specific customer segments, but generally available to any customer. Coupons are similar to promotions, but allow finer targeting because the customer must undertake a specific action to receive a lower price. These incentives are common in the Uniform and Cost Games but are much harder to implement in lower parts of the Hex. In the Custom Game, discounts are often discretionary or ad hoc, because the sales force makes decisions on a customer-by-customer basis. Discretionary discounts are also used in the Choice Game but, if too high, they can undermine the carefully crafted price hierarchy implemented in the offer lineup.

FIGURE 6.6 Competitors can match transaction incentives, exerting a downward force

Competitor matching is a commitment to match net prices. Many industries use this incentive, but retailers use it frequently and e-commerce retailers often implement it dynamically. Giveaways mean exactly what the word implies: a customer receives ancillary goods or services for no payment. Practically speaking, they are a form of nonmonetary discount and generally find use in longstanding relationships with large customers. In the Value Game, fearful of undermining their value proposition, companies tend to shy away from explicit discounts or promotions. One frequent tactic is to organize exclusive events where guests will have the privilege of buying at a lower price.

Fees and functional discounts

Suppliers use these tactics to bring prices and costs into alignment. As we can see in Figure 6.7, fees and functional discounts tend to shift a company toward the Cost Game. Fees and functional discounts have so many forms that we could not possibly list them all here, so we will highlight only a few.

Sellers may add a fee to a customer's invoice to account for extra variable costs incurred to serve that customer. Some manufacturers use raw

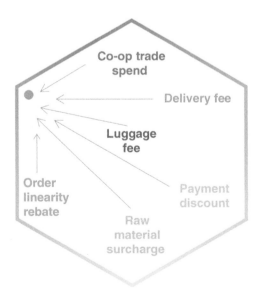

FIGURE 6.7   Fees and functional discounts are associated with cost

materials surcharges, for example, to cover the cost of inflation in raw materials if they exceed certain thresholds. This creates a reasonable justification for customers. Unbundling luggage from an airline fare and charging a luggage fee served a similar purpose. It helped major airlines align their prices with costs and allowed them to compete better against the fares of low-cost competitors.

Suppliers may also subtract an amount from a customer's invoice – in the form of a functional discount – when the customer adjusts their behavior in a way that will reduce the supplier's costs. Think about product delivery. A supplier can charge a fee for it, or charge less if the customer picks up the product in store. Another example of a functional discount is an order consistency rebate, which rewards a customer for keeping their order amounts consistent rather than ordering in a way that could disrupt a supplier's production schedule.

These incentives should be consistent with the nature of the pricing game. It is not a good idea for a company in the Value Game to spend a lot of time and effort thinking about functional discounts or surcharges. But these measures are commonplace in the Custom Game and the Cost Game.

The challenge with fees and functional discounts is that they can accumulate to an overwhelming level if the supplier does not continually evaluate each on its merits. Failure to do that can create the impression of nickel-and-diming.

Key takeaways

The pricing model comprises a set of strategic decisions that business leaders must make before their company ever sets a price point. Leaders need to decide how to implement price variations, either by changing their pricing architecture or publicized prices, or by creating pricing adjusters.

- The pricing model elements shown in Figure 6.1 form an integrated system, which means that pricing model decisions are interrelated, not independent from each other.
- Pricing model options have different positions in the Hex, which means that companies should pick ones that are compatible with their intended position in the Hex.

- Pricing architecture decisions are fundamental, because companies cannot change them quickly, and each shift requires significant change management. But such changes are often necessary and effective when a company decides to move to another game. We explore such moves, and the associated change management, in Part III.

- Pricing adjusters are faster to implement and provide more flexibility than pricing architecture or publicized prices, but they can also cause a company to drift from its position in the Hex. It is important to make sure these moves are consistent across the three types of adjustors and compatible with the desired game.

Before you move on to Part II . . .

Our objective with Part I was to encourage you to rethink pricing. The Strategy Hex provides a means for you to accelerate your decision making with confidence, and to view pricing from a broad and deep strategic perspective instead of viewing it narrowly as a static, zero-sum "numbers" game of value extraction.

Three Questions Shaping Your Pricing Strategy

Question 1: How do you create and share value?

1a. What do you do to create **measurable value** for your customers?

1b. What are your main **drivers of value** and the **limitations** to value creation?

1c. How do your **differentiation and growth objectives** justify how you share value with your customers?

Question 2: What pricing game do you want to play?

2a. Which game aligns best with the **characteristics of your market**?

2b. Which game aligns best with your **current pricing approach**?

2c. Which game aligns best with the **market forces** and your **competitive advantages**?

Question 3: What pricing model best fits your value creation strategy?

3a. What should your **pricing architecture** be (i.e., pricing basis, offer structure, and pricing mechanism)?

3b. What should drive your **price variation** (e.g., geography, channel, and time)?

3c. What price **adjustment** levers should you use (i.e., customer programs, transaction incentives, and fees and functional discounts)?

△ Sellers   ⬜ Offers   ◯ Buyers

FIGURE 6.8 Offer, seller, and buyer characteristics by game

Let's now revisit the three questions that help you develop a pricing strategy. At the end of the Introduction, we asked you to answer the first fundamental question, which addressed your strategy for value creation.

We would like you to review your answer to that question in light of what you have read in Part I. What questions or issues now come to mind with what you wrote down? In what ways did the six chapters in Part I reinforce your answer or lead you to rethink it?

Then we would like you to answer the second question: What game would you like to play? Please write down your answer along with a brief rationale for your choice.

To help you make the decision, let's look at Figure 6.8, which you first saw as Figure 3.3. It summarizes market characteristics that determine the best fit to a game. You'll notice that the number of triangles – which represent the sellers – differs across games to show the concentration or fragmentation in a market. The triangles also differ by size within a game, representing the seller's relative strength in terms of revenue or reputation.

Which triangle in Figure 6.8 best represents your company?

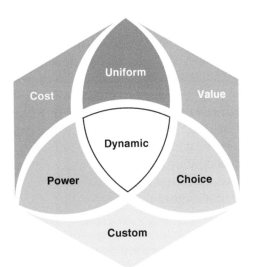

PART II

Winning the Seven Pricing Games

Part I laid the foundation for understanding the Strategic Pricing Hexagon by explaining the interactions across sources of information (cost, competition, and value), economic frameworks (elasticity, differentiation, game theory, and supply and demand), market characteristics, and market forces.

Part II closely examines the seven games within the Hex. Each chapter discusses the characteristics of one game and how leaders can excel in playing that game. Chapters will progress counterclockwise through the Hex, starting with the Value Game and ending with the Dynamic Game. For each game, we:

- Describe how the game works.
- Outline the special nature of pricing in the game, which includes the analytics underpinning value sharing and the most prevalent pricing model
- Provide two to four steps that leaders should take to excel in playing each game

Each chapter in Part II therefore has a similar structure, but the depth and detail vary depending on the twists and new perspectives we provide on the seemingly familiar aspects of some of the games.

We do cite many cutting-edge developments – especially in big data, technology, and artificial intelligence – in Parts II, III, and IV, and we have anonymized most of those stories. In many of the chapters, though, we bring the concepts to life with stories about companies in industries ranging from trucks to computer hardware to coffee and soup, with a broad representation across industries and company sizes.

You will notice that some of the core stories cover events that are more than a decade old. We have three important reasons for this. First, the passing of time makes it easier to observe the full, long-term impact of these pricing strategies. They are complete, self-contained stories that also show how an individual game still works today and beyond. Second, companies are not as sensitive to the disclosure of strategies they employed years ago, because their levels of sophistication have since evolved well beyond those events. Finally, we think the fundamental principles of success in each game are very resilient, which makes these examples timeless. They are as relevant today as they were 10 or more years ago and will remain relevant 10 years from now.

CHAPTER 7

The Value Game: When Art Trumps Science

With contributions from Jean-Sébastien Verwaerde,
Joël Hazan, and Rodrigo Garcia-Escudero

I n the early days of MP3 players, consumers could buy a device with portability or high capacity, but not both. Devices such as the Rio PMP300 offered portability but could store only a couple dozen songs. The Creative NOMAD Jukebox or the PJB100 stored gigabytes of music, but their bulk and weight limited their portability.

Then came Apple.

The iPod, launched in 2001, erased that frustrating tradeoff for good by offering room for up to 1,000 CD-quality songs on a 6.5-ounce device that featured unprecedented ease of use, sleek design, and an iconic scroll wheel.

Supported with an annual advertising budget on the order of hundreds of millions of dollars, the iPod swept the market. By 2004, it claimed a share of 82% in the US retail market for hard-drive-based digital music players.[1] iPod sales peaked at almost 55 million units in 2008. The iPhone, which debuted in 2007 with an even stronger value proposition, would eventually replace the iPod and revolutionize the market for cell phones. Apple's complementary products have achieved similar success. If the

AirPods or the Apple Watch were standalone companies, they would be in the Fortune 500.

After being around 90 days away from going broke in the late 1990s, Apple may have accomplished the most remarkable turnaround in corporate history to become, at one point, the world's most valuable company.[2] Its brand value, estimated at more than $480 billion in 2022, topped the popular Interbrand Best Global Brands ranking for the 10th consecutive year.[3] This brand equity is over 70% higher than Microsoft's, the runner-up in the ranking, and over five times higher than Samsung's, a more direct competitor. In 2022, Apple became the first public company with a market capitalization of over $3 trillion.[4]

While breakthrough innovations are not a prerequisite for success in the Value Game, Apple's story exemplifies how companies can bring products to market that are better aligned with the true drivers of customer value. Such products create tremendous economic value for the company to share and can lead to enviable and durable market positions.

Figure 7.1 summarizes the market characteristics of the Value Game that we introduced in Chapter 3. The most defining characteristic of the Value Game is the presence of a unique offer with a far superior value proposition than alternatives, a criterion the iPod fulfilled.

When an offer delivers much more value than any of its competitors, it tends to attract a broad set of customers and, as a result, the customer

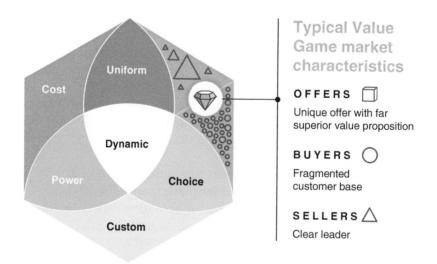

FIGURE 7.1 The market for the iPod was ideally suited to the Value Game

base is often very fragmented. Virtually all iPods were purchased by individual consumers, meaning that customers numbered in the millions. A far superior offer together with a fragmented customer base gives a seller such as Apple a lot of latitude to decide how much value to share with customers and to set prices accordingly.

Competitors struggled to catch Apple in the MP3 player market. In 2008, SanDisk's Sansa was the iPod's closest competitor, but with only 8% of the market.[5] The Rio PMP300 was among the very first MP3 players when it launched in 1998, selling around 200,000 units in 1999, but by 2003, its manufacturer had filed for bankruptcy.[6]

The special nature of pricing in the Value Game

Pricing in the Value Game starts with a breakdown of the differential value of a clearly superior offer. A tool such as the value ladder shown in Figure 7.2 helps you assess and quantify value and then decide how much of it to share with customers.

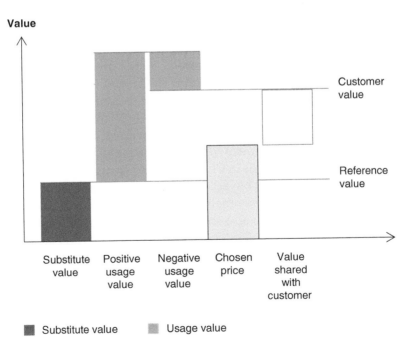

FIGURE 7.2   The value ladder representation

The value for customers comprises substitute value and usage value. Substitute value reflects the value of the Next-Best Competitive Alternative (NBCA). Usage value accounts for relative value differences, both positive and negative, to that next-best alternative. Usage value breaks down further into functional value and emotional value, both of which are almost always prerequisites for success in the Value Game.

As we described in Chapter 1, functional value includes utilitarian benefits that are measurable and quantifiable in terms of time, money, or capacity. Emotional value derives from the customer's intangible, subjective benefits. Companies often overlook or underweight the influence of emotional value, because it is harder to quantify than functional value.

The value ladder is a living document, not a one-off exercise. Net usage value can decline over time as functional and emotional value diminish, while substitute value can increase as viable competitors catch up with their own innovation. Successful companies in the Value Game monitor and manage the value ladder to identify potential value erosion and to develop measures to mitigate it or reverse it.

The pricing model shown in Figure 7.3 helps a company assess and decide not only how much value to share with customers, but also how to share it. The most important pricing model levers in the Value Game are in the pricing architecture. Price variations and price adjusters, such as functional fees or transaction incentives, have limited use. Customers are already paying a significant premium, which makes additional fees unnecessary. Discounts, as we mentioned in Chapter 5 with the example of Porsche North America, may cheapen the perceived value.

For the pricing mechanism and basis, Apple followed a common approach for the iPod by setting a fixed price per unit. More sophisticated alignments between mechanism and value are possible, however, as we showed with Google AdWords in Chapter 6. The pricing unit for search ads is outcome-oriented because buyers only pay per click. In other words, buyers only pay when they realize their objective of funneling traffic to their website. The auction system also shifts the value-sharing decision to customers because value varies significantly across keywords and customers.

Companies also need to consider how value-sharing decisions can affect the entire customer lifecycle. Apple's broader pricing model for the iPod encompassed the pricing of hardware, software, and content. Apple intentionally shared a greater amount of value up front on the bundled

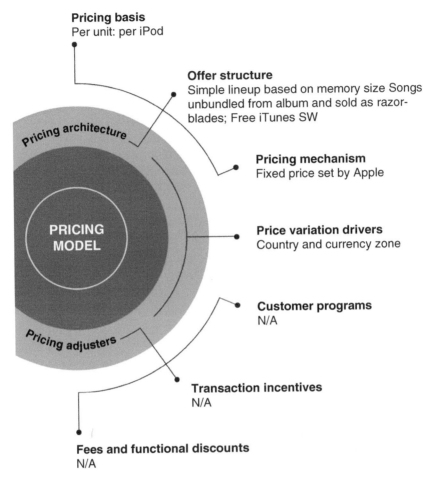

Pricing basis
Per unit: per iPod

Offer structure
Simple lineup based on memory size Songs
unbundled from album and sold as razor-
blades; Free iTunes SW

Pricing mechanism
Fixed price set by Apple

Price variation drivers
Country and currency zone

PRICING
MODEL

Customer programs
N/A

Pricing architecture

Pricing adjusters

Transaction incentives
N/A

Fees and functional discounts
N/A

FIGURE 7.3   The pricing model levers for the iPod in the Value Game

hardware and software sale with the goal of earning a higher share of
value later from loyal customers on the content. While iPod owners could
upload their own music to the devices, they could also buy music downloads directly from Apple via the iTunes store, with Apple taking a 30%
cut of that revenue. By February 2010, Apple's total direct downloads from
the iTunes store had exceeded 10 billion songs.[7] This resembled the classic
razor-and-blades model we described in Chapter 6.

Winning the Value Game

Step 1: Build the value ladder

Estimating usage value depends on the drivers of functional and emotional value versus the NBCA. Apple has a few points of comparison for the iPod. The improved storage and memory, the sleek design, and Apple's brand premium enhanced the iPod's positive usage value relative to the Rio PMP300. The negative usage value – such as the need to download iTunes to manage music – was minor. After all, iTunes provided easy access to legal downloads of songs. Figure 7.4 shows the results.

For some consumers, the iPod's reference point was not the Rio PMP300, but rather the Creative NOMAD Jukebox (Figure 7.5), which had storage capacity of 20GB. Significant positive usage value of the iPod derived from its portability, countered by negative usage value because the first iPod only featured 5GB of storage capacity.

Companies often use primary market research, such as customer surveys and focus groups, to estimate usage value either before a product

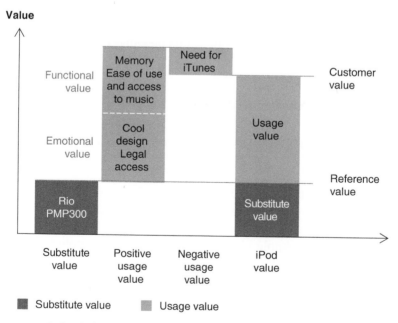

FIGURE 7.4   Value ladder for the iPod at launch, versus the Rio PMP300

Value

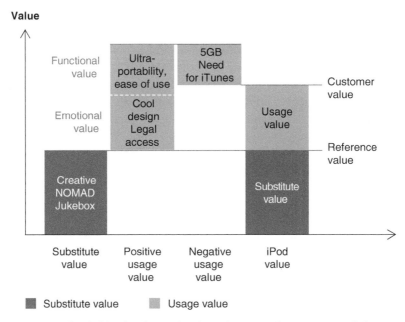

FIGURE 7.5   Value ladder for the iPod at launch, versus the NOMAD Jukebox

launch or on an ongoing basis. Based on Apple's brand value and the higher prices of newer iPod models introduced in later years, we estimate the usage value of the iPod at launch at between two and three times its substitute value.

Indirect analytical approaches such as economic value can help estimate usage value in certain situations. The Bloomberg Terminal, for example, provides real-time feeds to Bloomberg News, which breaks market-moving stories. When Bloomberg released an exclusive interview about Amazon's new tablet device, Amazon's stock price rose by 5%, increasing market capitalization by $4 billion.[8] Investors can derive immense economic value when they can trade instantly on the basis of such information.

Step 2: Choose how much value to share with the customer

Maximizing "value extraction" may be a leadership team's first instinct when setting prices in the Value Game. We recommend that companies resist this instinct and instead ask themselves: How much money should we share with customers and channel partners in order to create long-term advantages? First, as we explain in more detail in Chapter 21, it is usually not in a seller's best economic interest to "extract" all the value, because the loss of customers will be more than offset by the additional margin they will capture. Second, the wide gaps between net usage value and substitute value create many degrees of freedom for companies to drive behaviors in the market. There are two main strategies when it comes to sharing value with customers, depending on a company's goals and positioning.

One strategy is to share more value with customers to sell a high volume of products and penetrate a market quickly. Companies that adopt this strategy often prioritize total profit over unit margin. The original iPod went on sale in November 2001 at a price of $399 for 5GB of memory.[9] At the time, the Rio PMP300 cost around $200, while the Nomad Jukebox cost $269 after launching at $500 the previous year.[10,11] The iPod quickly won market share despite its significant premium over competitors. By August 2002, less than one year after its launch, the iPod held 33% market share, which then almost doubled to 64% in the ensuing 12 months.[12] This showed that Apple had priced the iPod in a way that accelerated penetration while allowing Apple to also retain a fair portion of the value the iPod created.

The other strategy, followed by some companies such as luxury goods manufacturers is to share less value with customers and focus instead on very high unit profit margins. Hermès, for example, limits the production of Birkin bags to create a sense of scarcity and make the bags highly sought after by fashion enthusiasts. Hermès reportedly limits the sale of these bags to their best customers, offering some other customers placement on a waiting list for up to six years.[13,14] The tradeoff, though, is that Hermès serves a narrow niche of customers who have a very high ability to pay the luxury premium.

Step 3: Invest to ensure continuous improvement

The Value Game attracts competition because of the size of the profit pool it generates. As competition increases and improves, it raises substitute value and forces a company to create new usage value or risk losing its existing leeway for pricing. Apple achieved that by aggressively reinforcing the emotional value of its products, by owning a reputation for simplicity and ease of use, and by releasing versions with new features on an almost annual basis.

Apple's brand identity, like most successful and enduring ones, is multilayered. It's built on messaging, storytelling, the visual elements of the retail design, customer engagement strategies, and its relationship with employees, investors, and ecosystem partners. The aura of secrecy that surrounds its inner workings and the hype surrounding its product releases amplify these effects.

Marketing is the function with the strongest influence on pricing, because of the importance of sustaining the brand value and the price premium. Apple invests in that strong brand image, spending around $1.8 billion on advertising in 2015, the last year it separately reported advertising costs.[15] It won the Emmy Award for best commercial in the year 2014 by successfully tying real product benefits to emotion. It also maintains continuity in its brand messaging, for example, by anchoring taglines on the word "hello" for almost four decades. An advertisement for the iPod in 2001 said "Say hello to iPod" and the message in a 2017 ad for the iPhone X ad was "Say hello to the future." These taglines date back to the launch of the Macintosh computer in January 1984, when it introduced itself by saying "Hello. I'm Macintosh. It sure is great to get out of that bag" at Apple's annual shareholders meeting.[16]

Perhaps the best reflection of the emotional value of Apple's brand strength is the way consumers view the products. Apple loyalists don't think *"I want this smartphone because it's a Dual-SIM, 64GB, 12-megapixel hexa-core processing smartphone."* They simply want the new iPhone. Loyalists prefer the iPhone to Samsung's smartphones even if features don't always compare favorably.

Impact: Long-term value

In 2022, BCG released its ranking of the world's most innovative companies, with well-known multinationals leading the list. For the second consecutive year, Apple ranked first. Its pipeline of product releases over the past two decades demonstrated how it has mastered the Value Game and achieved continued success.

The immense value Apple created and shared, starting with the iPod, helped drive long-term success in two other ways. First, it promoted integration with the Apple ecosystem, which expanded with the launch of iTunes and the App Store. In 2022, this larger ecosystem – which later included offerings such as Apple TV+ and Apple News+ – comprised around 20% of Apple's total revenue.[17]

Second, and perhaps most importantly, the iPod paved the way for the iPhone, which became the platform for products such as AirPods and the Apple Watch. When Apple released the iPhone in 2007, it also changed its name from Apple Computer, Inc. to Apple as a reflection of this broader consumer orientation.[18]

Key takeaways

The value ladder plays a critical role in how a company makes pricing decisions in the Value Game. We recommend the following approach:

- **Understand the product's usage value:** Quantify the incremental value – both functional and emotional – relative to the next-best substitute.

- **Decide how much value to share with your customers:** Depending on your strategic goals, share more value to penetrate the market quickly or less value for higher profit margins.

- **Establish a pricing model aligned with how value scales for customers:** Auctions can make sense when capacity is limited, and customer value is uncertain. A razor-and-blades model can help to encourage repeated follow-on purchases. In some cases, pricing per outcome or performance can also make sense.

- **Mitigate potential value erosion:** Invest in innovation and branding to ensure continuous improvement, with marketing as the lead function.

CHAPTER 8

The Uniform Game: The All-Time Classic

With contributions from Javier Anta, Matt Beckett, and Sebastian Bak

T he supermarket chain Whole Foods announced in January 2023 that it wanted to work with suppliers to reduce prices for shoppers as inflationary pressures began to ease.[1] That posed a daunting challenge, because their stores at the time carried as many as 20,000 items.[2] How could suppliers and Whole Foods guide themselves to that new equilibrium?

Such questions are vitally important for a smaller supplier such as Nona Lim, an entrepreneur who pioneered home meal-kit delivery service in the early 2000s. Drawing on her background as a competitive athlete and her knowledge as a nutrition consultant, Nona had experimented relentlessly to develop commercial versions of the recipes she loved growing up in Singapore. Her California-based company launched prepackaged healthy broths in brick-and-mortar retail with Whole Foods in 2014 and has since created a national brand for soups and broths.[3]

She had learned to defend her margin equation in previous negotiations. One key to her success is "to say 'no' to business that's not going to give you the minimum gross margin target that you have set."[4] That often means turning down retailers that demand too many concessions. This consideration of costs is important to the Uniform Game, which sits at the intersection of value and cost, thus requiring balanced consideration of both inputs.

In negotiations between suppliers and retailers, the outcomes often hinge on the answers to this deceptively simple question: How sensitive are consumers to price changes? The underlying concepts and tools that help companies answer that question – which we explore in this chapter – are the same for small suppliers seeking to create and own a niche as they are for global conglomerates seeking to improve their position in a mass market with equally powerful retail partners. More broadly speaking, they are the concepts and tools that help any seller who needs to set or change a nonnegotiable (fixed) price offered to all potential or eligible buyers. They help business leaders understand and apply their pricing agency to shape demand, share value, and win the Uniform Game.

Figure 8.1 summarizes the market characteristics for the Uniform Game. In Nona Lim's case, as we described in Chapter 3, the market for soups and broths fits these characteristics.

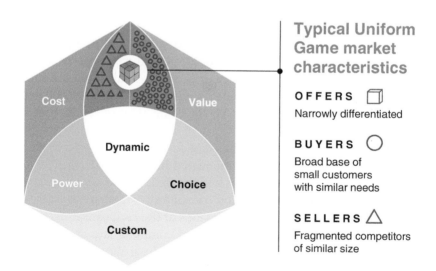

FIGURE 8.1 The typical characteristics of the Uniform Game

The special nature of pricing in the Uniform Game

The foot traffic and scale at Whole Foods and other retailers create a staggering number of potential consumer interactions, even for a small company such as Nona Lim. If any of those shoppers wants to grab Nona Lim's Miso Ramen Broth from the refrigerated section at their local Whole Foods, the price is exactly the same, no matter who they are or why they came to the store that day. It's $8.99 for the 20-ounce bag.[5]

Such single transparent price points are the hallmark of the Uniform Game. Because all customers pay that single uniform price, suppliers – and often their intermediaries – are always trying to make profitable trade-offs between price and volume in order to find the right equilibrium for sharing value.

The starting point to evaluate price–volume tradeoffs is a demand curve, shown in Figure 8.2. Companies often use estimates of price elasticity as shorthand to understand the impact of price changes within certain price ranges. The linear demand curve shown on the left is the easiest one to model but is unfortunately an anomaly in the real world. With multiple comparable competitors, the demand curve tends to have an S-shape.

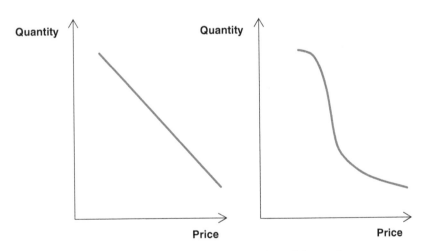

FIGURE 8.2   Demand curves showing linear and S-shaped demand

It is flatter on the left with demand saturated and on the right with less-price-sensitive customers, but steeply decreasing in the middle because of the large number of alternatives in your ideal price range.

The combination of a demand curve with marginal unit costs results in the profit function, shown in Figure 8.3. This is the key analytical tool for playing the Uniform Game. Successful pricing in the Uniform Game means finding prices that sit within a narrow range dictated by a product's elasticity and its costs. The range is narrow because of the steepness of the demand curve. Winning the Uniform Game, in turn, means not only having the ability to draw these curves, but also influence their shapes by influencing the price sensitivity of customers. This is where Nona Lim has pricing agency.

The gulf between textbook theory and market reality widens – and the fun begins – when we stop holding other aspects of someone's purchase

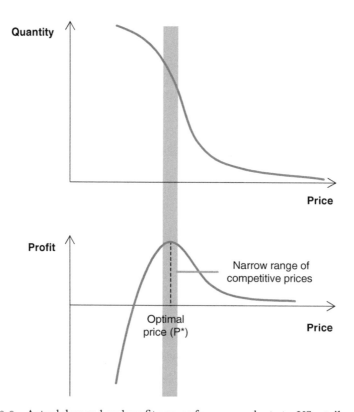

FIGURE 8.3   Actual demand and profit curves for one product at a US retailer

decision constant and start understanding the factors that influence price elasticity. As a reminder, low price elasticity is linked to lower price sensitivity, which means that the effects of price changes are muted. High price elasticity is linked to higher price sensitivity, which means the effects of price changes are amplified.

- **Substitutes:** Price elasticity increases as the number of available close substitutes increases.[6] The easier it is for consumers to switch, the greater the volume loss or gain for a company when it changes prices. The fragmented nature of competition drives the high elasticity we find in the Uniform Game.

- **Household budgets:** Price elasticity can change depending on how a price change affects the purchasing power of a consumer's income.[7] The effect may be less for a frequently purchased staple (such as shampoo or laundry detergent) than an infrequent purchase that they could defer, such as a new pair of shoes.

- **Differentiation:** Price elasticity tends to decline if a company can stress value arguments, create a trusted brand, or carve out some level of differentiation. Recall from Chapter 2 that the elasticity framework lies at the intersection of cost and value. Marketing still makes a difference, despite the apparent emphasis on mathematical relationships in the Uniform Game. The greater the perceived differentiation, even if slight, the greater the likelihood that a customer views fewer products as substitutes. Higher brand equity, which contributes to higher usage value, can also decrease price elasticity.

- **Relative market share:** Price elasticity tends to decline as a company's relative market share increases. Let's look at an extreme example. A company with a market share of 1% in a stable, low-growth product category might double its volume if it cuts its prices in half.[8] But if a company with a market share of 20% cuts its prices in half, it is unlikely that their action would double their volume in this category. Their relative volume increase – and therefore their elasticity – would likely be much lower.

These factors influence how a player in the Uniform Game can use specific pricing model levers, as shown in Figure 8.4 for Nona Lim.

In the Uniform Game, setting the pricing model primarily focuses on price adjusters. For consumer packaged goods (CPG) companies that sell

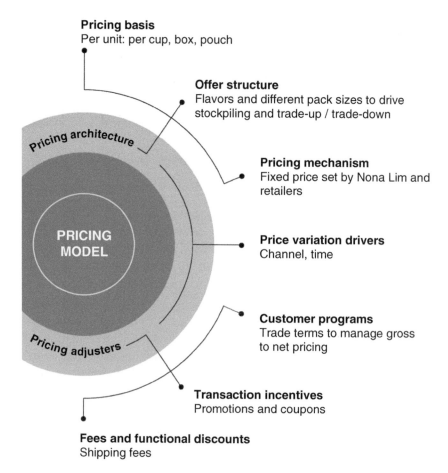

Pricing basis
Per unit: per cup, box, pouch

Offer structure
Flavors and different pack sizes to drive
stockpiling and trade-up / trade-down

Pricing architecture

Pricing mechanism
Fixed price set by Nona Lim and
retailers

PRICING
MODEL

Price variation drivers
Channel, time

Customer programs
Trade terms to manage gross
to net pricing

Pricing adjusters

Transaction incentives
Promotions and coupons

Fees and functional discounts
Shipping fees

FIGURE 8.4   Levers that Nona Lim can use in the Uniform Game

through retailers, customer programs are typically "gross-to-net" trade
terms, most of which are discounts that reward cumulative volume. The
retailer can then invest these savings to support in-store sales. Nona Lim's
trade terms were relatively simple when she launched her business, but
progressively grew in sophistication as her business scaled.

Transaction incentives, such as promotions and coupons, help increase
demand and volume. Promotions are one of the biggest pricing levers in
the Uniform Game, due to the tight linkage between price and demand.
However, if companies don't use them judiciously, promotions risk shifting volume between suppliers without expanding the overall market.

Nona Lim worked with retailers to define promotional schedules to encourage trial of her products and assessed the impact that promotions had on price elasticity and volume over time.

Offer structure is the most important pricing architecture lever in the Uniform Game, as the rest of the pricing architecture tends to be mostly standardized: transparent and fixed pricing per product, set by the seller. Nona Lim varied her offer structure by using different flavors, like Indian Lentil and Turmeric Chicken, as well as different pack sizes and bundled meal kits. Most of Nona Lim's products had fixed prices per unit of product, be it cups of soup, packages of noodles, or pouches of broth. When the optimum price range is narrow, offering new flavors at the same price is the most natural way to expand the offering and create new demand.

In addition, Nona Lim opted to sell directly to consumers through her own e-commerce website. That gave her a channel in which she had full control over pricing. Nona Lim could choose when to run promotions, and how much to promote. Orders placed through her website generally had a flat shipping fee. In the Uniform Game, fees and functional discounts usually play a limited role, but they can be a useful way to cover an extra variable cost such as shipping.

Working out a single optimal price is hard enough when a company sells directly to its customers, which many players of the Uniform Game do. But finding that price becomes more difficult when it reflects the symbiotic relationship between a retailer and a seller. Each party has its own objectives and financial equation to solve, and the two do not necessarily overlap. The steps that companies follow become increasingly complex, but we begin by returning to one simple example using Nona Lim's products at Whole Foods as a reference point.

A visit to a Whole Foods store in early 2023 revealed the competitive situation for Nona Lim. In the refrigerated section, her 20-ounce bag of Miso Ramen Broth stood next to a 24-ounce bottle of bone broth from Roli Roti, a company founded by a third-generation Swiss butcher named Thomas Odermatt.[9] Two variants of her ramen noodles stood next to a Miso Ramen meal kit from Sun Noodle, a company founded by Hidehito Uki, who immigrated to the United States from Japan in 1981 and, like Nona Lim, had a passion for the foods and recipes he grew up with.[10]

The Sun Noodle product had a promoted price that was a little over 20% below its normal shelf price. The promoted price for members of Amazon Prime was even lower, representing a discount of almost 30% off the normal shelf price.[11]

These prices and products, while not perfect one-to-one substitutes, illustrate the key pricing decisions facing Nona Lim. Can Nona Lim afford to price the broth to match Bone Broth's price of $7.39? Should they? Should Nona Lim promote ramen noodles? If yes, how deeply, and how frequently? Further, how should Nona Lim think about the price gaps between their products and on-shelf competition? And are Nona Lim's prices in line with what a typical Whole Foods shopper expects?

The complexity of the Uniform Game can increase exponentially when a company factors in more and more aspects of customers' buying behavior. Retailers and suppliers often face very similar market conditions, but the retailer's pricing strategy may be aligned with or opposed to a supplier's pricing strategy.

Shaping demand and elasticity to drive pricing strategy

Step 1: Understand profit-and-loss flexibility

Recall that the fundamental question for players of the Uniform Game is to understand how sensitive customers are to price changes. The seller's revenues and profits depend directly on the answer to that question. Each seller therefore needs to know how much resilience it has to withstand fluctuations in prices and volumes. This requires a strong understanding of fixed and variable costs and some basic financial modeling acumen.

Let's take Nona Lim broth, currently priced at $8.99. Figure 8.5 shows a hypothetical view of Nona Lim's financial resilience, that is, how her profit will change with a change in price.[12] Nona Lim would have a lot of resilience if her product's elasticity were moderate (2.1) because her profit would be relatively stable whether prices go down by 5% or up by as much as 20%. She would have much less resilience at a low elasticity (1.1) or high elasticity (3.5), because her profits could easily vary up or down by 15–30%.

Such simple financial models are the starting point to better understand how to win the Uniform Game. Companies can use several methods to calculate price elasticities, ranging from surveys to controlled experiments to

		Elasticity		
		Low (1.1)	Moderate (2.1)	High (3.5)
Price change	+20%	21%	1%	−22%
	+5%	−7%	1%	−6%
	−5%	−7%	−2%	5%
	−20%	−33%	−16%	14%

FIGURE 8.5 Change in Nona Lim's profits from different price changes and elasticities

quantitative analyses of natural market variations. We have two observations from applying these methods over many years. First, the methods tend to be very sensitive to the assumptions embedded in their analytical approach. They will therefore yield a range of elasticity estimates. Second, elasticities vary widely depending on local market conditions. This makes elasticity estimates subject to significant uncertainty and explains why it is important to understand the range of financial outcomes linked to different elasticity estimates.

Step 2: Set prices based on your own price elasticities

Once the company knows its profit-and-loss resilience, it can use elasticity values as a guide for how to change prices to drive strategic outcomes. These outcomes are tied to the strategic aspirations for the product, such as gaining market share or improving margins. The outcome provides the direction of the move, and the elasticity values inform the precise distance to move.

Elasticities also differ depending on whether a product is on promotion; therefore, it is necessary to distinguish between two types of elasticities:

1. **Everyday:** This quantifies sensitivity to list price changes, which the company typically does not advertise.
2. **Promoted:** This quantifies sensitivity to advertised price reductions from the list price. Promotional prices typically only last a few weeks, but the associated elasticity is much higher than everyday elasticity.

Because estimates of elasticities are uncertain, deciding on everyday and promoted prices requires business judgment and experience. These general observations should help guide your decision-making:

- Higher-than-average elasticity means the profit-maximizing price will be lower and vice versa, as shown in Figure 8.5.
- The larger the planned price change, the less predictive power the elasticity has.
- Elasticities are not constant, and they increase significantly beyond the thresholds at "magic" price points such as $9.99 or the price points of major competitors.
- Elasticities are also asymmetrical around clusters of competitor prices. They tend to be higher above them and lower below them, which helps explain why prices tend to converge into a narrow range, as we saw in Figure 8.3.
- Elasticities can vary by a factor of 5 when they are estimated at the most granular level, by store, segment, and at different times. It is hard for large companies to take advantage of these variations, because of the complexity of managing prices at such a granular level. But they represent a potential opportunity for smaller firms as well as for firms that develop tools with flexible capabilities like artificial intelligence (AI).
- Elasticity estimates will be inaccurate if competitors change their prices as a result of a price move. But the fragmentation of competitors in the Uniform Game ensures that elasticities have some relevance, because many uncoordinated moves by competitors will cancel each other's effect on any company's elasticity.

The use and interpretation of promoted price elasticities requires extra care because so many factors besides price can explain the higher volume (the "lift") generated during the promotion. The timing (month, day of the week) and the product merchandising (features and displays) can have a greater influence on volume changes than price.

The origin of the lift itself also may not be obvious. Where does that incremental volume come from? Some may come from competitors' volume, while some may represent more purchases by price-sensitive consumers or purchases by new or lapsed customers interested in trying the product. But in some cases, the company is simply pulling forward its own future sales, but at a lower price.

The lack of clarity explains why many promotions fail to yield a positive return on investment. By aggregating findings across more than 100 analyses of promotion programs, we have found that at least 20–30% of promotions run by consumer companies and retailers have negative ROIs.

Let's come back to Nona Lim's Ramen noodles. Figure 8.6 shows how to use one's own everyday and promoted price elasticities to derive target prices that deliver a strategic outcome of profit maximization. The pattern in the chart is quite common. With lower elasticity, the optimal profit curve for the list price is flatter as price increases, so the immediate profit risk of raising prices is low. Nona Lim may not want to push prices past the peak around $9.70, however, because achieving the same profit with lower volumes would create long-term risk that fewer consumers taste her broths. This is in stark contrast to the promoted price curve, which has a clear maximum around $7.30, but comes down quickly when the price starts to deviate on either side. This illustrates that while promotions can be a very powerful lever, lowering the price too much could easily cut profits in half. This is one of the reasons why so many promotions have negative ROIs.

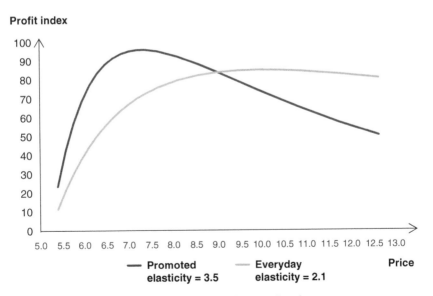

FIGURE 8.6   Finding the profit-maximizing price or price change

Elasticities are influenced by many factors beyond the difference between promoted and everyday price. These factors include product investments and flavors, brand investments, packaging, size and form, marketing collateral investments, retailer activity, and so on. Leading companies use AI models to track elasticity in a very granular way depending on all these factors. The more granular your measured elasticities are, the more precise and targeted your guidance will be.

Step 3: Reset pricing architecture based on cross elasticities

One's own elasticities help shape the direction and magnitude of unilateral price moves. But the combination of price transparency and multiple competing suppliers ensures that there are very few price moves in the Uniform Game that remain unilateral and unreciprocated. Businesses need to understand the impact of both their own and competitive price actions.

Misunderstanding the relevant elasticities could inadvertently spark a price war. If one seller makes a small price change that results in a large volume shift, for example, its competitors may feel compelled to undercut that price change to reclaim some of that lost volume. Overall volumes remain static, but price levels decline.

Cross elasticity describes how changes in the price of one product can affect demand for another good. Cross elasticity of two goods can vary depending on whether the two goods are substitutes, complements, or unrelated. A positive cross elasticity indicates that the two goods are substitutes. Negative cross-price elasticity indicates they are complements (e.g., coffee grounds and coffee filters). Cross elasticities are especially important for retailers, who may manage tens of thousands of SKUs.

Figure 8.7 is a simplified view of volume flows driven by cross elasticity for five products: A, B, C, D, and E. For each product, the row represents the volume flows when the product raises prices. When A raises its price, E gains the most volume, C and D gain moderate volume, and B gains just a little volume. However, when D raises its price, only E gains a little volume.

Managing the interplay between prices and volumes across multiple products is a significant opportunity in the Uniform Game. Sophisticated companies make strategic choices to steer these volume flows. This is

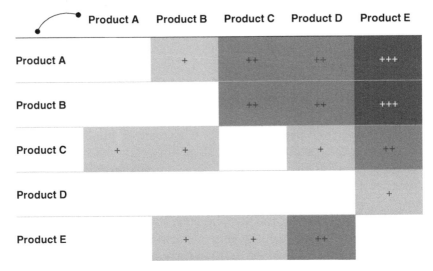

FIGURE 8.7 Cross-elasticity analysis reveals potential volume movement

why consumer goods companies often have multiple brands and variants within a category. If you own both A and E, then raising A's price makes sense, provided the volume is recaptured by E at the right margin.

Figure 8.7 provides the 2D map of the Uniform Game. The pricing team thinks across all pricing model levers on how to create advantage. We have observed CPGs:

- Modify retailer programs to ensure that substitute products are located as far apart as possible in the store.
- Promote complementary products together (e.g., beer and chips).
- Define and actively manage price indices between specific products.

For Nona Lim, the broth and noodles are complements while the Nona Lim broth and Butcher brand broth are substitutes, as are Nona Lim Ramen and Miso Ramen. If Miso Ramen followed Nona Lim price increase as described in Step 2, Nona Lim would lose substantially less volume than its own elasticity would predict.

This opens up a range of opportunities. Could Nona Lim raise the price of only certain flavors of Ramen? Could she introduce a new, smaller pack size to recapture any lost volume due to the price increases?

Step 4: Influence how customers select and buy

Understanding transactional elasticities (own and cross) helps a company achieve robust outcomes in the Uniform Game. But too much focus on these numbers can lead the company to overlook important insights into why customers shop at a specific location or make certain types of shopping trips.

This is especially true for retailers who manage hundreds of thousands of SKUs. Even sophisticated AI algorithms cannot keep up with the exponential increase in own and cross-elasticity relationships for so many SKUs. That is why companies use basket analyses to identify the key value items (KVIs) that drive value perception or drive traffic to stores. KVIs play an important role for retailers, because customers tend to compare KVIs across stores to make quick, general assessments on whether a store generally has higher or lower prices than their alternatives.

Sharing more value on KVIs can lead to higher revenue across other categories, an effect that transactional elasticity may not capture. Most retailers manage a list of KVIs based on past sales and overall customer penetration. When a company identifies and invests in less obvious KVIs, it can improve outcomes even more.

Leading retailers also set pricing zones by geography, which enables them to share more value in elastic zones while retaining more value in inelastic zones. The same logic applies for different channels.

Transactional elasticities could help a company such as Nona Lim make profitable price moves. But how can Nona Lim and Whole Foods enhance the targeting of the products? The needs and the drivers of price variance are presumably much different for a single mom in Plano, Texas, than a single male in midtown Manhattan. Understanding these differences could help Nona Lim find ways through Whole Foods, other channel partners, and her own website to create win–win experiences for smaller and local target segments.

The impact: More sophisticated Uniform Game pricing

General Mills reported in early 2023 that its elasticity was 27% lower than key branded competitors across its top 10 categories.[13] It seems as if General Mills has been able to shape its demand better than its competition has, resulting in lower elasticities. This demand shaping translates into 2–5% higher EBITDA.

At the 2023 CAGNY (Consumer Analyst Group of New York) conference,[14] it came as no surprise to us that the leading consumer goods companies identified revenue management as the key lever to drive profitable growth. Revenue management is currently a well-embedded discipline within most leaders in the Uniform Game. The function has broad strategic and tactical pricing responsibility, similar to what we described in Chapter 5 as the pricing team's responsibility.

Demand shaping does not happen by chance. The elasticity models set the stage for all the strategic choices. In our experience, a demand-centric portfolio[15] helps the pricing team or revenue management team make the subsequent complex tradeoffs that define success in the Uniform Game.

Key takeaways

Price elasticity is the economic framework that determines success in the Uniform Game. We recommend the following approach:

- **Understand elasticities in a very granular way:** Estimate how volume will shift in response to price changes and to factors that influence price elasticity, such as substitutes, household budgets, differentiation, and relative market shares.
- **Use elasticities as a guide for pricing:** Set and change prices by using everyday, promoted, and cross elasticities to model the impact of the potential changes. The more granular the measurements, the more precise the price setting can be.
- **Establish a pricing model to optimize the profit function:** Focus on price adjusters and offer structure to influence the elasticities. Even if your short-term goal is not to maximize profits, knowing the shape of the profit curve and the profit-maximizing price point is essential for understanding the financial consequences of any pricing decisions in the Uniform Game.
- **Differentiate how much value you share and where:** Share more value on key value items (KVIs), establish more granular pricing zones by geography and channel, and target specific customer segments with special offers.

CHAPTER 9

The Cost Game: Where Efficiency Reigns

With contributions from Camille Brégé, Drew Donovan, and Shaveen Garg

I n some industries, such as construction, the availability of substitutes and the high number of suppliers give customers significant bargaining power. In such markets, suppliers compete primarily on price, with the lowest bid most likely to win the project.

The CEO of Wrightway Contracting believed that it was impossible to win projects without having the lowest bid.

Wrightway specializes in roadwork, which includes building and maintaining local roads and highways, as well as airport runways and logistics hubs.[1] Their market fit the typical Cost Game characteristics shown in Figure 9.1. The company's survival depended heavily on effective cost management, which allowed them to offer the lowest bids their CEO considered essential.

But the CEO also knew that cost reductions have practical limits. If too extreme, they can erode quality and ultimately lead to lower revenue. Where could Wrightway's leadership team find additional levers – beyond cost management – to remain successful?

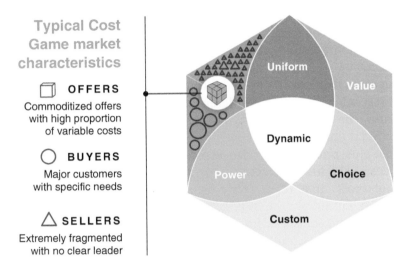

Typical Cost Game market characteristics

🗋 **OFFERS**

Commoditized offers with high proportion of variable costs

◯ **BUYERS**

Major customers with specific needs

△ **SELLERS**

Extremely fragmented with no clear leader

FIGURE 9.1   Construction market was ideally suited to the Cost Game

The company learned that understanding the roles and the impact of pricing levers could help them win more bids and thrive in a game that seemingly offers little upside for pricing. Despite the apparent constraints of the Cost Game, companies such as Wrightway have several ways to improve outcomes significantly by driving efficiency and sharing value thoughtfully. The story of Wrightway, which we elaborate on in this chapter, demonstrates how leaders can achieve powerful differentiation, greater customer trust, and steady predictable profits by tightly aligning their pricing model with their costs to drive efficiencies.

The special nature of pricing in the Cost Game

Cost-plus may sound like a simple pricing method that requires little analysis. It has also fallen out of favor with many pricing advisors over the past few decades, because it does not use customer value as the basis for pricing. How can a company claim to share value when its pricing does not focus on customer value?

It turns out that cost-plus pricing, accompanied by a cost-leadership strategy, can enable a company to gain market share profitably and even gain additional cost advantages, as we describe later in this section. It is a natural fit for companies in crowded markets, whose products or services have limited differentiation and whose customers have high bargaining power.

But accurately identifying and estimating costs can be a complex process. Most offers have many different cost elements, which means that calculating the total cost of a product or a project accurately requires a fine and granular tracking of costs.

Cost-plus pricing must also account for the expected changes in those costs. The first concept to understand in this context is the "BCG slope" of a cost curve, a term originally introduced by BCG founder Bruce Henderson. Put simply, the BCG slope represents the rate at which a doubling of volume translates into unit cost savings. For instance, a slope of 80% suggests that unit costs fall by 20% every time volume doubles. We will use BCG slopes to describe the three key influences of how costs evolve: scale, experience, and complexity.

Understanding scale effects is critical to predict changes in costs. Once a company understands its costs in detail, it is critical to categorize these costs into fixed, variable, or semi-variable depending on how they scale with overall volume. Figure 9.2 illustrates this concept. A purely variable cost does not change with volume and therefore has a BCG slope of 100%. It translates into a flat line on the chart. When production doubles, cost per unit does not change. Purely variable costs play a natural role in pricing, as they represent the marginal costs used in elasticity calculations and their drivers tend to be used as a pricing basis.

A purely fixed cost would have a BCG slope of 50%. If volume doubles, the same cost is spread over twice the number of units, so the cost per unit falls by 50%. These are the costs that microeconomic theory advises companies to ignore when they try to maximize profit as a function of price, because all fixed costs only reduce overall company profits. In our experience, however, very few costs are truly fixed.

Most costs turn out to be semi-variable in practice and often result in a 60–70% BCG slope. This means there is roughly 30–40% improvement in unit costs every time volume doubles. A precise understanding of the scale-driven BCG slope allows the Cost Game player to use its capacity and size optimally. Semi-variable costs are also often a sign that those costs can be decomposed further into more discrete cost drivers. Companies should look there first for insights into potential new pricing bases, because their

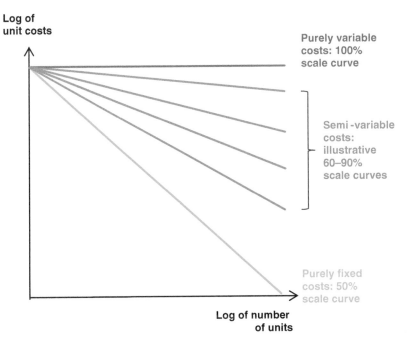

FIGURE 9.2   Illustrative scale curves related to different types of costs

pricing formula should reflect the interplay between different underlying cost drivers.

Wrightway's cost of labor to repair roads, for example, depends on the total length of the roads to be repaired. But this cost doesn't scale linearly, which makes it semi-variable. A closer examination reveals that the number of different roads to repave impacts the management overhead required, but not the rest of the labor. Each disaggregated labor cost will be closer to a purely variable cost and thus have a higher BCG slope. As we discuss later in this chapter, this will influence the choice of pricing bases.

Experience, or cumulative volume, is the second critical factor influencing unit costs. Henderson also discovered that cumulative production was an excellent predictor of cost declines.[2] This is still relevant today, particularly in markets destined for high growth over decades. Lithium-ion batteries, for example, have grown in usage by a factor of 100 over the past 25 years and are destined for further growth with their usage in electric vehicles. Although the annual reduction of the costs per kWh has slowed down from 13% to 6% in the same period, its BCG slope has stayed at around 81%, which means costs fall by around 19% when cumulative volumes double.[3] The most reliable way to plan for the price of lithium-ion batteries five years out is therefore to forecast cumulative volume, not annual price reductions.

Complexity is the third factor influencing unit costs. Complexity increases as the number of products and managed activities increases. This leads to higher unit costs, because coordination needs increase and costs related to a specific offering are amortized over lower volumes. Complexity curves highlight this effect. They plot the relationship between costs and a dimension that measures complexity, as shown in Figure 9.3. Like scale and experience curves, we use the BCG slope value to report the rate of increase in unit costs as the measure of complexity doubles. In our experience, complexity slopes range between 110% and 150%. A precise understanding of complexity-driven BCG slopes allows players to better manage their offering and control costs.

A company can use scale, experience, and complexity curves to predict future costs, based on a volume forecast. Thus, a solid understanding

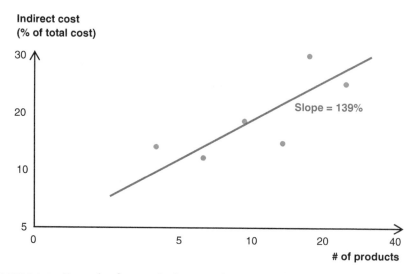

FIGURE 9.3   Example of a complexity curve for six manufacturing plants

of these curves allows Cost Game players to incorporate expected future costs when determining prices. If a company can forecast how much its costs will decline as production or volume increases, it can decide to price its first commercial units lower to stimulate demand. These initial sales might be less profitable, but they change the value equation, as greater demand drives faster cost declines over time. This is a critical part of making the tradeoff between sharing more value with customers to stimulate growth or prioritizing profitability.

The granular understanding of costs translates into pricing model choices in the Cost Game. Figure 9.4 summarizes the levers for Wrightway.

The choice of a pricing basis is the most important pricing architecture decision in the Cost Game. Choosing pricing units is not trivial, because it is crucial to align them well with the cost drivers. Think of auto insurance policies. The traditional pricing basis is per car, but the number of miles driven correlates much better with the actuarial risk of an accident and therefore with the insurance carrier's costs. Insurers have increasingly introduced pay-per-mile models with monthly base rates and mileage rates to target people who drive infrequently.

Using more than one pricing basis makes sense if important cost drivers do not correlate across customers. Utility bills, for example, often have a consumption basis and a capacity basis. Costs to serve depend on the amount consumed, but also on the capacity needed to serve peak demand. In the case of Wrightway, every construction project is tied to a long list of cost drivers, such as materials, labor, and overhead. Each cost driver has different units and needs to be estimated separately. The overall price for a project depends on the sum of all these costs.

The pricing mechanism and the offer structure play less important roles in the Cost Game. Sellers usually set fixed prices for their offerings. Another common price mechanism is a bidding process, such as a tender for a project with predefined specifications. For Wrightway, the offer structure for their bid is either unbundled with many different line items or a quote for the overall project. The buyer sets the mechanism in some cases by deciding whether to implement a bidding process or to demand a fixed price.

In terms of price adjusters, the Cost Game is the home of fees and functional discounts. Wrightway used fees and discounts to help align prices better to their costs, such as by guiding customers to select lower-cost

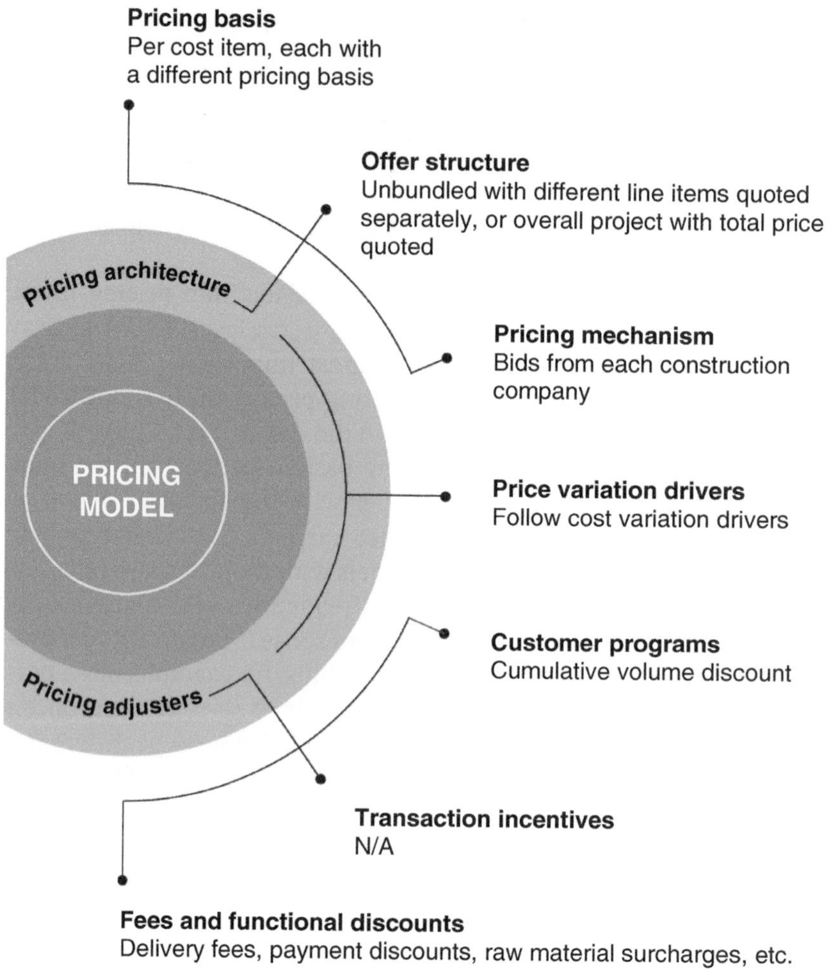

Pricing basis
Per cost item, each with
a different pricing basis

Offer structure
Unbundled with different line items quoted
separately, or overall project with total price
quoted

Pricing mechanism
Bids from each construction
company

Pricing architecture

Price variation drivers
Follow cost variation drivers

PRICING
MODEL

Customer programs
Cumulative volume discount

Pricing adjusters

Transaction incentives
N/A

Fees and functional discounts
Delivery fees, payment discounts, raw material surcharges, etc.

FIGURE 9.4   Pricing models for Wrightway & Sons

options or by incentivizing customer behaviors that resulted in lower costs for Wrightway. It is also common to have cumulative volume discounts as a price adjuster in the Cost Game, because they are the main customer program that contributes to gaining scale advantages.

Pricing to cost to gain scale and drive efficiencies

Step 1: Build an understanding of current and future costs

Cost Game players need a clear view of both the current and future states of their costs. This means understanding the cost drivers as well as understanding how costs are likely to change with experience, scale, and complexity.

One type of cost may have a diverse set of drivers, while disparate costs may have a common set of drivers. Marine shipping costs, for example, include the costs of the vessels, bunker fuel, crew, maintenance, insurance, and port fees. While crew and bunker fuel are clearly different cost items, they share cost drivers, such as the distance the goods need to be carried.

Cataloging all these costs at a granular level allows the company to estimate the cost-to-serve accurately. Low-margin businesses need to track even the smallest and irregular cost areas, because in aggregate they can have a material effect on profits. Developing expectations for future costs requires estimates of scale, experience, and complexity of BCG slope values.

Wrightway's finance team explored the details of all its costs to deeply understand all the drivers. The team then built precise projections on how these costs would evolve over time based on scale, experience, and complexity. As a result, Wrightway was fully prepared to define its optimal pricing model.

Step 2: Define the pricing basis

Once a company understands its current and future costs in depth, it can begin defining its pricing architecture. Deciding on the pricing basis or bases is the first step. If all cost drivers are strongly correlated, then the pricing basis can build off one cost. But that is not always the case. Shipping costs, for example, usually have three main drivers with no strong correlation to each other.

- **Weight:** The heavier the cargo, the costlier the shipping, because heavier loads require more effort to move.

- **Size:** The bigger the cargo, the costlier the shipping. Large cargo loads take up more space in a vessel and may require special handling.
- **Distance:** The farther the distance, the costlier the shipping. Cargo shipped between two locations in Europe will result in lower shipping costs than cargo shipped between Asia and Europe, for instance.

This lack of correlation means that decision-makers need to take all of these drivers into account when pricing. They need multiple pricing bases to ensure that they accurately reflect the cost-to-serve.

Events beyond the control of the buyer or seller can also severely impact costs and thus margins. Companies can gain some flexibility by, for example, indexing prices or surcharges to relevant commodity costs. Contracts often contain price-revision clauses to account for major disruptions such as changes in regulation or taxes, or hardships caused by a catastrophic event.

Coming back to Wrightway, the finance team analyzed the details of their project-based cost drivers. The team started with the primary cost drivers for any project-based organization – the costs of time and materials – and soon started to unearth useful insights. For example, Wrightway had always believed that the time costs to repair roads depended solely on the total length of the road. But the finance team saw that the BCG slope of these costs was not 100%. In other words, these costs were semi-variable. Digging deeper, the finance team realized that increasing the number of roads being simultaneously repaired also increased the required project management overhead. The road repair time costs therefore depended on both the length of the road and the number of roads being repaired. This insight allowed Wrightway to adopt two pricing bases for road repair time costs: the length of the road and the number of roads.

This exercise, repeated across every single cost item, helped Wrightway define more precise pricing bases, thus setting the stage for it to use pricing to drive the right behaviors and efficiencies.

Step 3: Use pricing to create efficiencies

Finding ways to influence customer behavior can contribute to long-term success in the Cost Game. Having customers become partners in lowering costs can result in a virtuous cycle that benefits both parties. Customers receive lower prices, while the seller earns a higher margin and gains additional volume that will push costs further down the scale curve.

A major food distributor went further in influencing customer behavior by combining price transparency with incentives that efficiently share value from cost optimization. Historically, customers would maintain relationships with several food distributors to get multiple quotes to keep distributors "honest" on price. This practice was highly inefficient and expensive for distributors, because each would need to send smaller trucks of the same food to multiple locations.

To address this issue, the food distributor fostered a closer relationship with its customers through price transparency and by offering incentives for customers to help lower its costs. These incentives included discounts for reduced delivery frequency, ordering on off-peak days, and buying private-label products. The discounts could be up to 60% of the standard margin, depending on how much the customer could reduce the distributor's costs. The food distributor saw its sales volumes double on average in accounts where it implemented this relationship-based model. The profit per customer increased by 30% even at the discounted rates, due to the increase in volume and reduction in expenses.

Some companies impose functional fees on outliers as a means of encouraging customers to modify or limit their behavior. Electricity companies, for example, charge higher fees for peak-time consumption to alleviate stress on the electricity grid and incentivize customers to use electricity in off-peak times. Customers then change their usage by running their dishwasher at 10 p.m. instead of 6 p.m., because they are motivated to decrease their own costs.

Construction companies like Wrightway can also help their customers better understand the costs associated with different aspects of the construction process by providing clear and detailed information about their pricing structures. Wrightway used price transparency to build trust and encourage closer collaboration and identify areas for potential cost savings.

Let's go back to the road cost example from Step 2. Wrightway educated customers on the need for the two distinct pricing bases – length of road and number of roads. Wrightway's updated project prices reflected these two bases and the Wrightway team often proactively reached out to educate customers on how to think about road repair projects. By fostering strong relationships with their customers, Wrightway positioned themselves as trusted advisors and consultants on project design. This gave them the opportunity to make recommendations regarding materials, delivery method, value engineering principles, and other variables that could significantly reduce construction costs and produce higher-quality work. This set the stage for the final step.

Step 4: Optimize the markup

Setting margins or markups – the "plus" in cost-plus – can be a complex process, with little room for error. Similar to the challenge the caterer faced in the introductory chapter, the right margin is the one that yields prices high enough to cover expected costs, but low enough to improve the chances of winning a bid. Margin decisions are even more important in markets where companies have limited scope for cost management, that is, when sellers share the same suppliers or draw from the same pool of labor.

Creating a range of target margins – rather than one universal target margin – helps maximize profits in the long term. The optimization parameters depend on the market. Let's take the example of a cement company that has lower costs to serve customers than its competitors', due to the proximity of its factories to major construction sites. They may choose to set their margins based on their competitors' costs, using parameters such as costs and capacities of each factory and transportation costs between factories and destinations. Using competitors' costs allows them to find a margin that sets prices significantly above their own costs, but below their competitors', so that they maximize the chances of winning customers.

Models based on probability theory can help determine the likelihood of winning customers at different price points. In the construction industry, such models typically rely on a competitor's past bidding behavior, based on data of the company's own win–loss record (see Figure 9.5). In some cases, for government contracts, information on previous bids is publicly available. Computing and analyzing this data for Wrightway revealed two valuable insights:

1. For 10% of the bids Wrightway lost, their pricing was lower than the winning bid.

2. For a substantial amount (49%) of lost business, pricing was very competitive. The winning bid was within 10% of Wrightway's price. Getting the markup and price right was critical here.

This analysis disproved the assumption that the lowest bid always wins. The Wrightway team started to focus more on optimizing the "plus" part of their pricing model. The probability model identified a range of target margins based on multiple parameters:

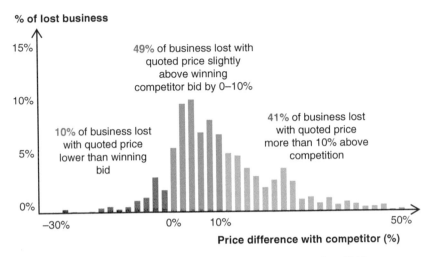

% of lost business

FIGURE 9.5   Wrightway's historical bids pricing versus competitors' bids

- Client sector (e.g., private industry, public department)
- Deal size
- Technical complexity
- Deal constraints (e.g., noise reduction, time constraints)
- Level of activity at work start
- Level of competition (e.g., backlog of the competitors in this area)

As they dug into the data, they realized that:

- The bids Wrightway lost despite being the lowest price (10% of all lost bids) were all high-complexity deals. The leadership team committed to focus on delivering the technical specs for these deals without being restricted by markups.
- The competitively lost deals (49% of all lost bids) – the ones in which Wrightway was no more than 10% higher than the winning bid – mostly involved mid-sized deals in two client sectors. The Wrightway team agreed to reduce markup expectations for these deals.

These targeted actions helped Wrightway win more deals and drive profitable growth.

The impact: A win–win for customers and sellers

Cost-plus pricing has an unfavorable reputation. Nonetheless, countless companies have thrived in the Cost Game by delivering more efficient and less costly solutions. The cost-conscious culture of many of these companies has created processes that relentlessly look for opportunities to improve efficiency. These improvements allow them to maintain low-cost operations and offer lower-priced solutions that pass much of the savings to their customers. They ultimately grow faster than their competitors. The more experience or scale a company gains, and the better it aligns prices to cost, the more it can lower its costs further and pass on part of the savings to customers in a true win–win fashion.

Wrightway achieved around five percentage points of EBIT impact after 24 months by aligning their prices more closely with costs and by using pricing to shape customer behavior. This kind of impact is completely game-changing for a business with relatively low margins.

Key takeaways

Cost-plus pricing in the Cost Game can help you grow your business, gain market share, increase profitability, and ultimately gain a strong position in your market. We recommend the following approach:

- **Understand your costs in depth:** Use experience, scale, and complexity curves to understand your current and expected fixed and variable costs.
- **Optimize all components of the cost-plus formula:** Select pricing bases that align to cost drivers and create a range for margins or "plus" portions based on customer and market characteristics.
- **Influence customer behavior to save costs:** Use fees and functional discounts to nudge customers to minimize costs, then share the value of the resulting cost savings with customers.
- **Tailor the plus:** Adjust the markup depending on the intensity of the competitive situation. Higher markups are warranted by even small offer differentiation or a lower number of competitors likely to win.

CHAPTER 10

The Power Game: When Every Move Counts

*With contributions from Federico Fabbri and
Jan Gildemeister*

H ard disk drives (HDDs) – the whirring, clicking memory banks inside personal computers – are characterized by their capacity and performance. Introduced by IBM in 1956, these data storage devices played a pivotal role in the explosion of general-purpose computing and became critical components of personal computers in the 1990s and beyond.

But from the late 1990s to the early 2000s, profitability plunged in the HDD market. From the beginning of 1995 to the end of 1999, the median annualized total shareholder return for HDD makers was –7%, in stark contrast to the annualized return of the tech sector's S&P 500 IT at 52% and the broader S&P 500 at 29%.[1]

Why did this happen?

Part of the answer lies in Moore's law, which predicts that the number of transistors in dense integrated circuits grows geometrically every year.[2] The equivalent metric in HDD technology is areal density. Gigabits per square inch had increased geometrically since the 1990s and even faster than what Moore's law predicted. *Scientific American* dubbed this trend

Kryder's law, after Mark Kryder, the CTO of Seagate, one of the leading HDD manufacturers.[3]

A key implication of exponential growth is continuously declining costs. As a result, pricing for technology products can be akin to negotiating a descent on a sheer rock face. Resisting the inevitable price erosion puts short-term revenue and volume at risk because competitors are likely to keep the same pace of price decline and pick up share.

Under those circumstances, it is not surprising that many companies believed that they were price takers. If they deviated from standardized features or prices customers demanded, they were courting disaster.

HDD buyers expected prices to continue dropping steadily, based on historical trends. However, the technology was approaching a physical limit to HDD performance, because mechanical limitations prevented faster rotation speeds. This would force the pace of innovation to slow down, which meant HDD suppliers needed to temper customer expectations of price erosion.

Unlike players of the Cost Game, though, HDD manufacturers were not in a market with concentrated buyers and fragmented sellers. Concentration was present both on the supply and the demand side. In this context, how could sellers really feel forced to be price takers?

The companies in the HDD industry eventually discovered their handholds and footholds on that rock face and learned how to maneuver to exercise some control over their downward descent. This chapter discusses the steps and the tools one player in this market implemented in the early 2000s to succeed in the Power Game. But the lessons apply well beyond markets with heavy price erosion. Even in markets with relatively stable prices, sudden cost shocks can squeeze profits and put players in a situation similar to what the HDD players overcame.

The special nature of pricing in the Power Game

One defining concept of the Power Game is market concentration, as Figure 10.1 shows. Hundreds of millions of consumers worldwide used hard disk drives, but the leading HDD manufacturers had only a handful of direct customers.

The essence of pricing in the Power Game is high-stakes negotiations in a repeated prisoner's dilemma. A limited number of suppliers with a portfolio of relatively comparable solutions battle for a set of opportunities

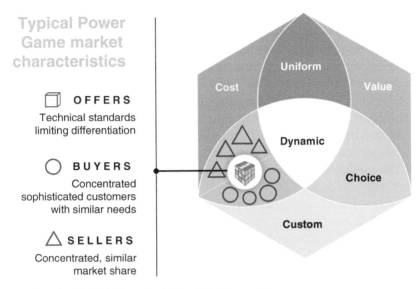

Typical Power Game market characteristics

⬜ **OFFERS**
Technical standards limiting differentiation

◯ **BUYERS**
Concentrated sophisticated customers with similar needs

△ **SELLERS**
Concentrated, similar market share

Uniform

Cost

Value

Dynamic

Choice

Custom

FIGURE 10.1   Typical characteristics of the Power Game

in a relatively open game with customers who are familiar to all parties. With few exceptions – such as strong customer preference, geopolitical interference, or missed product cycles – all suppliers compete for opportunities on an equal plane. Long-term contracts do exist, but because customers tend to negotiate and buy repeatedly, they rarely lock out a supplier from opportunities completely.

The outcome of each deal in the Power Game matters materially. The loss of any customer contract will have a significant negative impact on a company's financial performance. In the case of hard disk drives, Western Digital was straightforward about the pressure that manufacturers face:

> *The hard drive industry is intensely competitive, with hard drive suppliers competing for sales to a limited number of major customers. If we lose a key customer, or if any of our key customers reduce their orders of our products or require us to reduce our prices before we are able to reduce costs, our operating results would likely be harmed. In addition, if customer pressures require us to reduce our pricing such that our gross margins are diminished, we could decide not to sell our products to a particular customer, which could result in a decrease in our revenue.*[4,5]

Within this context, prices had eroded by 3–5% per quarter on average for years, but every few quarters, the erosion would temporarily accelerate and depress margins. This relatively predictable erosion reinforced the perception of the sales team – and most of the organization – that an HDD manufacturer was a price taker. The customers claimed the lion's share of the value in the industry, leaving suppliers with a share of value that was not sufficient to deliver a healthy return on capital for investors. The purchasing departments of the OEMs seemed to hold all the power.

A superficial analysis of the HDD industry may lead to the impression that power, stakes, and incentives were in perfect symmetry across buyers and across suppliers. The market would resemble a flat vertical granite slab. Look more closely, however, and many nuances appear. The HDD market also had tiny ripples that served as footholds to stop a free fall down the rock. A supplier's relative value to different customers was similar, but not identical.

In other words, HDD manufacturers had real imbalances to exploit. The Power Game in the HDD market was not a game of clones. The leading manufacturers did differentiate their products, an outcome of investing between 5% and 10% of their revenue into R&D.[6,7,8] Their customers also had preferred suppliers who had differentiated themselves in terms of supply chain reliability, product integration, or the frequent introduction of drives with higher capacity and speed.

We have found that these imbalances – or what we call advantageous asymmetries – exist in almost every Power Game market, not just in the market for HDDs. We have also found that recognizing these asymmetries is an important step in overcoming the mindset of a price taker. Players who do not recognize these asymmetries see themselves at the mercy of market forces, resulting in unconstrained price erosion.

In our experience, these asymmetries or competitive advantages are the only sustainable way to gain share in the Power Game. Share gained through lower prices can only be temporary because competitors will quickly lower their own prices in response. Time and time again, companies use lower prices to compensate for product quality weaknesses or product delays. This approach never works in the long term, primarily for two reasons: pricing cannot solve nonpricing problems, and such price cuts risk amplifying or compounding the effects of the existing price erosion.

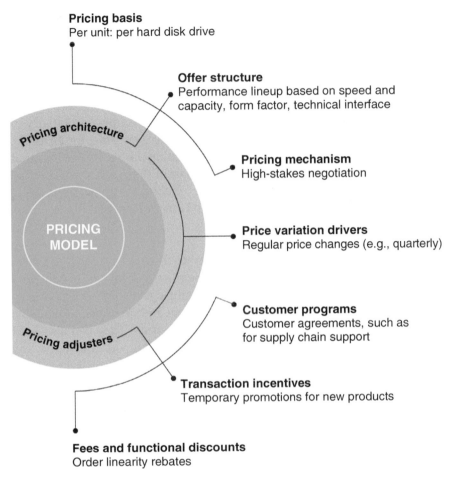

Pricing basis
Per unit: per hard disk drive

Offer structure
Performance lineup based on speed and
capacity, form factor, technical interface

Pricing architecture

Pricing mechanism
High-stakes negotiation

PRICING
MODEL

Price variation drivers
Regular price changes (e.g., quarterly)

Customer programs
Customer agreements, such as
for supply chain support

Pricing adjusters

Transaction incentives
Temporary promotions for new products

Fees and functional discounts
Order linearity rebates

FIGURE 10.2   Pricing model in the Power Game for HDD manufacturers

Figure 10.2 shows the pricing model for HDD manufacturers. The
most important element in the Power Game's pricing model is high-stakes
negotiations, which we have already discussed for the HDD sellers and
buyers. The typical pricing basis in the Power Game is per unit, and HDD
sellers used it as well because of the importance of cost as an input and the

aligned incentives of both buyers and sellers to obtain scale efficiencies. The offer structures typically comprise a lineup with standardized technical interfaces but different levels of capacity and performance. These standards ensure that the products from different competitors are good substitutes and that customers can buy from multiple HDD sellers at any time with few switching barriers.

Some price adjusters make sense in the Power Game, particularly to drive efficiencies. If a customer orders regularly over time, for example, the HDD seller can reduce its costs by minimizing production swings that can result in higher costs. They pass along part of those savings to the customer in the form of a functional discount or rebate. Later in this chapter, we also discuss how HDD sellers have used customer programs – such as engineering and supply chain support or supply guarantees – as negotiating levers.

The riskiest behavior for any player is to act as if they have no agency. Getting a fair share of value depends on company's individual choices, which makes understanding and using agency immensely important. Players can differentiate across customers and products, sell relative value, and plan their strategies for a repeated game. They can also hold themselves accountable for every move, so that they do not undo any progress they've made.

The rest of this chapter explains how to execute high-stakes negotiations successfully in the Power Game to manage price erosion and avoid a price freefall.

Finding handholds and footholds

Step 1: Map market asymmetries to define a consistent strategy across all accounts

Individual negotiations are typically zero-sum games. One competitor's gains are another's loss and vice versa. This version of the prisoner's dilemma incentivizes each player to race to the bottom to clinch the deal. Companies in most Power Games, however, play a repeated game, over time and across customers. Always bidding the lowest is no longer the winning strategy in a repeated game because it depresses future prices.

Players therefore need to strike a balance between remaining competitive and slowing price erosion.

The Power Game Pricing Chessboard in Figure 10.3 helps business leaders recognize asymmetries and think through their behaviors and actions. The framework in Figure 10.3 is unique to the Power Game, because of its highly concentrated markets. Players in the Custom Game or Choice Game – which also have high concentrations on the supplier side – can adapt the Chessboard to the games by replacing individual customers and products with customer and product segments. But it is much less useful in markets with low concentrations of suppliers and buyers, because it would be impossible to track transaction prices across all customers and determine each competitor's exact market share.

In the hyper-rational markets of the Power Game, the Chessboard provides a valuable bird's-eye view of the balance of power between competing sellers – depending on costs and value – as well as the balance of power between buyers and sellers, depending on market demand cycles. When companies and their sales organizations instead focus on one deal at a time, especially when each deal is big, they can easily lose sight of the balance of power in the market.

The Chessboard also allows companies to map profit pools and their relative share, first by using their own transaction and cost data and then adding any competitive intelligence they can gather. Analyzing margin and share for each customer and product combination allows the company to identify what we refer to as castles, grasslands, battlefields, and deserts, and their relative positions within them.

Each of these situations calls for different strategic moves:

- **Castles:** These are market segments in which a company has high margins and high share, fortified by competitive advantages such as cost, relationship, quality, or supply chain. The strength of these advantages guides how a company responds to competitive threats. If a competitor attacks your castle by offering much lower prices, a small concession should be enough to keep the share. You should not need to match the low price in full. If a small concession is not sufficient, the competitive advantage is weaker than imagined, and the castle walls are crumbling. Assuming the castle has strong fortifications, the optimal strategy in a repeated prisoner's dilemma is tit-for-tat, by attacking the competitor's castle.

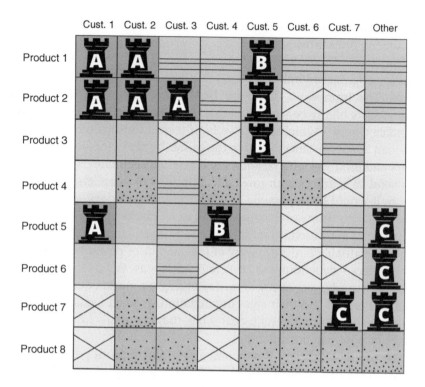

FIGURE 10.3   Power Game Pricing Chessboard, from the lens of Company A

- **Grasslands:** These are fluid territories in which share is balanced because no company has a competitive advantage that could justify a higher share. Companies have two goals in the grasslands. The first is to identify places where they can build a sustainable advantage, such as by understanding customers' unmet needs or improving collaboration on new products. If they succeed, they can turn a grassland into a castle. The second goal is to keep a fair share of the grassland and its relatively large profit pool. To do this, companies should minimize price erosion by avoiding aggressive negotiations on grassland deals. But if a company starts to lose more than its fair share of deals, it should aim to regain share using the tit-for-tat strategy characteristic of the prisoner's dilemma.

- **Battlefields:** These segments are less attractive than grasslands because they have lower margins and no share advantage for any competitor. In battlefields, historical price erosion is highest and customers expect that erosion to continue. This typically occurs because competitors have used lower prices to gain share, which they can't hold because they lack meaningful differentiation. Competition usually remains intense, though, because these segments often represent a large volume. The overall goal in battlefields should be to achieve lower erosion without losing a lot of market share.

- **Deserts:** These market segments have very low margins. These are often former battlefields in which margins have eroded so much that they are no longer worth fighting for, even when some competitors may believe there is some untapped profit. Products in these segments are typically at the end of their life cycles. Contagion is a significant risk in deserts. It arises when lower prices attract attention internally or externally and set the tone for a company's sales force. When competitors realize they have lost a deal, they might spread the contagion themselves by lowering their prices to win the next one, causing the desert to expand. The right strategy is typically to stop the spread, try to reduce price erosion drastically, and accept the lower share that results. After all, if a company devotes a lot of their capacity to defend deserts, it may leave opportunities open for their competitors to make gains in segments with higher margins.

This simple segmentation and the resulting Chessboard in Figure 10.3 make it clear that a coherent, consistent, and comprehensive negotiation strategy is superior to a sequence of negotiations that focus on one deal at a time. This is one reason why senior leaders play a critical role in managing pricing strategy in the Power Game. Understanding the Chessboard and the different competitive and margin contexts helps leaders clarify the stakes and develop an optimal negotiation plan. They understand what creates and fortifies an advantageous asymmetry, for example, an established relationship or product differentiation.

Markets are granular and may require a more nuanced segmentation than what we have laid out in Figure 10.3. But in every market, it is beneficial to have differentiated and consistent goals across segments to avoid deal-by-deal myopia.

Step 2: Use the Pricing Grid to drive consistent pricing

All prices in the Power Game are related to each other. To codify ideal price relationships across volume and products, companies can define a Pricing Grid, which has three dimensions:

1. **Performance:** Product lines in the Power Game are typically organized by level of performance. In the HDD market, capacity was a primary performance feature.

2. **Volume:** This is an important metric, because larger customers can usually negotiate lower prices. In aggregate, we have found a negative correlation between price and the order of magnitude of a customer's volume. We call this relationship the Natural Volume Slope[9] and describe it in more detail in Chapter 11 when we explore the Custom Game.

3. **Price:** This is a function of performance and volume. There is often a relationship between prices across products because products are partial substitutes for each other. There are likewise relationships between the prices that customers pay for the same product.

The combination of products with increasing level of performance, customer size, and price yields a three-dimensional grid such as the one shown in Figure 10.4, with a $20-million customer relationship and Product C highlighted.

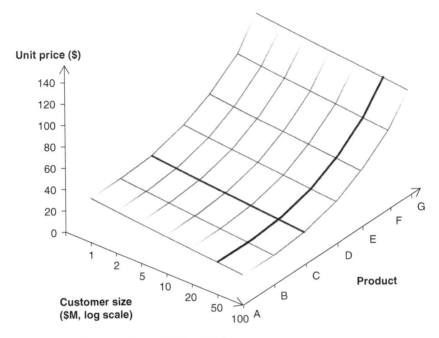

Unit price ($)

Customer size
($M, log scale)

Product

FIGURE 10.4   Example Target Pricing Grid

The Pricing Grid helps a company to minimize the contagion of lower prices. Imagine that in one quarter, a customer succeeds in negotiating a price that is lower than what the grid indicates for that combination of product and customer size. It is likely that the customer will soon use that lower price as leverage to negotiate lower prices for other products. Once a competitor observes a loss of volume on their directly competing product, they will also tend to lower the price, either in current negotiations with other customers or in subsequent negotiations. That one decision to pierce the safety net of the grid starts a race to the bottom, distorting the grid and eventually forcing it downward.

Companies should use the Pricing Grid to define target prices for every product in every negotiation. They should firmly resist pressures to comply with the largest negative deviations, that is, prices well below the grid. At the same time, companies can consider balancing this firm stance by conceding some of their positive deviations (prices above the grid) for two reasons. First, as we explained earlier, lower prices are more visible and therefore more contagious. Second, positive deviations usually result from imbalances that are likely to disappear over time rather than from enduring competitive advantages. Using positive deviations to maintain price consistency in other parts of the Grid enables a company to preserve margins better over the long term.

The Pricing Grid is a tactical tool that complements the Chessboard. It reinforces the importance of price consistency across customers and product lines. The pricing team's role is to manage the pricing grid very tightly and support the rigorous centralized planning for negotiations. Salespeople should have neither independent incentives nor the leeway to make significant direct price concessions. Their incentives need to include a collective success component, because the independent actions of one salesperson can adversely affect the rest of the business. In lieu of price concessions, they can offer their customers value-added services and bundles.

Step 3: Shape the evolution of the game for long-term success

In the Power Game, any inconsistency has ripple effects that reverberate negatively across the portfolio for several quarters. Imagine a company that is coming up short of its commercial target commitments a few days before the end of a quarter. It can be tempted to use an attractive lower price to close one more high-end deal if that deal would allow the company to achieve those targets. Figure 10.5 shows an example of this in the HDD industry. We can clearly see that the company exceeded the plan, because the additional deal had a positive impact on all five traditional metrics. Even if the company tracked price erosion, erosion of 3.4% did not seem to be that much worse than 3.2%. The company was already on its way to missing the 3.1% target for price erosion anyway, so why would a few more basis points matter?

If ambitious share gains are not supported by differential value, however, they will not be sustainable. In this case, the plan was too ambitious, and it backfired. One quarter later, the company achieved its volume target, but the incremental erosion created by that additional deal further eroded prices by 1.3 percentage points more than the plan, as shown in Figure 10.6. After accounting for the volume mix effect, the high-end product sold in that additional deal drove prices lower by 2% and profits down by more than 10%. Three quarters later, the impact had spread from one customer to most of the market margin. Profits were down 40% in that segment.

	Plan	In-quarter results – without additional deal	Additional deal	In-quarter results – with additional deal
Volume (M units)	20.0	19.1	1.3	20.4 ✓
Revenue ($M)	1.048	999	77	1.077 ✓
Average unit price ($)	52.4	52.3	59.4	52.8 ✓
Margin (%)	19.7%	19.6%	20.5%	19.7% ✓
Profit ($M)	107	96	16	112 ✓
Like-for-like quarterly erosion	–3.1%	–3.2%	–6.7%	–3.4%

Price erosion usually overlooked

FIGURE 10.5 End-of-quarter deal helps the team meet all short-term goals

The important metric for price erosion is what we call "like-for-like erosion," which is calculated holding the volume mix constant. This eliminates the effect of the volume of each product, which tends to migrate every quarter to the higher performance products as their prices go down. Prices in the Power Game are very sensitive to the balance of power. A company cannot manage them precisely unless they can measure their effects with a high degree of sophistication.

This HDD example is a severe example of contagion for three reasons. First, the high-end product in that additional discounted deal was starting to pick up volume. Lowering its price faster than normal resulted in lower prices for the entire lineup. Second, the customer who benefited from this great discount was a mid-size customer who used the resulting advantage to lower their own prices and gain market share. The customer's competitors

	One quarter later		One year later	
	Plan	**Results**	**Plan**	**Results**
Volume (M units)	20.0	20.0	20.0	20.0
Revenue ($M)	1,056	1,038 ↓	1,056	1,015 ↓
Average unit price ($)	52.8	51.9 ↓	52.8	50.7 ↓
Margin (%)	20.1%	18.7% ↓	20.8%	17.6% ↓
Profit ($M)	106.9	94.6 ⇓	119.8	78.9 ⇓
Like-for-like quarterly erosion	−3.3%	−4.6% ⇓	−3.0%	−4.2% ⇓

↓ Decrease <10%

⇓ Decrease >10%

FIGURE 10.6   Same deal causes mid-term decrease of margins and revenues

were eager to avoid losing share, so they matched the low price. To make the economics work, they all asked the supplier for that same great discount. Third, other suppliers observed higher erosion and felt like they had to lower their own prices as well. Thus, the price erosion – triggered by that one incremental and apparently innocent end-of-quarter deal – spread through all customers and all products in that segment.

This story illustrates that markets have equilibria driven by the balance of power between suppliers and buyers as well as between different suppliers, depending on the strength of their value propositions. Market share and price gains are sustainable when they are substantiated by differentiated value propositions. If not, we observe the meltdown shown in Figure 10.6.

To alter the balance of power, Power Game players can take actions that deepen the sources of value for both sellers and buyers. These can help build a castle in a grassland or reinforce the walls of an existing castle, while sharing value appropriately with the customer. Suppliers can:

- Invest in engineering resources at key accounts to optimize product integration and system quality.
- Optimize their own supply chain by introducing functional discounts, such as linearity rebates to ensure regular, smooth order cycles.
- Provide co-marketing funds to bring innovations to market.
- Provide supply guarantees or dedicated hubs close to a customer's assembly lines, so that buyers can optimize their supply chain.

As we have discussed, Power Game players find themselves in a repeated game. Evaluating the strategic impact of moves across several negotiation cycles is critical to success. This is another reason why we stressed in Chapter 5 that the C-level leaders have the pricing leadership in the Power Game. Implementing a pricing strategy in this game requires a high level of organizational resolve and operational discipline, especially when public investors apply pressure to see short-term share growth. When market share slips or quarterly earnings targets come under threat, it is tempting – and, unfortunately, common – for a company to suspend its internal pricing rules and "buy" market share without regard for the lower margins.

C-level leadership needs to engage in defining the strategy and holding the organization accountable to the pricing guidelines. Their companies need to build the language, frameworks, metrics, and competitive intelligence that allow the organization to speak about pricing decisions in the right terms.

Impact: Getting a firm grip on pricing

HDD manufacturers used their pricing agency to take action and reduce the price erosion that resulted from technical constraints. The poor total shareholder returns in the late 1990s and early 2000s prompted HDD manufacturers to consolidate further and start playing the Power Game. By recognizing how much agency they had and choosing their own path forward, HDD manufacturers were able to balance the value sharing in their market. They identified the existing asymmetries and crafted a consistent, portfolio-wide strategy.

Total shareholder returns turned positive by the late 2000s and early 2010s, reversing a years-long trend. Between 2010 and 2017, the total shareholder return for HDD manufacturers was 23%, 8% higher than for the IT sector of the S&P 500. Furthermore, research has shown that the consolidation in the HDD industry did not undermine innovation.[10]

Key takeaways

To strengthen your agency in the Power Game, we recommend the following approach:

- **Stop seeing your company as being at the mercy of market forces:** Go beyond the impression that power, stakes, and incentives are in perfect symmetry across both buyers and suppliers.
- **Execute high-stakes negotiations successfully:** Use the Chessboard to evaluate asymmetries based on the different competitive and margin contexts and to develop a targeted negotiation plan.
- **Avoid price freefall:** Use the Pricing Grid to predict the impact that one price change will have on other prices, to enforce price consistency, and to focus the organization on long-term success.
- **Establish a pricing model to drive efficiencies:** Increase the value delivered to customers by using price adjusters, including customer programs such as supply chain support and guarantees.

CHAPTER 11

The Custom Game: Making Sense of the Chaos

With contributions from Cesar Torres, Lionnel Bourgouin, and Steven Greene

W hen Chris Patterson took over as the CEO of Freightliner LLC in spring 2005, the market for medium- and heavy-duty commercial trucks in the United States was experiencing a boom. That prompted him to make a surprising declaration, something that CEOs rarely say when times are good.

"Our pricing model is broken," he told his team. "We can't keep pricing trucks the same way we have for decades."

A veteran of 25 years in the North American trucking industry, Chris knew that Freightliner, which would later become Daimler Trucks North America (DTNA), needed to figure out how to maintain its strong share and margins when – not if – the bubble of the mid-2000s burst.[1] He knew that DTNA would not only need the right equipment to remain competitive and profitable, but also required the right commercial strategy as a bulwark against whatever upheavals the inevitable downturn would cause.

The first event to trigger that downturn was already on the horizon and was already partly responsible for high demand: stricter regulations from the US Environmental Protection Agency (EPA) set to take hold in

2007. Yet neither Chris nor any other executive could have known at the time that the Great Recession also lurked around the corner. It would cause the US market for commercial trucks to crater worse than anyone could have imagined.

How Chris and his team prepared for a downturn exemplifies how leaders can understand and apply their pricing agency to shape demand, share value, and win the Custom Game, regardless of the economic conditions they face.

Figure 11.1 shows the typical market characteristics for the Custom Game. As we described in Chapter 3, DTNA's market fit these characteristics very well. How did DTNA's diverse customer base – which ranges from hundreds of thousands of commercial customers to logistics companies or retailers with large fleets – buy their highly customized commercial vehicles? We explore that in the next section.

The special nature of pricing in the Custom Game

The majority of volume came from customers who bought multiple trucks at negotiated prices with steep discounts, independent of distribution channel. Some 80% of the volume involved a concession – usually a discount to dealers – that reduced the price the customer paid.[2]

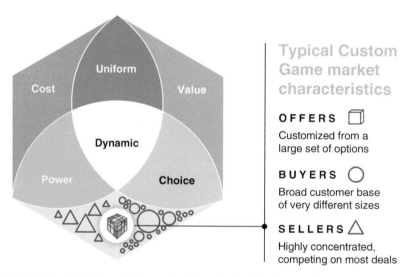

Typical Custom Game market characteristics

OFFERS
Customized from a large set of options

BUYERS
Broad customer base of very different sizes

SELLERS
Highly concentrated, competing on most deals

FIGURE 11.1   DTNA's market was ideally suited to the Custom Game

Customers always had some uncertainty about prices because limited information made it hard for them to make direct comparisons. Any given customer knew that it was unlikely that someone else had purchased the exact same configuration of base model and options. The negotiation process offset some of this uncertainty by providing customers with context as well as a sense of trust and fairness that they were getting the best possible deal.

This situation applies not only to commercial trucks, but to any company playing the Custom Game, regardless of industry. It also leads to the chaos shown in Figure 11.2.

Each dot in Figure 11.2 represents an individual transaction. The x-axis shows the sales volume for an individual deal. The y-axis shows the realized price, expressed as a percentage of the list price less marginal costs. Even at second or third glance, there seems to be no relationship

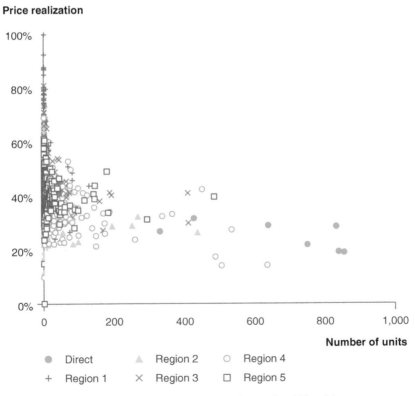

FIGURE 11.2 Every player in the Custom Game has a cloud like this one

whatsoever between prices and volumes. This holds true regardless of what the x-axis (e.g., revenue, sales volume) or the y-axis (e.g., discount percentage, margin percentage) shows. It also holds true for companies that consistently earn high margins and for those whose margins lag their competitors. These clouds all have a few things in common:

- **They are pervasive:** They can be found in industries as diverse as industrial equipment, chemicals, technology, and corporate banking, to name a few. They occur when an industry sets prices by negotiating heavy discounts on custom deals and the customer base is fragmented across a wide range of volumes. It wouldn't matter which company's data we used for Figure 11.2, because all the patterns would look similar.

- **There is massive variance:** The realized price for a deal can differ by a factor of two or three for any given volume. At the same time, a certain level of price realization – say, 40% – happens at almost any volume. This holds true for the company and for its competitors, which makes it difficult – if not impossible – to determine a market price or establish general competitive benchmarks.

- **Incremental deals rarely matter:** Except for some of the largest deals at the far right of Figure 11.2, you could remove a handful of data points from any Custom Game cloud without having a material effect on the aggregate revenue and profit of the business. The win or loss of any incremental deal rarely matters in the grand scheme.

- **Leadership is indifferent:** In the minds of many leaders, individual deals reflect market forces and are negotiated at the best possible price. If aggregate revenue and profit are acceptable, why make pricing changes? And if they are not acceptable, then the likely causes are usually something else besides pricing, such as product quality, marketing effectiveness, or production efficiency. These beliefs can be especially strong in a growing market, such as the one that DTNA experienced in the mid-2000s. The overall US truck market had grown by 33% to 288,800 vehicles in 2004, as the US economy's recovery gained steam and companies made truck purchases they had deferred in previous years.[3,4] Sales volumes rose by another 17% in 2005.[5]

Chris did not share those beliefs. He knew how the sales negotiation processes worked in his industry, and he knew that DTNA's current processes left its market share and its margins vulnerable to shocks. The coming EPA regulations would have two effects that could amplify the randomness and unpredictability. First, customers would likely face significant, industry-wide price increases at a time when it would be harder than usual to calculate the true cost of any truck. Second, if prices came under pressure, as they usually do in downturns, the vast price variance of Figure 11.2 would mean that some desirable truck configurations would barely break even or even lose money, depending on the margins for individual options and the extent of discounts.

Chris identified four improvement areas that correspond to four factors that are essential to success in the Custom Game: speed, business logic, predictability, and control.

- **Speed:** DTNA's deal desk seemed to take a long time to approve deals. "It's not just the time it takes to get back to the customer, but the number of times we need to go back and forth," Chris noted. How could DTNA have fewer, shorter conversations with customers and with each other?

- **Business logic:** The sales teams, dealers, and deal desk each had a justification for every concession and discount. But their stories showed no discernible patterns. How could DTNA make the prices – and the stories behind them – follow a consistent logic?

- **Predictability:** The lack of patterns in the stories diminished DTNA's ability to predict how trends and events will influence buying behavior. The new EPA regulations – which were expected to impose significant cost increases and warrant more variations across trucks – would not only make it harder to forecast demand, but also more difficult to predict costs, which could add between $5,000 and $10,000 to the price of a truck in 2007.[6]

- **Control:** The variance in individual customer negotiations made prices increasingly hard to manage. The outcome of negotiations depended on the capabilities and experience of at least four individuals: the buyer, the dealer's salesperson, the DTNA salesperson, and the approver at the deals desk. Get a few rookies in any of these positions, and margins could swing wildly up or down.

How can a company in the Custom Game improve its speed, business logic, predictability, and control, when it can't make sense of the chaos shown in Figure 11.2? That is the central pricing challenge not only for commercial vehicle manufacturers such as DTNA. It is one of the central challenges for any company that plays the Custom Game.

The conventional way for leaders to impose some order on the chaos is to change their transaction incentives.[7] Specific measures often include changes to salespeople's discount authority, a greater burden of proof for discount requests, earlier triggers for escalation procedures, and short-term incentives for salespeople and their managers to meet arbitrary price targets.

While such changes have some merit, they often result only in short-term improvements. They fail to address the root cause of the chaos: companies are using discretionary discounting to address too many sources of price variation that are either difficult for salespeople to manage or are beyond their control. A more fundamental and powerful change is to transfer some of the price variation driven by discretionary discounts into other pricing levers.

There are three levers to do that, as shown in Figure 11.3.[8] Fees and functional discounts can account for differences in costs. Formalized customer discounts and programs can help the company manage price variations driven by market conditions. Third, the company should manage product-related variations by adjusting option prices.

Pricing architecture plays a less important role in Custom Game pricing models because the pricing mechanism and basis are tied to the unique offer structure for each customer.

Imposing order on the chaos

Step 1: Get cost variance out of the way

Between 2005 and 2007, global growth fueled sustained demand for metals and raw materials. Iron ore and copper prices almost doubled,[9] and oil prices went from around $50 per barrel in 2004 to more than $100 in 2007.[10] These cost increases drove up the cost of manufacturing a truck so significantly that it was putting margins at risk if it was not passed on to customers.

Truck manufacturers usually account for raw material inflation in their annual model year price increases. That approach works well when the cost inflation is in the range of 2–4%, but in DTNA's case, the inflation

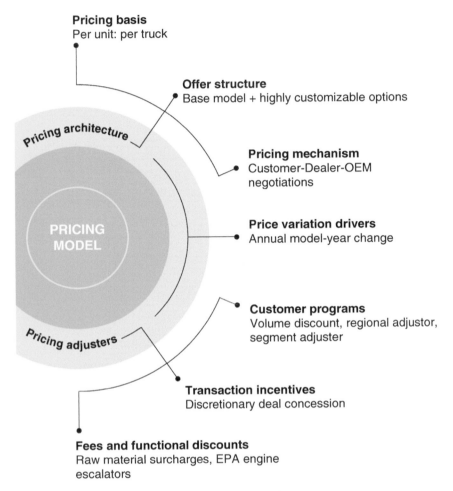

Pricing basis
Per unit: per truck

Offer structure
Base model + highly customizable options

Pricing architecture

Pricing mechanism
Customer-Dealer-OEM
negotiations

PRICING
MODEL

Price variation drivers
Annual model-year change

Customer programs
Volume discount, regional adjustor,
segment adjuster

Pricing adjusters

Transaction incentives
Discretionary deal concession

Fees and functional discounts
Raw material surcharges, EPA engine
escalators

FIGURE 11.3   Shifting from discretionary price variance

occurred so rapidly that it warranted taking action during the year. As a short-term solution, companies often reduce the amount of discounts, but this makes discounts even harder to manage, because inflation isn't the only factor the company usually faces. Customer mix and other market conditions also play a role.

The best solution in such cases is to do what DTNA did: add a raw material surcharge to the net price of trucks. It indexed the surcharge to a basket of raw material prices based on publicly available market data.

By making the effect of raw material costs transparent, DTNA made it clear that they did not intend to take advantage of cost inflation to boost their margin. Their added value came from the design, manufacture, and delivery of reliable, fit-for-purpose trucks, not in trading raw materials. Making the raw material a separate line item in the price of trucks was also a commitment that if the prices of raw materials were to go down, truck prices would adjust accordingly.

DTNA applied a similar logic to the price increase driven by the new EPA regulation. They and other OEMs imposed EPA surcharges that varied by model year, class of truck, and type of engine. Salespeople could not discount the surcharges, which amounted to roughly 10% of the price of a truck and applied to the net price. The transparent rationale for this surcharge was that the price driver was beyond the truck manufacturer's control. Customers tend to accept these forms of price increases in the Custom Game.

Step 2: Find the Natural Volume Slope

With cost out of the way, the next step to create some order and limit the randomness of discounting is to control for quantifiable market factors such as volume, geography, or customer segment. Aggregate market volume is broadly distributed across all customer sizes, which makes volume a critical driver in the Custom Game. For instance, the top 10 largest customers do not represent more than half of the market volume. If they did, this would be a Power Game and the price given to any single large customer would influence the entire market. In the Custom Game, a seller can make up lost volume from any large customer with volume from many smaller customers. This tempers the negotiation power of the largest customers. In such circumstances, sellers should carefully calibrate the discount that larger customers can receive as a function of their size.

We have uncovered a quantifiable relationship that codifies the negotiation power of large customers. We call it the Natural Volume Slope (NVS), a phenomenon we have observed so consistently across industries, across geographies, and across time periods that we consider it an essential and universal tool for playing the Custom Game. It is also applicable in adjacent games such as Choice and Power, as we discuss in those chapters.

The NVS is so robust that we can show you how to draw it by hand in your own version of Figure 11.2, without the need for sophisticated analyses. Here are the steps.

1. Convert the volume on your x-axis to a logarithmic scale. You'll notice in Figure 11.4 that the equal increments on the x-axis differ by a factor of 10, rather than to 50-unit increments in Figure 11.2. This replotting helps you understand what is happening at lower volumes.

2. Place two marks on the chart: one at the 80th percentile on the y-axis, and one in the middle of the cluster of the three to five largest deals at the lowest right part of the cloud.

3. Draw a line between the two marks.

That will give you an image that looks like Figure 11.4.

The cloud of deals becomes denser just below the line and seems to hug the line all the way. In other words, the line anchors the deals, and they all hang from that line with a few exceptions located above it. That line indicates the difference in negotiating power between a customer and another customer, which is 10 times larger, regardless of the volume. Let's say the NVS is 2%. That means a customer buying 10 trucks can negotiate an incremental discount two percentage points better than a customer buying one truck. A customer buying 100 trucks, in turn, can on average negotiate an incremental discount that is two percentage points higher than the customer buying 10 trucks and four percentage points higher than the customer buying one truck.

It may seem curious that the lines anchor at the 80% percentile in low volumes but in the middle of the largest-volume customers. There are two reasons for that. First, companies apply less scrutiny to the deals on the low-volume end because they matter much less individually. They often tolerate higher discounts until prices reach a floor. If you look closely at Figure 11.4, you can see a floor at around 20% for volumes up to 50 and 15% for larger volumes. The driver behind the triangular pattern observed in the dots is not the market, but rather the internal policies for approving deals. This highlights a significant improvement opportunity.

Second, larger deals have greater weight in average profitability of the business and are therefore subject to great scrutiny. The most experienced key account managers negotiate those deals, often with the involvement of very senior leaders. It makes sense, then, that the line is well anchored in the middle or 50% percentile of these deals.

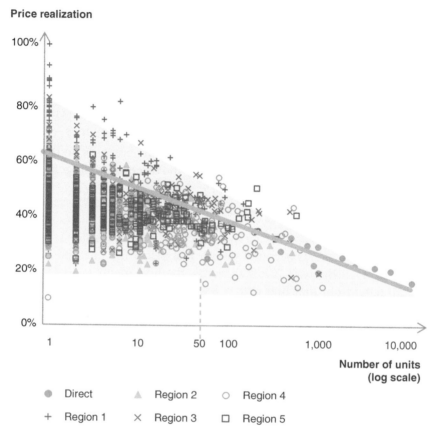

FIGURE 11.4   The NVS provides the anchor for modifying your pricing model

For the NVS in most businesses and markets, there is no practical difference between what the eye and hand will draw and what the computer will reveal. We have validated this by performing in-depth multivariate regression analyses, and every time the results of the two approaches are almost identical. The NVS serves as an invaluable anchor because it remains stable for years or even decades, despite managerial changes, policy choices, technological breaks, market shifts, and other disruptions.

Step 3: Determine market adjustments

The company can consider other sources of variations once it has anchored volume variations with the NVS. It can use what we call market adjusters to manage discount variance driven by factors that it can define and quantify objectively. In specific customer segments, the company may have advantages or disadvantages that can justify incremental discounting. The same goes for geographic areas where one brand's dealers might provide better and more reliable service.

To evaluate these factors, one starts by observing whether discounts on average are higher or lower in a segment or region, all else being equal. Multivariate statistical techniques facilitate this exercise. After quantifying the differences, the seller needs to look at their statistical significance and their business logic, which in turn reflects the three information sources – costs, competition, and value – that we discussed in Chapter 1. For example, how are differences in the channel structure keeping costs lower? How much higher is the competitive intensity there, and how does it vary within the region? How are differences in customer needs affecting the mix of products they buy and their willingness to pay?

In the case of DTNA, the mix of competitors differed by segment and could justify many adjustments. But this is not always the case. A global financial services company playing the Custom Game observed that prices in Switzerland tended to be 3% lower than in other European countries. But there was no discernible difference between a Swiss customer's needs and those of other European customers, nor was there any difference in cost or level of competition. What explained the difference? A few years earlier, the head of sales in Europe had used lower prices in an aggressive move to gain market share in Switzerland, where he was based. The action resulted in sustained lower prices there. When the company decided to stop giving incremental discounts to Swiss customers, it found it could replace their volume with higher-paying customers in other countries.

After using the NVS to determine the volume discount, a company can apply market adjusters to arrive at a target price. That target price, validated both by statistical analysis and business logic, provides the salespeople with critical information. It represents where the company has already negotiated deals with similar objective characteristics. But the target price does not take momentary competition into account, nor does it account for the customer's ability and stance as a negotiator. To account for those factors, the salesperson can use their experience and judgment to negotiate the final price, because they have the most relevant information.

We refer to that gap between target price and final price as sales discretion. Figure 11.5 shows how volume discounts, market adjusters, and sales discretion fit together.

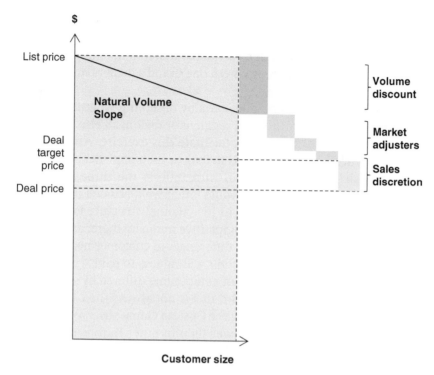

FIGURE 11.5   How DTNA made changes to win the Custom Game

Sales discretion has several powerful uses. First, it allows the company to assess the evolution of discount levels over time, independent of any mix effects. Let's say that average discounts have increased in one quarter, either because more large customers are buying or because deal sizes have increased. How salespeople have used their discretion allows the company to tease these two effects out. Average discretion is also a great way to evaluate and incentivize salespeople, because it screens out factors that are beyond their control.

Step 4: Adjust option prices

The sales discretion metric is also an effective way to assess the perceived value of options. For a particular truck option, it provides a view of whether willingness to pay for it is higher or lower, independent of all mix effects. If customers on average negotiate less intensively for one option than for others, the list price for that option may not yet reflect its value.

The company should therefore consider incorporating the discount variance into the list price variance when it updates prices for options.

But the company should not automate this process. First, the company must determine whether the discretion difference is statistically significant. Then it needs to figure out the underlying reasons behind the difference. Does the option have unique value, or does it appeal to a specific segment of customers that generally has a higher willingness to pay? If the option provides unique value, the seller should explore whether it should offer that option on more products or to more segments. Regardless of the answers, the process of analyzing these differences is usually a very fruitful exercise that helps the team learn a lot about the value of individual options.

Impact: Less chaos, more order

DTNA's extensive restructuring of its discounting practices in 2006 led to a new negotiation process ahead of the new EPA regulations and launch of its new Cascadia truck line in 2007. Figure 11.6 shows how the transactions shifted toward the NVS. Market adjusters absorbed some of the other variance. The new process led to several benefits beyond the price points themselves, not only during the extreme downturn, but in the upswing that followed it.

- **Faster quotes:** Sales teams could generate quotes faster and limit the back-and-forth of negotiations and discount approval escalations, because the quoted prices reflected objective rules rather than a reliance on gut feeling when pricing a new deal or follow-up purchase.
- **More backbone:** Despite their lower discretionary discount powers, salespeople now had more confidence when they quoted a price. The market adjusters replaced a black box with a transparent and logical process.[11] Instead of reflexively looking at previous deal prices or last year's price to the same customer, salespeople could determine a price from the ground up and believe in the underlying story.
- **More control:** The breakdown of price variance into its constituent drivers and the development of the discount market adjusters gave DTNA a small number of discrete levers to apply and tweak as needed to reflect shifts in the market. It also gave target prices for individual deals that would prevent salespeople from chasing business at artificially low prices.

Price realization

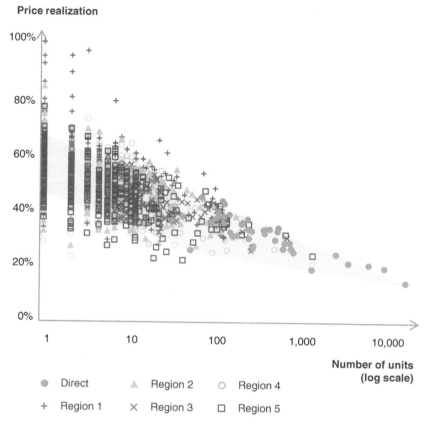

FIGURE 11.6 New logic shifting prices to their own natural optimal levels

- **Fairer prices:** Keep in mind that prices in DTNA's market, as in most Custom Games, were opaque. Having a step-by-step logical basis for a price quote conveys important information to customers and helps them perceive quoted prices as fair. If they compare two disparate prices, they can understand the rationale behind the differences.

- **Better reads on market trends:** The discount discretion of salespeople, despite being lower than in the past, served as a powerful barometer of price sensitivity. Greater usage of discretion could indicate more intense competition. If win rates show that most successful sales required maximum use of discretion, it may also indicate the start of an overall downturn. Less usage of discretion, in turn, could indicate shifts in customer needs or an imbalance in supply and demand.

- **More accurate list prices and predictable margins:** The new pricing model reduced gaps between list prices and realized prices by almost one-third, which meant that discounts would create a smaller range of variance for the margins. In addition, the raw material and EPA surcharges kept the cost variations – which were very substantial in that period – uncoupled and isolated from the discount logic.

Conventional business wisdom claims that a company cannot increase its market share and its margins at the same time. Higher prices boost margins and cut volumes, while lower prices boost volume but cut margins, right?

In 2006 and beyond, DTNA defied that presumption by simultaneously increasing prices, margins, and market share over a period of years. The US market for Class 5–8 trucks still achieved double-digit volume growth in 2006, as customers pulled purchases forward in anticipation of the new EPA regulations.[12,13]

Then the market imploded.

In 2007, overall volume sank by a shocking 35% thanks to "weaker market conditions," then dropped by another 18% in 2008 as the Great Recession began.[14,15] Nonetheless, DTNA remained the North American market share leader in heavy-duty (Class 8) vehicles and also became the leader in Class 6–7 trucks for the first time in its history in 2007, with a share of 31.5%, up 3.5 percentage points from 2006.[16]

By 2010, the market began to recover and DTNA's sales "significantly exceeded expectations." It maintained its leading share position in medium- and heavy-duty trucks, and even grew its Class 6–8 market share in the United States, Mexico, and Canada by another two percentage points.[17,18,19]

Key takeaways

In the Custom Game, it is critical to control the high level of discretionary discounting very tightly to provide both customers and the sales force with a sense of fairness for the pricing process. We recommend the following approach:

- **Establish a formula to define a target price for each deal:** This usually involves anchoring on the Natural Volume Slope and defining specific market adjusters.

- **Track the usage of sales discretion:** The difference between actual net price and target price contains valuable information on market trends and sales performance.

- **Incentivize the sales force on revenues and price discretion:** Combining the amount of revenues and the quality of revenues provides a much better balance than margin incentives.

- **Isolate the discounting process from large cost fluctuations:** Use separate surcharges to account for externally driven cost shocks that affect all competitors.

CHAPTER 12

The Choice Game: Framing Options for Customers

With contributions from Martin van den Heuvel, Matthew Kropp, and Santiago Aviles

I nspired by a week-long immersion in Milan in 1983, Howard Schultz presented the leadership team at Starbucks with plans to adapt the "romance" of the premium Italian coffee experience to the US market.[1,2] The coffeehouse he envisioned would sell espresso beverages in addition to whole beans.

"Premium" also applied to the proposed prices. The new coffeehouse would charge 95 cents for a cup of coffee, nearly double the 50 cents that a coffee drinker paid at the average diner back then.[3,4] A 14-ounce bag of whole beans would cost around $7, more than double the prevailing average of $3.00.[5]

Starbucks agreed to pilot the concept at one Seattle store. Soon, that pilot store attracted 800 customers per day, over three times as many as Starbucks' best-performing retail stores.[6] More important to Schultz, however, was that the test store "became a gathering place, and its atmosphere was electric."[7]

Starbucks' next move, however, caught Schultz by surprise. It decided against a rollout.

Undeterred, Schultz founded his own company, called Il Giornale, named after Milan's daily newspaper.[8] In 1987, that new venture acquired the existing assets of Starbucks – including the rights to the name – and eventually grew into a global company with one of the world's most valuable brands.[9,10]

Schultz's early marketing plans emphasized "quality and service, not price."[11] Starbucks was therefore managing a value equation. This translated into a carefully curated selection of premium products that consumers could self-select. Rather than optimizing the price points for each menu item individually, what mattered most at Starbucks was the assortment of products, how products compared to each other, and the way these were presented coherently for customers to choose between them.

Starbucks succeeded in the Choice Game by introducing a new mentality to the coffee category. Its lineup of products and prices guides customers to choose a beverage that fits their needs at that moment. Starbucks' commitment to the Choice Game and to maintaining the integrity of its value equation has helped the company weather commodity price spikes, global recessions, shifts in consumer tastes and behaviors, and, in the early 2020s, a global pandemic and inflation rates not seen in decades.

Companies playing the Choice Game typically have a large and fragmented customer base with heterogeneous needs, as Figure 12.1 indicates. In Chapter 3, we showed how these typical market characteristics fit to Starbucks.

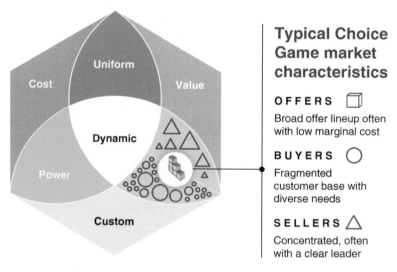

Typical Choice Game market characteristics

OFFERS
Broad offer lineup often with low marginal cost

BUYERS
Fragmented customer base with diverse needs

SELLERS
Concentrated, often with a clear leader

FIGURE 12.1   Starbucks and the Choice Game

The special nature of pricing in the Choice Game

Pricing in the Choice Game revolves around carefully planned offer structures. A coherent lineup of offerings must match customer segments defined by their different needs and value perceptions. Understanding customer behavior and influencing choice is much more important than defining any individual price point with precision. The profitability of the portfolio or the store is the key objective, not the isolated optimization of any individual product price point.

The ideal lineups in the Choice Game are easy for customers to understand, usually to the point that they can self-select their preferred package. The ideal lineups also prevent customers from cherry-picking best-in-class features from different sellers. In addition, by tailoring each offer to address the needs of a specific customer segment, offers can be more attractive to customers than competitors' offers. The challenge lies in achieving balanced and disciplined differentiation by bundling and unbundling features based on value perceptions and anchoring prices to these value perceptions rather than to the underlying marginal costs.

Players of the Choice Game can lose their balance and discipline when they design offers that are excessively feature-rich across the lineup – far beyond customer needs – in an attempt to offer and retain more value. They also lose balance and discipline when they neglect their segmentation and make too many bespoke offers, as if they were playing the Custom Game. In both cases, they are breaking the logic for customers to self-select into different packages and trade up or down.

Schultz consciously designed the Starbucks coffeehouse business for the taste-driven consumers, writing in a 1986 memo that "we will offer superior coffee and related products" and be "genuinely interested in educating our customers."[12] The education aspect mentioned in Schultz's memo illustrates how companies implement one cornerstone feature of the Choice Game: intentionally influencing customers to trade up or down across the portfolio. Without that kind of intervention, the Choice Game could appear to be little more than several independent versions of the Uniform Game. Instead, the Choice Game – which Starbucks has mastered – relies on customer self-selection across the whole portfolio. One customer may order a venti (20-ounce) caramel macchiato with an extra shot, while the more price-sensitive person behind them orders a tall (12-ounce) drip coffee and a third person orders an espresso – and none of them agonizes over the decision because the small sets of options and combinations on the menu board allowed them to find exactly what they wanted.

Successful players in the Choice Game create effective offer structures by carefully selecting the offer lineup model, considering customer behavior and designing paths for revenue expansion.

Offer lineup models

Good-better-best – the most common offer lineup in the Choice Game – comprises packages whose value and prices increase together, but not necessarily in lockstep. Figure 12.2 shows how this structure allows sellers to both share and retain more value than they could with a single offering at one fixed price. If buyers never moved across the three packages discussed, this offer structure could be considered three different instances of the Uniform Game. However, in the Choice Game this lineup is designed specifically to influence customer selection across the good-better-best options and provide a path to trade up.

Another common lineup is package sizes. Think of Spotify, the Swedish streaming provider, which offers Individual, Duo, and Family plans.[13] The services in each plan are identical, but the Family plan has six accounts versus two for Duo and one for individual. The price per user is cheaper in plans with more users, so package sizes fill more of the area under the demand curve shown in Figure 12.2. This offer structure, however, goes well beyond a simple volume discount. Spotify's intention is to nudge individual customers to trade up in predefined steps. They have identified that individual customers can encourage their significant other or their entire family to purchase plans and are providing them with an easy migration path to do so.

In either lineup model – good-better-best or package sizes – sellers can offer add-ons to allow for some customization. They can also create hybrid models in which each package differs by both value and volume. Starbucks coffees fall into such a matrix because each drink – regardless of value – can come in up to five different cup sizes.

All lineups should meet a few criteria:

- **Balanced:** Features, volumes, and prices form an integrated system that aligns offers with value perceptions.
- **Simple:** Customers need to be able to either self-select an offering or choose with limited help from a sales associate.

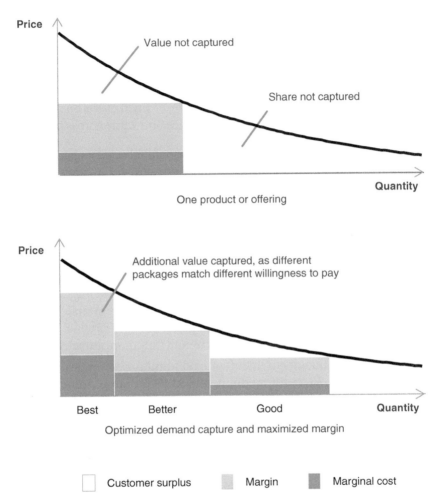

FIGURE 12.2   A good-better-best lineup allows for more value sharing

- **Fenced:** A fence either creates or reinforces the price–value separation between offers in the lineup. Misaligned or missing fences can encourage customers to choose less expensive alternatives or discourage them from trading up as their needs change. Some fences have strict enforcement, such as an ID check for seniors to obtain a discount. But when the objective is to have customers self-select into the right packages, the fences include different features and sufficient gaps between price points. In Netflix's streaming options, the presence of advertisements serves as an effective fence, because some customers are willing to pay a significant premium to avoid them.[14]

Customer behavior

Insights from behavioral science can help sellers develop ways to nudge a customer's choices in certain directions. Three of the most-studied and well-documented ways to nudge customers are the compromise effect, the decoy effect, and the anchoring mechanism. [15,16,17] Each exerts an influence on how customers perceive differences in price and value across offerings.

- **Compromise effect:** When Williams Sonoma released its latest bread-making machine, it observed a doubling of sales within a few weeks.[18] But the new product didn't drive the growth. Instead, it was sales of an older model that saw a sudden spike.[19] This reflects the compromise effect, which means that consumers are more likely to choose the middle option of a set of products over more extreme options. Classical economic theory asserts that consumers are rational actors, and thus will choose the option that yields the most value. In practice, however, sellers can expect higher uptake of offerings by juxtaposing them against high-end and low-end offerings. In the Williams Sonoma example, the new, more expensive product made the original, cheaper product immediately look like a wiser, more economical, and thus more attractive choice.

- **Decoy effect:** Imagine a lineup of cold fountain beverages priced at $1.00 for small, $1.75 for medium, and $1.99 for large. Some customers may feel compelled to purchase the large, even if they originally did not want to consume over a liter of liquid. The reason is that the large seems to be a much better deal than the medium. This imbalance negates the compromise effect. The "decoy" option is usually significantly inferior to one option (the "target"), but has no clear advantage over the other option. The addition of this decoy option alters customers' perception of the original two choices, resulting in a more favorable perception of the target option.

- **Anchoring mechanism:** Sellers can use this widely studied technique to influence customers' price perception by carefully determining the first price they see, which then serves as a reference point.[20]

Paths for revenue expansion

Well-planned offering structures provide sellers with several paths to increase sales and revenue over time. These paths include initial product evaluation and trial, increased consumption, and customer decisions about repurchase or renewal. Companies with Software-as-a-Service (SaaS) subscription models draw a continuous revenue stream from customers, which allows the business to focus more resources on ensuring that customers receive, and pay for, ever-increasing amounts of value. This is commonly known as the land-and-expand strategy.[21,22]

Even if they do not employ an X-as-a-Service (XaaS) model, businesses should strive to manage the entire customer life cycle. Starbucks uses its app to deliver personalized and gamified offers, communications, and services that provide value to customers and support them at every point in the life cycle. They began by segmenting customers into three distinct categories: occasional, loyal, and frequent. This allowed them to provide tailored experiences to drive desired behavior, which maintains the customer's ongoing revenue, and helps to move them to the next phase of the life cycle. For example, occasional visitors received recommendations and deals designed to increase the frequency of visits. Loyal customers are prompted to attach other products to their orders to increase basket size. But this revenue expansion approach requires the right offer structure and lineup.

Other pricing model elements

As we have discussed, offer structure is the predominant lever within the Choice Game pricing model (see Figure 12.3). We discuss the specifics of Starbucks' offer structure, as well as that of other companies, throughout this chapter.

In general, the pricing mechanism and basis are a fixed price per unit, set by the seller. The pricing basis aligns with the way value scales for customers. Starbucks' prices are per unit of drink, which aligns both to value and cost. A family ordering a drink for each family member gets more value than a person ordering a single drink.

Nuances in the definition of the pricing basis are important, as Workday, a human capital management software company, demonstrates. Workday bases its prices on the total number of employees of their customers, rather than the number of employees using the Workday software. The underlying assumption is that the value of Workday software is proportional to the size of the employee base.

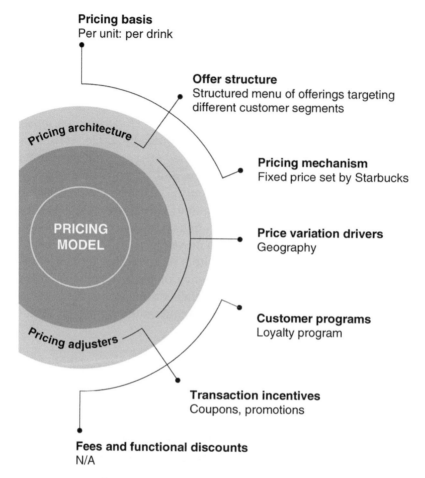

Pricing basis
Per unit: per drink

Offer structure
Structured menu of offerings targeting different customer segments

Pricing architecture

Pricing mechanism
Fixed price set by Starbucks

PRICING MODEL

Price variation drivers
Geography

Customer programs
Loyalty program

Pricing adjusters

Transaction incentives
Coupons, promotions

Fees and functional discounts
N/A

FIGURE 12.3   Offer structure is the main pricing model element

Starbucks follows the common Choice Game approach when it comes to price adjusters. First, they effectively use both customer programs and transaction incentives, which align to value and competition. In 2022, customers enrolled in Starbucks' loyalty program, Starbucks Rewards, drove 53% of its US revenue.[23] Starbucks and other Choice Game players also limit their use of fees and functional discounts – which align with marginal costs – because such costs are often low or negligible in markets suitable for the Choice Game.

Optimizing the lineup to serve more customer needs

Step 1: Segment your customer base

Success in the Choice Game rests on two foundations: an understanding of how customers perceive the value of offerings and their constituent features, and an understanding of how customers make their choices. This in turn requires a robust customer segmentation based on value perception, so that the company can design product offerings, align prices with value perceptions, and guide customers to make trade-offs and choices. Such companies keep a fair share of that value across the offering lineup and over the entire customer life cycle.

Regardless of what tools and techniques a company uses to measure differences in value perceptions, the first step is to break offerings down into a set of features or attributes. This process requires input from many functions – not only product development – in order to ensure that the list includes features whose value is more objectively measured (e.g., performance differences such as a car's horsepower) and more subjectively measured (e.g., a car's ease of handling or comfort). In addition to current features, this list should also include new and upcoming ones as well as ones currently offered only by competitors.

The building blocks of offers are extremely product-specific, which makes it difficult to generalize this process. But estimates of perceived value should reflect data collected directly from customers. Helpful tools and techniques for data collection include, but are not limited to, conjoint analyses, maximum differential analysis,[24] usage pattern identification,[25] and A/B testing.[26] The most important outputs of this customer research are defined customer clusters, usually ordered from low value to high value, and the value perception of product features and attributes for each of those clusters.

The Starbucks menu provides good examples of segmented customers and offers designed to align with each segment's value perceptions, as shown in Figure 12.4. For customers seeking a more flavorful beverage, Starbucks offers signature drinks such as the Frappuccino, as well as seasonal beverages such as the Pumpkin Spice Latte and the Peppermint Mocha.

	Traditional	**Low Calorie/ Healthy**	**Flavorful**
Sample offerings	Americano Brewed Coffee Cappuccino Espresso	Refreshers	Frappuccino Seasonal
Sample key features	Flavors and Toppings: None	Flavors and Toppings: Fruit/Fruit juice	Flavors and Toppings: Syrup/Sauce/ Drizzle/Whipped cream
Pricing	$2.95–$4.65	$4.75–$4.95	$4.95–$5.95

FIGURE 12.4   Drinks targeting different customers with different price points

Source: "Menu," Starbucks, March 2023, https://www.starbucks.com/menu/, with prices shown for Grande size, except for espressos.

For health-conscious customers, Starbucks offers low-calorie and plant-based options, such as the Mango Dragonfruit and Pink Drink Starbucks Refreshers. Within each of its distinct customer segments, Starbucks also created good-better-best lineups as well as volume progressions.

But some Choice Game players use lineups that are only segment-specific. The financial data provider FactSet, for example, has identified customer segments with distinct value perceptions, as shown in Figure 12.5.[27] A wealth management customer needs data products that are quite different from what a hedge fund customer needs. But hedge fund customers tend to have a higher willingness to pay for the right solution, because they are generally more profitable and have larger budgets. FactSet ultimately mapped an optimal set of features to the needs of around a dozen segments, then created and priced the packages.

Step 2: Design the lineup of offers

The outputs of your customer research become the primary inputs for offer development. Companies should define the highest-value offer first and the lowest-value offer last. Working in this order makes it less likely that the company will include high-value features in low-value offers, which would undermine the balance of the lineup.

	Wealth Management	**Hedge Fund**
Sample key features	Data	Data
	Summary statistics	• Comprehensive datasets
	Relevant market events	• Relevant real-time news
	Tools	**Tools**
	• Advisor dashboard	• Open, programmatic environment
	• Prebuilt model portfolios	• Multi-asset class portfolio analysis
	• Relationship management and reporting	• Research and execution management
Pricing	Lower	Higher

FIGURE 12.5   FactSet packages for Wealth Management and Hedge Fund clients

Source: "Wealth Management Firms," FactSet, March 2023, https://www.factset.com/solutions/clients/wealth-management-firms; "Hedge Funds," FactSet, March 2023, https://www.factset.com/solutions/clients/hedge-funds.

Packages or bundles also risk becoming unbalanced when a company focuses solely on features that customers like instead of selectively distributing features across packages. Calibrating the distribution of features not only creates and preserves the clear differentiation between packages, but also creates the pathways for revenue expansion as customers trade up.

Good-better-best lineups work best when they have three or four tiers and a price ratio of approximately 5-to-1 between the top and bottom tiers. The entry-level tier should provide the lowest common denominator features, that is, the ones that all customers will need.

This process has two steps:

1. **Creating an ideal lineup:** Creating your highest-value offer starts with identifying the customer segment for whom you can add the most value. Then you identify the specific needs that separate this highest-value segment from the one below it, and match features with needs. This process of identifying customer segments and fencing the features continues until you have created your lowest-end offer.

2. **Balancing and reinforcing the lineup:** In almost all cases, your real-world lineup exists neither in a vacuum nor in a completely rational world. That means you need to adjust and balance your ideal lineup to take competitive and behavioral influences into account.

This takes us back to competition and value, the two inputs that underpin the Choice Game, and to competitive differentiation, the framework we described in Chapter 2. This framework powers the value-driven elimination of uniformity, because it acknowledges that having one offering with a uniform price is an inferior way to share value when diverse customers have a wide variance in their wants and needs and have competing alternatives to meet those needs. When value differentiation is significant, companies and competitors shape and reshape demand by using multiple price points, segment-specific offerings, and alternative price models.

Returning to Starbucks, Figure 12.6 shows how it designed its lineup for customers seeking flavorful coffee beverages. Since flavor drives the perception of value in this segment, increasing the numbers of flavors increases the value perception. Thus, the highest value offers have multiple flavorings, compared to one flavoring for mid-value offers, and no additional flavorings for the lowest value offer. The entry-level Coffee Frappuccino provides the lowest common denominator features, by blending only coffee, cream, and sugar.

One way to reinforce the ideal lineup in competitive markets is to reduce opportunities for customers to make head-to-head comparisons. When two or more offerings are functionally equivalent, customers can pit the sellers against each other and make their decision primarily based on price. The better you can design your offers in ways that prevent head-to-head comparisons, the weaker price becomes as a decision criterion. The emphasis shifts instead to your differentiated and valuable features.

	Coffee Frappuccino	Caramel Frappuccino	Mocha Cookie Crumble Frappuccino
Flavorings	None	Caramel Syrup and Drizzle	Mocha Sauce and Drizzle Cookie Crumble Topping
Pricing	$4.95	$5.45	$5.75

FIGURE 12.6   Starbucks' Frappuccino lineup

Source: "Menu," Starbucks, https://www.starbucks.com/menu/, with prices shown for Grande size.

Companies also put the balance of their lineup at risk when higher-value features migrate to lower-tier offers without a corresponding addition of new value to the higher tiers. The more intense the competition, the more pressure a company might feel to pack the lower-tier offers with more value. It is important for lower-tier offers to remain competitive, but it is essential for higher-end offers to maintain value.

Some of the most consequential decisions in the Choice Game focus on which features to flow down over time. If Spotify chose to extend ad-free listening, a key fencing feature, down to the Free tier, they would likely experience a collapse in demand for their Premium tier. However, if Spotify flows down nonfencing features, such as access to their exclusive content, they can increase the value of lower tiers with limited devaluation of the higher tiers.

In general, a company should add new features as it moves old features down. The introduction of new features – whether through incremental or step-change innovation – preserves and grows value at the high end while maintaining a competitive position at the lower end. Put another way, players in the Choice Game should focus on greater differentiation through added value instead of optimizing individual price points with precision.

Step 3: Monitor and shape the customer journey

"Customer journey" is an overused marketing expression, but in the Choice Game, the term applies very well to how customers navigate their way through a series of decisions as they try to self-select their best option. It applies to daily decisions in a coffeehouse or to buying a car.

Best-in-class personalization in promotions and overall marketing activities helps Starbucks customers navigate choices and nudges them to try new things and trade up.[28] Starbucks has continued to refine and innovate their menu and product lineup to adapt to ever-evolving customer needs. Saying the lineup gets creative is an understatement. In 2023 Starbucks launched Oleato, a line of coffee infused with olive oil.

Companies playing the Choice Game also need to build resilience to weather business cycles. Impact from external shocks – such as recessions, the high inflation rates that dominated 2022, or the Covid-19 pandemic – can change how customers perceive value. The competitive set may also change, as customers discover alternative ways to meet their needs. This often means that players of the Choice Game find that their carefully crafted lineup and pricing no longer match market realities.

The key to establishing resilience in the Choice Game is discipline. Companies need to resist the temptation to abandon their principles. Starbucks faced this test when it encountered twin crises between 2006 and 2008. Skyrocketing coffee and milk prices and a global recession meant that Starbucks' costs were rising as their customers' incomes were falling. Starbucks acknowledged this new reality in their 2008 annual report, citing consumer confidence "approaching all-time lows" as a reason for "slowing growth, store closures and cost reductions."[29] These shifts in customers' value perception would throw the Starbucks lineup out of balance.

At first, Starbucks applied a cost-plus method instead of reassessing its customers' value perceptions across subsegments. The company increased prices by an average of 5 cents per drink in 2006 and 9 cents per drink in 2007. Investors initially welcomed the latter move, as the company's shares rose by 1.7% after the announcement of price increases.[30] However, by January 2008, Starbucks had fired their CEO at the time, Jim Donald, and the stock price had fallen by 35% since the day they announced price increases in 2007.[31]

When the Great Recession hit in 2008–2009, however, Starbucks remained disciplined in the Choice Game. When they evaluated customers' new value perceptions relative to price, they realized that customers perceived the highest value in their signature, complex beverages, such as the Frappuccino.[32] This understanding led them to raise prices of such beverages by an average of 10 to 15 cents. They also realized that customers now perceived less value in lattes and brewed coffees, in part because the quick-service restaurant (QSR) competitors had eroded Starbucks' differentiation by offering higher-end coffees and espresso-based drinks. Thus, Starbucks simultaneously decreased the prices of those beverages by an average of 5 to 15 cents. Starbucks stock price increased by over 20% within a year.[33] In comparison, the S&P 500 increased by around 1% over the same period.[34]

Impact: An offer for every customer segment

In 50 years, Starbucks transformed itself from a single coffeeshop to a chain of 30,000 coffeehouses worldwide. It achieved this success by understanding its customers and carefully designing a lineup with offers that matched the needs and willingness to pay of different segments.

This process is never-ending, as customer needs change and competitors catch up. Starbucks has continuously reshaped its lineup, tweaking its prices and introducing new offers like the Frappuccino, the Pumpkin Spice Latte, and the Oleato. These active adjustments to its lineup allow Starbucks to continue to deliver what customers need at prices they're willing to pay. By adhering to the Choice Game approach, Starbucks became the largest and most successful coffee seller in the world, with over $32 billion of revenue in 2022.[35]

More broadly, our experience shows that redesigning your offering lineup can have a tremendous impact. We often see companies achieve revenue growth of 5% to 15% by redesigning their packages, tiers, and bundles. This impact stems from both new customer acquisition and from higher revenue with existing customers.

Key takeaways

Success in the Choice Game depends on a company's ability to create packages and prices that align to the needs and preferences of customer segments. We recommend the following approach:

- **Define a coherent offer lineup:** Segment your customers based on their value perceptions and design a balanced, simple, and fenced portfolio that provides sellers diverse paths for revenue expansion.
- **Anchor prices to these value perceptions:** Involve the product team when defining the offer structure (good-better-best, package size variation, or a hybrid approach) and develop customer programs and transaction incentives.
- **Help customers navigate choices:** Use behavioral science to guide customer choice and incorporate insights from the compromise effect, decoy effect, and anchor mechanism into your portfolio design and communication.
- **Build resilience to weather business cycles:** Adapt your offer lineup and prices to changing value perceptions over time.

CHAPTER 13

The Dynamic Game: When Everything Matters

With contributions from Alberto Guerrini, Fabian Uhrich, Gabriele Ferri, and John Elder

T he airline industry is the poster child for the Dynamic Game – the automated, real-time setting of price points, using live data on costs, demand, and supply.

But for the better part of the twentieth century, the opposite was true: Every customer paid the same price as everyone else in the same class of service. Until 1978, regulations in the United States defined which routes an airline could operate and the fares they could charge. Prices were fixed and published in price lists. With limited competition, airlines were guaranteed a profit, and they lavished flyers with costly services covered by expensive airfares.

But the silverware and cloth napkins came at a high social cost: the vast majority of Americans couldn't afford to fly at all.[1]

When oil prices skyrocketed during the energy crisis of the 1970s, a team of economists and US senators pushed to deregulate the industry, resulting in the Airline Deregulation Act of 1978. With more airlines entering the market and competing for passengers, American Airlines realized they needed a way to optimize their revenue. They developed a system called DINAMO (Dynamic Inventory and Maintenance Optimizer), which used algorithms to determine the optimal price for each flight, based on factors such as the time of day, day of the week, season, and expected demand.[2,3] By adjusting prices in real time, American Airlines filled more seats and increased revenue.

Yield management was born.

The Dynamic Game came about in the airline industry when American paired DINAMO's sophisticated price-setting algorithms with Sabre, its computer reservations system. Sabre automated the process of making flight reservations and handled the necessary complex calculations and data analysis.

The Dynamic Game benefited consumers as well as the airlines. The wide dynamic range of price points democratized air travel, because they provided greater access to consumer segments that previously couldn't afford flying or never even viewed it as an option. Air travel's growth would not have been possible on the same scale if airlines had consistently charged all passengers one uniform price to fly from point A to point B.[4]

We use the word dynamic to describe this game for two reasons. First, it is the word businesses use to describe the pricing approach adopted by airlines, hotels, e-commerce, and all businesses with either perishable inventory or fluctuating supply and demand. The word also implies constant change, which is the more traditional and colloquial use of the term.

The Dynamic Game is a good fit for organizations that have mastered one of the six peripheral games and want to integrate aspects of the games on the other side of the Hex into their pricing approach. This moves the company toward the center of the Hex. A company traditionally playing the Uniform Game, for example, may want to understand more precisely what each of its competitors is doing in different channel, product, and customer segment combinations. Taking that complexity into account leads to a pricing approach that is inherently more dynamic, because the relevant inputs are in constant flux. A company playing the Power Game may want to rethink or adjust their pricing strategy by incorporating a granular view of customer needs and how their customers' value perceptions vary.

In other words, the Dynamic Game is not strictly the home of airlines, hotels, and e-commerce sites. It is open to any company that wants to incorporate all the economic frameworks (elasticity, differentiation, game theory, supply and demand) and information sources (cost, value, competition) simultaneously into their decision making. This combination increases the general instability of prices and the complexity of managing them.

We have seen organizations from all games successfully implement a more dynamic approach to pricing, but the move required significant investments in data science: analytical sophistication, team, and processes. Each player must commit to becoming smarter, faster, and fairer with the way they share value, as they gain a richer and more reliable understanding of the factors that drive buying behavior. They find themselves in a continuous loop of self-optimization, using all the inputs and paradigms simultaneously with a growing level of complexity. Whenever they think they have mastered the game, it's time to change the game.

Take, for instance, the San Francisco Giants baseball team. In August 2007, Barry Bonds was on the verge of breaking the all-time record for home runs. Russ Stanley, the head of ticket services for the Giants, realized there were large differences in the fans' willingness to pay for tickets. "Some tickets for that game were priced at $10," Stanley told *CIO Magazine.* "But if that ticket was $100, people would have bought it."[5]

This inspired the Giants to implement a dynamic algorithm-based system that enabled them to charge high prices for some seats on high-demand days, and lower prices to fill seats on less attractive days. By 2010 the Giants let the algorithm set 3.4 million prices dynamically over the course of the six-month season. Ticket revenue for the Giants increased by 7% in the 2010 season and by the summer of 2012 the team had sold out 140 games in a row.[6,7]

As shown in Figure 13.1, sellers in the Dynamic Game can be quite concentrated, given the scale required to play the game effectively. In addition, sellers and their offers are often undifferentiated, even though their value may differ greatly by customer and fluctuate over time. Sellers also need to monitor the actions of other sellers, because any player's moves impact all other players, but the set of relevant competitors can also vary by customer and time. The Dynamic Game is especially well suited to situations when short-term capacity is fixed and offers are perishable, but these are not prerequisites.

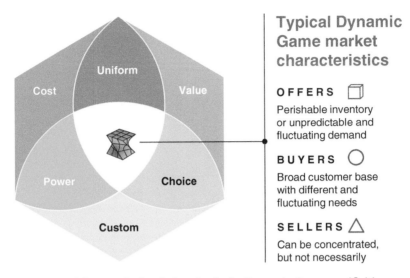

OFFERS

Perishable inventory
or unpredictable and
fluctuating demand

BUYERS

Broad customer base
with different and
fluctuating needs

SELLERS

Can be concentrated,
but not necessarily

FIGURE 13.1   Airlines and other industries fit the Dynamic Game specificities

The special nature of pricing in the Dynamic Game

Pricing in the Dynamic Game requires constant price adjustments based on live data, as well as a continuous inflow of additional data as both the players and the game become increasingly sophisticated.

One absolute prerequisite is the ability to secure access to large amounts of data across the three information sources. The data help the pricing algorithms to "learn" and set prices. Capturing this data across the market and reacting to it with speed and precision is critical. Players may change prices dozens of times across hundreds or even thousands of offers over the course of a single day. The sheer number of price actions and reactions across various players reinforces the need for sophisticated algorithms, because this volume of information would overwhelm any human analyst.

Having granular data is a necessary but insufficient condition to play the game. Players also need a supply–demand model that reveals the narratives within the data. Specifically, what are the supply and demand signals that matter, and how should the company respond to these signals?

Figure 13.2 shows a simplified and sanitized example of the supply–demand model for a retailer. In contrast to the classical supply–demand

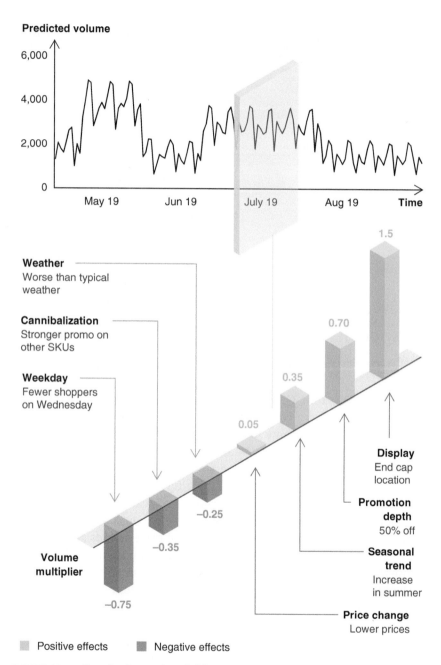

FIGURE 13.2   Supply–demand model for a category at a retailer

matching in a static elasticity framework, such models look at the inter-relationships across dozens of underlying drivers, ranging from weather to display location in the store. The model also reveals patterns that show similarities from week to week, but whose amplitudes fluctuate across months or seasons due to that same range of drivers. This pricing engine – in the state shown in Figure 13.2 – produced over 10 million unique prices per week, improving the company's revenue and profits far better than pricing methodologies did or could have.

With the sophistication of current AI methodologies, companies can create supply–demand models with unprecedented granularity, precision, and accuracy. At that point the model can guide prices to reflect strategic intent, such as maximizing volume, revenue, profit, or a specific balance of those metrics.

Let's work through an example we'll call OutfitOracle, a simple company that sells licensed merchandise such as T-shirts on its own e-commerce site.[8] Its pricing model is typical for an e-commerce seller, as shown in Figure 13.3. OutfitOracle sets the price on a per-unit basis for its broad range of products. It deploys a supply–demand model, supported by AI, to optimize prices and promotions based on how a range of inputs varies and to provide insights into how to use price adjustment levers.

We next describe what OutfitOracle needs to do to win their game and become the leading T-shirt seller on the internet.

Optimal pricing in real time

Step 1: Build the bespoke model

Players start by building v1.0 of their own supply–demand model, often from the ground up, working with a data science team. Such models are usually proprietary, because they are bespoke for the company's unique competitive context. That is why major e-commerce companies such as Amazon and Wayfair protect their pricing algorithms, and why airlines have resisted standardization of the pricing platforms.

This model combines the factors that have a meaningful influence on the supply–demand equation for the player, and these typically include the sources of variation we described in Chapter 1: location, time, customer segment, and capacity. The models also need inputs on price – the

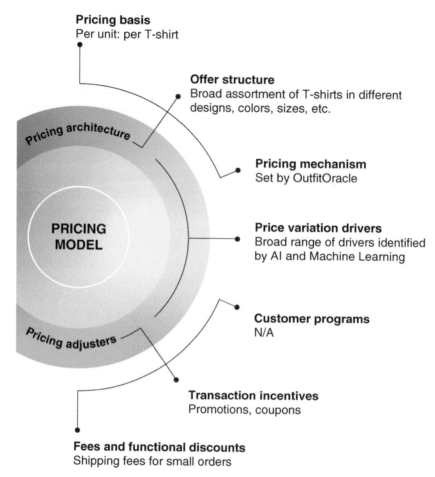

Pricing basis
Per unit: per T-shirt

Offer structure
Broad assortment of T-shirts in different designs, colors, sizes, etc.

Pricing architecture

Pricing mechanism
Set by OutfitOracle

PRICING MODEL

Price variation drivers
Broad range of drivers identified by AI and Machine Learning

Customer programs
N/A

Pricing adjusters

Transaction incentives
Promotions, coupons

Fees and functional discounts
Shipping fees for small orders

FIGURE 13.3 Price variation drivers are a key pricing lever in the Dynamic Game

company's own current and previous prices, price gaps to all competitors, and whether those price gaps are driven by promotional activity. Depending on the offer and company, models can include factors such as variable costs, macroeconomic inputs, and weather, each of which could be critical for making accurate demand forecasts. The company then tests the model and its algorithms until it can automatically set and reset prices.

Regardless of how robust this model is, a company needs to keep "humans in the loop" to understand, pressure-test, and identify patterns in the outcomes of the model, from individual price points to patterns of pricing behaviors.

OutfitOracle's model incorporates the prices of its own T-shirt portfolio, prices of some specific competitors (scraped from the web), its current inventory of shirts and holding costs, some seasonality patterns, and some rudimentary information about the consumers who are shopping on its site, based on data such as overall traffic, source IP location, and how they got to the site. Once the leadership team, working with the data science team, understands how each factor influenced their supply–demand balance – say, the number of T-shirt purchases and the available inventory by shirt – it can establish guardrails for the model. These include answers to questions such as:

- What is the maximum and minimum allowable algorithmic price change before an analyst must intervene?
- Are there some portfolio pricing relationships that must be maintained, for example, line pricing of all black T-shirts that fans can customize themselves?

With model v1.0 finished, OutfitOracle started a pilot program to price its T-shirts dynamically. Figure 13.4 shows how a pricing algorithm would manage price points over time for a single product, although this now happens for the full portfolio in almost real time.

Volume

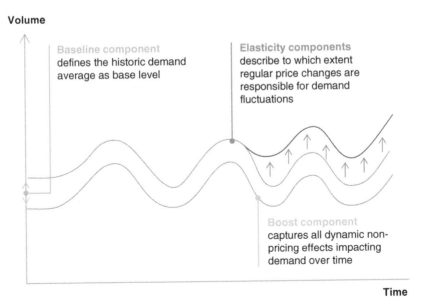

Baseline component defines the historic demand average as base level

Elasticity components describe to which extent regular price changes are responsible for demand fluctuations

Boost component captures all dynamic non-pricing effects impacting demand over time

Time

FIGURE 13.4 Illustration of dynamic pricing managed by an AI algorithm

Step 2: Add more information to improve model outcomes

The magnitude of changes to costs, competitors, and value – based on the several sources of variance – can occasionally be strong enough to create imbalances in a market. Players in the Dynamic Game treat these imbalances not only as challenges, but also as learning and improvement opportunities for their models. In many cases, the improvement comes from the inclusion of more granular data or improved precision of existing data. The improvement could also come from the quality of competitor data, richer cost data, or customer data that enables the company to personalize offers and prices.

These improvements can lead to fundamental changes in the pricing model itself, such as when airlines introduced a new pricing basis in the early 2000s by unbundling luggage options and seat choice from the core offering. Successful players of the Dynamic Game quickly realize that the range of customer willingness to pay is often broader than initially observed. Thoughtful dynamic pricing can access value at both ends of that spectrum: the less price-sensitive but hard-to-reach customers as well as more price-sensitive but easy-to-reach ones.

As the model encompasses more and more data and information sources, it progressively creates more opportunities for the company to exploit or correct supply and demand imbalances and to enhance the sophistication of the model itself. The finance industry is an excellent example of such ongoing optimization. The sophistication of trading algorithms has continuously increased, to the point where some trades are updated from millisecond to millisecond.[9]

The humans in the loop remain critical here. Sophisticated analysts will start to see patterns of behavior and identify opportunities where the company can intervene to shape demand. The analysts also ensure that additional data is adding value and not an effort to add data for data's sake.

Combining human talent with algorithms creates outcomes that are far superior to outcomes from the algorithm alone. Extreme examples of a "rogue" algorithm include a book about flies that was priced online for over $23 million in 2011.[10] Analysts receive a list of potential actions with quantified impact to choose from, based on their judgment. We have observed increases of more than 15 percentage points, as analysts free up time to focus on strategic topics and decisions. An adaptive AI feedback loop assesses the actions that drive such improvement and uses the insights to improve future recommendations.[11]

Step 3: Drive continuous improvement in the race for sophistication

Once the leadership team is comfortable that the model and the humans in the loop are driving continuous improvement, it is important to take a step back. The model's optimization is based primarily on the elasticity framework embedded within it, and it is getting continuously better at augmenting information sources across cost, competitor, and customer value. The company is now ready to evaluate how to use the two remaining frameworks: price differentiation and game theory.

- **Differentiation:** It is always useful to look at opportunities to differentiate offers based on the needs and value that different customer segments derive. The ride-sharing sector has implemented dynamic pricing. In the United States Uber and Lyft have developed a lineup of offers to cater to different segments beyond the basic type of car categories. Riders in a hurry, riders with pets, riders who can plan their trip ahead of time, and riders ready to share a car with others all have different needs and different budgets. This is the equivalent of what airlines have done with business travelers or with charging for luggage and food. Regular dynamic pricing models usually do not manage these customer differences well. Applying lessons from the Choice Game can be very effective.
- **Game theory:** Understanding competitor behavior and pricing accordingly is critical in the Dynamic Game, but a pricing engine does not always do that systematically and automatically. Dynamic Game markets can be concentrated on the supply side, which means that companies need to understand the intent of their competitors' moves. The Chessboard, which we introduced in Chapter 10, can serve as a powerful tool to do that. It usually is based on a matrix of offers (rows) and customer segments (columns) and will require some automation to gather relative prices and share in each cell. Yet the same logic around castles, grasslands, battlefields, and deserts applies and helps leadership teams interpret what may otherwise seem like random markets movements. When the underlying economics are similar to a prisoner's dilemma, we find that competitive algorithms that price against each other can automatically converge to some very low-margin Nash equilibrium. These correspond to what we call deserts in the Power Game, implying they are usually not worth fighting for. A

mapping of the broader Chessboard can often redirect resources and strategies toward more profitable segments.

Leaders have a critical role in the Dynamic Game to make sure the overall strategic context does not get lost in the focused effort to optimize the algorithms. They need to steer away from the "black box" syndrome, which turns an organization into "price takers" from its own algorithms, without a deeper understanding of all the supply and demand impacts. Offer differentiation is a powerful way to reshape the demand, and the Chessboard is an insightful and compelling way to shift the supply toward the most productive use of capacity.

OutfitOracle's leadership team stepped outside the algorithm and pricing model to explore some strategic questions:

- Why is one competitor always undercutting our prices? Should we manage the price gap to this competitor more intentionally?
- Sales of the all-black shirts have grown and occasionally spike. Should we consider providing personalized messages for a fee?

Exploring these questions involves critical thinking, not better algorithms. It highlights once again the critical element to success in the Dynamic Game: sophisticated, continuously improving algorithms that are augmented by humans in the loop who maintain a strategic perspective. No one masters the Dynamic Game, but the winners continually evolve.

Impact: Sustained value creation in the Dynamic Game

Both Uber and its competitors play the Dynamic Game with advanced AI pricing algorithms that manage every transaction. But Uber's recent evolution shows what can happen when leaders take a step back, reflect on strategy, and redirect algorithms. Uber attributes some of its superior performance in late 2022 and early 2023 to the strategic choices it made after its CEO got behind the wheel and drove customers himself. This gave him first-hand experience with how the algorithm's efficiency optimization affected drivers.[12]

These kinds of strategic resets are the essential driver of progress for companies in the Dynamic Game. They also illustrate the enduring role that humans play in the Dynamic Game, no matter how advanced the algorithms become. Leaders need to identify opportunities to reset the algorithmic competition with new types of data, a new scope of optimization, or a new pricing model. The airline industry has followed this pattern, as it has moved from yield management to hub-and-spoke flow optimization to unbundling.

The company then supports the strategic reset with new analytical capabilities, which can lead to incremental revenue growth of between 2% and 4%.[13] These strategic resets and the resulting model enhancements are invaluable for companies that want to establish stronger and more durable competitive advantages. But the improvement from the new analytics wanes after a few years, as the old models reach diminishing returns and competitors develop similar capabilities. If a company doesn't seize the opportunity for a fresh strategic reset at that point, one of their competitors will.

Key takeaways

Pricing in the Dynamic Game requires taking a comprehensive range of inputs into consideration. Optimizing prices and profit requires continuous investment in sophisticated analytics, a readiness to react to competitor moves quickly, and an ability to step back and reinvent the pricing model. We recommend the following approach:

1. **Capture your supply and demand signals:** Understand how each driver influences prices and use AI to build a precise predictive model that manages the elasticity framework.

2. **Improve your algorithms:** "Dynamic" also describes a Dynamic Game player's organization, which is in a constant state of evolution. Successful players test and adjust their models continuously, using the latest data and technologies.

3. **Don't lose sight of fairness:** Algorithms can successfully optimize price points, but customers will reject unfair prices regardless of the underlying analytical elegance. Clear communication about the logic of every change is critical. We explore this in much greater depth in Chapters 20 and 21.

4. **Keep the humans in the loop:** Integrating human talent and advanced analytics delivers superior outcomes and ensures that the algorithm does not become a "black box" within your organization.

5. **Explore and pursue regular strategic resets:** The impact of analytical improvements fades, and if you don't seize the initiative for a strategic reset, your competitors will. Stepping back and looking for new opportunities has always been important in the Dynamic Game. It will become even more important as AI makes algorithms more powerful.

We recommend this pricing game to companies with sophisticated pricing capabilities, even if their market characteristics don't fit the Dynamic Game perfectly. The center of the Hex is a destination worth exploring for companies that have developed advanced pricing capabilities in one of the peripheral games. This will be one of the moves we study in Part III.

Before you move on to Part III . . .

Our objective with Part II was to give you a more practical description of the pricing games, what characterizes them, and what it takes to succeed in each.

Three Questions Shaping Your Pricing Strategy

Question 1: How do you create and share value?

1a. What do you do to create **measurable value** for your customers?

1b. What are your main **drivers of value** and the **limitations** to value creation?

1c. How do your **differentiation and growth objectives** justify how you share value with your customers?

Question 2: What pricing game do you want to play?

2a. Which game aligns best with the **characteristics of your market?**

2b. Which game aligns best with your **current pricing approach?**

2c. Which game aligns best with the **market forces** and your **competitive advantages?**

Question 3: What pricing model best fits your value creation strategy?

3a. What should your **pricing architecture** be (i.e., pricing basis, offer structure, and pricing mechanism)?

3b. What should drive your **price variation** (e.g., geography, channel, and time)?

3c. What price **adjustment** levers should you use (i.e., customer programs, transaction incentives, and fees and functional discounts)?

At the end of Part II, we asked you to validate your answer to **Question 1** and answer **Question 2** of our pricing strategy questions.

Please remind yourself of your answer to **Question 1** about your value creation strategy.

We would like you to review your answer to **Question 2** in light of what you have read in Part II. Do you still want to play the same game? Are there other games that you have considered? Which game or combination of games would you now like to play in?

Then we would like you to answer **Question 3**: Considering your value creation strategy and the game(s) you would like to play as given, what pricing model will you need to succeed? How should you change your current pricing model?

Please write down your answer along with a brief rationale for your choice.

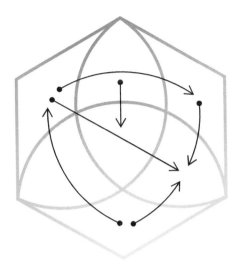

PART III

Changing Your Pricing Game

In Part II, we described each of the games of the Hex in detail, and explained how companies can succeed at their chosen game. Business environments evolve rapidly, though, and the pace of change is accelerating. Companies need to constantly reassess what game they are in, and whether a move to a different game is desirable or necessary.

Despite the strong pull and push of market forces, companies often have the power to choose the pricing game they want to play. We frequently observe that leaders underestimate their agency to control the fate of their firms, defaulting to the established models in their industries. Players who execute bold moves to change the game often reap outsized benefits.

Part III describes the motivations, actions, and consequences when one or more players decide to use their pricing agency for truly game-changing moves across the Hex.

We begin with the story of how the launch of innovation empowered a company to move from the Cost Game to the Value Game. Chapter 15 shows how progressive digitalization prompted one company to move to the Choice Game with an "as-a-Service" offering. Chapter 16 explains how Covid-19 provided the burning platform for a CPG player to embrace AI to optimize its promotions, moving it closer to the Dynamic Game. Chapter 17 explains how some companies disrupt their distribution channels to their advantage. In Chapter 18 we describe the deliberate strategy of Amazon Web Services to play a Cost Game when it changed the game in the IT infrastructure market. Finally, Chapter 19 explores how Intuit shifted down from the Value Game into the Choice Game to respond to Microsoft's entry into its market.

Each of these companies continuously reflects on how they create and share value, and whether their prevailing split still makes sense. Business leaders should ask themselves what game they are playing, whether a change to a different game is desirable and feasible, and what pricing model elements will help them achieve the best outcomes.

CHAPTER 14

Innovation: Seizing a Step-Change Opportunity

With contributions from Camille Brege, David Langkamp, and Ricard Vila

A company can disrupt its industry, reshape demand, and gain a significant advantage over its competitors by launching a new product with an innovative technology or by approaching its market in an innovative way. This game-changing product or service gives the company immense degrees of freedom to reset their pricing strategy, particularly when the product offers usage value that is far higher than its substitute value or the Next Best Competitive Alternative.

But those degrees of freedom go to waste if the company doesn't recognize them and exercise them in the market.

Breakthrough innovation that disrupts an industry does not always make the headlines, as the story of a company we call Emerald Engineering exemplifies.[1] Most people would not recognize the company name unless they lived close enough to read its factory sign, despite likely having used Emerald's white-labeled devices. It was barely a household name in the families of its employees. But within Emerald's multibillion-dollar industry, it had a leading market share and a strong reputation for quality. Its ongoing success and stability had made Emerald look like a well-oiled machine, but intensifying competitive pressure and slower industry growth had caused the machine to sputter.

That's when Emerald came up with a new generation of machines, supported by a new software and service platform. The new machines offered multiple sources of value to customers and were much cheaper to make and deploy. Emerald's innovations in design and manufacturing promised to deliver double-digit percentage point reductions in production costs.

There was one question on everyone's mind at Emerald: How much should we charge for this new system? The sales team had its own answer based on obvious arithmetic: lower costs mean lower prices. Seeking relief from the competitive pressures and eager to have a chance to spark some sales growth, they wondered how much of those double-digit cost reductions they could pass along to customers.

Fortunately, Emerald's senior leadership realized that this question was the wrong one to ask and the sales team's arithmetic was the wrong way to answer it. By stepping back and examining the overall pricing strategy, not just individual price points, Emerald asked themselves what pricing strategy would deliver maximum benefit for both Emerald and its customers. This customer-centric approach led Emerald to the Value Game.

How Emerald defined a new pricing strategy

Developing a pricing strategy for a new or next-generation product follows the same steps as for any pricing strategy. Emerald's leadership sought the answers to three questions: How do we create and share value?, What game do we want to play?, and What pricing model best fits our value creation strategy? These are the questions that elevate pricing from an afterthought or a necessary evil to a fundamental strategic issue.

How did Emerald create and share value?

By combining complex configurations, hardware, software, and after-sales services, Emerald had the potential to create a significant competitive advantage. After years of hard work, Emerald's product team was confident they had a platform that could revolutionize the customer experience, due to their improved outputs, reduced operating effort, and enhanced security.

But for a company accustomed to playing the Cost Game, expressing that value in money terms did not come naturally. This new platform had strong usage value, driven by functional value. The company analyzed the key value drivers, such as operational cost savings, and quantified them for key customer segments and geographies. This allowed Emerald to build the value ladder shown in Figure 14.1. The analyses of its new platform showed positive value differentiation that massively outweighed the negatives.

Once Emerald established its usage and substitute value, it knew that its innovation could quickly make the existing installed base of machinery – both its own and its competitors – obsolete in a hurry. The success of the

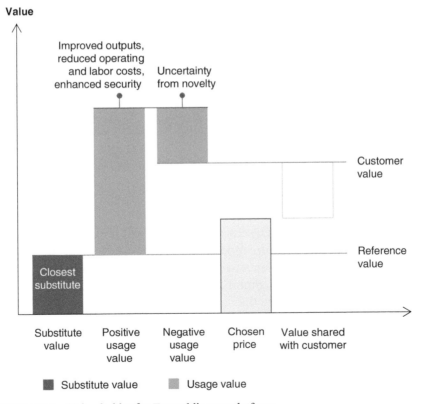

FIGURE 14.1   Value ladder for Emerald's new platform

new platform depended on the speed of that replacement. These considerations gave Emerald a strong incentive to share its additional value up front in a way that accelerated adoption and created opportunities to adjust that level later.

It undertook several steps to strike the right balance between sharing value up front and recalibrating the share in its favor over the platform's lifetime. The strong usage value could have easily led to an up-front price far out of line with the market. To prevent this, Emerald defined an attractive base offer – at a moderate premium to competition – and a series of upgrade options throughout the lifecycle. To arrive at a fair share of value, Emerald analyzed analogous implementations in similar industries, including the launch of new platforms and the implementation of new, service-rich offerings. Using these benchmarks as a guide, the leadership team decided to retain only between 5% and 20% of the value on the up-front machinery sales. This resulted in a much lower premium than the one initially indicated by simplistic assumptions such as splitting the difference, that is, retaining half the value rather than 5–20%. The team boosted their confidence in that decision by stress-testing value-selling arguments and prices with customers.

What pricing game did Emerald want to play?

Like its competitors, Emerald historically used the cost-plus pricing approach to set prices for its products. As with many industries, they used this approach more by default than by conscious choice because it delivered stable and comfortable margins for mostly standardized products.

Emerald's organization was built around playing the Cost Game, but a look at the market characteristics showed that its fit to the Cost Game was not pure. First, its market was more concentrated on the supplier side and less concentrated on the demand side. Second, Emerald historically sold thousands of options and combinations on top of its base product, making it impossible to analyze the value of individual components. Finally, Emerald's sales force was also a source of price variation because the ability to sell complexity varied significantly from salesperson to salesperson. Some of these dynamics resembled the Custom Game and pushed Emerald downward in the Strategy Hex to the lower part of the Cost Game.

But the insights from the value ladder in Figure 14.1 gave Emerald a compelling reason to change games. The potential competitive advantages from the vastly superior value proposition were powerful indicators that the Cost Game was no longer the most appropriate game. Emerald knew that it would be difficult to translate that value into the existing price model. Recall that the new system had much lower production costs, so if Emerald applied its cost-plus pricing logic, it risked transferring the bulk of the new value directly to its customers. Staying in the Cost Game would doom Emerald to unnecessarily low margins, a lower valuation, and fewer resources to invest in future innovations. The lower prices would also have likely ignited a price war that would have diluted Emerald's margins even more. Without a change to its pricing practices, Emerald would waste a win–win opportunity for itself and its customers.

From this point on, Emerald's leadership decided that the company would no longer build its organization and its go-to-market strategies around a margin equation. It would build them around a value equation.

Two clear options emerged as Emerald moved to the right side of the Strategy Hex: the Value Game or the Choice Game. The leadership team knew they had already overcome the barrier to entry to the Value Game, because the value of the new platform's unique combination of functional benefits would effectively make the rest of sellers in the market irrelevant, at least temporarily. But at the same time, they anticipated that competitors would catch up on capabilities over the medium term. That meant Emerald needed to move quickly and resolutely. Emerald's leadership team also felt that if they followed a strict value-based pricing logic, the resulting price point would lie far outside existing market perceptions and price levels.

These two factors led the team to consider moving to the lower half of the Value Game, closer to the Choice Game. By moving to the lower part of the Value Game as shown in Figure 14.2, Emerald could enjoy high margins, while also using some aspects of the Choice Game to insulate itself from competitors who may quickly catch up. The success of the transition would depend on the changes to the pricing model.

How should Emerald adjust its pricing model?

Under its existing pricing model based on a cost-plus approach, Emerald had sold its machines as a one-off device purchase at prices that it set itself. But Emerald knew it couldn't use that model for the new platform, as we mentioned, because the resulting low prices would transfer almost

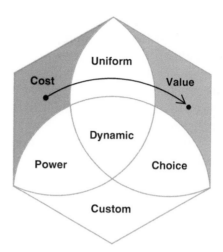

FIGURE 14.2 Emerald's changing position in the Strategy Hex

all the incremental value of the entire platform – hardware, software, and services – to customers. Nor could Emerald use a strict value-based approach, because charging customers up front for the full additional value would make their machines prohibitively expensive. Selling fewer machines would also compound the revenue sacrifice, because it would reduce opportunities for sales of upgrades and after-sales services.

Emerald thus needed to change the offer structure and shift more of its value share to later in the customer lifecycle. This required the right balance between selling base machinery and selling future upgrades and after-sales services. Given the value creation opportunity for customers, the leadership team considered outcome-based pricing formulas, but deemed them impractical. The company ultimately decided to implement a razor-and-blades model and achieved nearly 90% replacement of its older-generation machines within a short period after launch, despite challenging market conditions. This helped them achieve significant growth, stop their margin decline, and then quickly improve margins in the first few years after launch. During these years, Emerald maintained a perception of high value for their new platform by avoiding price adjusters such as functional fees and transaction incentives, because they could erode that value perception.

How Emerald implemented its value-driven strategy

Emerald's successful move toward the right of the Strategy Hex required significant organizational changes. A shift in pricing strategy is a matter of neither semantics nor mathematics. Changing a pricing strategy and a pricing game anywhere in the Strategy Hex – especially when the old and new games are not adjacent – will necessitate changes that touch many aspects of a company, including organizational structures, responsibilities, processes, and training.

The biggest implementation challenge – and the most significant and impactful transformation for Emerald – occurred in sales. Selling value was outside the comfort zone of a sales team hired and trained for the Cost Game. Emerald needed to overcome its sales teams' fears that the customers would reject the new value logic and the prices that result from it. To adapt to a whole new product and pricing strategy, sales reps needed training in value-based selling. Emerald approached this challenge in two steps.

First, Emerald ensured that the sales reps were knowledgeable about the platform and capable of selling it effectively. The company laid a strong foundation in value-based selling by deploying a variety of methods, from informational videos to war gaming. This helped sales reps hone their ability to explain the new pricing logic to customers in a simple but comprehensive manner. The company also provided them with demos that gave them hands-on experience. Once sales reps appreciated the value of the platform, they could understand how it met client needs and practice realistic selling exercises.

But the decisive step to bring the sales teams onboard was "self-discovery." Rather than issue a top-down command to the sales reps to "sell at price x," Emerald's leadership presented them the facts, including customer value assessments and feedback from sales reps who had already sold the next-generation machine in the pilot stage of implementation. Then they asked the sales reps to vote on a fair price premium. The overwhelming majority expressed a preference for a sizeable premium, closely in line with what the value models had suggested. This reflected a true change in mindset from cost to value.

The second step in the mindset shift was a change in incentives and ongoing support. Emerald set incentives to motivate sales reps to continue to learn about the platform and change their sales behaviors. The company tracked performance and monitored whether sales reps effectively sold the new machines.

Emerald then appointed high-performing sales reps to act as ambassadors with hands-on roles and responsibilities in the overall launch. The ambassadors delivered follow-up training and also coached sales reps when they entered the field. The product, marketing, and sales teams worked hand in hand to make sure the messages to the market remained aligned with the value proposition. For example, they provided the sales teams with value quantification manuals.

Key takeaways

Emerald Engineering's success shows that one of the biggest clichés about pricing – that a company must abandon cost-plus pricing and embrace value-based pricing – is an oversimplification. Business leaders need to not only recognize their degrees of freedom for their pricing strategy, but also understand which levers they should pull. We recommend the following steps to help with the transition:

1. **Recognize the full scope of the opportunity:** The introduction of an innovative product or service with a far superior value proposition gives you an opportunity to change established market equilibria and move toward the Value Game.

2. **Understand value over the entire life cycle:** You should consider how to share value along the full customer life cycle, even if it means sharing more value with customers up front and recalibrating the share later.

3. **Focus on training and incentives:** Success will depend on how well you transform capabilities in your commercial functions through a mix of training and incentives, including a multifaceted approach that allows the sales teams to immerse themselves in the new product or service.

CHAPTER 15

As-a-Service: Growing with Your Customer

With contributions from John Pineda, Matthew Kropp, and Steven Greene

I n the 1990s, as digitalization started to revolutionize business, an idea about the nature of software progressively emerged. Why couldn't it be an easy-to-consume, constantly evolving digital capability, instead of a static piece of code licensed in perpetuity like a physical product? In other words, couldn't companies sell software as a service, like electricity or gas?

Companies usually sold customer relationship management (CRM) software, for example, as part of larger enterprise resource planning solutions that required expensive up-front investments, long and complex on-premise implementations, and large IT teams to maintain and upgrade it. This was a prototypical Custom Game, as buyers negotiated custom deals at very high discounts to purchase perpetual licenses from companies such as SAP or Oracle.

This cumbersome business frustrated Marc Benioff, an executive who had spent 13 years at Oracle. In his mind, business applications such as CRM should be "as easy to use as a website."[1] To implement this vision, he founded Salesforce.com in 1999 to allow companies to subscribe to their

CRM on a per-user basis and pay per month. In just under three years, his fledgling company gained over 3,000 customers and brought in $22 million in revenue.[2]

Software as a Service (SaaS) was born.

This revolutionary pricing model – paying per user per month – became an integral part of Salesforce.com's success. It lowered barriers to entry by an order of magnitude, because customers could start small, with just a few users for a few months. These low entry barriers, combined with the model's flexibility, made large discounts and long negotiations obsolete.

Benioff's success reshaped his company and an entire industry by moving them in the direction of the Choice Game. As Salesforce grew and evolved, it formalized the "land-and-expand" strategy we described in Chapter 12. A freemium model enabled the "land" part of the strategy by allowing the first five users from any company to use Salesforce's CRM for free.[3] The "expand" part relied on a lineup of different offers introduced at different price points published transparently on the website. Salesforce created a "Customer Success" department with the mission of ensuring that customers derive the full benefits of the software they bought and discover the capabilities of more expensive options.

Benioff's groundbreaking model is now helping leaders in many other industries to reimagine and rewrite their own pricing strategies. This chapter explores the key challenges of adopting the "as a service," or XaaS, model as well as the necessary conditions for success.

The industrial manufacturer Maricross Machinery has demonstrated how an XaaS model can succeed far afield from the software sector that spawned it. Maricross sold specialized equipment to manufacturers whose products ultimately make their way into the hands of consumers.[4] Like Emerald Engineering in Chapter 14, Maricross built a strong global reputation within its industry, but was relatively unknown to the general public.

Maricross was effectively playing the Cost Game with a cost-plus pricing approach. Like most manufacturers, Maricross also competed for customers by trying to differentiate itself along several technical and measurable dimensions. At some point, its leadership identified a new point of differentiation that was so powerful it could reshape the entire market.

Sensors on their newer machines gave Maricross access to vast amounts of operational data that they could analyze to gain a deep understanding of their customers' machines. This meant Maricross would eventually know how customers' machines operated better than their customers did. The existence of this trove of data begged another important question, which often goes unasked and unanswered as companies develop their pricing strategies: "So what?" IBM has estimated that "[a]s much as 90 percent of all data generated by devices such as smartphones, tablets, connected vehicles, and appliances is never analyzed or acted on."[5] If consumer-driven companies fail to find valuable opportunities for their data, could industrial companies do better?

Maricross's CEO sensed that the company's "smart" machines could create new opportunities for value if the company shifted away from their traditional pricing model for selling machines. How Maricross chose to change demonstrates, once again, that defining and implementing a pricing strategy involves much more than changing the numbers or the semantics. It means changing the pricing game, which changes how the entire organization operates.

How Maricross defined a new pricing strategy

Like Emerald Engineering and the other game changers in Part III, Maricross revisited its pricing strategy by seeking new answers to the three key questions: how they create and share value, what game they want to play, and what pricing model best fit their value creation strategy.

How did Maricross create and share value?

Maricross could now access a large amount of data on the behavior of their growing base of installed "smart" machines around the world. They were part of the growing trend known as the industrial Internet of Things (IoT), which describes the exchange of data and the analysis of performance across interconnected devices and machines used in industrial settings.

But the challenge of establishing the value of that data and connectivity gets to the heart of what value creation really means. IoT services "create flows of value in a network rather than along a traditional value chain. In a network, it is harder but no less essential to define who creates value for customers, who creates value at other nodes in the network, and who derives that value."[6]

By developing algorithms to use the collected data, Maricross could identify high-leverage failure points on machines and monitor them to identify abnormal behavior. It could then trigger alerts and actions to line operators, thus helping their customers avoid downtime or yield loss. These valuable services gave Maricross a competitive advantage and an opportunity to gain market share.

Maricross knew that their customers would be willing to pay for improvements in uptime and yield, because they placed a high value on minimizing maintenance operations and downtime. But downtime was much more critical in some industries than others, which meant that customers would have a wide variance in their willingness to pay for the benefits Maricross offered. Maricross needed to determine how much value they should share across their customer base.

The journey to that new pricing strategy began not with price points, however, but with an understanding of their current game, their options to change the game, and the right way to implement a new pricing strategy.

What game did Maricross want to play?

Maricross had operated as two relatively independent organizations, with one focusing on new equipment sales and the other on aftermarket parts and services, for example, field visits from service technicians. Its primary method for setting prices was "time and materials" or cost-plus, although it occasionally used a "per use" pricing model. As mentioned earlier, this approach placed the company in the Cost Game.

The incremental costs of the new technology in their machines, however, were negligible. Sticking to a cost-plus pricing model would not only severely undersell the value of their differentiated service, but also limit the revenues it would generate, making it less attractive for the company to continue to invest in it. The new machines also meant that the company no longer had a pure fit to the market characteristics of the Cost Game. Instead of offering a commoditized product with a high variable cost, Maricross would be selling a "smart" product that could offer various services to their customers. These services included providing granular data on key variables such as vibration, temperature, and tension, generating detailed performance reports, identifying critical failure points, triggering alerts, and suggesting action plans.

Customers would appreciate different features in their mix of advanced services, in order to find the best match to their own needs. The more sophisticated customers may want access to the full range of capabilities, while others may only appreciate break-fix alerts. Ideally, Maricross would give all customers the opportunity to select the package of features best aligned with their capabilities, objectives, and aspirations.

The combined forces of innovation and digitalization made Maricross realize that it needed to move toward the right side of the Hex. The CEO, with the support from the board, decided to move away from Maricross's traditional cost-plus pricing model when it launched its new offering of digital services. The natural transition was to move toward the lower right in the Choice Game, as shown in Figure 15.1, where it would create a lineup of offers with different value propositions and different prices. Customers would "land" in an entry-level offer and "expand" as they either chose higher-value offers or increased their purchase volumes.

How should Maricross adjust its pricing model?

Maricross decided to shift to a subscription-based as-a-service (XaaS) pricing model. The new pricing basis would be a fixed amount per machine and per month. This model strongly aligned with how customers realized value. The more machines a customer had, the more value they received over the lifetime of those devices.

The rest of the elements of the pricing model followed from that decision, as shown in Figure 15.2. Maricross would set the price, but would

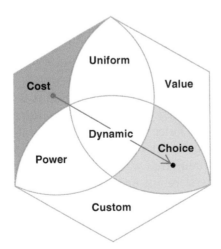

FIGURE 15.1   Maricross's move from the Cost Game to the Choice Game

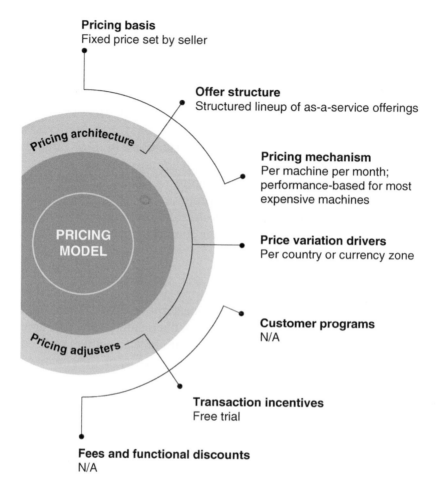

Pricing basis
Fixed price set by seller

Offer structure
Structured lineup of as-a-service offerings

Pricing mechanism
Per machine per month;
performance-based for most
expensive machines

Price variation drivers
Per country or currency zone

Customer programs
N/A

Transaction incentives
Free trial

Fees and functional discounts
N/A

FIGURE 15.2   Maricross's pricing model for the XaaS offering

uncouple it from the hardware sales negotiations to prevent sales teams from giving away an offering with a minimal marginal cost for free.

As a player of the Choice Game, Maricross's most important task in defining a new pricing model was to determine the right offer structure. It needed a product lineup that was priced in a way that would help them acquire new customers, retain existing ones, and expand revenue over time. Customer retention and revenue expansion is especially important in XaaS models, since they create a customer base the company can grow with.[7] Without customer retention, Maricross would lose many of the benefits from adopting the XaaS model.

Maricross designed an XaaS model with two target metrics. The first is a threshold of at least 90% customer retention, which in many cases requires a significant reduction in churn rates. The second is a 20% incremental revenue from cross-selling and upselling activities, which in turn depends on the choices the pricing model creates and the actions the company takes to upsell customers.

With these targets in mind, Maricross set subscription pricing at attractive ROIs for customers, between 2× and 5× depending on their original machine platform, with a payback period of less than one year. To alleviate concerns that its new price points might be unacceptably high, the company tested the offer with a small group of commercial team members, who acted as a secondary check on price points.

Maricross's pricing model was designed with the goal of achieving long-term sales growth and revenue expansion. Besides offering a free trial, the company also trained its sales teams to present customers with the most expensive offer first. If customers were unwilling to purchase the highest-end offer, which included all the available services, the teams would present lower-end offers that only contained subsets of the available services. This approach anchored customers to the highest price and made them more open to considering higher prices for the lower-end offers.

A performance-based subscription for the highest-priced machine platforms further reduced the perception of high prices. For that offer, Maricross charged a fixed retainer to cover costs and linked additional revenue to operational KPIs, for example, changeover time reduction and increases in throughput and yield.

Most people associate XaaS with online services and software. But the ubiquity of IoT and connected devices means these pricing models are now broadly viable in hardware. They open up new opportunities in the Strategy Hex.

How Maricross implemented its as-a-Service strategy

Making the transition to XaaS is not a quick or easy process. Despite clear CEO guidance and strong support from the board, Maricross's XaaS change was lengthy and complex. It took time and dedication to transform an organization that operated across machine platform "fiefdoms" to one with a successful digital offering that spanned machine platforms. The multiyear transformation touched almost every key function in the company.

Maricross faced significant internal resistance to change. First, there was opposition from the existing engineering teams to assemble a new product development organization with data scientists, data engineers, user experience and user interface (UX/UI) designers, and product developers. The aftermarket sales force also strongly resisted, because they felt they lacked the right customer relationships, value-selling capabilities, and incentives to make the new model work. They also had concerns about the ability to prove value and to identify and capitalize on upsell and cross-sell opportunities.

These and other challenges required perseverance from the CEO and board to overcome. They sponsored a holistic transformation program covering three areas:

1. **Product and offer:** Maricross created and staffed an entirely new digital product organization. It conducted customer interviews to understand value drivers in depth, then built the digital offer, iterated it with test customers, and crafted the value creation story for customers.

2. **Go-to-market:** Maricross developed professional sales and marketing collateral, including customer testimonials and professional demos. They also launched a training program for after-market sales reps.

3. **Delivery**: Maricross created and staffed a customer success organization from scratch. It rolled out a series of playbooks and templates to measure customer value, establish compelling proof of value to ensure renewals, and identify and capture upsell and cross-sell opportunities.

A rigorous program management office anchored the effort to deliver this cross-functional transformation. With strong support from the CEO and the board – which provided the resources and held the organization accountable – Maricross delivered a new high-margin offer that deepened customer relationships and accelerated growth.

Key takeaways

Maricross's starting point likely rings true for almost all OEMs that have manufacturing and parts-and-service business. Any business where customer usage is continuous and measurable lends itself well to an XaaS model. This is especially true in IoT services, which represent an opportunity no company can afford to ignore. How well a company seizes it will depend on its "imagination, willingness, and ability to look beyond existing business models and ideas about whom the company serves."[8]

We recommend the following steps to help with the transition to an XaaS model:

- **Answer the "so what?" for the information they collect:** The flows of data and information that you collect can help customers run their operations better throughout the product life cycle.
- **Define land-and-expand opportunities:** Defining an offer lineup aligned with customer value perceptions will help you acquire customers, retain them, and encourage them to trade up.
- **Create an organization to play the Choice Game:** Implementing an XasS model represents more than a change in pricing. It requires changes to the entire organization and its operating model, with a special focus on the product organization and new commercial functions.

CHAPTER 16

AI: Perfecting Price Differentiation

With contributions from Javier Anta, Jean-Sébastien Verwaerde, and Sebastian Bak

One important pillar of Starbucks' enduring success in the Choice Game is its mobile app, which is second only to Apple Pay in usage among US consumers.[1] Over 31 million customers used the Starbucks app to complete a payment in 2021,[2] but as we described in Chapter 12, Starbucks also uses the app to provide its most loyal customers with support and added value at every point in the life cycle.

The app also enables Starbucks to fulfill one of the biggest promises of sophisticated artificial intelligence (AI): personalized pricing on a large scale.

For each customer, the app creates offers based on a wide range of inputs, including prior purchases, menu preferences, and location. It embeds gamification to drive customer behavior, from trial of a new product category to more store visits. Its individualized offers have massively increased customer engagement and member revenue. This high level of precision targeting means that Starbucks almost never runs mass promotions to drum up sales.

One could argue that Starbucks' position in the Choice Game creates such an opportunity for large-scale personalized pricing. A CPG company in the Uniform Game probably has little chance, however, because it has a functionally undifferentiated offering with 100% price transparency to both customers and competitors.

Companies in this game often believe that they are price takers with very little agency to share value differently with customers. But even in the Uniform Game, customers are quite heterogeneous when you look closer. The underlying needs and motivations for why the customer makes the purchase are often quite different, even if the transaction price is the same for every customer.

Think of a bag of candy purchased at a grocery store for $3.99, or 20% off the regular price of $4.99. The motivation for the purchase is very different for the family of four buying the candy to replenish their pantry versus the college-aged person who wants to have snacks on hand for late nights.

It would be incredibly powerful for the candy company to identify opportunities to share value differently with consumers. The difficulty is that while the CPG companies know such differences exist – and often have segmentations that reveal them – they treat consumers equally in terms of pricing because the important sources of variation we described in Chapter 1 are too subtle or slight for them to be detected reliably with old-school analytics. The rough accuracy of uniform prices served as an acceptable, practical, and generally profitable compromise.

But a few companies are already making giant strides in harnessing the full power of data and AI to understand these subtle differences, activate precision personalized pricing, and create immense value for both consumers and themselves.

We describe the story of Montclaude[3] and how its implementation of AI-driven personalization moved it to the frontier between the Uniform Game and the Dynamic Game. Montclaude is a global CPG company with a portfolio of many well-known brands, categories, and price points. It competes in the Uniform Game in many fragmented fields with products that have limited functional differentiation. One such product, which we focus on in this chapter, is chocolate.

The endless loop of promotions

Montclaude found itself in an endless loop when it tried to answer the question of how much value to share. Competitors met any price decrease or promotion with similar price reductions or promotional activity of their own. If both companies engaged in lowering prices to attract more customers, the result would likely be lower profits for both players. Margin sacrifices may marginally shift market shares, but they contribute little to growing the overall size of the category.

Finding a way out of such endless loops is difficult because it involves changing the incentives and behavior for the company and consumers.

Then came Covid-19 and its disruptive economic effects, including supply chain issues and the inability to physically change prices in stores to promote products. Forward-thinking companies like Montclaude sensed an opportunity to escape the Uniform Game and move downward in the Hex toward the Dynamic Game via AI-driven personalized pricing.

How Montclaude defined a new pricing strategy

Montclaude and its competitors were stuck in a stable competitive equilibrium: transparent prices, stable shares, and a predictable cadence of pricing and promotions that effectively trained customers to wait for and buy on deals. Value sharing was limited to the narrow range of price promotions permitted by elasticity and ensuing competitive response.

How should Montclaude create and share value?

Montclaude's marketing teams had focused on analyzing the effectiveness of historical promotional activity and planning responses. The team took a step back and realized that Montclaude was sharing too much value, because its promotional activity was simply subsidizing base volume. Promotions showed short-term volume lifts, but there was no long-term category gain. Category shares stayed stable because everyone promoted at the same cadence. Legacy promotional optimization efforts were limited to fixing the weakest-performing promotions without taking the overall promotional portfolio into consideration.

Montclaude wanted to break the endless loop, but without abandoning the idea of promotions. The team still felt that promotions were the ideal transaction incentive because they could change their depth and frequency in response to the ongoing volatility. The challenge was to find ways to share value differently for the box of chocolates via more targeted promotions.

Some of the needs and occasions were clear. Shoppers at a candy store are clearly there to buy sweets, which means that store promotions need to convince the shopper that Montclaude's product was the best fit for their needs. Shoppers at a grocery store, meanwhile, need a reminder that the store carries Montclaude chocolates and maybe it is time for a treat. Chocolate promotions over the holidays need to address a very different need, as people exchange gifts and host parties.

What pricing game should Montclaude play?

Montclaude traditionally used the classic elasticity framework to optimize the uniform prices of their products. But buyers' needs and willingness to pay depend on factors such as timing, channel, occasion, and other circumstances of their purchase.

Montclaude's leadership realized that they needed to be nimbler and more responsive if they were to succeed in sharing value via targeted promotions. They needed to move closer to the Dynamic Game, as illustrated in Figure 16.1.

They needed to differentiate their targeted promotions by consumers, retailers, seasons, and other factors. But doing that at scale added another difficult dimension to the challenge. In 2021, consumers purchased

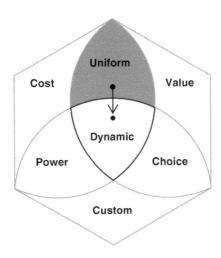

FIGURE 16.1   Montclaude moving from the Uniform Game to the Dynamic Game

over seven million tons of chocolate confectionery across countries and brands.[4] How could any marketer – or any team of human beings – know exactly what to promote, and when, how, and at what price? To make matters worse, the volatility of the pandemic and the behavioral changes it induced in consumers rendered the historical promotional analyses of Montclaude and most CPG companies irrelevant as a basis for future modeling.

Montclaude needed robust streams of data and stronger AI capabilities to gain a deeper understanding of its customers and to develop its targeted recommendations. Fortunately, it already had access to a wealth of data. In addition to legacy third-party syndicated data sources such as Nielsen, IRI, Kantar, and JD Power, companies could also use the proliferation of first-party data they collect by nurturing one-on-one relationships with their customers. Furthermore, multiple platforms are available to mine customers' online footprints and provide increasingly valuable insights from this data. To get to the insights that would allow them to build targeted promotions, Montclaude decided to build a sophisticated AI engine that could recommend flexible promotion strategies that were both bespoke – by brand, retailer, and time – and quickly adaptive to changes in demand signals.

How should Montclaude adjust its pricing model?

Montclaude saw no need to change the elements of its pricing architecture elements – pricing mechanism, unit, and offer structure – as it made the move toward the Dynamic Game. Its primary focus was the transaction incentives: a program of promotions designed and implemented so that Montclaude could respond to small market variations quickly and potentially in real time. Successful "smart" promotions would increase Montclaude's overall sales and drive incremental growth in the category, with minimal impact on margins.

Finding the right number of promotions presented an additional optimization problem. Chocolates are a heavily promoted category, which means every additional promotion brings less and less value in this saturated environment. The saturation also makes it harder for a promotion to stand out and leaves many undifferentiated promotions running in parallel. The other two negative effects are also clear, but they are harder to gauge precisely with conventional analytical approaches. First, when customers see frequent promotions and discounts, they begin to expect lower prices and become more price sensitive. Second, cross-promotion cannibalization limits or eliminates potential revenue and volume gains, as promotions simply end up stealing volume from one another.

It's easy to say that Montclaude needed the right combination of human guidance and AI to solve these problems. But the company found no off-the-shelf AI solutions that would fit its needs, given the complexity and nuances of the market for chocolates. Montclaude decided that it needed to build and scale its own in-house dynamic AI solution to optimize its promotions.

How Montclaude implemented its AI-driven promotion strategy

Montclaude started on the path to success by viewing this strategic change as something much broader than a souped-up version of a "numbers game." It laid out a vision and ambition that looked beyond the number, depth, and frequency of its chocolate promotions.

First, these advanced capabilities might enable Montclaude to build deeper relationships with retailers by growing the category and identifying opportunities for retailers to create more value. This would elevate Montclaude from "one supplier among many" to the role of category captain.

Second, Montclaude felt that its decision to internalize the required competencies would create a sustainable competitive advantage, not only because these capabilities would be harder for competitors to replicate, but also because they felt the new internal tools and processes would be more efficient and effective than any standard solution.

Finally, the new strategy would help redefine how Montclaude measured the success of promotions. By retraining consumers to buy at the right price at the right time rather than anticipating and expecting deals all the time, Montclaude felt it could expand the chocolates category, improve its margins, and see a noticeable reduction of the volume sold on deals.

Montclaude committed to making significant investments to upgrade its analytical capabilities, specifically around data scientists and advanced data analytics tools and platforms to help them make informed, data-driven pricing decisions. The new data science team built the data platforms and collected the large amounts of historical data – sell-outs, promotional events, execution support, financials, and competitive activity – required to train the AI models on how the category has worked.

The Montclaude data science team then built the predictive and prescriptive AI tools, using leading-edge machine learning methods to identify what made previous promotions successful or unsuccessful and use the underlying patterns to predict future outcomes. The predictive model could then generate billions of scenarios and choose the optimal one, subject to refinement by team members, often sales representatives.

As compelling and insightful as these outputs were, the leadership team recognized that success depended on execution. It worked in parallel with the commercial team to refresh its promotion planning and execution processes, on the assumption that 30% of the value from this transformation would come from the tool and the remaining 70% from behavioral changes, as shown in Figure 16.2.

The teams had to overcome two key challenges to make the behavioral changes stick. First, commercial teams would reject any "black box"

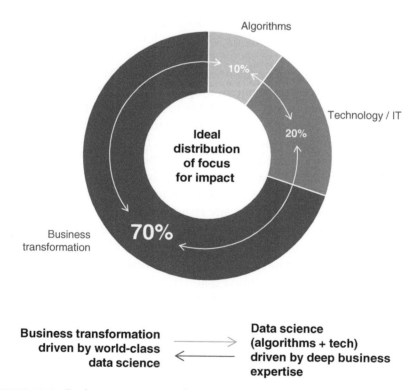

FIGURE 16.2   Business processes need more attention than algorithms and tech

solutions because they didn't understand the rationale. Second, general internal resistance to change would hamper Montclaude's efforts to implement the model's recommendations with retailers.

To address the "black box" concern, Montclaude ensured that all end users of the AI recommendation engine took part in several working sessions and trainings to understand how the technology worked, its limitations, and the data it used. This helped build confidence in the tool and reduce fears about the unknown. Montclaude also encouraged collaboration between the commercial teams and the data scientists to ensure that the end users had channels to provide their feedback on the decisions made by the model.

Montclaude also customized its new operating model to fit each market's business, data, and process realities. Business leads, for example, were responsible for conducting business data validation as part of a redefinition of roles and responsibilities to ensure that everyone stayed aligned and worked effectively toward the desired outcome. Montclaude also recruited new talent to fill gaps in its expertise and developed new KPIs around portfolio performance, including cross-brand KPIs.

These efforts enabled Montclaude to transform its promotions from a somewhat haphazard mechanism to a data-driven calendar that set promotions by SKU, by week, and by retailer, with continuous adjustment and optimization of the tools and processes in real time. Success was almost immediate, and over time the new calendar increased category retail sales by 3–5%, yielded a margin improvement of 300 basis points, and reduced the volume sold on deal by 5%.

Key takeaways

Companies playing in the ostensibly transparent Uniform Game still have significant agency to share value differently and change their game through targeted precision pricing. This moves a company close to the frontier between the Uniform Game and the Dynamic Game. While the environment in the wake of the Covid pandemic provided a strong motivation for Montclaude to act quickly, its success shows that the financial and commercial improvements alone make these transformations worth pursuing.

We recommend the following steps to help with the transition:

- **Look beyond the prices:** The journey to targeted precision pricing begins not with price points, but with an understanding of the current game, the best options for a new game, and the right way to implement the new pricing strategy.

- **Seek a first-mover advantage:** Companies that implement AI-based tools – and their capacity to generate and evaluate billions of scenarios – can create and retain a significant amount of value and sustain it due to a first-mover advantage.

- **Avoid a "black box" implementation:** AI and a sophisticated data infrastructure create only 30% of the value from this transformation. The remaining 70% of impact derives from changing internal behaviors and processes.

CHAPTER 17

Channel: Going Direct to Consumers

With contributions from Andrej Levin and Jacob Konikoff

B usiness leaders in any game often assume that their sales and distribution channels are a fixed, external constraint for every player in the game. This leads them to focus their energies on internally driven levers such as R&D and advertising, and less on optimizing their mix of channels.

But this assumption is flawed. Channel mix is a critical lever available to almost every business and is an important way for companies to increase their agency and shape strategic outcomes.

In broad terms, businesses need to decide whether they will sell directly to customers, use one or more intermediaries, or pursue a hybrid strategy with a mix of direct and indirect business. But this decision has no easy or obvious answer, because of the complex tradeoffs of each option.

Let's look at tradeoffs involved in using intermediaries. Retailers, distributors, resellers, wholesalers, service providers, and all other kinds of channel partners expand the breadth of customers a single company can reach and lower customer acquisition costs. If these intermediaries become true channel partners, they act as strong advocates for the products and services of the partner company and even build their own solutions on top of them.

The downside is that these channel partners maintain the direct relationships with end customers, which means they can collect and analyze a rich set of first-party data. These intermediaries affect – and, in some cases, control – the messaging and positioning of the partner company's offerings and brand and also control the assortment. Pricing is an issue, because the intermediaries negotiate price points, decide on promotions, and create the risk of overpricing the offerings and thus reducing sales because of the double marginalization effect.[1] That effect occurs when the supplier and the intermediary both try to build their own independent margin objectives into the end-customer price instead of jointly sharing the value.

In Chapter 15 we highlighted the benefits of having first-party data, but neither Starbucks nor Montclaude disrupted the fundamental structure of their channel strategies based on the data's availability and value. Starbucks has been selling coffee directly to consumers since its inception, as we described in Chapter 11, and Montclaude still sells its chocolates through intermediaries after transforming its pricing strategy. The advent of e-commerce in the 1990s triggered a massive wave of channel disruption, but in most cases, online sales eventually became just another channel, sitting alongside legacy channels and playing by the rules of the company's original game.

True channel disruption can lead to a new equilibrium in shared value, shifting the disrupting business to a new pricing game. But few companies deliberately use channel mix as a way to motivate and accelerate a move to a new pricing game. The two examples in this chapter – one from the apparel industry and one from the automotive industry –show how decisions of channel mix can reshape a business and an industry.

Companies in the apparel market have traditionally used third-party retailers to reach customers. However, as consumers increasingly focused their attention online and shifted their shopping habits to e-commerce, consumer brands found opportunities to adopt a direct-to-consumer (D2C) model. Earning additional margin by cutting out the middleman may be the most obvious benefit of the model, but the more important benefit is often the ability to analyze data gathered directly from consumers. This gives them the marketing insights to improve personalization. Companies also gain more control of pricing, including promotions. They can keep their prices aligned with their overall strategy instead of accommodating the strategies of retailer partners who may have different strategic objectives.

Nike has successfully shifted away from retailers and toward their own storefronts and online channels. At the 2017 annual shareholder meeting, Nike's CEO Mark Parker described the rationale: "From strengthening member benefits to creating branded retail environments, Nike Direct reflects one of our biggest opportunities. Bringing our brand closer to the consumer drives growth."[2] Nike's strong position in the sports apparel and footwear categories meant that many retailers had no choice but to accept its D2C strategy. For some independent or specialty retailers, Nike accounted for up to 70% of their shoe sales.[3] Any such retailer that stopped carrying Nike would inflict massive damage on themselves, but no meaningful harm to Nike.

From 2011 to 2022, Nike's D2C revenue jumped from $2.8 billion to $18.7 billion. This represented an increase in percentage of total revenue from 16% to 42%.[4] In North America, wholesale sales to third-party retailers grew by 6% from 2021 to 2022, while Nike Direct revenues increased by 25%, fueled by 30% growth in digital sales.[5,6]

The automotive market also has potential for channel disruption. Automotive OEMs have sold their products through dealerships for over 100 years, but this sales channel is often inefficient, especially in terms of customer experience and pricing. As any car buyer can attest, the purchase process at the dealership involves onerous negotiations, which frustrate customers and erode the dealer's margins.

These markets show the hallmarks of the Custom Game. Dealers negotiate prices individually for each transaction, which will have its own composition of discounts applied, including cash bonuses, trade-in bonuses, residual value support, and interest-rate discounts. Price transparency is low for both OEMs and customers, because almost nobody pays the list price and end-consumer discounts can range from 8% to 15% for most vehicle models.[7] Few customers also buy the exact same vehicle, because OEMs offer a wide range of features and options. The Toyota Corolla, one of the best-selling vehicles of all time, offered nine sub-models, two engines, two tire packages, and almost 30 supplementary add-ons in the United States in 2023.[8]

When an OEM sells 500 units of a vehicle, it will likely sell them at 500 different price points within the same market, even for cars with the exact same configuration.

The tradeoff of using intermediaries still makes sense for the OEMs, however, because the dealers play an almost essential role in the maintenance and repair of vehicles. According to a 2020 report from J.D. Power, dealer service centers – staffed by technicians specialized in the OEM's models – captured 88% of customers' annual service visits in the first three years of ownership.[9] Even after five years of ownership, dealers still captured 21% of service customers.

The importance of maintenance and repairs has diminished, however, as electric vehicles (EVs) have claimed a growing share of the market. Research from *Consumer Reports* and the US Department of Energy shows that pure EVs need less maintenance and cost less to repair than the conventional fuel vehicles.[10,11] This is largely because the EV battery, motor, and associated electronics require little to no upkeep, and EVs have far fewer moving parts than a conventional car. Brake pads wear down much slower due to regenerative braking, and EVs also have fewer fluids that require changing.

The diminished role of maintenance and repairs changes the tradeoff balance to such an extent that EV manufacturers may feel they are better off without a dealership network. Why should they tolerate the inefficiencies of dealerships when there is no longer a substantial additional benefit (dedicated and reliable service) to compensate?

In 2012, Tesla was poised to enter the automotive mass market with the launch of the Model S. This was Tesla's new flagship model: a luxury, high-performance sedan, which also happened to be all-electric. Tesla aimed to accelerate the shift to sustainable electric vehicles across the world. To that end, reaching the consumer directly became a key priority.

How Tesla defined a new pricing strategy

How should Tesla create and share value?

Tesla knew it had a revolutionary product with a superior value proposition for a large segment of customers. As a premium brand, it needed a customer experience that matched the high price for its vehicle. In that spirit, Tesla made the groundbreaking decision to avoid the dealer channel completely. It would display all its cars in Tesla-owned locations and sell them directly to customers online. This channel mix bolstered Tesla's premium positioning by allowing the company to provide transparent pricing with no discounting, as well as an unprecedented seamless customer experience. Customers looking to buy a Tesla saw one non-negotiable price, saving them numerous hours of research and haggling. In addition, Tesla offered high-end services such as "Tesla Personal Delivery," which delivered Model S orders directly to a location of the customer's choosing.[12]

BCG benchmarks show that sales operations account for 25–30% of revenues for legacy OEMs, compared to 7–12% for D2C OEMs.[13] By using the more efficient D2C sales channels, Tesla gained around 10–15 percentage points of margin, giving it more room to invest in innovation or share additional value with customers.

What pricing game should Tesla play?

Most automotive OEMs and their associated dealership networks play the Custom Game. But Tesla's desired position and market were not pure fits to the Custom Game's market characteristics. By deciding to offer a far simpler selection of cars with transparent, fixed pricing, Tesla decided instead to play the Choice Game, as shown in Figure 17.1. In 2023, the company produced four models, compared to the 19 models that Toyota produced. In addition, each Tesla model offered few variations, with the Model S offering no submodels, two engine options, two tire package options, and only two add-ons.[14]

The trend toward EVs is growing as consumers become more aware of the environmental impact of gasoline- and diesel-powered vehicles. This trend also spurred more demand for affordable EVs with similar main options. In addition, many car buyers are increasingly looking for a simpler, more streamlined car-buying experience, and are less interested in negotiating with dealerships with no price transparency.[15] Tesla recognized these trends and capitalized on them to build a competitive advantage.

How should Tesla set its pricing model?

Tesla's pricing model focused primarily on pricing architecture, specifically on developing the right offer structure. The first step was creating a structured lineup with offers designed to target different value perceptions. The next step was to set price points that aligned with the value of each offer.

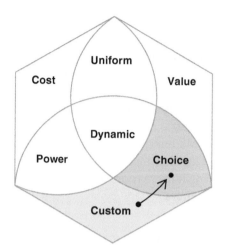

FIGURE 17.1 Tesla moving from the Custom Game to the Choice Game

As we recommended in Chapter 12, Tesla built its lineup by starting at the top end of price and performance. CEO Elon Musk described this approach in a blog post in 2006: "The strategy of Tesla is to enter at the high end of the market, where customers are prepared to pay a premium, and then drive down market as fast as possible to higher unit volume and lower prices with each successive model."[16]

The Tesla Roadster hit the market in 2008, selling for around $100,000. Beyond the high price point, it projected a new image of very high performance and desirability for EVs, anchoring consumers for the rest of the lineup to come. When Tesla unveiled its model Model S in 2009 with a base price of $57,400, comparisons to the Roadster were inevitable in customers' minds, whether conscious or not. The price they were willing to pay for a Model S was influenced by the higher price of the Roadster. The same logic applied later to the Model 3. When Tesla introduced its SUVs, it followed the same pattern. It priced the Model X as the high-end model, anchoring customers who chose the Model Y instead.

When designing its product lineup, Tesla needed to identify key fencing features. In other words, it first needed to identify attributes that drove the choice of a car, such as size, range, and interior finishes. Then it needed to establish levels for these attributes and ensure that models at the top of the lineup had the highest-level features. For example, Tesla's highest-priced car is the Model X, an SUV with seven seats and a range of around 350 miles. The lowest-priced offer is the Model 3, a sedan with five seats and a range of around 270 miles.[17]

Tesla made little use of price adjustments. It offered no customer programs, transaction incentives, or fees or functional discounts. Transaction prices were almost always the same as the list price. Customers never needed to worry about whether they got the best price, because everyone buying at the same time paid the same price.

Tesla managed list price changes centrally to ensure consistent alignment with value and to reflect Tesla's real-time understanding of the market, thanks to its direct relationship with buyers. While the auto industry traditionally used annual list price adjustments, Tesla could change prices much more frequently. In 2023, for example, Tesla changed prices in the United States four times in two months.[18]

How Tesla implemented its D2C strategy

Tesla's implementation of its D2C model, and the associated change in pricing strategy, focused on creating a retail network and building out its e-commerce infrastructure. While it launched the Model S in both in-store and online channels, Tesla has since shifted its channel mix and strategy many times to adapt to the company's growth and maturity.

Tesla's initial goal for its retail network was to reach people before they decided to buy a new car.[19] As a result, Tesla deliberately positioned showrooms in high-foot-traffic, high-visibility venues, such as malls and shopping thoroughfares. This allowed Tesla to interact directly with a large number of potential customers and educate them about Tesla cars and about EVs in general. Showrooms were designed to be interactive, and the staff – which received no commissions from sales – focused on ensuring customer enjoyment and education.

After brand awareness and customer demand became well established, Tesla started shifting from storefronts in high-end retail venues to standalone stores in cheaper locations,[20] similar to traditional dealerships. Tesla could afford to stop meeting customers where they were, because customers had begun to seek out Tesla locations. This shift allowed Tesla to reduce its rent obligations and to create better showcases for its vehicles and technology. It also added more service centers to its network, thus providing better access to maintenance and repair services for its growing customer base.

Tesla also sharpened its focus on e-commerce, which allowed it to reach customers more efficiently and to reduce its operational costs even more. Online sales were initially a necessity, because it was illegal for Tesla to open its own stores in many regions. To get around these dealership laws, Tesla opened "galleries" where it neither took orders nor discussed prices. Instead, employees showed off Tesla cars and told customers to buy them online. By 2019, Tesla was exclusively selling online, a move that Musk said could cut costs by 5–6%.[21]

Tesla's channel disruption proved to be immensely successful. From 2012 to 2022, its revenue exploded from $412 million to $81 billion, making it the top-selling EV brand, with around 65% of the market as of late 2022[22] and deliveries of 1.31 million vehicles in that year.[23]

Tesla resolved the tradeoff of using intermediaries because the advantages of a D2C approach significantly outweighed the benefits of the automotive industry's legacy dealership approach. Tesla also maintains a direct ongoing relationship with its customers, thanks to its frequent updates and its network of charging stations. Such ongoing contact can help an OEM to create a self-reinforcing loop, with customer input and data inspiring personalization that strengthens the relationship.

Whether other OEMs follow Tesla's lead will depend on how this same kind of tradeoff works for them. Most OEMs have announced D2C channels for some regions, mainly Europe, and often for specific parts of their portfolio, such as EVs.[24]

Key takeaways

It is easy to stay in your existing lanes and play by the rules of your current game. Deciding whether to sell through intermediaries, sell directly to customers, or implement a hybrid model starts with the question: "Are we truly serving our customers the way they want to be served?"

The question is sometimes difficult to answer because of the numerous tradeoffs involved. That's why you should continuously examine your channel mix and gauge how well it meets customer needs and delivers a high-quality customer experience. How customers search, select, and purchase products or services is not a given. There are degrees of freedom around channel mix that can, and should, influence your decisions on how to share value and what pricing game to play.

We recommend the following steps to help with the transition, independent of market or industry:

- **Define your own channel tradeoffs:** This depends on how well you understand the drivers of value and knowing whether you or intermediaries are the best match to those drivers of value.

- **Actively control the channel mix to your advantage:** This includes having a pricing architecture customized for the channel mix you have chosen.

- **Manage the costs:** The best channel match for customers may also be too expensive to maintain. The costs are always an important part of the tradeoff equation, and cost savings can open up opportunities to share more value with customers.

CHAPTER 18

Scale: Achieving the Ultimate Cost Advantage

With contributions from Ipshita Bhattacharya and Lionnel Bourgouin

A irlines once enjoyed monopolistic pricing power due to government regulations on fares, routes, and market entry of new airlines. As we explained in Chapter 13, deregulation starting in the late 1970s eventually led to a dynamic pricing methodology known as yield management.

However, some airlines took a radically different approach. Instead of managing yield to optimize prices for each customer, they reimagined costs as a way to drive down prices and pricing as a way to create cost efficiencies. They built their businesses around a tight alignment between prices and costs, the key success factor in the Cost Game. Airlines such as Southwest in the United States, Ryanair in Europe, and AirAsia in Asia focused on improving efficiency to lower costs and prices, accelerate their growth, improve profitability, and generate the funds to invest in innovation or further cost advantages.

Unlike legacy airlines, these low-cost carriers (LCCs) viewed air travel as a commoditized service to move passengers from point A to point B. As a result, they seized an opportunity to expand the market for air travel by capturing consumers who were priced out by legacy carriers. An executive from Southwest once said, "We're not competing with other carriers. We want to pull people out of backyards and automobiles and get them off the bus."[1] Similarly, AirAsia's slogan was "Now everyone can fly," clearly targeting customers previously outpriced by flag carriers.[2]

LCCs' cost-plus pricing was very successful. Southwest, Ryanair, and AirAsia became some of the largest carriers, by passenger volume, in their geographies.[3,4,5] In addition to winning market share, LCCs also consistently turned profits for decades, while many of the legacy players filed for bankruptcy or were forced to consolidate.

The story of LCCs demonstrates the magnitude of success that is possible with a cost-plus pricing model, even in markets with a broad base of small or individual customers, as opposed to the concentrated customer base we described in Chapter 9. This chapter explores a more recent example of successfully adopting the cost-plus model: Amazon Web Services (AWS).

Turning internal efficiencies into a business opportunity

AWS introduced the cost-plus model to the IT infrastructure industry, and experienced rapid growth, scale, and strong profitability as a result. In the early 2000s, Amazon realized it was adding a lot of software engineers without seeing a commensurate increase in the speed of software development. When Andy Jassy, then chief of staff to CEO Jeff Bezos, investigated the issue, he discovered that teams were slow to deliver software because they had to invest time into building database, compute, and storage components, activities that Amazon's leadership called "undifferentiated heavy lifting."[6] Amazon responded by building a set of common infrastructure services that all their teams could access through application programming interfaces (APIs), allowing engineers to spend more time on developing new features. Efficiency improved and development sped up.

Amazon's executive team soon realized that the success of this internal tool could portend something much bigger. They began to wonder whether external teams would also want to build applications without setting up their own infrastructure. Could they adapt this internal tool and turn it into an external offering? Amazon's leaders believed they could. They had the technology. But more importantly, they had a track record of running reliable, scalable, and cost-effective data centers, due to their experience working with low e-commerce margins.

In 2006, Amazon launched its first two AWS products, Simple Storage Service (S3) and Elastic Compute Cloud (EC2), with Andy Jassy at the helm.[7,8] If these basic offerings proved successful, Amazon could then offer a vast range of differentiated and value-add services for its customers.

How Amazon defined a new pricing strategy

IT infrastructure delivered as a service was a very different business from both e-commerce and IT infrastructure sold in boxes. Amazon had to find a new pricing model to fit this new industry. The choices Amazon made demonstrate how anchoring a pricing strategy to the Cost Game can, with the right scale, achieve outcomes that exceed everyone's expectations.

How should AWS create and share value?

Amazon carefully evaluated the existing market for IT infrastructure and identified opportunities to share value and differentiate itself from its competitors.

Back in the early 2000s, companies required significant capital investment and planning to procure and set up the IT infrastructure they needed. The process involved acquiring, installing, and maintaining infrastructure hardware, sold by companies such as Cisco, EMC, and IBM. Companies that could experience surge traffic, or that anticipated strong growth, would have to preemptively acquire excess capacity. Accounting firms, for example, would need enough capacity to support surges in January through April, even though the capacity would sit unused in off-peak months like May. Building or buying too little capacity could be disastrous. Building or buying too much would be wasteful.

Amazon realized that the core of its initial offering, like air travel, could be seen as a commodity. Access to any gigabyte of storage or any megabyte of RAM is the same. When products are interchangeable, price becomes the biggest differentiator. Amazon estimated that it could deliver the lowest overall prices if it changed how value was shared with customers. Instead of forcing customers to predict their peak usage and pay a large sum up front, Amazon would only charge customers for what they needed when they needed it. The peaks of some customers would likely be the troughs of others. This innovative way of sharing value allowed Amazon to compete effectively against established companies, quickly scale, and further reduce costs. In addition, having customer IT workloads and data within AWS would allow Amazon to offer value-add services and expand its profit pool. Thus, AWS would become the obvious choice for new cloud-native applications and workloads.

What pricing game should AWS play?

IT infrastructure providers were playing the Custom Game in the 2000s. They negotiated with each customer individually and discounted the deals down to the price point that would beat competition. Buyers were very fragmented, ranging from the largest corporations in the world to smaller businesses, each with very different needs. On the other hand, sellers were concentrated for each type of IT infrastructure hardware. For example, only a few companies were relevant suppliers of servers, networking equipment, or memory.

Amazon decided to let customers pay only for what they used, aligning price to cost-to-serve. They also intended to share more value with customers than IT infrastructure incumbents, so that they could grow quickly with the cloud business model. Rapid growth would allow them to walk down the scale curve before competitors did and thus be able to offer the lowest prices in the market. In other words, Amazon decided to disrupt the IT infrastructure market by moving upward and leftward in the Hex, toward the Cost Game, as illustrated in Figure 18.1. Amazon was confident in its track record of understanding and managing costs, a requirement for success in the Cost Game. Thus, they built the AWS organization and go-to-market strategies around a cost equation.

How should AWS set its pricing model?

In an interview in 2017, Andy Jassy claimed that "People gave us a lot of credit early on for the pricing model."[9] At launch, AWS focused primarily on developing its pricing architecture. It introduced different pricing bases – aligned with cost drivers – for different types of infrastructure services such as compute and storage.[10,11]

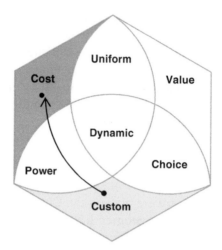

FIGURE 18.1 AWS moved IT infrastructure market toward the Cost Game

Unlike traditional IT infrastructure, AWS allowed customers to avoid the up-front capital expenses associated with purchasing and maintaining their own hardware. Customers could view list prices online and transact with a credit card, departing from the discount-based model of traditional IT infrastructure deals. In addition, AWS allowed customers to easily scale their computing resources up or down as needed, without the need to predict usage or purchase excess capacity. This often meant that AWS was a more cost-effective choice, in the long run, for businesses with fluctuating needs.

Incremental growth was especially high, as AWS expanded the market downward by capturing segments that had previously been underserved. Small developers and startups no longer needed to raise money to afford servers or data centers. Now, they could pay just for the computing power and storage they actually used.

SlideShare, an early AWS customer, acknowledged the reduced need for fundraising with a presentation dubbed, "Using S3 to Avoid VC."[12] The capital and time efficiencies that AWS delivered allowed small developers to become much more competitive with established companies. In 2008, a Silicon Valley entrepreneur and early AWS customer said that "Infrastructure is the big guys' most powerful asset. This levels the field."[13]

Initially, AWS did not make much use of price adjustments like customer programs or transaction incentives. At launch, there was one list price for each service, so every increment of capacity cost the same, regardless of total use. As it grew, AWS introduced value-added products and services beside the core IT infrastructure offering. It also implemented volume discounts and transaction incentives,[14] such as discretionary discounts for larger customers.

The rapid growth of AWS allowed it to build the sustained cost advantage essential to long-term success in the Cost Game. As we discussed in Chapter 9, scale effects mean that production costs fall as production and volume increase, leading to a positive feedback loop, in which lower costs lead to more customers, which lead to lower costs.

How Amazon implemented its cost-driven strategy

Amazon used a range of different approaches to keep costs and prices low. But all their initiatives were underpinned by their comfort with relatively narrow margins. "Commodity businesses don't scare us," Bezos said. "We're experts at them. We've never had 35 or 40 percent margins like most tech companies."[15] Amazon used the tight alignment between pricing and costs to expand AWS's coverage efficiently. Amazon also invested heavily and relentlessly to deliver cost savings, going as far as designing custom silicon for its cloud.[16]

AWS designed its go-to-market model to drive rapid adoption and growth. In the beginning, AWS targeted startups and small businesses that needed affordable and scalable IT infrastructure, to ensure the best match with its value proposition. For example, in 2007, AWS created the AWS Start-Up Challenge. That year, as part of the competition, over 900 new products and services were built using AWS.[17] In addition, AWS launched the AWS Start-Up Tour, which began with 10 North American and European cities. This tour allowed AWS to engage directly with startup founders and leaders and showcase how its products can support their interests and needs.[18]

Amazon used its skills in customer support, gained from its retail business, to "woo" the developer community on to its platform. AWS invested heavily in developer relations to deliver quality support and a positive user experience. Even before any products were launched, AWS had assembled a global team of evangelists to help future users understand how they can develop, deploy, and operate applications on the AWS platform.[19] In addition, Amazon created a variety of developer resources, including a public

Resource Center with AWS code samples and documentation.[20] Amazon also launched developer forums to facilitate discussion and knowledge sharing among users.[21]

Could established tech giants successfully duplicate Amazon's success and overtake AWS? When competitors like Microsoft and Google entered the market, Amazon had less cash and profits than they did, giving them much greater capacity to invest in the cloud. But Amazon had built up two key competitive advantages, which made it difficult for competitors to catch up. First, AWS already had significant scale, which provided a strong customer base, as well as lower per-customer costs. Second, Amazon had investors who were relatively more tolerant of lower margins, which gave them more room for lower prices. Amazon investors were used to the wafer-thin margins of e-commerce, while Microsoft and Google investors were used to the fat margins of software and search-based advertising. These investor expectations may explain why Microsoft and Google took so long to compete directly with AWS, as providing IT infrastructure would lower, rather than bolster, their profit margins.

Amazon's scale and acceptance of low margins allowed it to take regular price cuts. This ensured that AWS remained attractive to customers, by passing through some of the value gained from scale and, later on, technological advancements. Price cuts also helped AWS undercut competitors. For example, when Google slashed prices in the spring of 2014, Amazon immediately responded by pushing prices down further.[22] As of April 2021, AWS had reduced prices 107 times since its launch in 2006.[23] No other industry has shown comparable deflation.[24]

After gaining leadership in the emerging cloud IT infrastructure market, Amazon maintained its position by reinvesting profits into further growth. Over time, Amazon has built on its original AWS products with offerings for analytics, Internet of Things (IoT), and AI.[25] For example, Amazon has aggressively invested in capturing the AI market, through in-house efforts to design custom chips that provide improved capabilities as well as more favorable economics.[26] AWS also released industry- and domain-specific offerings, such as self-driving simulators in the automotive sector or emissions monitoring and surveillance in oil and gas.[27]

AWS became a remarkably profitable business. Besides adding value-added services on top of the Infrastructure-as-a-Service business, relentless cost efficiency passed on to customer prices played a key role. The lower the costs, the lower prices can go while still maintaining a profit margin. In Q1 2015, Amazon reported AWS as a line item for the first time, revealing $265 million in profit on $1.57 billion in sales, which is a 17% net margin.[28]

Almost 20 years after its inception, AWS was still the clear market leader, with 34% of global market share as of Q2 2022. Microsoft's Azure platform is next, with 21%, and Alphabet's Google Cloud trails at 10%.[29]

Key takeaways

Amazon changed the game by migrating the approach to pricing IT infrastructure from the Custom Game to the Cost Game. This pricing model allowed them to quickly gain a strong leadership position, as well as to share a large portion of the value they created with customers. The story of AWS demonstrates how the Cost Game can bring success and profitability if a company is able to achieve a sustainable cost advantage.

We recommend the following steps to help with the transition to the Cost Game:

1. **Identify potential sources of cost leadership advantage:** These include experience and scale, but you need to be able act on them. Your own internal advantages can become commercial opportunities.

2. **Design for scale:** Amazon created a common thread from customer needs to its own cost drivers, meaning that it could scale its offering easily as customer needs changed or customer volume grew quickly.

3. **Use the pricing model to drive efficiencies:** These occur when pricing in your customers' best interests drives your costs down or when charging a large customer for usage makes your utilization rates predictable.

4. **Manage margin expectations:** Margins in a Cost Game business with a cost-leadership strategy tend to be modest or low. The company should manage expectations accordingly.

CHAPTER 19

Free: Competing with the Most Magical Price Point

With contributions from Joel Weitzman, John Pineda, and Matthew Kropp

W ell-established players in any pricing game tend to disregard the low end of their markets. When competitors enter the market with "good enough" offerings at low prices, those incumbents will usually concede those seemingly unattractive, low-margin segments to them.

But these new entrants can become serious threats if they build strongholds in those segments and start to move upward in the market. In April 1990, Aldi, the German "hard discounter," opened its first store in the United Kingdom. Hard discounters have a heavy focus on private-label products and operate "minimally decorated outlets which sell a small assortment of foodstuffs and household goods – typically 1,000 to 1,500 SKUs."[1] This simpler operating model allowed Aldi to offer significantly lower prices than the British supermarket giants, whose 7% profit margins at the time were the world's highest.[2]

By 2022, Aldi had become the UK's fourth-largest supermarket chain, shaking up the "big four" lineup, which had remained roughly the same for nearly 20 years. That same year, Aldi and Lidl, another hard discounter based in Germany, combined to attract £1 of every £6 spent on groceries in UK.[3]

The difference between low price and no price

The American software company Intuit became an established leader in accounting and tax preparation solutions by implementing a pricing strategy built around sharing a significant amount of value with customers. Intuit's low prices relative to more advanced but also more expensive solutions opened up the low end of the market: small home-based businesses and mid-market firms with up to 500 employees. Its QuickBooks lineup – differentiated by its ease of use – became the most recommended product for small businesses by helping them keep their financial records organized, make informed business decisions, and comply with tax laws.

Then Microsoft came along.

In 2005, the software giant launched a product that would compete against the QuickBooks line. The next year, Microsoft introduced an entry-level version called Office Accounting Express at a price point that seemed impossible for anyone to ignore: "free."

Research has shown that a buyer's emotional responses to "free" can overwhelm rational decision making. Dan Ariely highlights this in his book *Predictably Irrational*.[4] In one experiment, people were offered a Lindt truffle for 15¢ or a Hershey's Kiss for 1¢. Some 73% of participants chose the truffle, while 27% chose a Kiss. But when the prices of both chocolates were dropped by 1¢ – to 14¢ and 0¢ respectively – suddenly 69% of participants opted for the free Kiss, even though the relative price gap between the two candies stayed the same.

For Intuit, conventional pricing wisdom suggested that it should not overreact by matching free with free. The volume Intuit would gain from its own free offering would not offset the loss in revenue and the margin declines.[5] In other words, gaining share in the lowest end of the market was not worth the price cut it would take to play there. The optimal, profit-maximizing price point for Intuit should therefore be much higher than the corresponding price point for Microsoft.

But Intuit could not ignore the threat. Doing nothing was a clearly risky strategy.

How Intuit defined a new pricing strategy

Intuit was already keenly aware of the potential threat Microsoft could pose. In the late 1990s, Microsoft launched an offering called Money to compete against Quicken, Intuit's first flagship product, and had gained a significant market share. When Microsoft introduced Office Accounting Express, Intuit realized it needed to reevaluate its offer lineup and pricing strategy to stay competitive.

How did Intuit create and share value?

Few small business owners eagerly look forward to managing their business finances, because the ever-increasing complexities of business accounting are intimidating. But this task is necessary to run a successful business, and serious legal implications can arise from noncompliance and improper record-keeping.

Intuit's QuickBooks' value proposition relied on its strong reputation for ease of use, a reflection of its motto D4D, which stands for Design for Delight. That philosophy traces its roots back to founder Scott Cook, who had learned about customer-centric product design while working at Procter & Gamble early in his career.[6] Intuit also developed a lineup of different products to cater to specific segments, because it recognized that businesses of different sizes have different accounting and financial management needs.

What pricing game did Intuit play?

From a differentiation standpoint, Intuit was clearly playing the Value Game in the mid-2000s. Prior to the entry of Microsoft, QuickBooks' primary competitors were complex accounting software solutions such as Peachtree Accounting and MYOB Accounting. But QuickBooks' feature set and user-friendly interface gave it a superior value proposition and made the QuickBooks lineup the clear market leader.

You may recall that the market characteristics of the Value Game have a lot of similarities with the characteristics of the adjacent Choice Game. The main difference is in the uniqueness or superiority of the offer (Value Game) compared to the intensity of the competition (Choice Game).

When Microsoft entered the market in 2005 with Office Small Business Accounting – the paid offer that preceded Office Accounting Express – it increased competitive intensity significantly, because the package's features matched a lot of QuickBooks' capabilities, and it came integrated with Microsoft's ubiquitous Office Suite. Competitive intensity also increased indirectly, because Microsoft had the financial means to invest as much as needed to compete with QuickBooks.

From the standpoint of market characteristics, Microsoft's entry pulled Intuit down from the Value Game into the Choice Game. Intuit was mostly there already from a pricing approach. QuickBooks catered to a diverse customer base with varying needs and budgets, and Intuit had a well-structured lineup of versions. Intuit also offered additional services to small businesses, such as payments, payroll, websites, and e-commerce. This broad set of choices enabled customers to start from any product or service and move to the others depending on their needs. It also left Intuit well prepared to make the transition from the Value Game to the Choice Game, as shown in Figure 19.1.

How did Intuit adjust its pricing model?

Brad Smith, the leader of Intuit's small business unit, opted to defy conventional wisdom and look beyond profit-maximizing price points.[7] He understood that Microsoft represented a serious strategic threat. When he met with his team the week after Microsoft announced its free product,

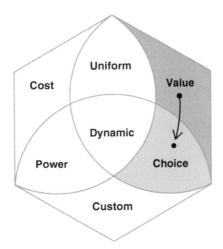

FIGURE 19.1   Intuit needed to move from Value Game to Choice Game

he reframed the "How do we respond?" question by posing his own game-changing question: "Who are the potential customers that Microsoft is most likely to convert, and how do we convince them we have a better value proposition?"

Brad's reframing of the question was powerful for two reasons:

1. **He didn't oversimplify the motivating power of "free":** Instead of assuming that "free" is by default a compelling offer, he urged his team to dig deeper and consider all the factors that drive a customer to choose an accounting solution. For a successful restaurant owner, for example, is it worth it to learn new accounting software, ask their accountant to change as well, and go through the pain of transferring, say, 10 years of data, just to save $200? Of course not. Brad's team concluded that neither Intuit's flagship QuickBooks Pro nor its advanced products such as QuickBooks Premier would lose any meaningful volume to Microsoft's free software.

2. **He freed up his team to think strategically:** By mentioning that he was ready to go free, Brad gave his team the degrees of freedom they needed to come up with solutions that might have a negative short-term impact on profit but would be in Intuit's long-term strategic interests. If some customers received so little value that they would find a free offer compelling, maybe Intuit should not charge those customers anything in the short term. Maybe they should bring those customers into their ecosystem of offerings, with the goal of creating value over time and then taking a share of that value at a later stage.

It turns out that the segment most easily swayed by a free offer for accounting software is people starting a new business. In the mid-2000s, Americans were filing over 2.5 million new business applications per year, and that number would surge to over 5.5 million per year by 2021.[8,9] Whether based in a garage, a storefront, a workshop, or a bedroom, such new businesses all have one thing in common: money is tight. Their main concern is creating a functioning business, and they rarely want to bother with accounting. In that context, a free offer makes sense. Without a free accounting package, these entrepreneurs would revert to pen and paper or an Excel spreadsheet to track their dollars and cents. Between the lack of funds and the long odds for success, they rightly perceive the value of accounting software as close to zero.

Intuit therefore decided to convert the small-volume product Simple Start into a free offer, effectively launching its own freemium model.

Matching Microsoft by reducing the price of Simple Start from $99 to free would reduce revenue in the short term, but Intuit could recover some of that revenue in the long run for two reasons. First, the new free offering would attract customers who may otherwise be priced out. Second, a sufficiently high conversion rate to paid offerings would reduce acquisition costs and could compensate for the short-term revenue loss.

This strategic pricing move was particularly powerful because Intuit had designed Simple Start specifically for a segment they had called "New to the world": startups and early-stage businesses. The product had a built-in onboarding process that guided new users and gave them confidence that they were doing things right. The name reinforced that value proposition. Simple Start also reflected the "Delight not dilute" philosophy for product development at Intuit, a corollary to its D4D motto. The product was not a stripped-down, bare-bones version of a more advanced product but rather a product designed organically to fit its target segment.[10]

How Intuit implemented its freemium strategy

The first year that Simple Start was offered for free, Intuit clarified its good-better-best lineup for QuickBooks. The highest-end offer was Premier at $449.95, and the mid-tier offer was Pro at $199.95.[11] In addition, Intuit also had volume progressions with Premier (three users at $1,199.95), Pro (three users at $549.95), and a five-seat offer called QuickBooks Enterprise Solutions which started at $3,000.

The primary fencing features between Simple Start and the paid versions were based on functionality, including inventory, accounts payable, budgets, and multiuser capability. Premier was fenced from Pro with industry-specific features, including different default settings, reports, and help screens. For example, QuickBooks Premier Accountant Edition allows accountants to toggle between other versions, enabling them to support clients in any industry.

Intuit did not stop at just making Simple Start free. They made Simple Start a gateway into the broader QuickBooks ecosystem by making it easy to upgrade to more advanced paid versions of QuickBooks and to contract with Intuit for additional small business services such as payroll or a website.

They also invested heavily in their high-end offers, to ensure that they were delivering sufficient value to their highest-margin customers.

In 2008, QuickBooks Accounting Pro Edition 2009 won *PC Magazine*'s Editor's Choice Award for the fifth consecutive time. The judges said that Intuit's offering had "more enhancements" and "more features than rivals Microsoft Accounting Professional 2008, MYOB Premier Accounting 2008, or Peachtree by Sage Complete Accounting 2009" and concluded that it was ". . . superior to all of those competitors."[12]

Intuit escaped the threat from Microsoft by looking beyond price points for ways to compete with a low-priced offer designed for customers for whom price mattered most. Had the Intuit team believed in the inevitability of market forces, the company might have become yet another name on that long list of once-successful companies that lost to a competitor. Instead, Intuit shifted to a new game by taking several steps to ensure a successful "freemium" implementation.

Embracing free beyond a competitive response

Companies playing the Choice Game should not only consider freemium as a competitive response in the low end of the market. Free is a valid price point with multiple advantages. It can help a company acquire users that would be otherwise left unserved, such as startups. It can also help a company acquire customers inexpensively by lowering the hurdles to trial and adoption, with the intent that many of these will eventually convert to paying customers.

The products from Atlassian – a collaboration software company with popular applications like Jira, Trello, and Confluence – always have a free option, which is usually limited to 10 users.[13] But beyond that, the free version has few limits on its functionality. Small teams can use the full tool such as Jira or Confluence for free for as long as they want, which means they are effectively adopting the tool instead of simply trying it out. The switching costs for Atlassian's products are high, however, because they are used in core workflows and quickly become embedded in the way teams operate. When a customer outgrows the free version, they are very likely to become paying customers.

One risk of the freemium model is to put so much value in the free offer that upselling and expansion becomes very difficult. Evernote, the note-taking software company, had a 3.75% conversion rate of registered users to paid customers in 2009.[14] Then in 2016, Evernote reduced the features of the free tier and raised prices of their paid tiers by around 40%.[15] Customers responded with anger, but a year later, Evernote announced that it had more than doubled the number of subscribers over the previous two years, and premium subscribers were at an all-time high.[16]

Avoiding such risk was Intuit's message behind the product design strategy of "Delight not dilute." Thinking along one dimension – more features or fewer – is a flawed design shortcut, because it leads you to believe there is an optimal number of features to include in the free option. The better approach is to focus on characterizing the customers who can only afford a free option. Who are they? What do they need? How do they use the current product?

A similar set of questions applies to the customers who derive value from the product and can afford to pay. What are the needs, and therefore the features, that this paid group requires but the "free" group does not? This guiding principle – focusing on the "who" more than the "what" – applies to the design of any lineup in the Choice Game.

Free is also often an essential component of two-sided business models, under which the users of the free product or service are not the direct customers. The company instead earns its money by selling the attention or data of the users to a third party. Radio stations and alternative newspapers have used that model successfully for decades, and social media companies such as Meta and Snapchat have also built successful businesses using that model.

Companies such as YouTube and Spotify use a hybrid business model by offering ad-supported free tiers and paid tiers free of ads. This gives them two distinct sets of paying customers – users and third parties – and increases their opportunities for revenue expansion.

Key takeaways

By reframing the problem and encouraging its team to focus on customer segments and needs rather than features, Intuit showed how a company can shape a market with pricing strategy rather than blindly following market forces.

The Intuit team triangulated a new pricing strategy that brought competitive price dynamics, Intuit's own short-term and long-term economics, and the needs of discrete customer segments into harmony. Three years after Intuit's response, Microsoft admitted it no longer had a strong enough offering or strategy to compete in the market for small-business accounting software. It announced its withdrawal from the market in October 2009.[17] Today, Intuit remains the leader in the accounting software market.

But free offerings can do more than fend off low-price "good-enough" competitors. We recommend the following steps to making free an important driver of success in the Choice Game:

- **Focus on customers and their needs, not features and functionality:** The low ends of markets usually have customers who are unserved or underserved by incumbents. Rather than offering them bare-bones versions of existing products, you should design offerings specifically for the needs of the most attractive segments in the low end. A company's long-term interests in the Choice Game are best served when it aligns its offerings with the value it creates for customers.

- **Use freemium as a gateway:** If some customers receive little value, consider a freemium model, so that customers can migrate to paid offers when their needs evolve, and they derive more value.

- **Take a long-term perspective:** Free becomes a long-term revenue generator when it succeeds as a short-term lead generator. But conversion to paid is not a given. The challenge for companies is to convert these leads by incentivizing customers to upgrade, and the behavioral science approaches we described in Chapter 12 can support this effort.

Before you move on to Part IV . . .

Our objective with Part III was to help you imagine what it takes to change your game and adapt your pricing model. Such a change takes time and requires a clear vision and persistence from business leaders in order to overcome organizational challenges and market obstacles.

Three Questions Shaping Your Pricing Strategy

Question 1: How do you create and share value?

1a. What do you do to create **measurable value** for your customers?

1b. What are your main **drivers of value** and the **limitations** to value creation?

1c. How do your **differentiation and growth objectives** justify how you share value with your customers?

Question 2: What pricing game do you want to play?

2a. Which game aligns best with the characteristics of your market?

2b. Which game aligns best with your current pricing approach?

2c. Which game aligns best with the market forces and your competitive advantages?

Question 3: What pricing model best fits your value creation strategy?

3a. What should your **pricing architecture** be (i.e., pricing basis, offer structure, and pricing mechanism)?

3b. What should drive your **price variation** (e.g., geography, channel, and time)?

3c. What price **adjustment** levers should you use (i.e., customer programs, transaction incentives, and fees and functional discounts)

At the end of Part III, we asked you to answer **all three** of our pricing strategy questions.

Please remind yourself of your answer to **Question 1** about your value creation strategy and **Question 2** about the game(s) you want to play in.

We would like you to review your answer to **Question 3** in light of what you have read in Part III. Do you still want to implement the same change in your pricing model? Did ideas for pricing model changes come to your mind? What barriers will you need to overcome in order to implement these changes?

Please write down your answer along with a brief rationale for your choice.

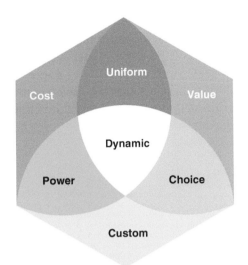

PART IV

Shaping Society Through Pricing Decisions

Whether they are business leaders or consumers, people are more accustomed to thinking about pricing in narrow terms: uniform prices, costs and value, and the power of the free market. They are less used to thinking about prices as a range of possibilities to accomplish a bigger objective.

In Part III we explored a wider range of strategic options that can benefit both businesses and their customers. Moving toward the right and bottom part of the Hex – toward the Value, Choice, or Custom Game – can open new opportunities to create and share value.

Now in Part IV we push those boundaries even further by exploring how strategic pricing can have a positive impact on many pressing social issues. These include how to make health care and education more accessible and how to accelerate efforts to mitigate the effects of climate change. We also cover deceptively simple questions such as, What is a fair price? or What is a fair way to share value between buyer and seller?

Few people think of strategic pricing as part of the solution to any of these problems. But each of the major issues we discuss in Part IV have core challenges that match up very well with one or more of the seven pricing games. Exploring these options can lead to solutions that can benefit society without diminishing or threatening the interests of buyers and sellers in a market.

CHAPTER 20

Fairness: How to Differentiate Prices Across Customers

With contributions from Ricard Vila

The human sense of fairness is so ingrained that we share those kinds of emotional responses with other primates. In his famous TED Talk, Dutch primatologist Frans de Waal shows a video of capuchin monkeys who are very content to receive pieces of cucumber as rewards when they bring a stone to a supervising researcher. That peace lasts until one monkey notices that her partner just earned a grape for the same task.[1]

The grape is a higher price, because to capuchins, like most humans, a grape full of sugar tastes much better than a slice of cucumber. To understand this difference, the "underpaid" capuchin brings the researcher a different type of stone. When she receives cucumber again, she angrily throws it back at the researcher, rattles the cage, and tries to make her discontent as clear as possible.

The cucumber slice is no longer a fair price. What's more, when offered a now inferior reward, the capuchin prefers to receive no reward at all. Paradoxically, getting no value is better than getting an unfair amount of value.

What applies to capuchin monkeys also applies in our vastly more complex $100-trillion global economy. Monetary transactions are essential for the smooth functioning of society, because they allow strangers to cooperate across different scenarios and vast distances. Conflict is unlikely to arise and collaboration is likely to continue, as long as all parties feel good about the exchanges. Because prices quantify value sharing, parties on both sides of the transaction use them to assess whether an exchange is fair. Thus, fair prices are essential to smooth and peaceful economic cooperation.

But what is a fair price?

A fair price is . . . ?

Answering that question is as complicated as it is important, so we will need to explore several potential definitions in depth. We start with the three types of fairness that psychologists have identified:[2]

1. **Outcome-based:** Fairness of outcomes focuses on end states that ensure that everyone achieves the same result, such as Google's pay-per-click pricing basis

2. **Needs-based:** Achieving fairness of needs calls for treating people differently, based on their individual needs. Unequal outcomes may be considered fair if they align with those discrete needs, as is the case with financial aid for college access

3. **Process-based:** Fairness of process focuses on how an end state is achieved. Unequal outcomes can nonetheless be perceived as fair if the process to achieve those outcomes is perceived to be fair. This perspective is important when the fairness of outcomes is difficult to assess. Free markets are often seen as a fair way to set prices in this context

Each of these perspectives will play a role as we attempt to define a fair price, and as we demonstrate that perceptions of pricing fairness are ultimately linked to how value is created and shared between buyers and sellers.

. . . a price accepted by both parties?

In *The Price Is Wrong*, a book devoted to pricing fairness, Sarah Maxwell starts with the personal perspective of the parties in a transaction. From their standpoint, a fair price is one that is low enough for the buyer and high enough for the seller. This definition assumes that the negotiation process was free and that neither party was under duress.[3]

But even with these assumptions, an acceptable price that is considered fair one day may seem unfair the next day, if new information arises. Feelings of unfairness can arise quickly when a buyer learns that their neighbor bought the same product from the same seller at a much lower price.

Amazon once faced massive backlash when reports revealed that they conducted random price tests that charged customers different prices for the same product. Amazon was forced to apologize publicly and refunded customers the difference between their purchase price and the lowest tested price.[4] In survey after survey, consumers show a strong aversion to paying different prices – and especially higher ones – for the exact same good.[5] In one survey, 76% of respondents agreed with the statement "It would bother me to learn that other people pay less than I do for the same products."[6] Some 87% disagreed with the statement that "It's okay if an online store I use charges people different prices for the same products during the same hour."[7]

A buyer and seller may have agreed to transact at a price that is acceptable to each of them, but new information and new comparisons can quickly flip the perception of that price from fair to unfair. A price accepted by both parties is therefore an insufficient definition of a fair price.

. . . a price that is the same for everyone?

Uniform pricing seems like an easy and logical alternative. That definition of a fair price reflects fairness of outcomes and addresses the key flaw of the previous definition, namely, that comparisons can create a perception of unfairness.

But this definition has its own flaw. In many real-world scenarios, people perceive different prices offered to different customers as fair. The BCG Henderson Institute (BHI) conducted an extensive global survey on fair pricing (see the Appendix, "About the Studies" for more details) that confirmed many such scenarios. Some 75% of respondents perceive discounts for seniors, students, or low-income customers to be fair, but such support is rarely universal. Japanese and French respondents, for example, don't think gasoline discounts for seniors are fair. Americans support gasoline discounts for seniors but feel that hotel discounts for low-income people are not fair.

Maxwell explains that social norms drive these perceptions, and we agree that they play a role. The French show less support for senior discounts than Americans do, because France has a relatively generous publicly funded universal retirement system, while US seniors rely on their individual retirement savings. In contrast, the French generally support discounts for students, while Americans are much less generous toward students than they are toward seniors.

Individual circumstances – especially self-interest – also drive how people accept price variation. In the United States, the perceived fairness of senior discounts increases with age, while the perceived fairness of student discounts decreases with age, as shown in Figure 20.1. The perceived fairness of discounts for low-income earners decreases as a person's income increases, although this decrease is much sharper for people who claim to be conservatives than for self-professed liberals.

These social norms follow some historical patterns of economic development. When rating fairness of a scale from 0 to 100, with 100 being the fairest, respondents from the United States, Japan, France, and Germany find the same kinds of price differentiation to be less fair than respondents from lower-income countries such as India, China, or Brazil. The difference of almost 15 percentage points may result from the greater prevalence of uniform pricing in developed countries. India, where haggling is still widespread, had the highest average fairness ratings for price variations.[8] Germany, where uniform pricing has been the norm for over 100 years, showed the lowest average fairness rating for price discrimination.[9]

While some may think that a uniform pricing model is fair – at least in theory – the types of price variations that people support show few discernible universal patterns. The table in Figure 20.2 shows the average fairness rating (scaled from 0 to 100) for six product categories by discount basis and country. Norms and social context may explain some of this variation.

One general trend is that people show less support for price discrimination for physical products (e.g., gasoline and consumer electronics) than for services such as hotels, movies, grocery retailing, or banking. This may be because customers personally consume services on premise, while discounts for physical products are prone to resale on secondary markets or to exploitation. If seniors receive large discounts on consumer electronics, for example, younger consumers could send them to the store to buy TVs for them. That does not seem like a good behavior to incentivize.

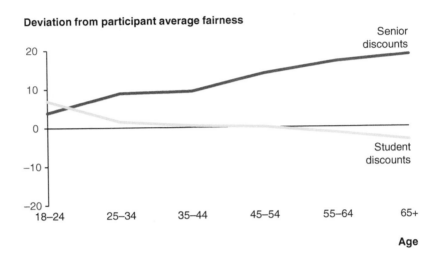

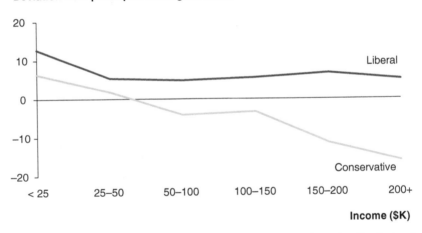

FIGURE 20.1 US survey respondents showed higher support for price discrimination that benefits themselves

Not only is uniform pricing an inadequate definition of fair pricing, it also poses a more fundamental problem. From the perspective of economic utility, uniform pricing exacerbates existing inequalities.[10] Money, like most things, is subject to diminishing marginal utility, which means that each additional unit gained provides an ever-smaller increase in

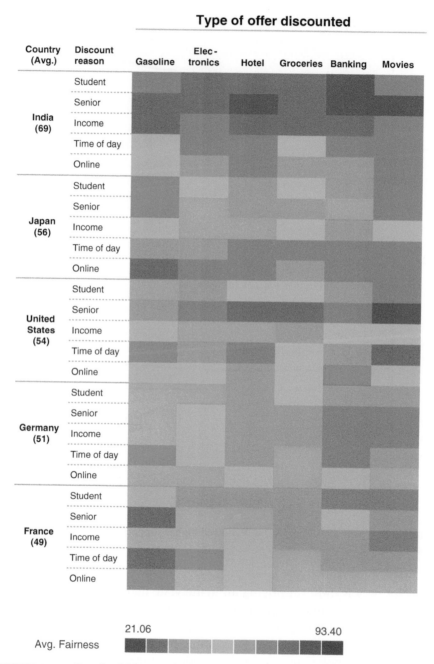

FIGURE 20.2   Perceived fairness of price discounting by country, product category, and rationale

subjective value. Practically speaking, uniform pricing benefits those with the most money, who lose less utility parting with a given amount than people with less money do. In other words, uniform pricing costs everyone the same dollar amount, but wealthier people sacrifice less utility than poorer people.

. . . a price set by the free market?

To overcome the issues raised in the first two definitions, many economists will define a fair price as the market price. This definition reflects fairness of process. Juan Elegido, a professor of business ethics at the Lagos Business School of the Pan-Atlantic University in Nigeria, asserts that a just or fair price is one set by a market that he defines not as a competitive market, but rather one devoid of a legal or natural monopoly.[11] In his view, when there are enough buyers to sustain a particular business at a particular price, the prevailing market price is a fair one.

This definition is intuitively appealing and has centuries of support, from the neoclassical economic thinking of the mid-twentieth century all the way back to the moral thinking of Aristotle.[12] In his book *Price Theory*, first published in 1962, Milton Friedman wrote that "[i]n a free market, the point of intersection of the supply and demand schedules . . . is of particular significance. At this particular price, and only at this price, will the desires of demanders and suppliers be simultaneously satisfied."[13]

The fairness of process inherent in the law of supply and demand continues to permeate economic thinking. At an OECD Roundtable in 2016 on the topic of price discrimination, one paper emphasized the social value of letting the free market set prices: "In a free market economy, price serves critical allocative functions. Price adjusts to balance supply and demand, and high prices often serve to attract investment to markets where it would create the greatest consumer benefit."[14]

In short, prices are fair when all parties let the open or free markets do their job. Ron Baker, a pricing specialist and founder of VeraSage Institute, put it this way: "The problem with a 'just' price is who gets to decide what is just? The free market already provides an answer to this question – whatever someone is willing to pay."[15]

If supply and demand in free markets are in relatively stable equilibrium, we could expect those markets to yield uniform prices. Yet we have already shown price uniformity to be an insufficient definition of fair prices. When open markets do not yield uniform prices, they can create more unfairness. Regressive pricing, for example, is uncommon, but does occur in open or free markets, including:

1. Higher prices for minority and female car buyers[16,17]
2. Higher food prices for poor people[18]
3. Higher risk-adjusted insurance rates for poor and middle-income drivers[19]
4. Higher drug prices for poor patients, even among the uninsured[20]

The definition suggested by Elegido thus faces two problems. It naturally favors uniform pricing and fails to condemn regressive pricing.

A free market, in theory, is efficient at setting prices by incorporating all available and relevant information. The market, in effect, acts as an enormous information processor that can save a business – especially a smaller one with limited resources – from doing that research and analysis work, assuming the market price is transparent or accessible with minimal effort.

But Sally Blount, a professor of strategy at the Kellogg School of Management and a former colleague at BCG, shows that an efficient market is not necessarily a fair one. Analyzing various market mechanisms, she concludes that while markets have some fair processes, their outcomes are not necessarily fair.[21] According to her logic, fairness for most people is a function of how buyers and sellers split the economic pie. There is no guarantee that market prices result in a fair sharing of value, as we have defined in this book.

Social norms also impose constraints on how fair people perceive market prices to be. Maxwell writes: "a socially fair price is one that . . . does not give [the] seller unreasonably high profits and does not take advantage of demand."[22] Of course, when a market faces a supply shock, there is a social understanding that prices will rise. If the increase is not too dramatic, people will accept it because it incentivizes suppliers to spend more and do what is necessary to bring more supply to the market. But if a natural disaster such as an earthquake caused the supply shock, people will consider a significant price increase to be unfair, because they perceive the seller to be benefiting from a random event rather than from a deserving action.

In our quest for pricing fairness, it seems we have come full circle, but have learned a lot on the journey. We started with an acceptable price for both buyers and sellers, then discovered we needed to compare outcomes and process between sellers, and then finally came back to consider the seller outcome in relation to the buyer outcome. If a large price increase for the buyer results in "too much" profit for the seller, the buyer perceives the price as unfair. Since the beginning of this book, we have asserted a view that is consistent with the perspective of Blount, Maxwell, and many others: pricing is the way to share value between buyers and sellers. How should we think about sharing that value in an equitable way? This is the definition of a fair price that we explore next.

. . . a price that shares value equitably between parties?

We defined the value created by an offering – from the customer's perspective – as the sum of its substitute value and its net usage value. From a seller's perspective, the value they retain is the difference between the price paid by the customer and the variable costs linked to that transaction.

All of our fairness research has confirmed that respondents find cost variations to be a good rationale for price variations, because that rationale depends the least on other circumstances. Therefore, we consider the best way to define the transaction value that buyers and sellers can share as the difference between customer value and variable costs. The position of the price within that range defines how the two parties will share that value. The buyer earns the surplus, which is the difference between customer value and the price. The seller earns a gross profit, the difference between the price and the variable cost, as Figure 20.3 shows.

This creates an opportunity for our last definition of a fair price: the price that shares value equally across buyers and equitably between buyer and sellers. We come back to what equitable means later. Let's focus first on the equal sharing across buyers. There are two ways to accomplish this:

1. Change the price for each customer to ensure that all customers receive a similar share of value in surplus.
2. Choose a pricing basis that sets the price at a fixed proportion of the value created for each customer.

Figure 20.4 illustrates these two perspectives for an even split of the value, that is, 50% for the seller and 50% for the buyer. Pricing based on

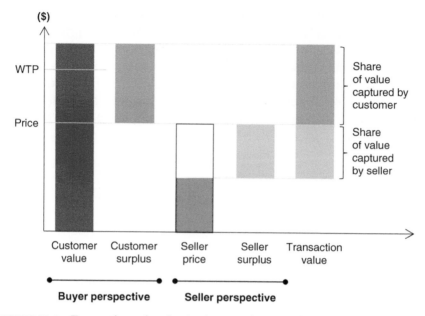

FIGURE 20.3 Transaction value sharing between buyer and seller

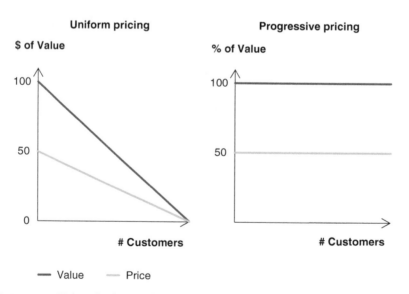

FIGURE 20.4 Value-sharing pricing is a form of uniform pricing, with the percentage of value as the pricing basis

value sharing is a form of uniform pricing when we look at the percentage of value shared instead of the absolute level of the surplus. In that case, the perception of price discrimination disappears, and both parties can see the fairness of outcomes that value sharing creates.

This definition of a fair price solves many of the issues of the other definitions. Unlike the acceptable price, the value-sharing price means that only true peers will be charged the same price. A seller can charge a higher price to a customer who derives much higher value, without perceived unfairness, as long as the seller communicates the clear rationale. The value-sharing price also improves on the uniform price, because it recognizes that the same price for everyone is not necessarily fair. It accounts for differences in utility and also avoids regressive pricing, because the price declines as a function of value all the way to zero.

One prerequisite is that the buyer and seller need to estimate and agree on value. We have seen that this is neither easy nor always possible. But the increase in availability of customer data and computing power – as we discussed in Part III – means that some companies in some markets can implement such a solution. Prime examples include XaaS models based on usage as well as B2B companies that are either playing the Value Game or can use outcomes as their pricing basis, as some industrial suppliers have.

Progressive pricing as practical application for low-marginal-cost offers

Figure 20.5 visually represents uniform pricing, as we first introduced in Chapter 2. It shows the outcomes of offering the same price to all customers, and thus highlights some of the issues we have mentioned. From a fairness perspective, the surplus is distributed very unevenly between customers, as the two triangular shapes show. It is also interesting to note that the last customer to buy on the right is economically indifferent, because they do not derive any surplus value. At that point, the capuchin monkey would be wondering whether the piece of cucumber is worth the effort of offering a stone to the researcher.

There is a subtle difference, however, between the graph in Figure 20.5 and the one we showed in Chapter 2 as Figure 2.2. We have reduced the

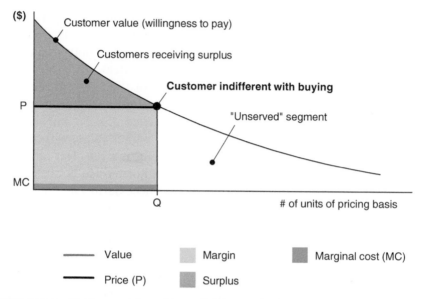

FIGURE 20.5 Uniform pricing with negligible marginal costs

marginal cost to a fraction of what it used to be. This is the situation for digital products and services such as software, music, news, games, data services or AI. There are hardly any marginal costs to produce and distribute digital goods to an incremental customer. In such a situation, any fixed price excludes all customers who derive a lower value than that price. This underserved segment on the right of Figure 20.5 represents a missed revenue opportunity for the seller and a significant reduction of the population that could get access to the product or service.

Trying to solve that access problem within a uniform pricing model has the unfortunate consequence of bringing the price to zero or close to it, thereby shrinking revenues to the point that it becomes impossible to cover the fixed costs of the business. Price adjusters usually cannot cover the price variation if the price is higher, because in practice, even discounts varying from 0% to 90% can only cover a price variation of a factor of 10, and the value differentials in many digital markets are even greater than that.

The most effective lever is usually to change the pricing basis to one that is completely proportional to value. By necessity, companies that serve these markets must therefore adopt a different pricing model, as we have seen in the Choice Game, Value Game, or even the Custom Game and Dynamic Game.

Figure 20.6 represents a new distribution of value. If the company sets the price proportional to the value and the marginal cost is considered negligible, then every customer – every unit on the x-axis – gets the same proportion of value. This is fair from the perspective of value sharing, even though it may at first seem unfair from a price perspective. We call this a **progressive pricing model,** because what customers pay always progresses proportionally to the value they get.[23]

Such a model makes sense when marginal costs are negligible and there is a wide variation in willingness to pay. The seller can serve the largest potential population and generate a revenue stream that covers fixed costs and allows the company to invest in more innovations. The wider the perceptions of value are – and thus the greater the variance in willingness to pay – the greater the incentive sellers have to vary their prices. Implementing progressive pricing as an advanced form of personalized pricing can be desirable and feasible on a large scale, if the company has comprehensive, reliable, real-time customer data. The more accurate and timely insights a company has into how each customer perceives value, the better they can fine-tune prices at the personal level.

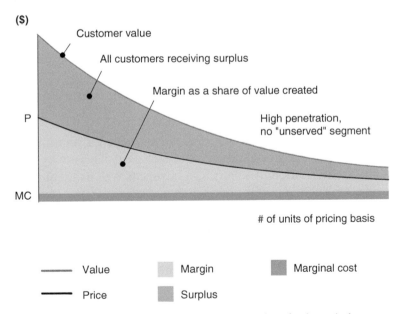

FIGURE 20.6 Progressive pricing – implementing a value-sharing mindset

Implementing a progressive pricing model requires compelling communication about why the model is fair. That can take time, but the result is a value sharing graph that looks like the right side of Figure 20.4. In Chapter 22, we show that this kind of model can improve access to drugs such as the ones that cure Hepatitis C.

Key takeaways

While there are no standard answers to the question of "What is a fair price?," business leaders can embrace market transparency, understand what drives the perceptions of fairness in their market, and ensure that they offer prices that customers will perceive as fair. With the right understanding and the right approach, they can practice price differentiation in ways that mutually benefit themselves and their customers, if not society as well.

- Price differentiation is a strong and significant pricing lever that business leaders should use more confidently. They have a lot of latitude in most societies to vary prices in ways that the majority of customers will perceive as fair.
- Price differentiation should be accompanied by strong and explicit justifications.
- A progressive pricing model can align prices and value in a uniform way across customers, who can perceive it as fair if the company communicates the rationale sufficiently.

How much value to share with customers depends on a number of factors usually linked to the alternatives of each party. This is why fragmentation and concentration of sellers and buyers as well as the uniqueness of the offer are such important market characteristics in the Hex.

CHAPTER 21

Equitable Pricing: How Buyers and Sellers Share Value

With contributions from Jerod Coker

We have contended throughout the book that sharing value is a more beneficial strategy than classical pricing approaches, and we have described many examples of companies that have grown and prospered with these pricing strategies.

In the previous chapter, we laid out the logic for why sharing value is the key to pricing fairness. Business leaders seeking to charge fair prices should view "leaving money on the table" as an opportunity to seize rather than a mistake to avoid. As Figure 20.3 implied, no seller has the right to all the value created by a transaction because both parties are needed for the value to materialize. Companies that share value through fair prices, reinforced with a transparent rationale, are rewarded with increased sales and higher profit over time.

We now share some perspectives about how much value should be shared and under what circumstances.

The fairest price – not the highest price – optimizes profits

The title of this section expresses one of the most fundamental and most provocative ways we would like you to rethink pricing. It runs counter to the classical economic theory and pricing dogma we mentioned in the Introduction to this book. But before we show you how to put this idea into practice, let's address the skepticism extent among many readers.

That skepticism is rooted in classic economic theory of the rational customer, for whom even a small benefit is enough to trigger a purchase, because they would be worse off otherwise. This theory is well tested in situations when a buyer and a seller negotiate the price of a product for the first and last time. Both parties are trying to maximize their benefit from the transaction, and the seller earns the most profit by extracting the maximum willingness to pay from the potential customer.

These situations – a single transaction between a buyer and a seller who have no alternatives and will not see each other ever again – combine all four flawed old-fashioned games we described in the Introduction – zero-sum, value extraction, static, and numbers. They are also extremely rare. Most businesses and most customers have alternatives, and buyers and sellers are bound to consider doing business again. Loyalty is a fundamental driver of success for many businesses and trust for customers.

Furthermore, value and maximum willingness to pay are not the same thing, even though the terms are often used interchangeably. One may interpret the expression "don't leave money on the table" as setting the price at the maximum willingness to pay or setting the price to the full value. When we assert that companies should "leave money on the table," we use the latter interpretation. As we have seen in Chapter 20, most people are not willing to pay the full amount of value. Asserting that companies should share value or leave some money (value) on the table is therefore not necessarily incompatible with the traditional pricing recommendation to never leave money (willingness to pay) on the table.

We have found that the share of value is a more useful way to conceptualize and solve the challenge of pricing than willingness to pay. First, focusing on value and the need to share it highlights that willingness to pay is normally lower – often much lower – than the value. Therefore, trying to extract all the value in a transaction is a mistake, both ethically and economically. Second, it forces companies to make the case for the value they should get.

Willingness to pay is a well-researched concept, but relatively little research has been conducted regarding how the value shared between buyers and sellers can influence buying behavior. What happens when we estimate demand not by estimating willingness to pay, but by looking at how a customer's purchase likelihood changes as the amount of shared value changes?

To answer that question robustly, we used the extensive BHI research – complemented by our own experience – to understand how the perception of price fairness changes as a function of the value shared. We tested six scenarios that covered B2B and B2C transactions and considered the value created either by cost savings or income/revenue increases. In each of these scenarios, we made the value created and the value shared explicit.

Let's take a deeper look at one of those scenarios. Assume that a customer shopping for a $500 TV could get a discount if they joined an online bulk-buying club. Buying through the club would save the customer $200, less a fee that the club retains. That fee could vary between 10% and 90% of the savings ($20 to $180). Different respondents were shown different amounts along this spectrum and expressed how fair the offer was on a scale from 0 to 100.

If the buyer received more than 70% of the value, it means that they would pay $360 for the TV ($500 – $200 + 30% commission for the club). In that case, the average fairness rating was 67 and the purchase likelihood was 85%. Conversely, when the bulk-buying club retained 70% of the value, the buyer would pay $440 for the TV ($500 – $200 + 70% commission for the club). In that case the fairness rating was 43 and the purchase likelihood was only 38%. Just like the capuchin monkey, a majority of respondents would rather throw away the opportunity to get a discount than pay what they perceive to be an unfair fee for the privilege.

Figure 21.1 shows how profits change as a function of the seller's share of value, for a seller with a unique value proposition, low substitute value, and high usage value. Even in these very favorable conditions, the seller's share that optimizes profit is slightly above 50%. The perception of fairness has a tangible impact on purchase likelihood. When the seller crosses the value-sharing threshold of 50%, the increase in the percentage of customers ready to forgo the benefits of a purchase more than offsets the increase in prices. It creates the risk of angering customers without any upside on profit. This supports our claim that fair prices, not maximum prices, optimize profits over time.

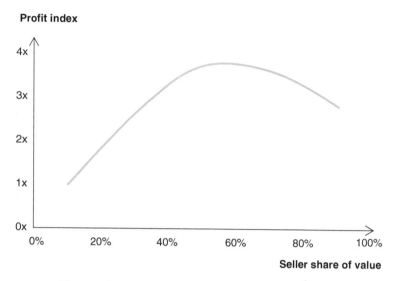

FIGURE 21.1   The margin-optimizing share of seller value is around 50%

When we studied how that optimal share varies, the survey confirmed many market observations we have made over the past decade. Figure 21.2 shares some examples:

- The seller's optimal share of value is higher in countries such as India, China, or Brazil, which have higher average levels of perceived fairness.

- The proportion of value to share with customers increases as the absolute value at stake increases.

- Customers are much more sensitive to the amount of value shared when it affects their income or revenue than when it relates to cost savings.

- Offers with unique value propositions that do not have competitive alternatives can get a higher proportion of value. But based on the survey, the benefit of uniqueness was only four to five percentage points, lower than what we observed companies try to achieve in many markets.

- B2B customers tend to be much more sensitive to the amount of value the seller retains. The optimal amount was around 20%, based on the survey. In practice we have found these optimal proportions to be even lower. A seller share of around 10% for revenue-enhancing solutions was often a good target.

Optimum seller share of value

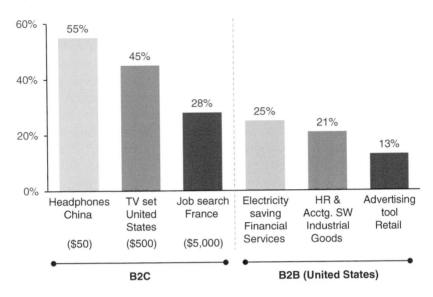

Types of solutions

   Cost saving, unique

   Cost saving, with competitive alternatives

   Income generating, with competitive alternatives

FIGURE 21.2   Profit-maximizing share of seller value

This research confirmed our work with many companies that sharing value is more beneficial than trying to extract the maximum amount of value. We found that many technology companies choose to retain only 10% of the available value and share 90% or more with their customers and channel partners. There are exceptions, of course, but the main motivation of those companies was usually to gain market adoption as fast as possible.

For many reasons, the pharmaceutical industry is at the opposite end of the sharing spectrum. One reason is that the price for a new drug often results from a one-time negotiation. Repeat purchase incentives are not as present. Another reason is that health economists tend to evaluate the benefits of a drug in terms of cost savings in a traditional way, by considering any cost saving as a benefit. One way to improve the perceived fairness of drug prices would be for the manufacturer and the payer to look at how they could share the total economic value of a new drug (cost of standard of care less marginal cost). Such calculations do happen in some cases, but they are rarely done in a disaggregated way by patient. We generally observe that both parties are satisfied with a sharing of value less beneficial to buyers than the benchmarks shown in Figure 21.2.

The level of emotions and public anger about drug prices is a clear sign that they are not perceived as fair. A Gallup poll conducted in August 2022 revealed that 58% of Americans have a negative view of the pharmaceutical industry, making it tied with the government as the second-most-hated sector, slightly below oil and gas. This negative perception has real consequences, as lawmakers around the world seek to act against pharmaceutical companies to reduce drug prices.[1,2] We hope that an explicit discussion of value sharing with the benchmarks we have shared can contribute to healthy debate that would increase the perceived fairness of drug prices.

How to implement fair pricing

The implementation of fair pricing comes down to resolving a tradeoff. The research and the logic we have presented in this chapter show that companies have numerous opportunities to differentiate their prices in ways that customers will perceive as fair and to share value in ways that benefit both customers and the company. Some companies have access to deep, rich sets of data that enable them to personalize prices to each customer's context and break away from the old-fashioned idea of seeking "the" uniform or optimal price.

But at the same time, we have shown that perceptions of fairness have inherent limits prescribed or influenced by social norms and local customs. Fair pricing must respect all the subtle, significant differences across countries, populations, and industries that allow multiple, often conflicting definitions of fair prices to coexist. Customers become angry and even react irrationally – such as opting for no value over some value – when a company crosses the lines.

Customers have also become more attuned to fairness, because the internet has given them the ability to make instant price comparisons and to explore the financial disclosures of companies to understand how much money they earn. Customers have also grown suspicious of how companies use their personal data for business purposes.

The means to strike the right balance and resolve the tradeoff is a well-communicated strategy of price differentiation based on value sharing. The critical decision – as we framed it in the Introduction and Part I – is the fair share of value that a company should pass on to customers. We have occasionally posed this in the form of the question "How much money should you leave on the table?"

Such communication – combined with a generous level of value sharing – will mitigate customers' concerns. It can also help smooth over customers' worries about the use of their personal data transmitted by their mobile devices, for example, as Anindya Ghose, a professor at NYU's Stern School of Business, described in his book *Tap: Unlocking the Mobile Economy*. Targeted communication can make a company's messages "truly contextual so that consumers perceive the device as a butler and a concierge, not a stalker."[3]

Companies used to be able to mask their price variation with opaque practices that took advantage of consumers' lack of awareness. In today's world, consumers post publicly about what they pay and compare prices with a few taps or clicks. A clear story that explains the reasons for price variation can turn this transparency into an advantage.

The value sharing and communication strategies will differ by game, because each game has its own degrees of freedom for price variation, its own limits, and aspects that matter in the communication strategy. We describe these for each game below, starting at the top of the Hex.

Uniform Game

As we described in Chapter 16, the biggest lever for price differentiation in the Uniform Game is promotions. Customers widely perceive time-based price discrimination as fair, provided they have the choice to buy at different times and benefit from the promotion. Targeting different segments with discounts is possible, but perceptions will differ depending on the product category and the country.

The justification for targeting a particular segment with lower prices is crucial. Lower cost-to-serve is usually a strong justification, and the ability of nontargeted consumers to take advantage of the promotion enhances its perceived fairness. Targeting segments because of their lower willingness or ability to pay tends to be problematic, because almost everyone thinks their budget is tight.

Matching competition is also the second-best justification for lower prices, because the bulk of value in the Uniform Game is substitute value, not usage value. It becomes problematic when prices increase, however, because it can raise suspicions of collusion or price gouging.

The percentage of value to share is especially relevant for retailers working with suppliers who want to run a promotion. Should the retailer pass on all of the cost savings to customers, or only a portion of it? Retailers who enhance their own margins by retaining more than 50% of the cost savings from supplier discounts may trigger a backlash. If consumers become aware of this, the anger associated with the sentiment of unfairness can cause just a few consumers to put campaigns on social media.

Cost Game

The main lever for price differentiation is cost, expressed through either the pricing basis, the sources of price variation, or price adjusters such as fees and functional discounts. The respondents in the BHI survey declared that cost was the most legitimate rationale to vary prices, which means that fairness should not be an issue if a company has a sound justification built on costs.

But the value-sharing proportion is not symmetrical as costs increase or decrease. Companies can pass on a cost increase – in the form of fees or surcharges – because margins tend to be thin. Keeping the same incremental margin on top of the new costs is generally perceived as fair. But if costs decline, the resulting efficiencies can lower costs for both the seller and the buyer. Companies can enhance their own margins –fairly – by not passing along 100% of the cost savings to customers.

Most players of the Cost Game are B2B companies that should share more than 50% of the value. When the incremental value comes from cost savings (as opposed to revenue enhancement), the two parties can measure it more reliably. It is easily perceived as fair when the seller retains 20–30% of that value. If a company has a unique and unmatchable cost advantage, it could consider testing whether it can retain between 30% and 40%. These parameters provide concrete guidance for companies looking to negotiate contracts with outcome-based pricing.

Power Game

Costs, volume, and competitor behavior are the biggest sources of price variation in the Power Game, which means that price changes justified by these variations are easily accepted as fair. Customers rarely raise the issue of price fairness, but large customers are likely to take exception if they learn that a smaller customer received a lower price. This can create lingering bad feelings with the larger organization's purchasing department.

Value sharing is rarely a major issue in the Power Game, because substitute value constitutes the bulk of the value. But there is an exception here as well. If a supplier comes with an innovation, the customer will have a tendency to expect a major share of the value. That can range from 70% to 90%, depending on the uniqueness of the value proposition and whether it is based on cost savings or revenue enhancement. The buyer's logic derives from the fundamental market characteristics that define the Power Game. Even when the seller has a truly unique innovation, the seller cannot profit from it without willing buyers. Each buyer has considerable leverage, because there are so few buyers in the concentrated markets of the Power Game. In the same spirit as the capuchin monkeys, the customers may decide to delay the introduction of an innovation – and forgo potential gains in market share – if sellers try to retain what the buyer perceives is too high a share of the value. An effective way for the seller to call the bluff of the buyers is to threaten to compete against them by going directly to end customers. The credibility of such a threat, of course, depends on the resources and capabilities of the seller. Under the right circumstances, the seller can significantly enhance the share of value it retains.

Custom Game

Similar to the Power Game, costs, volume, or competitor behavior are the biggest sources of price variation, and changes based on them tend to be perceived as fair. But in contrast to the Power Game, players of the Custom Game can use customization to improve the ratio of usage value to substitute value and create more opportunities for price differentiation.

We have asserted previously that seemingly random differentiation in the Custom Game is usually perceived as unfair by both customers and salespeople. That is why we recommended explicit price adjusters – and not a black box – to explain most of these variations. Value sharing can be a powerful rationale for price differences as long as the seller quantifies the value. In such cases, the supplier may retain a share value that is between 5 and 15 percentage points higher than in the Power Game. The reason, again, comes down to the underlying market characteristics. The fragmentation of the customer base gives the Custom Game seller more opportunities to find a customer who will have a higher economic interest in the additional value.

Choice Game

This game tends to have a higher proportion of value coming from usage value than from substitute value. The wide variation in the perceived usage value creates many opportunities to differentiate prices. The main levers to maintain perceived fairness are how the company packages features with varying value into different products or bundles as well as how it targets those products or bundles to different segments.

Customer programs can enhance effectiveness by improving the alignment between value and prices. Fairness is usually not an issue when those programs are based on customer behavior such as loyalty. Programs based on intrinsic customer characteristics, however, raise the risk that customers will perceive them as unfair. Success depends on the company's ability to quantify value differences and to demonstrate that prices align with share of the value. The most advanced way to do this is to pick a pricing basis aligned with value. The optimal share of value should follow the guidelines we introduce in Figure 21.3.

Value Game

The vast majority of value in this game comes from usage value. All the levers and guidelines mentioned above for the Choice Game apply, but there are some nuances. While players in the Custom Game look to upsell and find opportunities to justify price differentiation on the upside, players in the Choice Game tend to be neutral with justifications as prices move equally up or down in their portfolio. Value Game players often anchor prices high, which means most price differentiation involves lower prices. Justifying them is tricky, however, because the company cannot risk undermining its value proposition. The fashion industry, for example, needs a way to dispose of old inventory. Its lower value justifies a lower price, and beneficiaries of lower prices will rarely complain of unfairness, but using this lever too often or too conspicuously can backfire and harm brand perception. One approach that preserves fairness and brand perception is a private sale event reserved for a select group, whether influencers or loyal customers.

The share of value the company retains should align with benchmarks of Figure 21.3, with a focus on the uniqueness of value proposition.

	Main source of value	Main levers of price differentiation	Fairness perception (1–10)
Uniform Game	Mostly substitute	• Time-based promotions • Segment promotions	• 8 • 6
Cost Game	Mostly substitute	• Pricing basis • Cost + logic • Fees & functional discounts	• 10 • 10 • 10
Power Game	Substitute with some usage	• Cost, volume • Competitor • New product	• 10 • 8 • 5
Custom Game	Balanced between usage & substitute	• Cost • Offer • Discount adjustor • Discretionary discount	• 10 • 8 • 6 • 2
Choice Game	Usage	• Offer • Customer programs • Pricing basis	• 10 • 4 • 8
Value Game	Mostly usage	• Pricing basis • Offer lineup • Customer program	• 6 • 8 • 4
Dynamic Game	Depends	• Time • Offer • Fees	• 6 • 8 • 4

FIGURE 21.3   Price differentiation, fairness, and value-sharing proportions by game

Dynamic Game

Players of the Dynamic Game usually have a pricing engine that delivers different prices to different customers at unique points in time. Time is the usual driver of price variation, which means companies need to justify why their prices would vary with time.

Customers tend to perceive supply and demand as a valid and fair justification, except when spikes in demand leave customers concerned about price gouging. Critical in these moments is a company's ability to explain how a price increase helps them address a supply constraint, such as when ride-sharing services implement surge pricing at the end of a concert.

If there are rules or trends that make prices go up or down over time, the best justification for the changes is one that links the value and willingness to pay for customers who buy at different times. It is natural – and fair – for a business traveler to pay a high price for a hotel room booked three days before travel and a leisure traveler to pay a lower price for the same kind of room booked three weeks or three months in advance. In addition to their dynamic pricing engines, players in the Dynamic Game can also use a lineup of offers to align prices and value, following the rules of the Choice Game.

Companies need to be especially careful when they use dynamic pricing in a monopoly or quasi-monopoly situation. Randomness with no perceived control can feel very unfair to customers, as Ticketmaster experienced in 2023. Any existing lack of trust in a company's pricing engine is compounded when prices seem to go up dramatically and completely beyond the control or influence of customers. When a US senate panel alleged in early 2023 that Ticketmaster's "high fees, site disruptions, and cancellations" are symptoms of a lack of competition, the company said in a statement that it "has a significant share of the primary ticketing services market because of the large gap that exists between the quality of the Ticketmaster system and the next best primary ticketing system."[4]

Key takeaways

A fair price is the price that shares value equally across buyers and equitably between buyer and sellers. What we call equitable pricing may seem counterintuitive from the perspective of classical economics, but ironically, it is a more effective way to serve the goal of classical economics – higher profits – than conventional pricing approaches. In other words, companies that share value through fair prices – reinforced with a transparent rationale – are rewarded with increased sales and higher profits over time.

To implement equitable pricing, we recommend the following approach:

- **Focus on value sharing instead of willingness to pay:** Both allow companies to set prices, but determining the level of value sharing gives you more options to influence customer behavior and align your pricing with the drivers of variation in your market.
- **Understand what game you are playing:** The levels of value sharing and the rationales behind them differ from game to game.
- **Decide how much money to leave on the table:** That may sound like heresy to those who advocate the maximization of profit in a transaction, but equitable pricing treats "leaving money on the table" as an opportunity to seize rather than a mistake to avoid.

CHAPTER 22

Access: How Pricing Can Eradicate Diseases

With contributions from David Matthews, Suchita Shah, and Shashanka Muppaneni

Pharmaceutical innovations – particularly those that cure chronic or life-threatening diseases – create enormous value for society by preventing deaths, improving lives, and lowering health care costs. They fit very well to the Value Game, because a cure is much better than any chronic treatment, especially one with side effects. This is the case for the direct-acting antivirals (DAAs) that cure hepatitis C (HCV), and would apply to other medicines that hold great promise to cure other diseases, such as certain types of cancer.

But the pharmaceutical industry's predominant economic model – charging per treatment at the time of care – can limit society's ability to reap the full benefits of a cure. The problem: a mismatch in the timing of payment versus the timing of benefits. The prevailing model front-loads the payment to pharmaceutical companies while the treatment's value to society accrues over time, sometimes decades.

The advent of cures creates a true pricing dilemma for pharmaceutical companies and for the insurance companies and national health care systems that pay for medicines. If drugs were priced today to reflect all the value that accrues over time, the resulting (high) costs would strain payers, prompting some of them to limit patient access. Conversely, treating all patients as fast as possible – and in doing so, accelerating eradication – requires prices per patient so low that developing certain cures would become far less economically attractive to pharmaceutical companies, particularly compared with the economics of drugs that treat chronic diseases.

Is it possible to solve this dilemma and align the incentives of pharmaceutical companies, payers, and patients?

We argue that the answer is yes, by moving from a uniform pricing mindset to a model better aligned to outcomes in the Value Game. The solution is an alternative, population-based treatment-pricing model, which we call the payer licensing agreement (PLA). Its rationale lies in the differences in economics between "managing" and "curing" a disease. For most diseases, treatment focuses on the acute and follow-up regimens for individual patients whose current symptoms meet a specific profile. To align value and stakeholder incentives with that objective, pharma manufacturers traditionally apply a uniform pricing architecture with a fixed, per-patient pricing model.

Eradicating diseases, in contrast, should take an entire "population" or group of patients into account at a price that reflects the value of curing all patients. In this chapter, we use the case of HCV, whose cure was first introduced in 2013, to demonstrate the advantages of a PLA over traditional per-patient models. We presented this model in February 2018 at the 5th Annual Global Health Economics Colloquium held at the University of California, San Francisco.[1] At the time we called it the Netflix model, a nickname that was slightly misleading but very helpful to popularize the idea. In this chapter we stick with the more technical, if boring, term PLA.

Hepatitis C: The economic burden of a cure

According to the World Health Organization (WHO), 58 million people worldwide are chronically infected with HCV,[2] around 50% more than the number with HIV.[3] In the United States, HCV kills more people annually than the next 60 most deadly infectious diseases combined.[4] Prior to 2013, patients were treated using various therapies with challenging side effects. This discouraged many patients from taking the medicines, and some patients' conditions deteriorated so badly that they required expensive and risky liver transplants.

Innovative medicines introduced in 2013 can cure HCV in 8 to 12 weeks. Yet since their approval, more than 90% of the world's infected population remains uncured.[5] The target that WHO set for the eradication of HCV – 2030 – is now looking unrealistically ambitious. HCV persists as a global crisis.

Why haven't more people been cured? In addition to pricing, there are several other barriers to treating HCV patients, including inadequate patient awareness, screening, linkage to care, and access to physicians and medication.[6] The initial price per patient of HCV cures was so high because their costs were not spread over a long time horizon, whereas the alternative HCV treatment costs were. That made it impossible to provide treatment to all patients right away.[7,8] In some health care systems, the cost of curing the HCV population, under the per-patient model, would have been higher than the cost of all other treatments combined – and larger than many countries' annual budgets for all biopharmaceutical products. Many payers thus limited the access to cures to those HCV patients whose disease had reached an advanced state.

A uniform, up-front, per-patient pricing model is intrinsically flawed

When pharmaceutical innovation produces a cure, the value-maximizing approach for society is to distribute the medication as quickly and as broadly as possible. Pursuing aggressive eradication makes so much sense from the perspectives of both the health care system and the patients that nothing should stand in the way.

The current pricing model, however, is the major barrier hindering aggressive eradication, because its pricing basis fails to align stakeholder incentives. Instead, an up-front, per-patient pricing basis forces payers to choose between broadening access and incentivizing innovation. This intrinsic flaw stems from the characteristics of the diseases.

Curative medications often target diseases that are both chronic and progressive. This results in a mismatch between the timing of payment and the timing of benefits. When a disease like HCV is both chronic and progressive, its cures have a very skewed demand curve: very tall and thin on the left and low and flat toward the right, as shown in Figure 22.1.

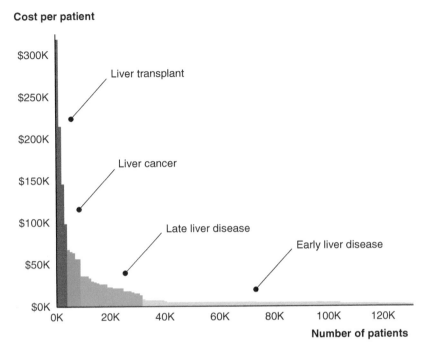

FIGURE 22.1 HCV 10-year health care costs variation[9]

The chart represents the cost to treat 100,000 patients in the ensuing 10 years, ranked from highest to lowest cost per patient. On the left are patients in advanced stages of the disease who might need a very expensive liver transplant. Fortunately, this is only a small proportion of the infected population. On the bottom right are patients at the early stage of the disease. It might not cost much to treat them, because the disease can be asymptomatic for many years, sometimes decades. The shape of such a demand curve is so extreme that the cost per patient on the left can be a thousand times higher than those on the right.

As a result of this large variation, it is hard for a pricing model with a single price point for the drug to adequately match that demand curve. Figure 22.2 displays, in a simplified way, how a uniform price of $22,000 per patient distributes value between the health care system and the pharmaceutical company. At that price, it is more economical for the health care system to treat only 23% of patients, with a total drug cost of $500 million and savings of $1.1 billion. Curing the rest of the patients individually

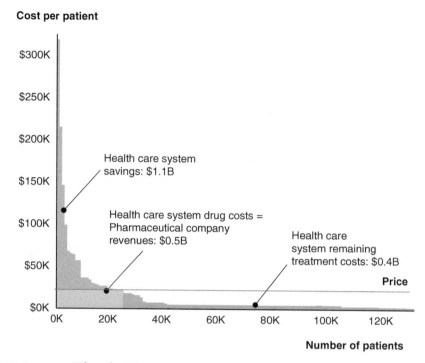

FIGURE 22.2 When the HPV cure was priced at $22,000 per patient, many payers limited its use, which allowed them to save $1.1 billion over 10 years, but only cured 23% of patients[10]

would cost the health care system less than $22,000 per person, but around $400 million in aggregate.

If you think this does not treat enough patients, you can try to figure out the uniform price that would be cheap enough to treat most of the population. That uniform price would have to be below $2,000 per patient and would result in revenues for the pharmaceutical company of around $200 million, far below the $500 million they can generate in the $22,000 price scenario.

Clearly, there is no uniform price that aligns the incentives of all societal stakeholders: patients, the health care system, and the pharmaceutical company.

Solving for such a demand curve may remind you of the Choice Game, which means that introducing different price points could solve the dilemma. But unfortunately, there is no way to create a lineup of different offers at different price points, because the drug is the same for all patients. The only way to vary prices in this uniform pricing model is over time, with the pharmaceutical company lowering the price after patients on the left side of the curve have received the cure.

Most countries have more or less adopted that approach. Yet even though the price for the DAA has fallen by more than 60% since its launch, some payers still limit access, partly because many patients are asymptomatic and partly because payers expect that prices will continue to fall. The price erosion has been among the most extensive the industry has seen, but it is still insufficient to encourage payers to look for and treat all HCV patients.

Exploring the Value Game: The payer licensing agreement

Now that we have ruled out the Uniform and Choice Games as options, let's consider the Value Game. It appears to have the best fit to the market characteristics. DAAs were breakthrough drugs at their introduction – far superior to interferon-based therapies – because they were more effective without side effects. A small set of pharmaceutical companies offered these drugs to a broad set of potential "customers," whether patients or health care systems.

To define a pricing model that fits the Value Game, it is critical to understand the drivers of value creation. If maximum value is linked to eradication of the disease, a pricing basis per population is better suited than a per-patient basis. In addition, curing patients at a population level delivers value to the patients right away, while the value delivered by DAAs accrues over time in the form of health care cost savings, because the system no longer needs to treat patients. These two simple facts were the inspiration for a pricing basis per population and over time.

The advantage of looking at the economics this way is that for large populations, the aggregate costs of care for HCV patients over time is relatively stable for a health care system. This means that an annual price per population and per year could be set in a way that generates savings every year. In addition, recurring payments can promote continued engagement and investment from health care system payers, who would have an incentive to use screening programs to look for patients.

The nickname "Netflix model" came from the comparison to the famous subscription model under which customers pay monthly to get access to a population of movies and TV shows. The analogy works best on the B2B side as Netflix pays content providers a negotiated licensing fee, regardless of the final number of viewers of that content. From this point of view, the model is parallel to the PLA. In the HCV case, it is better to have a mutual commitment of a few years to spread out the drug cost and have the capacity to screen and treat the maximum number of patients.

The best analogy is the enterprise licensing agreement (ELA) model pioneered by the software industry. Within an ELA, the value that different users derive from the product can vary by an order of magnitude. For instance, when Microsoft licenses its Office suite to a large company, it uses an ELA to charge a single annual fee for all the company's employees rather than selling unit licenses for individuals. That fee is estimated and negotiated on the basis of the mix of users across the organization – from experts to casual users – and represents the total value created and consumed.

This model is used widely throughout the industry to ensure that all eligible users of the software – even those who hardly use it – enjoy unrestricted access. In contrast, a fixed price per user would lead large companies to equip only high-value users with the software.

The payer licensing agreement (PLA) is the adaptation of the ELA to the pharmaceutical industry. The pharmaceutical company would sell health care system payers a license – on a per-population rather than per-patient basis – for universal access to a treatment for a few years at a fixed annual charge. Ideally, the period of the license would correspond to the length of time that a payer determines is required to cure most of the population. It promotes affordability and provides strong motivation for identifying, diagnosing, and treating as many patients as possible before the expiration of the payer's license.

Benefits of the payer licensing agreement

PLA implementation could expand treatment access to all patients, potentially achieving WHO's HCV targets before 2030 and reducing payers' total health care costs without jeopardizing the pharmaceutical manufacturers' revenues.

By aligning prices more closely with value, PLAs shift the model from value extraction (Figure 22.2) to value sharing (Figure 22.3). We can see

Cost per patient

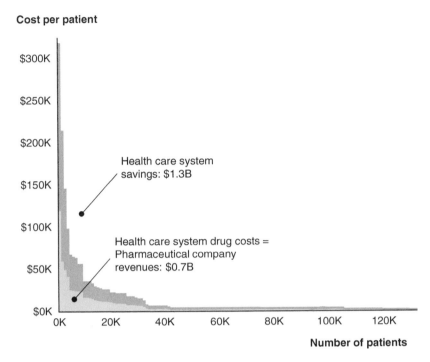

FIGURE 22.3   A PLA allows all HCV patients access to the cure, resulting in higher surplus value for payers, as well as higher revenue for pharmaceutical companies[11]

in Figure 22.3 how implementing a PLA increases the value shared by all HCV stakeholders, with manufacturer revenue rising to $700 million from $500 million, payers gaining an additional $200 million in savings, and all patients receiving access to the cure.

We have simplified the model shown in Figures 22.1 to 22.3 to illustrate the logic as clearly as possible. But we have also conducted a more detailed economic analysis in collaboration with the Center for Disease Analysis.[12] Our epidemiological and economic modeling related to HCV considers the current disease burden, disease progression rates, in-system health care, hospitalization and screening costs, and existing programmatic interventions to derive cohort-specific, direct economic costs of treatment.

Figure 22.4 illustrates the economic and social impact of three pricing scenarios over 12 years. The base scenario is the current fixed, per-patient

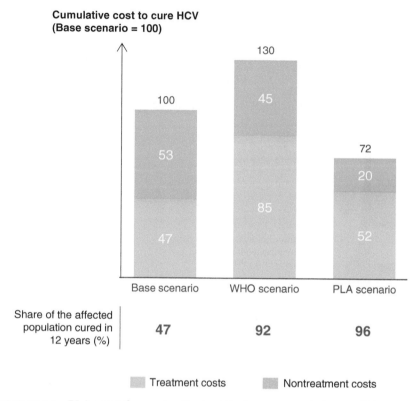

**Cumulative cost to cure HCV
(Base scenario = 100)**

	Base scenario	WHO scenario	PLA scenario
Share of the affected population cured in 12 years (%)	47	92	96

Treatment costs   Nontreatment costs

FIGURE 22.4   PLA cures the most patients at the lowest cumulative cost[13,14]

pricing model, which would cure less than half the population and split the costs roughly evenly between hospital and drug costs. The middle scenario shows how expensive it is to pursue the WHO's eradication goal with that uniform per-patient pricing model. While treating the majority of the population, the overall health care costs would be 30% higher.

The third scenario shows the win-win-win the PLA model imparts. More patients are cured and revenues for the pharma manufacturers are higher than in the base scenario, while overall costs are 28% lower. In the first two years, the PLA model cures three times as many patients as in the base scenario. This speed is one reason for the significant savings in hospital costs.

In every health care system we modeled, we found that a PLA works better for patients, payers, and manufacturers, regardless of variable disease burdens and health care economics. In the United States, for example, our modeling showed that a PLA would have significant impact:

- Tripling the number of patients treated and cured within two years
- Reducing the number of liver-related deaths by some 60%
- Reducing the total cost to payers by approximately 30%, because patients are treated much earlier, before the disease progresses to more costly stages
- Providing higher and more predictable revenues and profits to bio-pharma manufacturers

Setting the license price under a PLA starts with defining the value of curing all patients in a given population. Next, the payers and the pharmaceutical company must agree on how they will share that value and define the annual payments for the drug. That payment could be fixed, because the marginal cost of a DAA is extremely small. In the case of a drug that is more expensive to manufacture, one could consider a licensing agreement with a fixed part and a variable part per patient, designed to cover patient-specific marginal costs. Within that framework, market forces can work in the same way as they do with a uniform pricing model. If multiple pharmaceutical companies offer drugs with similar efficacy, it is likely that the competition between them would allow the health care system payers to negotiate lower prices per population and per year.

All these benefits are a powerful illustration that changing pricing models is not a zero-sum game. By better aligning the incentives of all parties – patients, payers, and providers – it is possible to get much closer to a social optimum.

The challenges of implementation

Like any pricing model change, implementing the PLA requires overcoming a number of barriers. First, the PLA model is best suited to single-payer systems, such as those in Canada, the UK, France, and Japan. In a multi-payer system, PLAs work best when all payers opt into the model, ensuring that, over time, fixed license payments represent the relative share of the covered population, thus avoiding patient churn to other payers as patients seek coverage.[15]

In addition, every health care system – single- or multi-payer – is complex, highly regulated, and slow to change. State-run payers face both legal restrictions on innovative contracting, as well as frequently changing priorities. Multi-payer systems have little incentive to consider long-term costs when their insured population is subject to high rates of attrition. Some payer systems separate the management of pharmacy and medical benefits, making it difficult to accurately calculate the profit-and-loss value of dispensing a cure. In the United States, for example, claims made at the doctor's office or hospital are often not connected to claims made at the drugstore. As a result, it can be complex and difficult for payers to connect the value of dispensing HCV pills with the reduced costs from hospitalizations and liver transplants. Vertical integration is improving these data connections, but these are still the main reason that value-based contracts have low penetration in the United States.

Dealing effectively with these various systemic challenges will be critical to successful PLA implementation. Nevertheless, we are convinced that in the near term, the model could be beneficial from health care and economic standpoints. As pharmaceutical companies prepare to bring other cures to market, they should explore population-based pricing models aligned more with the economics of cures than with treatments that manage disease. Our investigation into the effectiveness of the PLA approach for HCV has demonstrated the high potential of such models. Single-payer systems can seize the opportunity to work with manufacturers on the development of an eradication strategy supported by a population-based pricing model.

Over the past few years, we have seen examples of payers experimenting with new contracting models for HCV. None is identical to the PLA model we recommend, but all are inspired by similar ideas and goals: treating as many patients as possible as fast as possible at an affordable cost. One notable example is Australia, which committed A$1.2 billion over five years (March 2016 to February 2021) for unlimited access to cures. The details of the Australian deal are not public, but what is known is that the amount was meant to cover treatment for at least 62,000 patients.[16] This threshold was selected because the government estimated that around 62,000 HCV patients would be treated during the five-year period.[17] The total cost was capped at A$1.2 billion, so treatment for patients above the 62,000 threshold would have no incremental cost.

The program exceeded the government's expectations, treating around 90,000 patients over the five-year period, almost 50% more than expected.[18]

However, treatment rates declined every year, with only around 11,000 and 8,000 patients treated during 2019 and 2020, compared to around 30,000 and 20,000 in 2016 and 2017.[19] The Covid-19 pandemic may not be a contributing factor to the decline, which started in 2016.

Australia's approach is very similar to the PLA we proposed. The key difference is the pricing mechanism. In the Australian deal, the pricing mechanism was a cap, and not a true recurring payment. This reduced incentives to invest in finding and treating patients, after the cap was not hit about halfway through the agreement. At that point, the government had already met its target, and the incremental cost per patient returned to the uniform model, which limited the incentives to seek out and treat hard-to-reach patients. There would be continuous motivation to "get their money's worth" by treating more patients, however, if the A$1.2 billion were broken into five installments of $240 million per year, and not explicitly tied to a number of patients.

Many other payers have tried to follow in Australia's footsteps. In 2019, the US states of Washington and Louisiana both signed deals to purchase an unlimited supply of HCV medications for a set fee. This approach has many similarities to a PLA.[20] The agreements greatly reduced the budget impact of providing cures. Louisiana, for example, estimated it would cost $760 million to treat all of the HCV patients in its Medicaid program. The agreement meant that it would spend no more than $35 million per year for the five-year term, for a total of $175 million.

But the deals failed to supercharge treatment rates as much as expected. Louisiana's treatment rates increased between 2019 and 2020 by 18%, but then dropped by 22.8% from 2020 to 2021.[21] The Covid-19 pandemic may explain some of the decline. Nearly every aspect of Washington's plan, other than the DAA agreement, was cut due to budget shortfalls and the Covid-19 pandemic. Some of the canceled initiatives included screening programs in emergency rooms and busing providers to rural regions.[22]

Louisiana saw higher treatment rates than Washington, because it implemented more of the initiatives it planned. But it also struggled to treat hard-to-reach HCV patients, such as users of intravenous drugs.[23] Washington's and Louisiana's struggles underscore the need for a comprehensive, well-funded strategy beyond the drug cost.

Eradication requires more than adjusting the pricing model and aligning economic incentives. It also requires the right infrastructure and continued support. It is very encouraging to see that in 2023 the US federal government released a four-point plan to eradicate HCV:[24]

- **Step 1: Provide rapid, point-of-care testing.** Outside the United States, patients can undergo RNA tests at convenient locations and receive treatment in the same visit, if they test positive. But in the United States, tests have to be processed at offsite labs, forcing patients to return to obtain test results and treatment. The new program would accelerate approval of point-of-care RNA tests by enlisting the Independent Test Assessment Program, an NIH–Food and Drug Administration partnership.

- **Step 2: Broaden access to HCV cures.** The new plan proposes an agreement, similar to those of Washington and Louisiana, between pharmaceutical companies and the federal government. Federal health plans will receive unlimited access to the drug for a set fee, spanning a five-year period.

- **Step 3: Increase education and engagement.** By supporting grassroots organizations and trusted community partners, the new program will build trust and create the conditions for more people to seek testing and care. This includes supporting universal screening as part of routine care and scaling up training programs for clinicians.

- **Step 4: Invest in prevention.** The current curative drugs do not prevent reinfection. The new program seeks to bolster existing public health measures to prevent new infections. It also seeks to reenergize vaccine research, which might be accelerated by the advent of the mRNA platform.

We have focused our in-depth study of the PLA model on HCV, but we are confident that our findings are relevant to other treatments and therapeutic areas. PLAs would be most effective in areas that have three characteristics: value that accrues over time, vast value discrepancies among patients, and low incremental manufacturing costs. As in the case of hepatitis C, a new pricing model can be a critical step toward eradication, but the need to remove more implementation barriers is likely.

Key takeaways

For HCV patients, challenges aside, a pricing model borrowed from the tech industry could be just what the doctor – or the economist – ordered.

- Implementing the payer licensing agreement (PLA) for curative medications can align value and stakeholder incentives with the objective of eradicating diseases.
- Using per population as a pricing basis allows pricing to reflect the value of curing all patients.
- In addition to pricing, increasing treatment rates requires addressing several barriers, including inadequate patient awareness, screening, linkage to care, and access to physicians and medication.

CHAPTER 23

Green Premium: How to Shape Demand for Sustainable Solutions

With contributions from John Pineda and Lauren Taylor

B usiness leaders are realizing they have a responsibility to address significant environmental challenges, such as climate change, pollution, and resource depletion. Sustainability has become an imperative, as consumers and investors are increasingly pressuring them to reduce environmental impacts and contribute to the efforts to meet those challenges.

If businesses successfully develop and market green solutions – ones with an improved environmental impact compared to their legacy offers – they could bring economic and environmental benefits into alignment and create incentives to scale green options to more customers and sectors.

Some green offers have sold well but have struggled to generate a profit. Green products usually cost more than traditional products, and the average consumer's willingness to pay – their Green Premium WTP – does not always recover the incremental costs. When it does, the segment is usually too small to justify the at-scale investments needed to transform operations.

That difficulty has created a belief among many leaders that, in general, consumers are not environmentally sensitive enough for green products to scale. This is the Green Premium Quandary: the green premium average willingness to pay is inferior to the green premium cost as shown in Figure 23.1.

Facing this quandary, many environmental activists focus on the supply side of the green premium, by looking for ways to reduce costs. As Bill Gates stated in his blog: "lowering the green premiums is the single most important thing we can do to avoid climate disaster."[1] This thinking is largely inspired by a cost-plus approach.

We agree this is a very important action, but it is mostly relevant for businesses in the Cost Game and potentially the Power Game and Uniform Game. On the opposite side of the Hex, businesses have an opportunity to pursue an alternative course of action: shaping the demand for green solutions to increase Green Premium WTP by adopting an approach from the Choice Game playbook: segmentation.

With a segmented view of demand instead of an aggregate one, companies can take advantage of the heterogeneity of customers, who have different needs and different levels of willingness to pay. They can then define a coherent lineup of green solutions that covers segments with a much higher willingness to pay. That creates a green demand curve with a higher

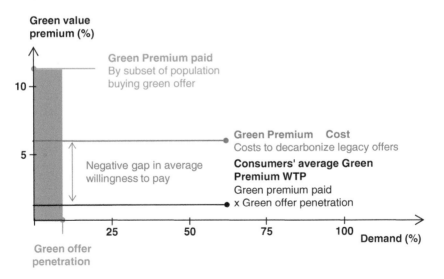

FIGURE 23.1   The Green Premium Quandary

average willingness to pay that exceeds the green premium cost. Businesses in the Value Game and Custom Game can also use this kind of approach.

In this chapter, we explore the demand side of the Green Premium Quandary and share global research we conducted with consumers about their climate and sustainability needs and attitudes, in addition to their willingness to pay a green premium in four product categories.

Quantifying the Green Premium Quandary

"Green premium" typically refers to the additional price that customers pay for a green product compared to a conventional one. If we go upstream in the value chain, the green premium is in fact a "green cost" for businesses. Producing green products typically results in additional costs, such as sustainable materials or energy-efficient manufacturing processes.

The green premium of "green" steel, for example, is 40% above the cost of conventional or "gray" steel. Green steel has limited differentiation relative to gray steel, and customers have high bargaining power. The cost-plus pricing method is therefore a natural fit. Potential green steel customers, such as automotive OEMs, may not be willing to pay this premium for a sustainable product and may opt to purchase gray steel instead.

The situation is a bit more positive when it comes to consumers. Our global survey on climate and sustainability found that up to 80% of consumers were concerned about the environment when making recent purchases (see the Appendix, "About the Studies"). The survey – which covered eight countries and 14 product and service categories – revealed a broad and encouraging sensitivity to environmental issues. In many categories, however, only 10–14% of respondents are purchasing sustainable products and an even smaller 3–4% are already paying a significant premium for sustainability, as shown in Figure 23.2.

The green premium cost varies significantly by sector. For consumer-facing offers, it often falls in a range of 5% to 25%, but it can be much higher upstream in the value chain. The average Green Premium WTP is often between 1% and 5%. So, the Green Premium Quandary is real and exists, to some degree, in all sectors. The gap is smaller for B2C businesses, however, so we focus our demand-side analysis there.

First, we recognize that "green" is not a binary attribute. Green products can have varying levels of sustainability, depending on their environmental

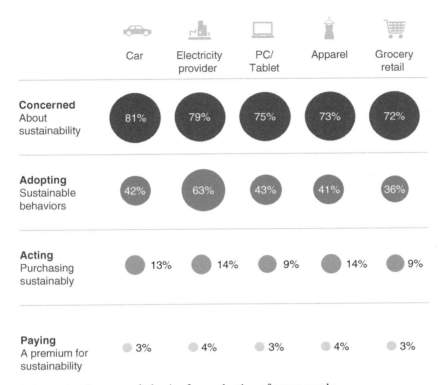

FIGURE 23.2 Consumer behavior for a selection of green goods

impact over the whole product life cycle. These aspects can include the energy and resources used, emissions generated, and waste produced during both the production and use of the product. We can split green products into "made" green and "used" green:

- **"Made" green** refers to reducing the environmental footprint of how a product is made and delivered to the customer. A net-zero car, for example, would have zero-carbon green steel, a natural leather substitute interior, and be delivered via electric truck charged with renewable electricity.
- **"Used" green** refers to a product designed for lower and net-zero emissions from use and disposal. An electric vehicle would have zero tailpipe emissions, be charged with renewable electricity, and recycled at end-of-life.

This leads to the various levels of green products and their green premiums. Customers may be willing to pay more for greener products and services, but companies need to engage with their customers to understand what truly drives their green willingness to pay and communicate their approach to green. Companies could increase willingness to pay for many customers with a multifaceted approach: net zero, fully recyclable, free of harmful chemicals, and so forth.

Segmenting consumers to understand demand for green products

The market revenue for green products grew at a 7.3% compound annual growth rate between 2016 and 2021, according to the Sustainable Market Share Index. This rate was 2.7 times faster than the growth rate for products not marketed as sustainable.[2] This indicates a growing demand for sustainable products among consumers, and that companies that prioritize sustainability in their offerings may have more runway for growth.

The percentage of consumers paying a green premium may be low today, but a closer look reveals a more nuanced landscape. When we conducted research on the Green Premium WTP in four product categories – electric vehicles (EVs), dog food, jeans, and laundry detergent – in the United States, Germany, and China, we found that consumers are willing to pay very different green value premiums, depending on their level of concern for the environment and their income or wealth levels.

Figure 23.3 shows a schematic demand curve that averages out our findings across the four product categories. Note that we are now talking about a "green value premium," rather than a green premium, to account for the fact that green solutions might not be as convenient as legacy solutions. In the EV market, for example, the range is more limited, there are fewer charging stations than gas stations, and charging takes longer than filling up an internal combustion engine (ICE) car. A high green value premium can reflect a combination of higher willingness to pay and a higher tolerance for inconvenience.

The following is a high-level description of the five segments shown in Figure 23.3.

FIGURE 23.3   Schematic demand curve

1. **The "Sustainability-First":** They are highly enthusiastic about the green movement. They are sustainability activists, trend-setters, and innovators. They want green solutions now and are not deterred by price or friction points.

2. **The "Green-Concerned":** They are genuinely worried about sustainability issues and are motivated to take action to drive positive change. Their sustainability preference may be linked to other factors such as health, security, luxury, novelty, and innovation. They will trade up for green features, but they will start considering price as a limiting factor.

3. **The "Green-Conscious":** They care about the environment, but sustainability is not a top priority when purchasing a product. While still willing to pay a small premium, their ability or willingness to pay is limited. Green will be considered alongside other value drivers to make purchase decisions.

4. **The "Green-Neutral":** They appear completely indifferent to sustainable alternatives as a choice driver. They can be convinced to switch to a green option at price parity or if offered an enhanced price–value proposition.

5. **The "Anti-Green":** They are willing to purchase a green product at a green discount, meaning that the green product price is cheaper. They are characterized by a strong desire to maintain the status quo. They are often skeptical of enhancement claims and marketing hype and tend to have negative associations with green products in terms of quality or functionality. Their top choice factors typically include considerations such as price, quality, safety, and brand recognition.

To illustrate more precisely the Green WTP, Figure 23.4 shows the actual curve for the laundry detergent in the United States. The Sustainability-First customers can have a value premium that exceeds 80%, which is a very high ceiling. They are willing to overcome many of the obstacles and difficulties that owning an electric vehicle might impose. This implies that companies do not need to remove all barriers to adoption for this segment, which is not necessarily the case for consumers in other segments.

This demonstrates that the green consumer market is far from homogeneous, and that the logic of the Cost Game is not optimal. By adopting a Choice Game logic instead, companies can find ways to target different customer segments to choose green options aligned with their willingness to pay. This ultimately enables greater overall value creation and greater sustainability impact.

Redesigning offers to reshape the green demand curve

Pricing in the Choice Game revolves around carefully planned offer structures. A coherent lineup of offerings must match customer segments defined by their different needs and value perceptions. Understanding consumer demand drivers and shaping the configuration of proposed choices is much more important than defining any individual price point with precision. We explore how this applies to sustainable products.

Sustainability-First

In this segment, consumers make purchase decisions based mostly on sustainability. They look for sustainable options and take the time to absorb information about technological innovations that bring new green

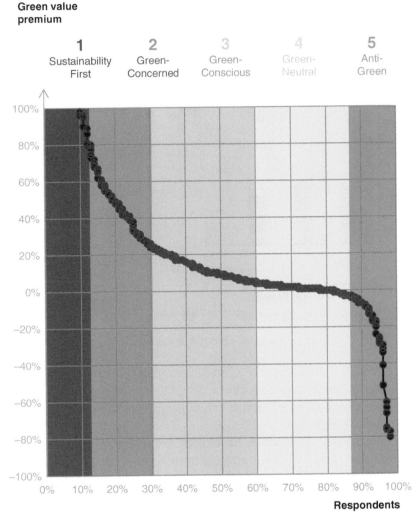

FIGURE 23.4   Actual demand curve for laundry detergents in the United States

solutions to market. For the right green offer, they are willing to pay up to double the price, but in return, their expectations are high, as is their ability to scrutinize empty claims. In some categories, green products targeting this segment already have a relatively high market share, despite higher prices, as evidenced in Figure 23.5. Depending on the category,

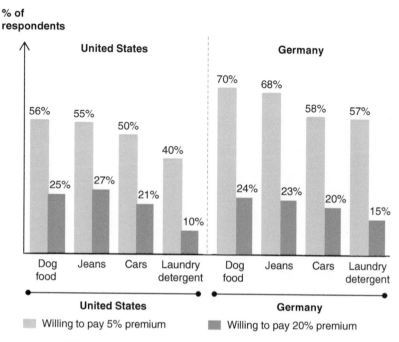

FIGURE 23.5   Willingness to pay for a product at a premium at 5% and 20%

these consumers represent between 5% and 10% of the population and they have a high green premium willingness to pay always north of 20%, sometimes as high as 80%.

Unfortunately, businesses have often not designed products for this segment that were ambitious enough from a green perspective. Too concerned about lowering green premiums, they have targeted premiums in the range of 5% to 15%, far below what this segment is willing to pay. To capitalize on the opportunity here, companies should focus on developing an attractive value proposition that combines sustainable production with extended life cycle and cutting-edge technology with superior quality standards. We think companies could achieve a green premium above 50%, while still sharing considerable value. With the right marketing campaigns, the Sustainability-First consumers will be evangelists for high-quality green products and feel good about their purchases.

Tesla successfully aimed to address the Sustainability-First segment in the automotive market with the launch of its Model S sedan and, prior to that, the Roadster. The Model S wasn't the first EV in the US market, but it effectively redefined what an EV is by combining the benefits of a battery-powered EV with the appeal of a mainstream luxury sedan. Tesla targeted the Model S sedan at high-end consumers and priced most of them at over $100,000.[3] At the same time, these consumers were ready to make tradeoffs to adopt a more sustainable product. Early adopters lacked the benefits of charging infrastructure, for example, but this did not deter them from buying an EV.

Green-Concerned

The Green-Concerned segment comprises individuals who are deeply invested in sustainability issues and motivated to drive positive change. The proportion of consumers in this segment varies from 10% to 20% depending on country and product. They are interested in green innovations and are ready to embrace and use some eco-friendly products daily. Their needs and priorities can lead them to assign higher value to certain green products over others.

They are willing to pay a 15–20% premium for green products. This is less than the Sustainability-First segment, but significantly more than the Green-Conscious. This segment requires advanced green products that they can feel good about and that allow them to brag about in social contexts. However, most current green offers are not differentiated enough from legacy products and do not take full advantage of the segment's willingness to pay.

Tesla diversified its portfolio of green offers by introducing a compact hatchback with a starting price of $43,000 (Model 3), a full-size SUV at $100,000 (Model X), and a compact SUV at $55,000 (Model Y). Ford also introduced variety by creating compelling EV models of iconic ICE brands, with the Mustang Mach-E starting at $45,000 and the F-150 Lightning at $58,000.[4]

Green-Conscious

Green-Conscious customers represent between 25% and 40% of the population, depending on country and product category. They and the first two segments usually represent more than half of the market. The Green-Conscious see sustainability as a plus in the product and are more likely to buy a product with a green benefit. They associate sustainability with other positive values, such as health and security. This segment is willing to pay up to a 5% green premium. Some 56% of dog owners in the United States, for example, are willing to pay a 5% green premium for eco-friendly dog food, while around 70% of German dog owners are willing to pay the same premium for the same product.

To target this segment, companies should use labeling to provide clear and transparent information about the environmental impact of products or services, for example, about carbon footprints. It is also important to inspire and empower customers to choose greener options. This can involve highlighting the environmental benefits of the products and providing incentives for customers to make more sustainable choices.

As mentioned previously, sustainability is not the top priority of this segment. To target customers effectively, companies should incorporate and highlight other benefits that are important to consumers and positively associated with the environment. Healthiness, high quality, and being socially responsible are attributes that are often well correlated with sustainability. The bundling of benefits creates a win–win situation for both the consumer and the environment. We call it "mainstream green" because it allows companies to bring the benefits of green to the consumer mainstream.

A company that sells EVs, for example, might highlight the fact that their cars are not only emissions-free and environmentally friendly, but also require less maintenance and have lower operating costs than traditional ICE cars. Highlighting this long-run monetary benefit could persuade consumers primarily concerned about cost savings to choose an EV. When a sustainable product offers tangible benefits beyond environmental sustainability, it can create more value for consumers, increase willingness to pay, and justify a higher price.

Green-Neutral

The Green-Neutral segment assigns similar value to both environmentally friendly and non-environmentally-friendly products. They do not prioritize sustainability and do not take it into account when making a purchase. They represent 25–35% of the customer population.

This segment of consumers tends to be more reluctant to buy green solutions, due to adoption barriers that we mentioned before. To engage this segment effectively, companies need to first eliminate these barriers.

In addition, affordability is typically the main concern for this segment. They have no additional willingness to pay for sustainable products. However, if sustainable products are available at comparable price points to nonsustainable products, then the Green-Neutral consumers may choose to purchase the sustainable option. Therefore, companies should work on making affordable green offerings, taking advantage of economies of scale they can achieve by serving the first three segments we described. Those three segments, again, comprise more than half of the customers and are willing to pay a premium. It should be possible to offer basic green products to the Green-Neutral segment at the legacy price. This should help to tilt the price–value proposition away from conventional or gray products.

Alternatively, companies could consider developing affordable "khaki" solutions, which serve as stepping stones to green products. Khaki refers to a product that incorporates both sustainable and conventional elements, such as a hybrid car that combines an electric motor with a gasoline engine. By balancing the use of eco-friendly materials and sustainable production methods with nonsustainable elements, companies can lower their costs and offer lower prices. These solutions can also help customers make the transition to more sustainable options gradually, without having to make a significant financial investment up front.

Anti-Green

These customers are doubtful about the benefits or importance of sustainability. They question the validity of environmental concerns and exhibit a general distrust of environmental activism and green solutions. They represent 10–15% of the population.

Their willingness to pay for green options is negative, which means they need a lower price for green options to become competitive with legacy options. This group will be the hardest to sway. However, when the rest of the population has switched to some form of green products, the economies of scale will work the opposite way they work today. Green products will become cheaper, and legacy products will become more expensive. Companies can then work on raising the price of conventional gray products, which will make green options more attractive for this group. Companies can also phase out support for gray solutions and heavily tilt the business case toward green products.

With this new demand curve, our new estimate of the average Green Premium WTP falls between 8% and 15% for the product categories we have studied. This lies above the Green Premium Cost and solves the Green Premium Quandary for these categories. This demonstrates that the Green Premium Quandary – at least in consumer markets – can be resolved by decisively reshaping the demand curve for green solutions, as illustrated in Figure 23.6.

The Sustainability-First segment is analogous to the traditional "first movers," because they will quickly adopt a new green product regardless of price. Many other consumers are expressing interest and signaling a path to action, but they are not currently purchasing sustainable products at a significant premium. These would be the "late majority" in a typical adoption curve.

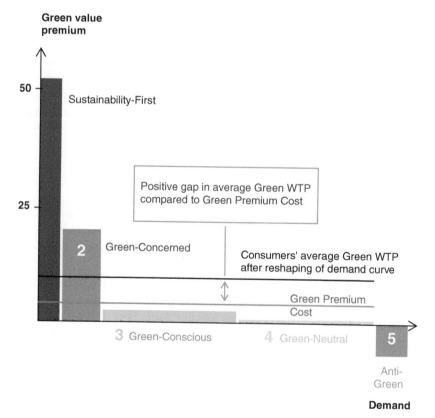

FIGURE 23.6 How a reshaped demand curve resolved the Green Premium Quandary

Some green products have achieved significant penetration across different consumer goods categories, despite elevated premiums in some cases, according to NYU's Sustainable Market Share Index.[5] The Sustainability-First and Green-Concerned are real people, and we have spoken with many of them. They often do not find the products that will satisfy their need for more sustainable solutions. When they pay a green premium, it is lower than their green willingness to pay, because companies either did not design the right product or ask them to pay a higher premium.

It is not uncommon for us to identify a higher ceiling of willingness to pay than companies had tested themselves. They later validated our findings by raising their prices or developing higher-value products. Based on the research findings and insights presented in this chapter, we believe that the true Green Premium WTP – when averaged across the market – is higher than the Green Premium Cost. We therefore feel confident that companies have a clear opportunity to reshape the demand for sustainable products.

Some companies have made similar analyses and set ambitious goals to increase adoption and drive their industry forward. Renault, for example, has announced that the "Renault brand aims to have the greenest mix in the European market in 2025, with over 65 percent of electric and electrified vehicles in the sales mix and up to 90 percent battery electric vehicles mix in 2030."[6]

Consumer-facing (B2C) companies have a clear path to capitalize on the existing demand potential for green solutions and to define strategies to achieve widespread adoption. The Choice Game's playbook is a strong fit. They also have an opportunity to send this positive signal upstream to B2B companies and encourage these companies to invest in green products. The questions of "Who will absorb 'green costs'?" and "Who will be able to pass on a 'green premium'?" should be an open discussion and commitment among all stakeholders in the value chain.

The premiums associated with using green raw materials can be significant. Green plastics, for example, can come with a premium of 70% to 200% per kilogram compared to conventional plastics, and green aluminum comes with a premium of 30% to 50%.

But the impact of these premiums on consumer end prices can be relatively low. A fully decarbonized car may cost an additional $500 compared to a conventional car, which translates to a less than 2% increase for a vehicle with a base price of $30,000. Companies can absorb or pass on a portion of the green cost associated with sustainable production methods, depending on how they are following the Choice Game strategies we described above. B2C companies and their suppliers can enhance this opportunity by cooperating to embed sustainability into their innovation cycle and co-design sustainable products and solutions with their suppliers.

One important component of the value chain for automotive OEMs is the production of green steel. We have observed a notable gap between the commitment of downstream players to decarbonize their upstream value chains, and the commitment of upstream players to provide the low-carbon materials required to meet these targets. This divergence creates a major scarcity risk for green materials.

Green plastic might be a priority for household and personal care, but it is less critical for the automotive sector, where it accounts for a relatively small share of emissions, as Figure 23.7 shows. Competitors in the plastic market could develop more competitive products with highest-value customers and deprioritize customer segments with limited long-term demand. They could also lower abatement cost competitiveness with alternative solutions.

Value chain position and market context can help inform a company's efforts to develop an effective pricing strategy for a new green offering. B2C companies have the greatest opportunity to realize higher margins if they can secure a premium positioning for their green products. Whether B2B players can realize a price beyond what the cost-plus approach yields will depend on the magnitude of market scarcity and their ability to produce low-carbon materials below market cost.

Key takeaways

The Green Premium Quandary encapsulates the challenge many companies have faced in getting consumers and customers to pay a premium above the incremental costs of green products. Companies have more options to resolve the quandary besides waiting for customers to change behavior and lowering green costs. B2C companies can reshape their demand curve for green products and create sustainable green demand for B2B companies upstream in the value chain.

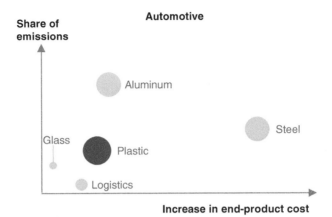

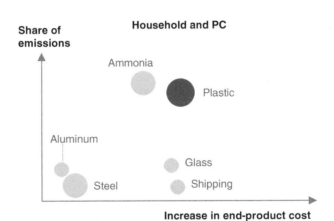

FIGURE 23.7   Share of emissions and cost increases for green raw materials

We recommend the following approach to start reshaping the demand curve for your business:

- **Recognize the opportunity:** Between 10% and 20% of consumers are passionate about the environment or concerned enough that they are willing to pay a green premium of 20% or more for the right product.
- **Work on justifying the premium:** B2C companies that redesign their offerings with the highest standards of sustainability and product functionality can justify this high premium.

- **Follow the Choice Game strategies:** After focusing on the Sustainability-First consumers, companies can target the Green-Conscious consumers, who have limited ability to pay a green premium, by bundling green features with other features they associate with the environment, such as health and safety. Broader adoption beyond that will depend on eliminating the green premium cost, which should be easier with scale.

- **Work with supply chain partners to reduce costs:** B2C companies can support the broader transformation of the upstream value chain by committing to create predictable demand for sustainable products and co-designing sustainable solutions with their suppliers and, in turn, with their suppliers.

CHAPTER 24

CO_2: How to Encourage Lower Carbon Emissions

With contributions from Christian Haakonsen, John Pineda, Matthew Gordon, and Paulina Ponce de León

F ending off damaging climate change is like a timed game of chess we can't afford to lose. The unregulated burning of fossil fuels by individuals, corporations, and nations alike contributes to the buildup of greenhouse gases in the atmosphere. As a result, addressing carbon emissions requires collective action and shared responsibility to avoid the "tragedy of the commons," the phenomenon that occurs when people collectively deplete a common resource by pursuing their own self-interest.

The odds of avoiding checkmate improve significantly if the world meets one target: keeping cumulative carbon dioxide (CO_2) net emissions under 350 gigatons between now and 2050. Failing to take steps to curb carbon emissions could lead to disastrous outcomes, including rising sea levels, extreme weather events, food and water shortages, and the spread of diseases.

Carbon credits can help accelerate progress toward this objective. They represent a specific unit: one metric ton of CO_2 either removed from or kept out of the atmosphere. Governments made some progress by implementing cap-and-trade mechanisms, with uniform market prices for one tonne of carbon emission rights. Companies that reduced their emissions beyond regulatory requirements could sell their emission rights to other companies, creating economic incentives to reduce emissions cost-efficiently across industries.

To complement these efforts, the voluntary carbon market (VCM) emerged as an additional mechanism for companies to compensate for (offset) their emissions – beyond regulatory requirements – by funding projects to remove CO_2 from the atmosphere or avoid CO_2 emissions.

In 2023, the VCM offerings consisted of carbon credits generated from individual projects – such as renewable energy, afforestation, or reforestation projects – sold to few buyers. These credits are sold at varying prices and their quality and impact are not always transparent. In fact, sellers in the VCM find themselves navigating the Custom Game and encounter numerous challenges to grow and scale up their efforts. The current offer structure does not match the buyers' broad range of willingness to pay and preferences across carbon offset projects. Moreover, buyers are reluctant to participate in a market with opaque pricing and an abundance of low-quality projects.

Capturing differences in willingness to pay with the right pricing can shape the entire market by redefining how value is created, assigned, and shared between buyers and sellers. We contend that moving to a Choice Game is crucial to incentivizing more funding to be deployed to a market that has vast potential and is likely necessary to reach net emission reduction objectives. If successful, this move will ultimately result in much greater value retained by sellers, while buyers further reduce their carbon footprints.

What is the voluntary carbon market?

Carbon-credits markets include the VCM and the compliance markets established by regulation. While compliance markets are currently limited to specific regions, voluntary carbon credits are significantly more fluid, unrestrained by boundaries set by countries or political unions. In 2021, the VCM transacted 500 million tonnes of CO_2 at a value of $2 billion, four times the value in 2020. Forecasts estimate the VCM value potential to be between $10 billion and $40 billion by 2030.[1]

Project developers represent the upstream part of the market. They offer avoidance projects that reduce emissions of CO_2 and removal projects that capture and store CO_2 from the atmosphere. Within each of these categories, there are different nature-based and engineered project types, as shown in Figure 24.1.

Avoidance levers
Levers to reduce *emission*
of CO_2 into atmosphere

Removal levers
Levers to remove CO_2
from the atmosphere

Nature-based solutions (NBS)

Reducing emissions from
deforestation and forest
degradation

- REDD+: Reduce
  emissions from activities
  implemented by group of
  individuals
- JREDD: Reduce emissions
  at the jurisdictional level
  (level of state or province)

Other nature-based
avoidance

Avoided peatland impact
Halt conversion of peatland

Forestry-based removals
Recover destroyed or
plant new forests

Other nature-
based removal

Soil sequestration
Store CO_2 through
alternative (regenerative)
agriculture techniques

Ocean fertilization
Introduce nutrients
into ocean to increase
food production

Engineered solutions

Renewable energy
Install renewable energy
sources for third party

Household devices
Provide cleaner-burning
stoves and/or energy-
efficient devices

Waste and industrial
Provide waste
minimization, source
separation, and recycling

Energy-efficiency,
fuel, and transport
Combine the use of
a traditional internal
combustion engine
with an electric motor

Direct air carbon
capture and storage
Capture and sequester
dilute CO_2 from atmosphere

BECCS
Use bioenergy to generate
electricity or heat, while
storing the resulting CO_2
underground

FIGURE 24.1   Different examples of projects resulting in carbon credits

Removal credits are highly valued in carbon markets due to their intuitive effectiveness in mitigating climate change. They often command a premium price compared to avoidance credits. This premium price is due to the higher level of investment required for the underlying project and the stronger demand for it.

In addition to the type of project, the size of the project and the delivery time also play a role in determining the value of carbon credits. In many cases, smaller-scale projects contribute greater relative societal impact on dimensions that go beyond CO_2 offsets. Carbon credits become more valuable per tonne of CO_2 as a result. Location can also be a decisive factor, as projects can be difficult to implement in areas with limited infrastructure and resources.

While all projects must deliver impacts on sustainability or emissions mitigation, different project types provide different levels of benefits. A large-scale wind energy project in France, for example, provides additional benefits, such as contributing to the country's energy independence. An improved cookstove project in a remote part of Africa benefits people living in communities in need. While the sustainable benefits of wind projects remain significant, the credits generated by cookstove projects are likely to command a higher price due to their added value of social impact.

Carbon credits can have a wide range of prices in current carbon markets. The price per metric ton of CO_2 can range from just a few cents to as much as \$15–\$20 for afforestation or reforestation projects. Tech-based removal projects, involving carbon capture, may command even higher prices, with carbon credits for such projects selling at \$100–\$300 per metric ton of CO_2 emissions.[2] This is also because they are seen as critical technologies to scale, and help enable future removals beyond those directly covered by the credit.

Therefore, all carbon credits are not created equal.

The VCM should move from the Custom Game to the Choice Game

Buyers in the VCM are companies that aim to reduce their carbon footprint, which makes the customer base very large, with varying sizes and objectives. When buying carbon credits, these companies have a choice from among a broad set of project options.

Most of the volume comes from customers who buy carbon credits from multiple projects at negotiated prices. Several factors influence willingness to pay and the price ultimately paid for a carbon credit. First, it depends on the buyers' greenhouse gas (GHG) intensity, which means how much carbon it emits to generate a unit of revenue. Companies with high GHG intensity need to offset a large amount of emissions, with a limited budget, enabling them to negotiate a discounted price for a larger volume of carbon credits. Second, companies with higher marginal abatement costs may incur greater expenses in reducing their emissions, making them more likely to purchase carbon credits at higher prices. Third, the extent of progress they have made toward their climate commitments is also a critical determinant.

In this context, buyers and sellers in the VCM are in the Custom Game. This poses significant challenges for both buyers and suppliers. Suppliers struggle with periodic oversupply of carbon credits. This is due to a proliferation of new carbon offset projects and a lack of one centralized registry for tracking carbon credits. Buyers, on the other hand, face challenges related to price uncertainty and lack of transparency, which makes it difficult for them to compare projects. These challenges constrain market growth and ultimate potential.

To overcome these challenges, it is necessary to structure a clear lineup of carbon credit projects, providing buyers with a better understanding of the available options at transparent and consistent prices. This can help to shape the demand, making it easier to match the supply of available credits with the specific needs and preferences of buyers. Therefore, moving to a Choice Game can reduce the risk of oversupply for suppliers and price opacity for buyers, ensuring that the VCM remains an effective tool for addressing climate change.

The VCM should evolve into a structured lineup of offers targeting different customer segments

The Choice Game revolves around a coherent lineup of offerings defined by the different needs, value perceptions, and willingness to pay of customer segments.

BCG conducted a survey with potential VCM buyers as part of a joint initiative with the Environment Defense Fund (EDF). The study showed that the VCM buyers are not a homogeneous group with similar needs and willingness to pay. They can be categorized along two primary axes:

1. The level of climate maturity, which involves, for example, tracking emissions in scope 3.
2. The carbon intensity of their business, which is related to the amount of greenhouse gas emissions in their operations and varies depending on the industry.[3]

This results in four distinct market segments, as shown in Figure 24.2:

- **Commodity buyers:** Low carbon intensity companies have few emissions in comparison to their income. When they have low carbon maturity, they tend to show less differentiation in their willingness to pay for quality. They consider carbon credits as commodities and focus on meeting the minimums of third-party quality standards.
- **Early days buyers:** High carbon intensity companies that start their carbon credit procurement journey. They tend to be price sensitive due to budget constraints.

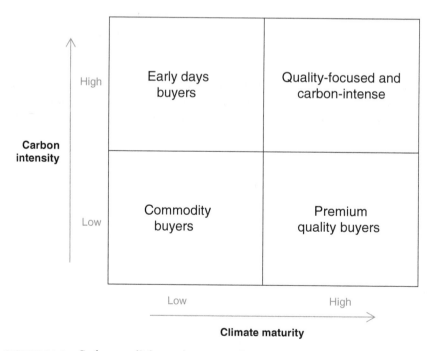

FIGURE 24.2 Carbon credit buyers' segmentation

- **Quality-focused and carbon-intense buyers:** High carbon intensity and high maturity carbon credit purchasers will make sophisticated tradeoffs between quality and price with resources dedicated to doing so.

- **Premium quality:** Companies with low carbon intensity and high climate maturity, such as many technology companies, have relatively low emissions compared to their revenues and high margins. Their customers and employees put pressure on them to be leaders on climate. They have developed expertise in buying credits and are willing to pay for quality.

Each segment has unique needs and preferences when it comes to carbon credits. Some buyers may be willing to pay more for credits that meet their specific needs or offer additional benefits. To turn all segments into buyers in the VCM, it is crucial for sellers to understand the value drivers that influence buyers' behavior and willingness to pay.

The survey included a conjoint analysis across the four buyer segments.[4] One of the main research objectives was to understand how customers value the quality of a carbon credit product and their willingness to pay a premium price for that quality. Quality evaluation criteria include five primary areas – additionality,[5] permanence, leakage, baseline, and quantification – as well as co-benefits such as biodiversity, soil quality, air quality, and improving community livelihoods. Some third-party organizations have developed frameworks to calculate carbon footprint scores to help understand the value perception of buyers. We used a quality score scale from 1 to 5[6] with the reference level for analyses set at $15/tonne for a rating of 3. Figure 24.3 shows the results of the conjoint analysis in terms of willingness to pay for different-quality projects.

The first conclusion is that having a rating with at least a score of "3 – moderate" out of 5 is considered a minimum or baseline. Most buyers are not willing to purchase credits tagged with a "2 – low" or a "1 – very low" quality score. Several factors such as a historical oversupply of lower-quality credits at low prices, undersupply of higher-quality credits, complexity of evaluating quality, and a general lack of market transparency have pushed buyers to express a high willingness to pay for quality that is defensible.

The second conclusion is that across all customer segments, each increase in level from "moderate" to "high" and "very high" confidence comes with high value premiums. More mature segments have a higher willingness to pay for quality.

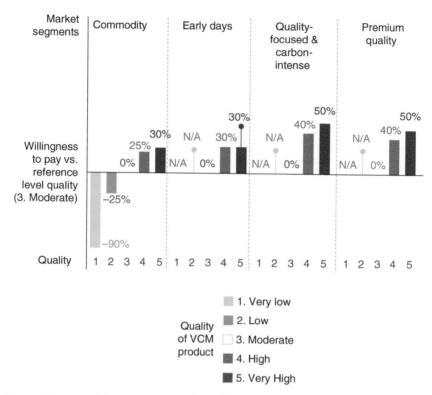

FIGURE 24.3   Conjoint analysis showing willingness to pay based on quality

The conjoint also aimed to understand what project type was the most important for each buyer segment. Figure 24.4 shows the results of this analysis, taking sustainable management of forests and their conservation, called REDD+ (Reducing Emissions from Deforestation and Forest Degradation), as the reference point due to their large volume.

All buyer segments value removals more than avoidance and are willing to pay high premiums for forestry-based and other nature removals. Companies see these projects as more defensible, particularly since the current Science-Based Targets initiative (SBTi)[7] guidance only accepts removals. Moreover, companies may find that forestry-based removals are the most straightforward and cost-effective option for meeting their emissions reduction targets, because the cost of direct air capture and other technologies is significantly higher than the cost of forestry-based removals, and their availability and the level of awareness lower. However, these credit purchases are often limited by supply.

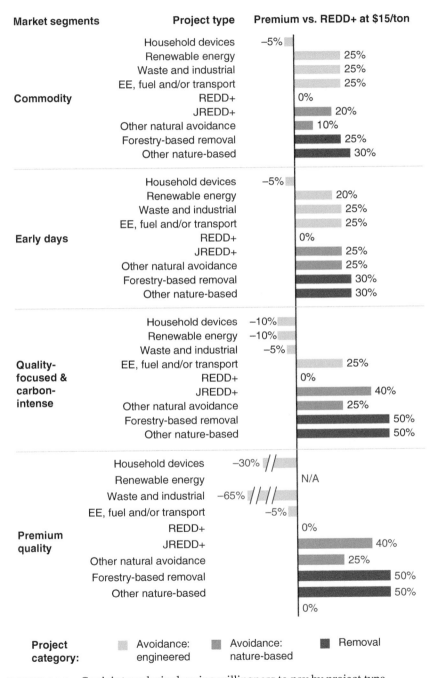

FIGURE 24.4 Conjoint analysis showing willingness to pay by project type

For avoidance credits, segments have different "hierarchies" in their preferences for renewable energy (RE) projects versus nature-based solutions (NBS). More mature segments prefer NBS over engineered avoidance credits, more aligned with the market's broader understanding of credit quality by project type. The Premium Quality segment is less likely to purchase waste and industrials, renewable energy, and household devices, while Quality-Focused would mostly not consider renewable energy credits. Less mature segments are largely indifferent in their preferences across avoidance credits, with even a slight preference for renewable energy, indicating potential low awareness of quality vis-à-vis project type.

Companies also care about how well the projects that generate the credit align with their image and brand. By selecting specific projects, buyers can demonstrate their commitment to certain sustainability goals and enhance their reputation with their customers, employees, and shareholders. In 2019, Patagonia launched its "Action Works" campaign, which included a series of advertisements promoting its carbon compensation efforts. One of the advertisements featured the Maasai Wilderness Conservation Trust, a carbon offset project in Kenya that Patagonia has invested in. The advertisement highlighted the positive impact of the project on local communities and the environment, and encouraged viewers to support the project by purchasing Patagonia products.

Given the variation in preferences among different buyer segments, it is possible to design a lineup of carbon offsets that caters to each specific need. The drivers of willingness to pay discussed here can become the primary inputs for offer development. It is therefore important for businesses to continue segmenting their product lineup based on quality and project type, while being transparent and consistent in their pricing model. Within the desired quality and type, customers can then easily identify specific projects that are a good match with their geographic locations and their climate and broader impact narratives.

A way to strengthen the chances of success of the product lineup is to create a high value offering with unique features and a premium price point. This offer can act as an anchor for buyers across all segments and increase demand for carbon credits at higher price levels.

We can draw a parallel to the market for smartphones in 2007, when it consisted of devices with physical keyboards and limited functionality, such as those sold by BlackBerry and Nokia. The iPhone transformed that market by changing the way people use and think about their devices. It also had a significant impact on consumer demand, by introducing a new level of user experience and functionality that consumers came to expect. It paved the way for the development of a wide range of high-quality devices.

Although the iPhone is a success story in the Value Game, we feel that the survey results we've presented indicate clear room for such a transformative offer at the high end of the VCM in a Choice Game. Developing and providing such a high end offering could help the VCM market to take off by attracting buyers with high willingness to pay from the Premium Quality and Quality-Focused and Carbon-Intense segments. For example, some suppliers can invest in developing technologies to provide highly durable carbon removal via Direct Air Capture (DAC). DAC is a method that captures large amounts of air through a mechanical process and uses a chemical filter to remove carbon dioxide. This process is expensive and not yet implemented on a large scale. But these apparent issues are not a problem for a high-end offer in the Choice Game.

The related carbon credit would attract new buyers, increase demand, and expand the overall market. The price premium of this unique offering would allow sellers to earn higher profits and reinvest in innovation and communications to educate the market, creating a virtuous circle. An offer with far superior value, priced at a high premium would also anchor buyers across all segments and offerings at higher prices. This would likely result in a healthier market.

At the same time, the VCM still needs carbon credits at a middle-low price point to appeal to customers with lower willingness to pay, such as the Commodity and Early Days segments. These credits are the entry-level offer into the VCM, with the objective of upselling buyers over time to more expensive and higher-quality projects. The credits still need to meet minimum benchmarks of quality that provide sufficient confidence in their impact. Education will be needed to improve awareness about the importance of quality and promote the adoption of higher-end offers.

Non-governmental organizations (NGOs) can play a key role in educating buyers, raising standards, and shaping policies to increase awareness and preference for undervalued attributes. Carbon standard setters (e.g., emissions reductions standards, carbon markets certifications) can assess raising standards to elevate the market, accompanied by an assessment of what prices carbon offset buyers may be able to bear.

Low-maturity customers can also work internally on their awareness and enhance the quality and value of their carbon credit portfolio by developing internal policies and procedures that align with industry standards, seeking guidance from industry experts, prioritizing credits based on essential quality attributes, and learning from leading buyers.

Shifting the VCM to a Choice Game in such a way would enable faster and higher-impact moves in the climate chess game, increasing our odds of success by breaking free of the constraints that come with the current Custom Game.

Key takeaways

Voluntary carbon market (VCM) offerings consist of carbon credits that are generated from individual projects sold to few buyers at different and negotiated prices. But VCM companies have encountered many challenges to grow in the Custom Game, such as pricing opacity and oversupply. We recommend the following approach to facilitate a move to the Choice Game:

1. **Segment the market:** Buyers can be split into segments based on their level of maturity and carbon intensity, and have different willingness to pay and preferences across carbon credits.

2. **Design a segment-specific portfolio of offerings:** Given the variation in preferences among different buyer segments, it is possible to design a carbon offsets lineup that caters to each specific need.

3. **Anchor the market at the high end:** The VCM needs high-quality anchor products with innovative features to appeal to high-end buyers and anchor the rest of the market in higher-quality, higher-value, and higher-price offerings.

CHAPTER 25

Impact: How Progressive Pricing Can Scale Social Ventures

With contributions from Marco Bertini and Richard Hutchinson

S ocial impact is the outcome of interventions that aim to address large, fundamental challenges such as poverty, disease, and inequity. Charitable nonprofits – funded by donations from benefactors and grants from funding institutions and foundations – traditionally lead these efforts by providing beneficiaries with free solutions. Examples include free food from local food banks or free health care from Doctors Without Borders/Médecins Sans Frontières.

But charitable nonprofits are in a perpetual state of having too many needs and ambitious goals and too little money to meet them. Fundraising is time-consuming, unpredictable, and loaded with conditional fine print, as donors often attach their own agendas to their contributions. They struggle to deliver consistently on their bold initiatives or scale as fast as they would like. These struggles slow the world's collective progress toward mitigating and resolving social injustices and challenges.

The struggles of nonprofits have also led to the emergence of other forms of social impact organizations (SIOs). Today, we can think of a spectrum from purely charitable nonprofits to for-profit social enterprises. In between are the earned income nonprofits, which derive related and unrelated income. The Girl Scouts of America, for example, has two streams of related income from their primary functions: membership fees and cookie sales.[1] Selling cookies directly helps the girls by developing entrepreneurship and financial empowerment,[2] and 76% of the cost of each box is reinvested in the troop.[3] Unrelated income, in contrast, lacks a direct link to the nonprofit's primary function. Out of the Closet, for example, provides medical care for patients suffering from HIV/ AIDS,[4] but also operates thrift stores. Some 96% of revenue from these stores goes toward funding prevention and treatment, but this represents unrelated income because selling secondhand goods does not directly help patients.

How could SIOs create significant new streams of related and unrelated income without jeopardizing the integrity of their missions or their nonprofit status? The answer – which should come as no surprise if you have read this far – is for the SIOs to change their pricing game. SIOs of all kinds tend to operate in the Cost or Uniform Game. We think they – and especially their beneficiaries and society as a whole – have a lot to gain from a move to the Choice Game by adopting price differentiation.

Many nonprofits can mitigate their financial issues by charging for the solutions they provide, turning beneficiaries into customers. As long as the SIO continues to provide solutions that customers pay for, the move to a "commercial" model would produce an independent and steady source of revenue. This would decrease dependence on fundraising from donors and institutions issuing grants, thus increasing the stability needed to make longer-term plans.

The commercial model also recognizes that social impact depends on more than giving beneficiaries access to something. Creating enduring positive impact is essentially value creation, which results from the combined effects of access, consumption, and performance. SIOs achieve it only when those in need have access to a solution, use the solution, and benefit from using the solution.

In other words, the commercial model shifts an SIO's mindset from what is essentially a margin equation – how can they give their beneficiaries something at the lowest cost? – to a value equation, which challenges them to create the best combination of access, consumption, and performance without calling the integrity of their mission into question. By introducing prices, SIOs give themselves an important tool to achieve greater social impact by optimizing access, consumption, and performance. If we consider social impact as a long-term proposition, the incremental earned revenue clearly contributes more to financial sustainability than no earned revenue at all.

Why nonprofits hesitate to become commercial

Most nonprofits have hesitated to charge for their solutions and convert beneficiaries to customers. One concern is that doing so would shift their focus from delivering on their mission to chasing revenue. That is a valid concern, but it depends both on how the organization generates the revenue and how it spends it. A nonprofit can commercialize activities that relate directly to their mission rather than focusing on unrelated activities that may be more lucrative but could call a nonprofit status into question.

Another concern is the perceived injustice associated with charging people money, even small amounts, to fulfill their needs. That is also a valid concern, but that perception arises when someone equates access with impact. Access is essential to driving impact, but insufficient on its own. What good is installing a water pump in a rural sub-Saharan village if no one uses it because it is not trusted? Or because it broke down quickly after installation due to poor quality? Or because the water it provides is not clean?

Witness the success of Project Maji, which uses a commercial model to increase access to clean water to villages in sub-Saharan Africa by installing and maintaining water infrastructure. Maji Cubes are solar-powered water kiosks that dispense a unit of water whenever a payment is made.[5] Customers pay using an automated cashless system as they get the value, and Project Mali uses the revenues to cover operating expenses, technical support, and long-term repairs. The dispensing fees allow each Maji Cube to be self-sustaining. Thus, Project Maji can conserve their donated funds for capital investments, allowing them to install more Cubes with the same amount of fundraising. By charging customers for using water, Maji expanded overall access.

A price, even an extremely small one, creates a "moment of truth" when the potential beneficiaries assess the value they could receive. Their acceptance of the tradeoff indicates their level of engagement. The price also provides ongoing feedback on how well each solution is truly addressing the needs of beneficiaries. It can reveal a lack of engagement in situations, for example, when an SIO has designed a solution to meet the desires of the donor who funded the initiative but has not met the real needs of the potential beneficiaries.

How charging for initiatives can increase their social impact

Price is often perceived by social entrepreneurs as nothing more than an obstacle to access, when access is the way the SIO defines successful impact. In that case, SIOs default to a logic of setting the price as low as possible (ideally, zero) and looking for ways to cut costs. Yet, paradoxically, charging a price can actually increase access. The problem lies in two flaws in the logic of that default strategy.

Let's look at Figure 25.1, which helps expose the perceived tradeoff – a choice between reaching more people or charging them something – as false. If you abandon the premise that everyone pays the same prices, you can differentiate prices based on value and expand the market because those who pay more cross-subsidize the others. First, not all prices need to be identical and certainly not all at zero. It is possible to differentiate. Second, not all costs play the same role in pricing decisions, as we explained in Chapter 1. If costs are largely fixed, it is still possible to have zero as a price for some beneficiaries. Third, not-for-profit does not necessarily mean not-for-revenue. As long as the incremental revenue matches the sum of fixed costs and marginal costs, the SIO achieves a steady stream of income that provides financial stability and sustainability, enables it to expand its reach, and broadens overall access.

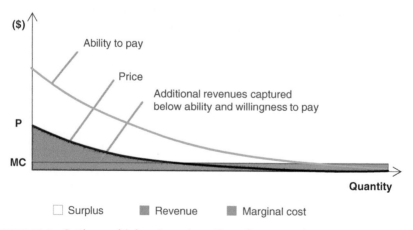

FIGURE 25.1 Setting multiple price points allows for more value capture

Charging for solutions can also increase impact by increasing consumption. Behavioral economics has shown that consumption can increase with the price people pay.[6] For example, customers who paid more for a theater subscription attended more plays.[7] However, the positive correlation between consumption and price is not universal.[8] In Madagascar, where the World Bank estimates that over 80% of people live on less than $2.15 per day,[9] a randomized experiment showed that prices above zero reduced both demand and use of insecticide-treated bed nets for preventing malaria.[10] But the constraint in that case is ability to pay, not willingness to pay. While an organization can shape willingness to pay by changing the value and the communication, ability to pay is an absolute constraint that is hard to overcome.

Another weakness of the default strategy of minimizing prices by minimizing costs can also reduce social impact – regardless of how much access it provides – because it reduces how well the solution performs. You might recall the "$100 laptop" once designed and produced by One Laptop per Child (OLPC), a nonprofit with the ambitious goal of delivering "hundreds of millions" of computers around the world to the lowest-income people, who would otherwise have no access to a device. In 2007 it launched its device, known as the XO, at a price of $188 at a time when entry-level laptops in the United States were priced between $599 and $1,099.[11]

OLPC thus achieved its goal of a low price, but it only delivered 50,000 machines to two countries. What happened? To achieve that low price, OLPC cut so many corners that the XO barely worked. To save costs on solid-state drives, the XO only had 1 GB of storage. It was powered by a hand crank that was difficult for kids to use.

How higher revenue drives greater scale and greater impact

In 1976, a Bangladeshi economics professor named Mohammed Yunus loaned $27 to 42 women in the village of Jobra, to support the purchase of raw materials for their bamboo furniture businesses. To his surprise, all 42 borrowers paid him back. But even more shocking was the change in their daily profits. They rose from 2¢ to $2, as the women no longer had to pay interest to usurious money lenders.[12]

Yunus had pioneered microfinance, which has evolved into a social impact initiative almost unrivaled in terms of uptake or influence. The World Bank has estimated that upwards of 100 million individuals have taken advantage of microfinance over the past four decades, with as much as $25 billion circulating in the industry.[13]

Those initial loans gave Yunus a valuable insight to the creditworthiness of the poor. They had trustworthiness and financial sensibility – what they lacked were resources. In 1983, after successfully piloting microloans throughout Bangladesh, he opened Grameen Bank. Grameen's 20% interest rates were significantly lower than traditional money lenders' rates of 100% to 120%.[14]

Today, thousands of microfinance organizations have spread throughout the world, with products customized to the diverse needs of the global poor.[15] Grameen Bank itself has lent to over 10 million members, with a historical repayment of 97%, which is higher than other banking systems.[16]

The successful global expansion of microfinance shows how SIOs can overcome one of their biggest challenges to creating more lasting social impact: scale. The missing accelerant for greater scale is profit, but many SIOs may shudder at the prospect of profiting from their initiatives. It seems antithetical to their mission and threatening to their legal status. Yet Grameen Bank is actually still a nonprofit, despite the profitability of its lending. Grameen Bank's overall profits are virtually zero, because its interest rates are low and because almost all of its interest income goes back to its owners, who are the borrowers themselves.

This logical link between profit and purpose is simple. If an SIO generates excess revenue instead of losing money, it not only becomes self-sustaining, but also gains incentives to expand, supported by markets as well as its mission. Generating revenue can increase social impact by improving access, consumption, and performance. Generating excess revenue – that is, profits – not only enables an SIO to deliver those same improvements on a larger scale, but also encourages other organizations to begin providing their own solutions. The scaling of social impact accelerates, because profit scales not only the SIO's own organization, but also scales the overall mission by bringing others into the effort.

Holding a nonprofit status means making no profit on a net basis, not making no profit on any individual transaction. A mix effect makes sense, with some transactions making money and some losing. This mindset opens up the left side of Figure 25.1 instead of keeping the SIO trapped on the right side, where direct income is at or below marginal cost.

We also contend that being a nonprofit, in that sense, comes with an obligation to develop the right pricing strategy. In the next section, we look at how SIOs can play the Choice Game and implement an approach we call progressive pricing, again, to tap into the market on the left-hand side of Figure 25.1.

Progressive pricing is an option for social ventures

In Chapter 20, which focused on pairing fairness, we laid out the ethical case for progressive pricing, which allows increased access to populations with low ability to pay while generating revenues from segments with high willingness to pay. Progressive pricing therefore avoids the artificial or false tradeoff between providing broad access and ensuring stable financing for social impact. Progressive taxation is the largest-scale implementation of such a strategy at a country level.

As in the Choice Game, a fundamental rationale for progressive pricing for SIOs is that people have different abilities and willingness to pay because they receive different amounts of value from the same or similar service. Some people also perceive that they have more means to contribute to a cause that benefits a group and are therefore willing to contribute more to express solidarity with others who have less means.

Some organizations implement this progressive strategy by letting people contribute as much as they want or can. The Wikipedia Foundation or National Public Radio (NPR), a US media nonprofit, regularly launch campaigns to request donations from their users and listeners, respectively. Over the years, NPR has developed a curated lineup of gift packages that correspond to different monthly contributions. This reflects the insights from behavioral science that too much choice confuses people, whereas an organized set of specific options makes it easier for listeners to self-select how to contribute.

Some organizations have implemented means-based variation for contributions, such as Playworks, a nonprofit based in California, which supports children's physical health through play. To increase social impact, they have created a set of offers with three different levels of services at three different price points, which also vary based on the income levels of the students' families at each school. The highest-end offer, Playworks

Coach, costs between $60,000 and $65,000 and includes an onsite coach to help manage recess, train students, and create activity schedules.[17] But schools can qualify for 50% subsidies of up to 50%, based on the income level of their students' families. By providing a range of services with price points that account for both ability and willingness to pay, Playworks generates revenue that helps it maintain financial stability and scale its services to more schools.

But we are not advocating this as a universal solution, because creating a mix of high- and low-value offers can be difficult or undesirable. For example, the Global Alliance for Vaccines and Immunization (GAVI), a public–private global health partnership, cannot create a lineup of vaccinations with different efficacies and different price points, nor does it want to. Nonetheless, we think progressive pricing is a solution worth exploring in many situations. In terms of social impact, the economic framing of the Choice Game is more powerful than the Cost or Uniform Game's, as we illustrate in the final case study of this chapter and book.

How the strategic pricing questions are also relevant for nonprofit organizations

In the Introduction, we presented the three pricing questions that leaders must answer to define their pricing strategy. Here, we show how Global Certifications, an education nonprofit organization, can review their pricing strategy – and increase their impact – by using these questions as their guide.

Global Certifications (GC) provides education services including curricula, lesson plans, teaching resources, and examinations. Its offerings are widely acknowledged as high-quality and proven to provide students with significant benefit. However, GC has not scaled its services beyond a 5% penetration rate in developed countries, even though its offerings are suitable for students anywhere in the world. How can GC create a pricing strategy that will help it broaden its social impact?

First, GC must examine how it creates and shares value.

- What do you do to create **measurable value** for your customers?
- What are the main **drivers of value** and the **limitations** to value creation?
- How do your **differentiation and growth objectives** justify how you share value with your customers?

GC creates measurable value in three main ways: designing courses and providing materials for learning and assessment, supporting professional development for teachers, and providing internationally recognized qualifications to students who pass its exams. The main drivers of this value creation are the number of schools that have adopted GC's courses, the number of teachers who benefit from its professional development, and the number of students who learn its curriculum and pass its exams. All three are correlated, but the difference within and across the three drivers could open up possibilities for differentiation.

As a nonprofit organization, GC is self-funding the costs of developing and updating high-quality courses, training, and qualifications by charging course and service fees to schools. The fees also take into consideration reinvestment in product and service innovation. But after careful evaluation, it realized that many schools and teachers, while interested in its courses, cannot afford them. GC was ready to consider a different pricing strategy that would allow it to reduce or remove this barrier and pursue greater social impact.

The next step was for GC to decide what pricing game to play. This decision derives from answers to the following three questions:

1. Which game aligns best with the characteristics of your market?
2. Which game aligns best with your current pricing approach?
3. Which game aligns best with the market forces and your competitive advantages?

GC's main competitive advantage is the reputation and quality of its curricula and lesson plans. Developing and maintaining them is primarily a fixed cost, largely independent from the number of schools and students served. The transition to remote learning during Covid opened up possibilities for other ways of learning.

So far, GC had played the Uniform Game, by default rather than by careful consideration. It applied the same transparent rate card to everyone and had no formal discount program.

GC realized that its business characteristics and competitive advantage were both aligned to the Choice Game. For example, it could increase the range and flexibility of the packages offered to both schools and teachers by varying the number of subjects offered to each school or by adding digital options to their professional trainings. The characteristics of the education market were also a good fit for the Choice Game. Schools form a fragmented customer base with diverse needs, and only a few competitors could match the breadth and depth of GC's offerings. Finally, GC wanted to serve a broader population of schools and students. The Choice Game is ideal to facilitate that goal by enabling GC to offer low-price options in a way that does not anger its existing base of schools.

The final step for GC was to define a pricing model that best fits its value creation strategy:

- What should your **pricing architecture** be (i.e., pricing basis, offer structure, and pricing mechanism)?
- What should drive your **price variation** (e.g., geography, channel, and time)?
- What **price adjustment levers** should you use (i.e., customer programs, transaction incentives, and fees and functional discounts)?

The offer structure is the most important component of the pricing model in the Choice Game. GC decided to offer a wide range of online courses in addition to the in-person training and conferences. They decided that keeping the same pricing mechanism (price set by seller) made the most sense but saw an opportunity to choose a pricing basis and formula that introduced more price differentiation. For example, GC explored changes to their school certification program and their exam pricing. Instead of charging per student, they could charge per school and lower the charge per student to the minimum possible fee to cover the test costs. They also created a program for school districts where the price per school would decrease as the number of schools enrolled in the program increased.

Next, GC considered what factors should drive its price variation. It chose two main factors: country and type of school. It knew that developed countries had a greater ability to pay for its offerings, but also that public schools tend to have tighter budgets than private schools, suggesting differences in ability to pay. Implementing these price variation drivers would allow GC to expand access by providing a targeted way to reduce prices.

Finally, GC also evaluated different price adjusters. It considered implementing a fee waiver program for schools that could not pay the fees for setting up GC courses.

As of this writing, GC is starting to roll out their new pricing strategy, which will take a couple of years to implement in full. So, there is no real outcome or hindsight perspective yet. But GC demonstrates how these simple questions can spark better conversations around pricing strategy and help organizations of all kinds explore their degrees of freedom in an efficient, constructive, and confident way. The Strategy Hex simplifies and clarifies seemingly complicated pricing questions that often elude precise answers. It also shows once again that a company can define an innovative pricing strategy without ever discussing specific prices.

Key takeaways

Despite plenty of great work from many social impact organizations, there is still much progress to be made on a number of important social challenges.

Nonprofit organizations unnecessarily shy away from prices and profits, for fear of reducing social impact. But pricing is an important lever for increasing and scaling impact. If used properly it can optimize access, consumption, and performance.

By designing a lineup of offers with price points that account for ability to pay and willingness to pay, social impact organizations can provide their target population with choices and have them become invested in the consumption and performance of solutions. We recommend the following approach:

- **Take a positive view of pricing:** Pricing is a strong and significant pricing lever that social impact organizations (SIOs) shouldn't be afraid to use more.
- **Understand the link between pricing and impact:** SIOs have a lot of freedom to charge for solutions in ways that protect, or even enhance, social impact.
- **Differentiate prices to influence behavior:** SIOs can use price differentiation to increase access and share how beneficiaries respond. Price differentiation should take both ability to pay and willingness to pay into account.

As you move on . . .

We assume you are now quite familiar with the Hex, the games, and our Pricing Strategy questions and how to answer them. We hope this gave you new ideas about how to change your business, your market, or maybe society.

If you are working in a nonprofit involved in a social venture or interested in a social problem:

- Can a new strategic pricing approach help?
- If yes, use the three strategic questions to determine whether and how it can help.

The Three Questions for Determining Your Pricing Strategy

Question 1: How do you create and share value?

Your answer to this first fundamental question derives from your answers to these three questions:

1a. What do you do to create **measurable value** for your customers?

1b. What are your main **drivers of value** and the **limitations** to value creation?

1c. How do your **differentiation and growth objectives** justify how you share value with your customers?

Question 2: What pricing game do you want to play?

2a. Which game aligns best with the **characteristics of your market?**

2b. Which game aligns best with your **current pricing approach?**

2c. Which game aligns best with the **market forces** and your **competitive advantages?**

Question 3: What pricing model best fits your value creation strategy?

3a. What should your **pricing architecture** be (i.e., pricing basis, offer structure, and pricing mechanism)?

3b. What should drive your **price variation** (e.g., geography, channel, and time)?

3c. What price **adjustment** levers should you use (i.e., customer programs, transaction incentives, and fees and functional discounts)?

Epilogue

Over the weekend before finalizing the manuscript of this book, one of us attended a wedding in New York City. A guest at the reception was the founder and CEO of an AI startup. After learning that we were working on a pricing book, he sighed.

"Pricing, I struggle with this every day," he said.

After several years of hard work and a few test customers, he was getting a very strong commercial response and scaling up of his business. But after observing differences in customer value across industries and seeing his marginal costs get lower and lower, he was not sure how to set a single appropriate price point. The Cost Game and Uniform Game price mindsets were in play, even though the Choice Game on the opposite end of Hex seemed like a much better fit to his situation.

Another guest was a successful serial entrepreneur in health care services. His latest venture had a revolutionary testing technology for a relatively common type of cancer. The technology not only had significantly better sensitivity and specificity but was also less costly and less invasive than other technologies. Most importantly, it could be used to screen larger portions of the population in routine doctor checkups and detect cancer very early on. His struggle, though, was finding a way to incentivize the medical community to adopt this test. While he was appropriately thinking in terms of the Value Game, he was also taking for granted that his pricing model couldn't deviate from established industry practices. The parallels with the hepatitis C story in Chapter 22 were stark.

These anecdotes – and the multiple and diverse examples in our book – show how pervasive pricing opportunities are across businesses, markets, and society. The power of the Strategic Pricing Hexagon and the pricing games it defines lie in its simplicity and broad applicability. Simplicity – because just naming a game provides clear guidance on a strategic path to grow or scale a business. Breadth – because once you have the Hex in your strategic toolkit, you will find applications all around you.

To illustrate this, let's briefly analyze yet one more market that touches almost all of us in some way in our lifetimes: the labor market. The wages we receive are the price set for our work. The Covid crisis brought this fact to the forefront, because it launched all kinds of fascinating conversations and reflections about how to compensate workers who had moved far from their headquarters to work remotely, say, from a village in the mountains. The debates on their compensation touched on the typical three sources of information – cost, value, and competition:

- "They are moving to a place with a much lower cost of living, so we should reduce their compensation."
- "Yes, but they are doing the same job and delivering the same value to the company, so why would we change how we pay them?"
- "Well, we should look at how much they would be paid if they were to work for another company and that should be our benchmark."

It is not a big stretch to go one step further and find situations that match each of the games. Let's switch the order in which we go through the games one last time.

We'll start with the Custom Game, which involves negotiations between workers and employers based on what that worker would get paid in the "market." This is very typical of knowledge workers, but extends far beyond them. Each job offer they receive will be customized to their specific role, experience, skillset, and other factors. After getting the offer, most knowledge workers will negotiate on the salary, bonus, and benefits, usually bringing arguments about what they were getting paid before or could earn elsewhere. As a result, the companies hiring such workers are more likely to have a chaos cloud, which captures the massive variation in the total wages paid to each worker. The best practice is for human resources to establish some guardrails by defining bands depending on qualifications.

When the employers become larger, and those bands become tighter, we move to the Choice Game. Most large corporations recruiting undergraduates for their first full-time job have fixed starting wages and do not negotiate with students. They will then have bands for different levels of employees, which are correlated to a certain extent with their title, level in the org chart, experience, and competitive opportunities. Promotions and pay raises are the paths to upsell in this game.

What happens when we get to senior leaders in these large corporations? New compensation mechanisms come into play with grants of stock and stock options that align compensation with shareholder value creation. In 2021, just over a quarter of compensation for the typical CEO at an S&P 500 company came from cash salary or bonus.[1] This is typical of the **Value Game** and one of the factors that drives income inequality. The ratio between CEOs and lowest-paid workers has increased more than tenfold since the introduction of these new compensation mechanisms in the 1970s and 1980s.[2] The pricing mindset is completely different and drives a different pricing structure.

Contrasting that approach are the ones that characterize the wages of most union workers. We are now at the top of the Hex in the Uniform Game. Union wages are typically set through a collective bargaining agreement between the union and the employer. In general, union wages are transparent to members, and unions will negotiate different fixed wages for different roles, similar to how a retailer sets different prices for different products.

The Cost Game can characterize the wages paid to minimum wage workers, who are not unionized. Across the world, minimum wages are often set based on the cost of living at the time. They typically increase periodically based on some measure of inflation.[3] The Pew Research Center found that at least 80 countries, including France, Germany, and the United Kingdom, have an explicit requirement to revisit minimum wages every so often – in most cases annually or once every two years.[4] Thus, the minimum wage, if periodically adjusted, should be equal to the minimum cost of sustaining one worker.

Unlike the Uniform and Cost Games, the Power Game characterizes the wages of rare and exceptional workers who have few employers to choose from. Sports superstars match this situation and, indeed, game theory and high-stakes negotiations regularly create riveting drama for sports fans. Soccer superstars, for example, are few and far between. But so are prestigious teams with the wallets to pay for them. Ronaldo, Messi, Neymar, Mbappe, and now Haaland can only play for Real Madrid, Liverpool, Barcelona, Manchester (City or United), Bayern Munich, or Paris St. Germain (PSG). Each deal heavily impacts every other deal in the market.

The Dynamic Game is the newest to the labor market and captures the pay of workers in the "gig economy." Payments for rideshare or food delivery jobs can vary minute to minute. They depend on numerous factors, including supply and demand of labor, location, route, time of day, and competing employment alternatives. These factors are often identified by AI and fed into algorithms that output optimal wages.

None of these applications is a pure fit. But the rules, best practices, and typical winning strategies associated with each game provide new perspectives and insights into the labor market and how to deal with issues like income inequality.

After advocating for the Strategic Pricing Hexagon, it is time to thank you for your curiosity and persistence and leave you with some reminders about the nuanced applicability of this unified pricing framework.

1. Despite its broad applicability, the Hex, the seven pricing games, and all the concepts associated with them only provide the building blocks to think about pricing strategically. Real-life situations usually have a combination of the characteristics we have described for each of the *pure* pricing games. In other words, the pricing games are often entangled. After all, this is what gives players the pricing agency they need to change their games. We hope that you find the process of decomposing pricing problems through the lens of the games as insightful and enjoyable as we do in our client engagements.

2. As we set out to write a pricing strategy book, we intentionally de-emphasized price points throughout the entire book. We are not saying they are unimportant and should be overlooked. As in chess and other games of skill, the best strategy can lead to a resounding defeat if it is not backed up by sound tactical play. We hope the Hex will be your trusted tool to help you determine which tactical decisions matter most and how to bring together diverse sources of expertise and wisdom to set prices and avoid devastating mistakes.

3. Finally, although it took us 10 years to "mature" the Hex and fine-tune its consistency, the Hex is not meant to be set in stone. Pricing strategy is inherently complex, ambiguous, and nuanced. Philosophers and economists have debated value and its exchange since the earliest days of commerce. Ongoing research, debate, and experimentation are necessary, whether to build on the Hex or highlight its weaknesses. We look forward to that process.

Appendix: About the Studies

This section references the various studies cited in Part IV.

Chapter 20: Fairness

The survey referenced throughout this chapter is based on consumer research conducted in collaboration between the Boston Consulting Group (BCG) and the BCG Henderson Institute (BHI).

- Survey date: June 2019.
- Number of respondents: 13,256.
- Countries surveyed: United States, China, India, Brazil, Japan, Germany, France, and Sweden.
- Product and service categories: banking, electronics, groceries, hospitality, movie theaters, pharmacy, internet, gas stations, universities.
- Sources of price variation tested: senior discounts, student discounts, geographic price differences, time of purchase, channel of purchase, relative income of purchaser, and so on.

In the first part of the questionnaire, respondents answered general questions about perception of fairness in various commercial situations. It helped respondents think about the various aspects or pricing fairness and validated the richness of perceptions of fairness that we had explored in earlier qualitative research.

In the second part of the questionnaire, respondents were asked about what they would do in hypothetical situations where the share of value flowing to buyers and sellers was explicit. This was the newest part of this research effort that was specifically designed to test how value sharing influences perceptions of pricing fairness.

In each situation, the potential buyer of a product or service had the opportunity to contract a third party that could generate some savings or additional income. The amount of savings and the fees the respondent would have to pay to get the savings was clearly stated as well as the resulting share of the savings the fees would represent. We tested two savings scenario and one scenario where the value was additional income:

- Shopping at a retailer for a $500 TV with the help of a bulk buying club that can save up to $200 but will charge a fee that will be taken out of the $200 savings.
- Shopping online for $50 headphones with the help of an online plugin that could save up to $20 but charge a fee to get the savings.
- A job search service that charges a proportion of the $10,000 salary increase.

In each scenario we asked respondents about the fairness of the offer and the likelihood they would contract the third party. After that we told them that someone had contracted the same third party but got a higher proportion of the value. We then asked them to reevaluate the fairness of their transaction. The survey measured fairness in two ways: by using the average "fairness" that respondents assigned to a scenario, on a scale from 0 = "completely unfair" to 100 = "completely fair" and by using a score of the respondents' open-ended comments, based on a natural language processing algorithm.

Chapter 21: Equitable Pricing

The fairness consumer survey just described supported the analysis in this chapter about the perception of how value is shared between consumers and companies selling them products or services. To complement that study, one year later, the Boston Consulting Group (BCG) and the BCG Henderson Institute (BHI) conducted a second survey about fairness with business decision makers:

- Survey date: September 2020.
- Number of respondents: 805.
- Countries surveyed: United States, Canada, United Kingdom, Singapore, Australia, and New Zealand.
- Respondents spanned all industries, but 53% of them were in five sectors: financial services (15%), technology (11%), industrial goods (10%), professional services (9%), and retail (8%).
- Revenues of companies that participants work for ranged from $5 million to more than $20 billion. Half of respondents worked for companies with less than $500 million revenues.

We tested relative fairness of hypothetical B2B purchasing situations. Like in the consumer research described in Chapter 20, the value shared and captured by the seller was made explicit and the same questions were asked about likelihood to purchase and fairness perception. Two scenarios were about creating savings and one scenario about incremental revenues.

- An energy-saving system that could monitor electricity usage in buildings and use AI to reduce the electric bill in exchange for a fee.

- A new software that combines HR and accounting capabilities that suggest cost-savings opportunities in the HR department but charges a proportion of the savings.

- An advertisement placement optimization software that increases company revenues by using machine learning algorithms and charges based on a proportion of incremental revenues.

Chapter 22: Access

In 2018, the BCG Henderson Institute (BHI) and the Center for Disease Analysis (CDA) collaborated to develop an analysis of the potential impact of a payer licensing agreement (PLA) to treat hepatitis C virus (HCV) patients. The model included three countries: the United States, Italy, and the UK.

The model was a dynamic systems-based Markov model tuned using historical epidemiological data to forecast disease progression and associated health system costs for HCV patients. The Markov model was used to forecast viremic HCV prevalence over time and followed individual five-year age segments as they evolved. The model used direct costs for economic analyses and, for quality-adjusted life year (QALY) analyses only, costs associated with the burden of disease and their impact to society. For each country, we modeled three scenarios:

- Status quo with direct-acting antiviral (DAA) treatments priced and prescribed as they have been historically.

- WHO scenario, where DAA treatments are priced as they have been historically, and screening and treatment is increased to meet or exceed ambitious WHO targets.

- PLA scenario, where DAA treatments are priced using PLA and screening and treatment is increased to meet or exceed WHO targets.

The model projected cost and impact from 2018 to 2030 because of the WHO 2030 elimination target and because the first novel DAA (Sofosbuvir) loses exclusivity in 2030.

This study had two key results regarding HCV treatment:

1. If the PLA model were implemented, the number of patients treated and cured would double in the first three years, while the liver-related deaths (LRDs) would decrease by around 40–50%, versus status quo.

2. Implementing the PLA model would result in a decline in total payer costs of more than 25%, with an increase in pharmaceutical manufacturer revenues of 10%. These results were true across the three health care landscapes studied, the United States, the UK, and Italy, and were robust against variations to critical model parameters through sensitivity analysis.

In summary, the PLA scenario consistently overachieved the WHO's health objectives for 2030 while reducing the total cost to the health system.

Chapter 23: Green Premium

The survey referenced throughout this chapter is based on consumer research from two sources: the global consumer research on climate and sustainability from BCG's Center for Consumer Insight (CCI), and specific research from the BCG Henderson Institute (BHI) on willingness to pay for a green premium.

The CCI research provides a comprehensive view of consumer-centric sustainability. Customers were asked about their behaviors, needs, and perceptions overall.

- Survey date: June–July 2022
- Number of respondents: approximately 19,000
- Countries surveyed: United States, Japan, Germany, France, Italy, China, India, and Brazil
- Product and service categories: Consumer packaged goods, specifically beverages, snacks, skin care, and home care, retail, specifically grocery retail and dining, leisure travel, apparel, streaming media services, electronic devices, building materials, luxury products, electric utilities, and cars

Respondents were asked about how sustainability mattered to them and how it related to their core needs and purchase drivers. They were also asked about their perceptions of green versus gray products and about the key barriers toward adopting more sustainable behaviors. All responses were analyzed by category and market to derive granular insights and consistent patterns.

The BHI research is based on a survey conducted to assess how consumers perceive sustainable products.

- Survey date: November 2022
- Participants: approximately 500
- Countries surveyed: United States, China, and Germany
- Product categories: cars, dog food, jeans, and laundry detergent

The survey asked consumers a range of questions about the importance of sustainability in their daily choices, including their preference for green products over conventional ones. For example, they were asked if they would be willing to pay a 20% premium for a sustainable car compared to a conventional car. Additionally, respondents were asked to rank the factors that influence their purchasing decisions and identify any barriers preventing them from buying more sustainable products. The survey also investigated whether customers associate particular brands with sustainability. The survey enabled the drawing of the demand curve for each sustainable product category.

Chapter 24: CO$_2$

BCG conducted a survey of carbon credit buyers as part of a joint initiative with the Environmental Defense Fund. The goal of the research was to better understand and segment the buyers of voluntary carbon credits, assess the most important quality indicators for those buyers, and better understand willingness to pay and tradeoffs for different types of carbon credits.

- Survey date: November 2022.
- Participants: 478 companies.
- Global coverage: United States (62%), UK (11%), France (4%), Germany (4%), India (5%), Italy (3%), Spain (3%), Canada, Mexico, the Netherlands.

- Respondents spanned all industries, but two-thirds of them were in six sectors: manufacturing and industrial goods (21%), energy (11%), technology (11%), oil and gas (9%), professional services (8%), and financial institutions (7%).
- The number of employees in companies that participants worked for ranged from fewer than 50 (12%) to more than 50,000 (8%); 44% were between 500 and 10,000 employees.
- Product categories: Avoidance and removal carbon credits.

Companies have been classified based on their level of climate maturity and carbon emission intensity. Climate maturity was assessed based on ambition of climate targets, scope of emissions tracked, and understanding of voluntary carbon market (VCM) prices. Carbon intensity was assessed as a function of GHG intensity (tCO2e/$ EBITDA), which also tends to correlate with level of pressure from external stakeholders (e.g., investors, NGOs, regulators).

The survey asked buyers a range of questions about their preferences and willingness to pay among carbon credits based on their quality and their type of project. Participants were also asked to rate all core quality dimensions, such as additionality, measurement/reporting/verification (MRV), permanence, project/program type, co-benefits, location, vintage, and price.

The research identified different patterns in VCM willingness to pay across buyer segments, the primary perceived drivers of credit quality among respondents (e.g., additionality, project/program type), and other value drivers for voluntary carbon credits that were less technical in nature (e.g., co-benefits or project/program location that were more closely associated with storytelling benefits for the buyer's company).

Notes

Introduction

1. "GDP, Current Prices," International Monetary Fund, September 2022, **https://www.imf.org/external/datamapper/NGDPD@WEO/OEMDC/ ADVEC/WEOWORLD**.
2. Richard Smirke, "IFPI Global Report 2023: Music Revenues Climb 9% to $26.2 Billion," *Billboard*, March 3, 2023, **https://www.billboard.com/pro/ ifpi-global-report-2023-music-business-revenue-market-share/**.
3. Utpal M. Dholakia, "When Cost-Plus Pricing is a Good Idea," *Harvard Business Review*, July 2018, **https://hbr.org/2018/07/when-cost-plus-pricing-is-a-good-idea**.
4. Leila Abboud, "Analysis: Hard-up Telcos Get Stingy with Mobile Give-aways," Reuters, May 2012, **https://www.reuters.com/article/us-mobile-subsidy/ analysis-hard-up-telcos-get-stingy-with-mobile-give-aways-idIN BRE84N10Q20120524**.
5. David Goldman, "The iPhone Is a Nightmare for Carriers," *CNN Money*, February 8, 2012, **https://money.cnn.com/2012/02/08/technology/iphone_ carrier_subsidy/index.htm**.
6. Roger Cheng, "Verizon Unveils 'Share Everything' Family Plans for Data," *CNET Media*, June 12, 2012, **https://www.cnet.com/tech/mobile/verizon-unveils-share-everything-family-plans-for-data/**.
7. David Goldman, "AT&T Scraps Voice Minutes for 'Shared Data' Plan Option," *CNN Money*, July 18, 2012, **https://money.cnn.com/2012/07/18/technology/ att-mobile-share-plan/index.htm**.
8. "T-Mobile Introduces America's Only Unlimited 4G LTE Family Plan," T-Mobile USA, December 8, 2014, **https://www.t-mobile.com/news/press/ unlimited-family-plan**.
9. "Sprint Corporation Form 10-K for Fiscal Year Ended March 31, 2016," U.S. Securities and Exchange Commission, 2016, **https://www.sec.gov/ Archives/edgar/data/101830/000010183016000066/sprintcorp201510-k.htm**.
10. "2015 Annual Report," T-Mobile, Inc., 2015, **https://s29.q4cdn.com/ 310188824/files/doc_financials/2015/ar/2015_Annual_Report.pdf**.
11. "2014 Annual Report," Telefónica S.A., 2014, **https://www.telefonica.com/ en/shareholders-investors/financial-reports/historical-archive-annual-eports/2014/**.
12. "2017 Annual Report," Telefónica S.A., 2017, **https://www.telefonica.com/ en/shareholders-investors/financial-reports/historical-archive-annual-reports/2017/**.

13. Rachel E. Greenspan, "'It's the Legacy of Slavery': Here's the Troubling History Behind Tipping Practices in the U.S.," *TIME USA,* updated August 20, 2019, **https://time.com/5404475/history-tipping-american-restaurants-civil-war/**.

14. Saru Jayaraman, *Forked: A New Standard for American Dining* (New York, NY: Oxford University Press, 2016).

15. Ibid.

16. Roberto A. Ferdman, "I Dare You to Read This and Still Feel Good About Tipping," *Washington Post,* February 18, 2016, **https://www.washingtonpost .com/news/wonk/wp/2016/02/18/i-dare-you-to-read-this-and-still-feel-ok-about-tipping-in-the-united-states/**.

17. Mike Rodriguez, Teófilo Reyes, Minsu Longiaru, and Kalpana Krishnamurthy, *The Glass Floor: Sexual Harassment in the Restaurant Industry* (New York, NY: Restaurant Opportunities Centers United Forward Together, 2014).

18. Michael Lynn, Michael C. Sturman, Christie Ganley, Elizabeth Adams, Mathew Douglas, and Jessica McNeil, "Consumer Racial Discrimination in Tipping: A Replication and Extension," Cornell University School of Hospitality Administration, January 1, 2008, **https://ecommons.cornell.edu/handle/ 1813/71558**.

19. "Minimum Wages for Tipped Employees," U.S. Department of Labor, January 1, 2023, **https://www.dol.gov/agencies/whd/state/minimum-wage/tipped**.

20. Restaurant Opportunities Center United, *Recipe for Success: Abolish the Subminimum Wage to Strengthen the Restaurant Industry* (New York, NY: ROC United, 2014).

21. Michael E. Porter and Mark R. Kramer, "Creating Shared Value," *Harvard Business Review*, January–February 2011, **https://hbr.org/2011/01/the-big-idea-creating-shared-value**.

Part I

1. "The Model T," Ford Motor Company, March 2022, **https://corporate.ford .com/articles/history/the-model-t.html**.

2. Austin Weber, "Ten Ways the Model T Changed the World," *Assembly*, September 2, 2008, **https://www.assemblymag.com/articles/85804-ten-ways-the-model-t-changed-the-world**.

3. Henry Ford, *My Life and Work*, Kindle edition, location 466. Originally published by Doubleday, New York: 1922.

4. Ibid., locations 489–490.

5. Ibid., locations 636–637.

6. Ibid., locations 624–625.

7. Ibid., locations 603–605.

8. Weber, "Ten Ways the Model T Changed the World."

9. Lindsay Brooke, "Mr. Ford's T: Versatile Mobility," *New York Times*, July 20, 2008, **https://www.nytimes.com/2008/07/20/automobiles/collectibles/20FORD.html**.

10. Weber, "Ten Ways the Model T Changed the World."

11. Mark R. Wilson, "Yellow Cab Co. (of Chicago)," *Dictionary of Leading Chicago Businesses (1820–2000)* (The Electronic Encyclopedia of Chicago, 2005), **http://www.encyclopedia.chicagohistory.org/pages/2912.html**.

12. Robert Tate, "A Brief History of Taxicabs 1907–1968," *Motorcities*, October 10, 2018, **https://www.motorcities.org/story-of-the-week/2018/a-brief-history-of-taxicabs-1907-1968**.

13. Walter L. Jacobs death notice, *Chicago Tribune*, February 10, 1985, **https://www.chicagotribune.com/news/ct-xpm-1985-02-10-8501080541-story.html**.

14. "GM Heritage," General Motors, March 2023, **https://www.gm.com/heritage**.

15. "Advertisement for General Motors, 'A Car for Every Purse and Purpose,' 1925," The Henry Ford, **https://www.thehenryford.org/collections-and-research/digital-collections/artifact/192114/**.

16. Steve Finlay, "The Rise and Fall of Automotive Leasing," Wards Auto, March 1, 2004, **https://www.wardsauto.com/news-analysis/rise-and-fall-automotive-leasing**.

Chapter 1

1. James Goodman, "Men's Haircut Prices – How Much Does A Haircut Cost?," *MensHairstylesToday,* January 3, 2023, **https://www.menshairstylestoday.com/haircut-prices-barber-tip/**.

2. "From Paper-Clip to House in 14 Trades," *CBC News*, July 7, 2006, **https://www.cbc.ca/news/canada/from-paper-clip-to-house-in-14-trades-1.573973**.

3. Kyle MacDonald, "What If You Could Trade a Paper Clip for a House?," YouTube, uploaded by TedXTalks, November 2015, **https://www.youtube.com/watch?v=8s3bdVxuFBs**.

4. Cathy Free, "A Guy Once Swapped a Paperclip to Get a House. This Woman Is Trying to Do the Same," *Washington Post*, August 20, 2020, **https://www.washingtonpost.com/lifestyle/2020/08/20/guy-once-swapped-paperclip-house-this-woman-is-trying-do-same/**.

5. "Roberto Goizueta," obituary, *The Economist,* October 23, 1997, **https://www.economist.com/obituary/1997/10/23/roberto-goizueta**.

6. "Rolls-Royce Celebrates 50th Anniversary of Power-by-the-Hour," press release, Rolls-Royce, October 30, 2012, **https://www.rolls-royce.com/media/press-releases-archive/yr-2012/121030-the-hour.aspx**.

7. "'Power by the Hour': Can Paying Only for Performance Redefine How Products Are Sold and Serviced?," Knowledge at Wharton podcast, February 21, 2007, **https://knowledge.wharton.upenn.edu/podcast/knowledge-at-wharton-podcast/power-by-the-hour-can-paying-only-for-performance-redefine-how-products-are-sold-and-serviced/**.

8. Rebecca Sadwick Shaddix, "How to Price Your Product: A Guide to the Van Westendorp Pricing Model," *Forbes,* June 22, 2020, **https://www.forbes.com/sites/rebeccasadwick/2020/06/22/how-to-price-products/?sh=69050a1555c7**.

Chapter 2

1. Jean-Manuel Izaret and Just Schürmann, "Why Progressive Pricing Is Becoming a Competitive Necessity," Boston Consulting Group, January 17, 2019, **https://www.bcg.com/publications/2019/why-progressive-pricing-becoming-competitive-necessity**.

2. Eugene F. Zelek, Jr., "Legal Tools That Support Value Pricing," Freeborn & Peters, **https://www.freeborn.com/sites/default/files/legal_tools_that_support_value_pricing_zelek.pdf**.

3. Jean-Manuel Izaret, "Solving the Paradox of Fair Prices," Boston Consulting Group, May 12, 2022, **https://www.bcg.com/publications/2022/considering-pricing-variation-to-help-solve-the-paradox-of-fair-prices**.

4. "Game Theory," *Stanford Encyclopedia of Philosophy*, Stanford University, March 8, 2019, **https://plato.stanford.edu/entries/game-theory/#Repeat**.

5. The Editors of Encylopaedia *Britannica*, "Alfred Marshall," *Britannica*, September 2018, **https://www.britannica.com/biography/Alfred-Marshall**.

Chapter 3

1. Pepe Rodriguez, Andres Garro, Aaron Snyder, and Ted Sisko, "Building Segments-of-One Supply Chains in Medtech and Biopharma," Boston Consulting Group, November 26, 2019, **https://www.bcg.com/publications/2019/building-segments-of-one-supply-chains-medtech-and-biopharma**.

2. "Worldwide Quarterly Mobile Phone Tracker," IDC, February 2023, **https://www.idc.com/getdoc.jsp?containerId=IDC_P8397**.

3. Ibid.

4. Apple Inc. Form 10-K for the Fiscal Year Ended September 27, 2008, U.S. Securities and Exchange Commission, 2008, **https://www.sec.gov/Archives/ edgar/data/320193/000119312508224958/d10k.htm**.

5. "Worldwide Quarterly Mobile Phone Tracker," IDC, February 27, 2018, **https://www.idc.com/getdoc.jsp?containerId=IDC_P8397**.

6. Rebekah Denn, "Magic or Mythic? Bone Broth Is at the Center of a Brewing Cultural Divide," *Washington Post*, August 22, 2017, **https://www .washingtonpost.com/lifestyle/food/trend-check-where-bone-broth-stands-now/2017/08/21/b7e45524-7ed2-11e7-9d08-b79f191668ed_story .html**.

7. "Our Top 10 Food Trends for 2020," Whole Foods Market, **https://www .wholefoodsmarket.com/tips-and-ideas/top-food-trends**.

8. "Company Info," Whole Foods Market, March 2023, **https://www .wholefoodsmarket.com/company-info**.

9. Data for the Whole Foods store at 3201 N. Ashland Ave. in Chicago, IL, sourced from the placer.ai website on February 7, 2023.

10. Campbell Soup Company Form 10-K for Fiscal Year Ended July 31, 2022, U.S. Securities and Exchange Commission, 2022, **https://www.sec.gov/ix?doc=/ Archives/edgar/data/16732/000001673222000093/cpb-20220731.htm**.

11. Stephen. J Bronner, "This Entrepreneur Who Left Tech for Food Got $3 Million in Funding After She Decided Not to Be 'Too Innovative,'" *Entrepreneur*, November 6, 2017, **https://www.entrepreneur.com/growing-a-business/ this-entrepreneur-who-left-tech-for-food-got-3-million-in/304151**.

12. Seagate Technology Form 10-K for Fiscal Year Ended July 2, 2004, U.S. Securities and Exchange Commission, 2004, **https://www.sec.gov/Archives/ edgar/data/1137789/000119312504136208/d10k.htm**.

13. Western Digital Form Corporation 10-K for Fiscal Year Ended July 2, 2004, U.S. Securities and Exchange Commission, 2004, **https://www.sec.gov/ Archives/edgar/data/106040/000095013704007712/a01568e10vk.htm**.

14. Western Digital Corporation Form 10-K for Fiscal Year Ended June 27, 2003, U.S. Securities and Exchange Commission, 2003, **https://www.sec.gov/ Archives/edgar/data/106040/000089256903002216/a93092e10vk.htm**.

15. Ibid.

16. Western Digital Corporation Form 10-K for Fiscal Year ended June 28, 2002, U.S. Securities and Exchange Commission, 2002, **https://www.sec.gov/ Archives/edgar/data/106040/000089256902001988/a83140e10vk.htm**.

17. Sean Captain, "Maxtor Rolls Out 80GB and 100GB Hard Drives," *Computerworld*, June 18, 2001, **https://www.computerworld.com/article/2582064/ maxtor-rolls-out-80gb-and-100gb-hard-drives.html**.

18. John C. McCallum, "Disk Drive Prices 1955+," November 2022, **https:// jcmit.net/diskprice.htm**.

19. Seagate Technology Form 10-K for Fiscal Year Ended July 2, 2004.

20. McCallum, "Disk Drive Prices 1955+."

21. Alexander S. Gillis and Sarah Wilson, "Hard Disk Drive (HDD)," *TechTarget*, **https://www.techtarget.com/searchstorage/definition/hard-disk-drive**.

22. McCallum, "Disk Drive Prices 1955+."

23. Fernando Cortes, "Zero-Sum: How Walmart Transportation Is Working to Reduce Emissions Now and in the Future," Walmart Inc., June 8, 2022, **https://corporate.walmart.com/newsroom/2022/06/08/zero-sum-how-walmart-transportation-is-working-to-reduce-emissions-now-and-in-the-future**.

24. FedEx Corporation Form 10-K for Fiscal Year Ended May 31, 2022, U.S. Securities and Exchange Commission, 2022, **https://www.sec.gov/ix?doc=/Archives/edgar/data/0001048911/000095017022012762/fdx-20220531.htm**.

25. *Today's Trucking*, March 2009, p. 19, **https://www.trucknews.com/digital-archive/2009-march/**.

26. "25 Years of Freightliner LLC as Part of DaimlerChrysler AG: A German-American Success Story," press release, Daimler Truck North America, May 31, 2006, **https://northamerica.daimlertruck.com/company/press-releases/pressdetail/25-years-of-freightliner-llc-as-2006-05-31**.

27. Howard Schultz, "When It Comes to 'Establishing the Il Giornale Difference," Il Giornale Coffee Company, May 1986, **https://brandautopsy.com/files/IL_GIORNALE_memo.pdf**.

28. "Starbucks Commitment to Wellness," Starbucks Corporation, January 2019, **https://stories.starbucks.com/wp-content/uploads/2019/01/Starbucks_Wellness_Timeline.pdf**.

29. SEC Filings, Form S-1, Registration Statement under the Securities Act of 1933 for Starbucks Corporation, June 25, 1992.

30. Citrix Systems, Inc. Form 10-K for Fiscal Year Ended December 31, 2021, U.S. Securities and Exchange Commission, 2021, **https://www.sec.gov/ix?doc=/Archives/edgar/data/877890/000087789022000019/ctxs-20211231.htm**.

31. Camille Brégé, Lionnel Bourgouin, David Langkamp, Michael Chu, Matt Beckett, Pierre Poirmeur, and Joana Niepmann, "Debunking the Myths of B2B Dynamic Pricing," Boston Consulting Group, November 20, 2020, **https://www.bcg.com/publications/2020/dynamic-pricing-b2b-myths**.

Chapter 4

1. Chavi Mehta and Ambar Warrick, "Factbox: Tech Giants Dominate Wall Street's Trillion-Dollar Club," Reuters, December 9, 2021, **https://www.reuters.com/markets/europe/tech-giants-dominate-wall-streets-trillion-dollar-club-2021-12-09/**.

Chapter 5

1. Julie Cantwell, "Porsche CEO Tells U.S. Arm No More Rebates in Wake of Boxster Giveback," *Autoweek*, August 25, 2002, **https://www.autoweek.com/news/ a2112676/porsche-ceo-tells-us-arm-no-more-rebates-wake-boxster- giveback/**.
2. Reed K. Holden, *Negotiating with Backbone: Eight Sales Strategies to Defend Your Price and Value*, 2nd ed. (Pearson Education, 2016).

Chapter 6

1. Google Inc., "Google's Targeted Keyword Ad Program Shows Strong Momentum with Advertisers," news announcement, August 16, 2000, **http:// googlepress.blogspot.com/2000/08/googles-targeted-keyword-ad- program.html**.
2. Google Inc., "Google Launches Self-Service Advertising Program," news announcement, October 23, 2000, **http://googlepress.blogspot.com/2000/ 10/google-launches-self-service.html**.
3. William Poundstone, *Priceless: The Myth of Fair Value (and How to Take Advantage of It)* (Hill and Wang, 2003).
4. The name and the basis for this model goes back to King Gillette, who pioneered the disposable razor blade over 100 years ago (**https://gillette.com/ en-us/about/our-story**).

Chapter 7

1. Tony Smith, "Apple iPod Grabs 82% US Retail Market Share," *The Register*, October 12, 2004, **https://www.theregister.com/2004/10/12/ipod_ us_share/**.
2. Jack Nicas, "Apple Is Worth 1,000,000,000,000. Two Decades Ago, It Was Almost Bankrupt," *New York Times*, August, 2018, **https://www.nytimes .com/2018/08/02/technology/apple-stock-1-trillion-market-cap.html**.
3. "Best Global Brands 2022," *Interbrand*, November 2022, **https://interbrand .com/best-global-brands/apple/**.
4. Paul R. La Monica, "Apple Has Become the World's First $3 Trillion Company," *CNN*, January 3, 2022, **https://www.cnn.com/2022/01/03/investing/ apple-three-trillion-dollar-market-cap/index.html**.
5. Ron Adner, "From Walkman to iPod: What Music Tech Teaches US About Innovation," *The Atlantic*, March 5, 2012, **https://www.theatlantic.com/ business/archive/2012/03/from-walkman-to-ipod-what-music-tech- teaches-us-about-innovation/253158/**.

6. rmbray, "The Failed MP3 Player That Changed the Music Industry Forever," *Yahoo!Finance*, November 5, 2018, **https://finance.yahoo.com/news/failed-mp3-player-changed-music-153556133.html**.

7. Dong Ngo, "Johnny Cash Song iTunes' 10 Billionth Download," *CNET*, February 25, 2010, **https://www.cnet.com/culture/johnny-cash-song-itunes-10-billionth-download/**.

8. "**Amazon.com**, Inc. (AMZN)," *Yahoo!Finance*, September 26, 2013, **https://finance.yahoo.com/quote/AMZN/history**.

9. Phillip Michaels, "Timeline: iPodding Through the Years," *Macworld*, October 22, 2006, **https://www.macworld.com/article/182065/ipodtimeline.html**.

10. Ryan Bray, "The Failed MP3 Player That Changed the Music Industry Forever," *Consequence*, November 5, 2018, **https://consequence.net/2018/11/the-failed-mp3-player-that-changed-the-music-industry-forever/**.

11. Jon Healey, "Portable MP3 Player Breaks Price Barrier," *Los Angeles Times*, April 2, 2001, **https://www.latimes.com/archives/la-xpm-2001-apr-02-fi-45741-story.html**.

12. Smith, "Apple iPod Grabs 82% US Retail Market Share."

13. "Hermès First Time Buyer Guide," *Baghunter*, February 2023, **https://baghunter.com/blogs/insights/hermes-handbag-first-time-buyer-guide**.

14. Ibid.

15. Apple Inc. Form 10-K for the Fiscal Year Ended September 26, 2015, U.S. Securities and Exchange Commission, **https://www.sec.gov/Archives/edgar/data/320193/000119312515356351/d17062d10k.htm**.

16. Walter Isaacson, *Steve Jobs* (Simon & Schuster, 2011), Kindle edition, location 170.

17. Apple Inc. Form 10-K for the Fiscal Year Ended September 24, 2022, U.S. Securities and Exchange Commission, **https://www.sec.gov/ix?doc=/Archives/edgar/data/320193/000032019322000108/aapl-20220924.htm**.

18. "Drop the Computer," *The Economist*, January 11, 2007, **https://www.economist.com/business/2007/01/11/drop-the-computer**.

Chapter 8

1. Jaewon Kang, "Whole Foods Asks Suppliers to Lower Prices," *Wall Street Journal*, January 31, 2023, **https://www.wsj.com/articles/whole-foods-asks-suppliers-to-lower-prices-as-costs-ebb-11675115155**.

2. Russell Redman, "Whole Foods Shelves 365 Store Concept," *Supermarket News*, January 11, 2019, **https://www.supermarketnews.com/retail-financial/whole-foods-shelves-365-store-concept**.

3. "Nona's Story," *Nona Lim,* **https://www.nonalim.com/pages/our-story**.
4. Ray Latif, "Why Profitability Means Saying 'No' More Often," *BevNET's Taste Radio,* February 7, 2020, **https://www.tasteradio.com/insider/2020/taste-radio-insider-ep-71-why-profitability-means-saying-no-more-often/**.
5. Prices observed during a store visit to the Whole Foods at 3640 N. Halsted in Chicago on February 7, 2023.
6. "The Price Elasticity of Demand," Chapter 5.1 in *Principles of Economics,* University of Minnesota, accessed April 2022, **https://open.lib.umn.edu/principleseconomics/chapter/5-1-the-price-elasticity-of-demand/**.
7. Ibid.
8. That corresponds to a price elasticity of –2, or a 100% volume increase divided by a 50% price decline.
9. "Our Story," Roli Roti, **https://roliroti.com/about-us/**.
10. "The Soul of Noodles," Sun Noodle Inc., **https://sunnoodle.com/About-Us-1**.
11. Amazon purchased Whole Foods in 2017.
12. This scenario reflects a change in the retail price of the product, with a related change (up or down) in Nona Lim's wholesale price of the product to a retailer. Nona Lim's gross profit change is measured as the wholesale level with specific assumptions about variable costs.
13. General Mills, 2023 CAGNY Conference, February 21, 2023, **https://s29.q4cdn.com/993087495/files/doc_presentations/2023/02/F23-CAGNY-Slides-Final.pdf**.
14. Based on presentations given at the in-person Consumer Analyst Group of New York (CAGNY) Conference in 2023 in Boca Raton, Florida, February 20–24, 2023.
15. Michael Silverstein, Dylan Bolden, and Dan Wald, "Demand-Centric Growth: How to Grow by Finding Out What Really Drives Consumer Choice," BCG, September 1, 2015, **https://www.bcg.com/publications/2015/marketing-sales-demand-centric-growth-finding-out-drives-consumer-choice**.

Chapter 9

1. Wrightway & Sons is a fictitious name.
2. Bruce Henderson, "The Experience Curve" (Boston Consulting Group, 1968), **https://www.bcg.com/publications/1968/business-unit-strategy-growth-experience-curve**.
3. Micah Ziegler and Jesica Trancik, "Re-Examining Rates of Lithium-Ion Battery Technology Improvements and Cost Decline," *Energy & Environmental Science* 14 (2021): 1635–1651.

Chapter 10

1. BCG ValueScience Analysis based on CapitalIQ data.
2. Gordon E. Moore, "Lithography and the Future of Moore's Law," *Proceedings SPIE 2439, Integrated Circuit Metrology, Inpsection, and Process Control IX* (May 22, 1995).
3. Chip Walter, "Kryder's Law," *Scientific American*, August 1, 2005, **https://www.scientificamerican.com/article/kryders-law/**.
4. Western Digital Form 10-K for Fiscal Year Ended June 27, 2003, U.S. Securities and Exchange Commission, 2003, **https://www.sec.gov/Archives/edgar/data/106040/000089256903002216/a93092e10vk.htm**.
5. Western Digital Form 10-K for Fiscal Year Ended July 2, 2004, U.S. Securities and Exchange Commission, 2004, **https://www.sec.gov/Archives/edgar/data/106040/000095013704007712/a01568e10vk.htm**.
6. Seagate Technology Form 10-K for Fiscal Year Ended June 27, 2003, U.S. Securities and Exchange Commission, 2003, **https://www.sec.gov/Archives/edgar/data/1137789/000119312503040541/d10k.htm**.
7. Western Digital Form 10-K for Fiscal Year Ended June 27, 2003.
8. Maxtor Corporation Form 10-K for Fiscal Year Ended December 27, 2003, U.S. Securities and Exchange Commission, 2003, **https://www.sec.gov/Archives/edgar/data/711039/000089161804000694/f96951e10vk.htm**.
9. The Natural Volume Slope (NVS) codifies a large customer's negotiating power. It can be drawn using three simple steps. First, convert the volume on the x-axis of your price realization graph to a logarithmic scale. This replotting helps you understand what is happening at lower volumes. Second, place two marks on the chart: one at the 80th percentile on the y-axis, and one in the middle of the cluster of the three to five largest deals at the lowest right part of the cloud. Finally, draw a line between the two marks. The NVS line represents the increase of negotiation power as purchase volume increases by 10×. For example, if the NVS is 2%, a customer buying 10 trucks can negotiate a 2% incremental discount from a customer buying one truck.
10. Anna Rita Bennato, Stephen Daviesz, Franco Mariuzzox, and Peter Ormosi, "Mergers and Innovation: Evidence from the Hard Disk Drive Market," *International Journal of Industrial Organization*, Elsevier, vol. 77(C) (2020).

Chapter 11

1. For simplicity's sake, we will refer to the company as DTNA throughout this chapter, even though the formal name change from Freightliner to DTNA did not occur until a couple of years after Patterson took over as CEO.

2. "Quarterly Census of Employment and Wages," U.S. Bureau of Labor Statistics, March 14, 2023, **https://data.bls.gov/timeseries/ENUUS000205484? amp%253bdata_tool=XGtable&output_view=data&include_graphs =true**.

3. DaimlerChrysler AG Form 20-F for Fiscal Year Ended December 31, 2004, U.S. Securities and Exchange Commission, 2004, **https://www.sec.gov/ Archives/edgar/data/1067318/000104746905004930/a2152389z20-f.htm**.

4. Ibid.

5. DaimlerChrysler AG Form 20-F for Fiscal Year Ended December 31, 2006, U.S. Securities and Exchange Commission, 2006, **https://www.sec.gov/ Archives/edgar/data/1067318/000104746905004930/a2152389z20-f.htm**.

6. Overdrive Staff, "The Next Round," *Overdrive by Randall-Reilly,* December 12, 2008, **https://www.overdriveonline.com/business/article/14872333/the- next-round**.

7. This figure was originally introduced in Part I.

8. This figure was originally introduced in Part I.

9. "Commodity Price Data (The Pink Sheet)," World Bank, **https://www .worldbank.org/en/research/commodity-markets**.

10. "Crude Oil Prices – 70 Year Historical Chart," Macrotrends, **https://www .macrotrends.net/1369/crude-oil-price-history-chart**.

11. For more information of salesforce confidence and "backbone," see books such as *Pricing with Confidence* by Reed Holden.

12. DaimlerChrysler AG Form 20-F for Fiscal Year Ended December 31, 2006.

13. Today's Trucking Staff, "Patterson Calls 2007 'Stressful and Disappointing,'" *Trucknews.com*, August 1, 2014, **https://www.trucknews.com/products/ patterson-calls-2007-stressful-and-disappointing-2/**.

14. Daimler AG Form 20-F for Fiscal Year Ended December 31, 2007. *EDGAR.* Securities and Exchange Commission, 2007, **https://www.sec.gov/ Archives/edgar/data/1067318/000104746908001782/a2182013z20-f.htm**.

15. DaimlerChrysler AG Form 20-F for Fiscal Year Ended December 31, 2008. *EDGAR.* Securities and Exchange Commission, 2008, **https://www.sec.gov/ Archives/edgar/data/1067318/000104746909001917/a2190793z20-f.htm**.

16. Truck News, "Daimler Claims Top Spot for Medium-Duty Market Share," *Trucknews.com,* February 19, 2008, **https://www.trucknews.com/ products/daimler-claims-top-spot-for-medium-duty-market-share/**.

17. Fleet Equipment Staff, "Daimler Trucks North America Leads Class 6-8 NAFTA, U.S. markets," Fleet Equipment, January 27, 2011, **https:// www.fleetequipmentmag.com/daimler-trucks-north-america-leads- class-6-8-nafta-u-s-markets/**.

18. "Daimler Trucks North America Leads Class 6-8 NAFTA and U.S. Markets," *OEM Off-Highway*, January 19, 2011, **https://www.oemoffhighway .com/engines/filtration/emissions-control-exhaust-systems/ news/10224236/daimler-trucks-leads-market**.

19. Daimler Trucks North America, "Daimler Trucks Sees Increased Profits," *OEM Off-Highway,* April 4, 2011, **https://www.oemoffhighway.com/market-analysis/press-release/10250336/daimler-trucks-sees-increased-profits**.

Chapter 12

1. Howard Schultz, *Pour Your Heart Into It: How Starbucks Built a Company One Cup at a Time* (Hachette Books, 2012), Kindle edition, location 52.
2. Howard Schultz and Joanne Gordon. *Onward: How Starbucks Fought for Its Life Without Losing Its Soul* (Rodale Books, 2012), Kindle edition.
3. Linda, "When Did Coffee Cost a Dime," *The Commons Cafe,* November 26, 2022, **https://www.thecommonscafe.com/when-did-coffee-cost-a-dime/**.
4. "Il Giornale," Starbucks Archive, Starbucks Corporation, 2023, **https://archive.starbucks.com/record/il-giornale**.
5. "Coffee Prices by Year and Adjusted for Inflation," US Inflation Calculator, **https://www.usinflationcalculator.com/inflation/coffee-prices-by-year-and-adjust-for-inflation/**.
6. Schultz, *Pour Your Heart Into It*, location 59.
7. Ibid.
8. Schultz and Gordon, *Onward*, location 10.
9. Schultz, *Pour Your Heart Into It*, locations 94–98.
10. "Best Global Brands," Interbrand, March 2022, **https://interbrand.com/best-global-brands/**.
11. Howard Schultz, "When It Comes to 'Establishing the Il Giornale Difference . . . ,'" Il Giornale Coffee Company, May 19, 1986, **https://brandautopsy.com/files/IL_GIORNALE_memo.pdf**.
12. Ibid.
13. "Premium Plans," Spotify, March 2023, **https://support.spotify.com/us/article/premium-plans/**.
14. "Plans and Pricing," Netflix, March 2023, **https://help.netflix.com/en/node/24926**.
15. Xinqian Li, "The Research Review and Prospect of Compromise Effect," *Open Journal of Social Sciences* 8, no. 4 (April 2020), **https://www.scirp.org/journal/paperinformation.aspx?paperid=99534**.
16. Ryan Pak and Andrew Ferdowsian, "The Decoy Effect and Risk Aversion," March 27, 2021, **https://stanfordeconreview.com/wp-content/uploads/2021/03/ryan_pak_comparative_advantage.pdf**.
17. Andrew J. Caceres-Santamaria, "The Anchoring Effect," Federal Reserve Bank of St. Louis, April 2021, **https://research.stlouisfed.org/publications/page1-econ/2021/04/01/the-anchoring-effect**.

18. Paul Lee, "The Williams-Sonoma Bread Maker: A Case Study," *Wall Street Journal*, April 10, 2013, **https://www.wsj.com/articles/BL-232B-784**.

19. Ibid.

20. Peter J. Scott and Colin Lizieri, "Consumer House Price Judgments: New Evidence of Anchoring and Arbitrary Coherence," *Journal of Property Research* 29, no. 1 (May 10, 2011): 49–68, **https://www.tandfonline.com/doi/abs/10.1080/09599916.2011.638144**.

21. Phillip Andersen, John Wenstrup, and Vikas Taneja, "Five Selling Secrets of Today's Digital B2B Leaders," Boston Consulting Group, April 5, 2016, **https://www.bcg.com/publications/2016/sales-channels-marketing-sales-five-selling-secrets-todays-digital-b2b-leaders**.

22. Meini Heuberger, Roger Premo, Mark Roberge, and Phillip Andersen, "Six Keys to Customer Success," Boston Consulting Group, October 2019, **https://web-assets.bcg.com/img-src/BCG-Six-Keys-to-Customer-Success-Oct-2019_tcm9-231198.pdf**.

23. "Starbucks Invests in New Rewards as Loyalty Members Help Inflation-Proof the Brand," PYMNTS, August 2, 2022, **https://www.pymnts.com/earnings/2022/starbucks-invests-new-rewards-loyalty-members-help-inflation-proof-brand/**.

24. Mariah Ore, "How to Use MaxDiff Survey Analysis for Feature Prioritization," User Experience Center, Bentley University, **https://www.bentley.edu/centers/user-experience-center/how-use-max-diff-survey-analysis-feature-prioritization**.

25. Stephanie Dutchen, "Pattern Recognition: New Visualization Software Uncovers Cancer Subtypes," Harvard Medical School, October 2, 2014, **https://hms.harvard.edu/news/pattern-recognition**.

26. Emilie Kaufmann, Olivier Cappé, and Aurélien Garivier, "On the Complexity of A/B Testing," *JMLR: Workshop and Conference Proceedings* 35 (2014): 1–23, **http://proceedings.mlr.press/v35/kaufmann14.pdf**.

27. "FactSet Solutions," FactSet, March 2023, **https://www.factset.com/solutions**.

28. Heidi Peiper, "Coffee Meets Olive Oil: The Story Behind Starbucks New Coffee Ritual – Starbucks Oleato Coffee Beverages," *Starbucks Stories & News*, February 21, 2023, **https://stories.starbucks.com/stories/2023/the-story-behind-starbucks-new-coffee-ritual-oleato-olive-oil/**.

29. "Fiscal 2008 Annual Report," Starbucks Corporation, 2008, **https://s22.q4cdn.com/869488222/files/doc_financials/annual/2008/SBUX2008ARv5_2008.pdf**.

30. Nichola Groom, "Starbucks Raising U.S. Drinks Prices Next Week," Thomson Reuters, July 23, 2007, **https://www.reuters.com/article/us-starbucks-prices/starbucks-raising-u-s-drinks-prices-next-week-idUSN2337368320070723**.

31. Melissa Allison, "Starbucks Shake-Up: Schultz Back as CEO," *Seattle Times*, January 8, 2008, **https://archive.seattletimes.com/archive/?date=20080 108&slug=starbucks08**.

32. Claire Cain Miller, "Will the Hard-Core Starbucks Customer Pay More? The Chain Plans to Find Out," *New York Times*, August 20, 2009, **https://www .nytimes.com/2009/08/21/business/21sbux.html**.

33. Prices shown for the Grande size for all drinks except espressos, "Starbucks – 31 Year Stock Price History | SBUX," Macrotrends, March 21, 2023, **https://www.macrotrends.net/stocks/charts/SBUX/starbucks/stock-price-history**.

34. "SNP – SNP Real Time Price. Currency in USD," Yahoo! Finance, March 24, 2023.

35. "Starbucks Reports Q4 and Full Year Fiscal 2022 Results," Starbucks Investor Relations, November 3, 2022, **https://investor.starbucks.com/press-releases/financial-releases/press-release-details/2022/Starbucks-Reports-Q4-and-Full-Year-Fiscal-2022-Results/default.aspx**.

Chapter 13

1. Sumit Singh, "How the Airline Deregulation Act Shook Up US Aviation," *Simple Flying*, December 3, 2022, **https://simpleflying.com/airline-deregulation-united-states/**.

2. Anthony W. Donovan, "Yield Management in the Airline Industry," *Journal of Aviation/Aerospace Education & Research* 14, no. 3 (Spring 2005), **https:// commons.erau.edu/cgi/viewcontent.cgi?article=1522&context=jaaer**.

3. Barry C. Smith, John F. Leimkuhler, Ross M. Darrow, "Yield Management at American Airlines," The Institute of Management Sciences, January–February 1992, **https://classes.engineering.wustl.edu/2010/fall/ese403/software/ Informs%20Articles/CH18%20Yield%20Management%20at%20 American%20Airlines.pdf**.

4. Jean-Manuel Izaret, "Solving the Paradox of Fair Prices," Boston Consulting Group, May 12, 2022, **https://www.bcg.com/publications/2022/ considering-pricing-variation-to-help-solve-the-paradox-of-fair-prices**.

5. Stephanie Overby, "For San Francisco Giants, Dynamic Pricing Software Hits a Home Run," *CIO*, June 29, 2011, **https://www.cio.com/article/282100/ business-intelligence-for-san-francisco-giants-dynamic-pricing-soft ware-hits-a-home-run.html**.

6. Joel Schectmann, "San Francisco Giants CIO Says Dynamic Ticket Pricing Helped Pack the Stadium," *Wall Street Journal*, August 6, 2012, **https://www .wsj.com/articles/BL-CIOB-719**.

7. Dwight K. Schrute, "Get Em While They're Hot: Dynamic Ticket Pricing in Major League Baseball," Digital Initiative, Harvard Business School, November 13, 2018, **https://d3.harvard.edu/platform-rctom/submission/get-em-while-theyre-hot-dynamic-ticket-pricing-in-major-league-baseball/**.

8. The name OutfitOracle is fictitious, and the industry disguised, but the stories and the underlying facts are based on the experiences of real companies.

9. Charles Duhigg, "Stock Traders Find Speed Pays, in Milliseconds," *New York Times*, June 23, 2009, **https://www.nytimes.com/2009/07/24/business/24trading.html**.

10. Rosa Golijan, "How a Book about Flies Cost $23.7 Million on Amazon," *Today*, April 25, 2011, **https://www.today.com/money/how-book-about-flies-cost-23-7-million-amazon-123532**.

11. Based on BCG project experience.

12. Preetika Rana, "What Happened When Uber's CEO Started Driving for Uber," *Wall Street Journal*, April 7, 2023, **https://www.wsj.com/articles/uber-ceo-started-driving-for-uber-5bef5023**.

13. Elizabeth Louise Williamson, "Airline Network Seat Inventory Control: Methodologies and Revenue Impacts," PhD thesis, Massachusetts Institute of Technology, Department of Aeronautics and Astronautics, June 1992, **https://dspace.mit.edu/handle/1721.1/68123**.

Chapter 14

1. The name Emerald Engineering is fictitious, but the story and the underlying facts are based on a real company's experience.

Chapter 15

1. Marilyn Much, "How Salesforce's Marc Benioff Revolutionized the Software Industry," *Investor's Business Daily*, February 11, 2019, **https://www.investors.com/news/management/leaders-and-success/how-salesforces-marc-benioff-revolutionized-the-software-industry/**.

2. "The History of Salesforce," Salesforce, Inc., March 19, 2020, **https://www.salesforce.com/news/stories/the-history-of-salesforce/**.

3. Kelvin Yu, "A Brief History of Salesforce and Key Lessons for B2B Entrepreneurs," *Medium*, June 24, 2019, **https://medium.com/profiles-in-entrepreneurship/a-brief-history-of-salesforce-and-key-lessons-for-b2b-entrepreneurs-5c9d8d5337e2**.

4. The name Maricross Manufacturing is fictitious, but the stories and the underlying facts are based on the experiences of real companies.

5. "The Internet of Things," IBM, March 22, 2023, **https://www.ibm.com/big-data/us/en/big-data-and-analytics/iotandweather.html**.

6. David Langkamp, Just Schürmann, Thomas Schollmeyer, Rolf Kilian, Amadeus Petzke, John Pineda, and Jean-Manuel Izaret, "How the Internet of Things Will Change the Pricing of Things," Boston Consulting Group, December 7, 2017, **https://www.bcg.com/publications/2017/how-internet-of-things-change-pricing-of-things**.

7. Jean-Manuel Izaret, Nicolas Hunke, John Pineda, Federico Fabbri, and Win Chia, "Cloudified Pricing – Coming to an Industry Near You," Boston Consulting Group, May 24, 2018, **https://www.bcg.com/publications/2018/cloudified-pricing-coming-industry-near-you**.

8. Langkamp et al., "How the Internet of Things Will Change the Pricing of Things."

Chapter 16

1. "US Proximity Mobile Payment Users, by Platform, 2021 (millions)," *Insider Intelligence,* March 1, 2021, **https://www.insiderintelligence.com/chart/245782/us-proximity-mobile-payment-users-by-platform-2021-millions**.

2. Sarah Lebow, "How the Starbucks App Is Energizing Mobile Payment Use," *Insider Intelligence*, April 2, 2021, **https://www.insiderintelligence.com/content/how-starbucks-app-energizing-mobile-payment-use**.

3. The name Montclaude is fictitious, but the story and the underlying facts are based on a real company's experience.

4. Estimation by Euromonitor, March 2023.

Chapter 17

1. Michael A Salinger, "Vertical Mergers and Market Foreclosure," *Quarterly Journal of Economics*, May 1988.

2. "NIKE, Inc. Annual Shareholder Meeting Transcript," NIKE, Inc., September 21, 2017, **https://s1.q4cdn.com/806093406/files/doc_downloads/NIKE-Inc-2017-Annual-Shareholders-Meeting-Transcript-9-21-2017.pdf**.

3. Nathaniel Meyersohn, "Nikes Are Getting Harder to Find at Stores. Here's Why," *CNN Business*, March 22, 2021, **https://www.cnn.com/2021/03/22/business/nike-independent-shoe-stores/index.html**.

4. "NIKE, Inc. Form 10-K for Fiscal Year Ended May 31, 2011," U.S. Securities and Exchange Commission, 2011, **https://www.sec.gov/Archives/edgar/data/320187/000119312511194791/d10k.htm**.

5. "NIKE, Inc. Form 10-K for Fiscal Year Ended May 31, 2022," U.S. Securities and Exchange Commission, 2022, **https://www.sec.gov/Archives/edgar/ data/320187/000032018722000038/nke-20220531.htm.**

6. Ibid.

7. Andrej Levin, Parmeet Grover, Karen Lellouche Tordjman, Alfred Wiederer, Alex Melnik, and Jonas Hiltrop, "Turbocharge Auto Sales with Advanced Analytics," Boston Consulting Group, January 25, 2022, **https://www.bcg .com/publications/2022/turbocharge-auto-sales-advanced-analytics.**

8. "2023 Corolla: Your Build," Toyota Motor Sales, U.S.A., Inc., March 12, 2023, **https://www.toyota.com/configurator/build/step/model/year/2022/ series/corolla/.**

9. "Coronavirus Fallout: Vehicle Service Customer Satisfaction Improves, but Dealers Should Prepare for Parts Shortages and Dissatisfied Owners, J.D. Power Finds," J.D. Power, March 12, 2020, **https://www.jdpower.com/ business/press-releases/2020-customer-service-index-csi-study.**

10. Benjamin Preston, "CR Research Shows That EVs Cost Less to Maintain Than Gasoline-Powered Vehicles," *Consumer Reports*, September 26, 2020, **https://www.consumerreports.org/car-repair-maintenance/pay-less- for-vehicle-maintenance-with-an-ev/.**

11. "Maintenance and Safety of Electric Vehicles," Alternative Fuels Data Center, U.S. Department of Energy, March 2023, **https://afdc.energy.gov/vehicles/ electric_maintenance.html.**

12. "Tesla Motors Delivers World's First Premium Electric Sedan to Customers," Tesla, Inc., June 22, 2012, **https://www.tesla.com/blog/tesla-motors- delivers-world%E2%80%99s-first-premium-electric-sedan-customers.**

13. BCG analysis and casework.

14. "Compare Models: Model S vs. Model Y," Tesla, Inc., March 2023, **https:// www.tesla.com/compare.**

15. Karen Lellouche Tordjman, Augustin K. Wegscheider, Mathieu Nemoz-Guillot, and Eric Jesse, "Are US Car Dealers Ready for Tomorrow?," Boston Consulting Group, November 16, 2022, **https://www.bcg.com/publications/ 2022/future-of-car-dealers-in-the-us.**

16. Elon Musk, "The Secret Tesla Motors Master Plan (just between you and me)," Tesla, Inc., August 2, 2006, **https://www.tesla.com/blog/secret-tesla-motors- master-plan-just-between-you-and-me.**

17. "Compare Models: Model X vs Model 3 Rear-Wheel Drive," Tesla, Inc., March 2023, **https://www.tesla.com/compare.**

18. "Tesla Changes U.S. Prices for Fourth Time in Two Months," *Reuters*, February 14, 2023, **https://www.reuters.com/business/autos-transportation/ tesla-changes-us-prices-fourth-time-two-months-2023-02-14/.**

19. Elon Musk, "The Tesla Approach to Distributing and Servicing Cars," Tesla, Inc., October 22, 2022, **https://www.tesla.com/blog/tesla-approach- distributing-and-servicing-cars.**

20. Fred Lambert, "Tesla (TSLA) Launches Major Shift in Retail Strategy: Cheaper Locations, Remote Working, and More," *Electrek*, July 28, 2021, **https:// electrek.co/2021/07/28/tesla-tsla-major-shift-retail-strategy-cheaper- locations-remote-working/**.

21. Tim Higgins and Adrienne Roberts, "Tesla Shifts to Online Sales Model," *Wall Street Journal,* February 28, 2019, **https://www.wsj.com/articles/ tesla-says-it-has-started-taking-orders-for-35-000-version-of-model- 3-11551392059**.

22. "New EV Entries Nibbling Away at Tesla EV Share," blog post, S&P Global, November 29, 2022, **https://www.spglobal.com/mobility/en/research- analysis/new-ev-entries-nibbling-away-at-tesla-ev-share.html**.

23. "Tesla Vehicle Production & Deliveries and Date for Financial Results & Webcast for Fourth Quarter 2022," press release, Tesla, Inc., January 2, 2022, **https://ir.tesla.com/press-release/tesla-vehicle-production-deliveries- and-date-financial-results-webcast-fourth-quarter**.

24. Paul Stenquist, "Why You Might Buy Your Next Car Online," *New York Times*, June 21, 2022, "**https://www.nytimes.com/2022/06/21/business/tesla- online-sales-dealerships.html**.

Chapter 18

1. Charlotte Thompson and Elliott N. Weiss, "Southwest Airlines," UVA-OM-0743 (Charlottesville VA: Darden Business Publishing, 1993).

2. "Annual Report 2006," Air Asia Berhad, 2006, **https://www.capitala.com/ misc/FlippingBook/ar2006/index.html**.

3. Arlene Fleming, "The Largest Airlines in the World," *TripSavvy*, September 9, 2021, **https://www.tripsavvy.com/the-largest-airlines-in-the-world- 53223**.

4. "Delta Now World's Largest Carrier; Ryanair Stays Top International Airline," CAPA Centre for Aviation, June 8, 2011, **https://centreforaviation.com/ analysis/reports/delta-now-worlds-largest-carrier-ryanair-stays-top- international-airline-53030**.

5. "AirAsia Nears 50 Million Annual Passenger/200 Aircraft Milestones, Having Transformed Asian Aviation," CAPA Centre for Aviation, January 15, 2015, **https://centreforaviation.com/analysis/reports/airasia-nears-50- million-annual-passenger200-aircraft-milestones-having-transformed- asian-aviation-203232**.

6. Geoff Colvin, "How Amazon Grew an Awkward Side Project into AWS, a Behemoth That's Now 4 Times Bigger Than Its Original Shopping Business," *Fortune*, November 30, 2022, **https://fortune.com/longform/amazon- web-services-ceo-adam-selipsky-cloud-computing/**.

7. "Announcing Amazon S3 – Simple Storage Service," Amazon Web Services, Inc., March 13, 2006, **https://aws.amazon.com/about-aws/whats-new/2006/03/13/announcing-amazon-s3---simple-storage-service/**.

8. "Announcing Amazon Elastic Compute Cloud (Amazon EC2) – Beta," Amazon Web Services, Inc., August 24, 2006, **https://aws.amazon.com/about-aws/whats-new/2006/08/24/announcing-amazon-elastic-compute-cloud-amazon-ec2---beta/**.

9. Ángel González, "AWS CEO: Luck Gave Amazon's Cloud-Computing Unit a Boost," *Seattle Times*, February 7, 2017, **https://www.seattletimes.com/business/amazon/aws-ceo-luck-gave-amazons-cloud-computing-unit-a-boost/**.

10. Jeff Barr, "Amazon S3," AWS News Blog, March 14, 2006, **https://aws.amazon.com/blogs/aws/amazon_s3/**.

11. Jeff Barr, "Amazon EC2 Beta," AWS News Blog, August 25, 2006, **https://aws.amazon.com/blogs/aws/amazon_ec2_beta/**.

12. Spencer Reiss, "Cloud Computing. Available at **Amazon.com** Today," *Wired*, Apr. 21, 2000, **https://www.wired.com/2008/04/mf-amazon/**.

13. Ibid.

14. Jeff Barr, "Amazon S3 – Busier Than Ever," AWS News Blog, October 8, 2008, **https://aws.amazon.com/blogs/aws/amazon-s3-now/**.

15. Reiss, "Cloud Computing. Available at **Amazon.com** Today."

16. AWS for Every Application, "Improve Performance, Lower Costs, and Enhance Security with AWS Silicon, 2023," Amazon Web Services, Inc., March 31, 2023, **https://aws.amazon.com/silicon-innovation/**.

17. "Announced: AWS Start-Up Challenge Winner," Amazon Web Services, Inc., December 6, 2007, **https://aws.amazon.com/about-aws/whats-new/2007/12/06/announced-aws-start-up-challenge-winner/**.

18. Jeff Barr, "2008 AWS Start-Up Tour," AWS News Blog, August 14, 2008, **https://aws.amazon.com/blogs/aws/2008-aws-start/**.

19. Jeff Barr, "A Few Words on Technology Evangelism," AWS News Blog, February 3, 2006, **https://aws.amazon.com/blogs/aws/a_few_words_on_/**.

20. Jeff Barr, "Finding AWS Code Samples," AWS News Blog, September 20, 2006, **https://aws.amazon.com/blogs/aws/finding_aws_cod/**.

21. "Announcing Launch of New Developer Forums," Amazon Web Services, Inc., February 8, 2006, **https://aws.amazon.com/about-aws/whats-new/2006/02/08/announcing-launch-of-new-developer-forums/**.

22. Frederic Lardinois, "In Response To Google, Amazon Announces Massive Price Cuts For S3, EC2, ElastiCache, Elastic MapReduce And RDS," *TechCrunch*, March 26, 2014, **https://techcrunch.com/2014/03/26/in-response-to-google-amazon-announces-massive-price-cuts-for-s3-ec2-and-rds/**.

23. Bowen Wang, "Amazon EC2 – 15 Years of Optimizing and Saving Your IT Costs," Amazon Cost Management Blog, August 17, 2021, **https://aws.amazon.com/blogs/aws-cost-management/amazon-ec2-15th-years-of-optimizing-and-saving-your-it-costs/**.

24. Chris Haroun, "Amazon Web Services: This Generation's Berlin Wall Tear-Down Deflationary Event," *VentureBeat*, July 5, 2015, **https://venturebeat .com/business/amazon-web-services-this-generations-berlin-wall-tear-down-deflationary-event/**.

25. "Discover Solutions from AWS and AWS Partners," AWS Solutions Library, March 31, 2023, **https://aws.amazon.com/solutions/**.

26. Ben Schermel, "Benchmarking the AWS Graviton2 with KeyDB – M6g Up to 65% Faster," *KeyDB*, March 1, 2020, **https://docs.keydb.dev/blog/2020/03/02/blog-post/**.

27. "AWS for Industry," Amazon Web Services, Inc., March 31, 2023, **https://aws .amazon.com/industries/**.

28. "**Amazon.com**, Inc. Form 10-Q for the Quarterly Period Ended March 31, 2015," U.S. Securities and Exchange Commission, 2016, **https://www .sec.gov/Archives/edgar/data/1018724/000101872415000038/amzn-20150331x10q.htm**.

29. Eoin Higgins, "AWS, Microsoft, and Google Each Offer Different Cloud Solutions – Here's How They're Competing on the Market," *IT Brew*, December 7, 2022, **https://www.itbrew.com/stories/2022/12/07/aws-microsoft-and-google-each-offer-different-cloud-solutions-here-s-how-they-re-competing-on-the-market**.

Chapter 19

1. Jan-Benedict E.M. Steenkamp and Nirmalya Kumar, "Don't Be Undersold!," *Harvard Business Review*, December 2009, **https://hbr.org/2009/12/dont-be-undersold**.

2. Xan Rice, "The Aldi Effect: How One Discount Supermarket Transformed the Way Britain Shops," *The Guardian*, March 5, 2019, **https://www.theguardian .com/business/2019/mar/05/long-read-aldi-discount-supermarket-changed-britain-shopping**.

3. Zoe Wood, "'Big Four No More': Where Now for UK Grocers as Aldi Overtakes Morrisons?," *The Guardian,* September 17, 2022, **https://www.theguardian .com/business/2022/sep/17/big-four-uk-grocers-aldi-morrisons-cost-of-living-crisis**.

4. Daniel Ariely, *Predictably Irrational* (HarperCollins Publishers, 2009), chapter 3.

5. Mathematically speaking, the offerings of established firms have lower price elasticities than the offerings of new entrants.

6. Richard Backwell, "Intuit Founder Scott Cook: Keeping the Books on Innovation," *Globe and Mail*, January 20, 2013, **https://www.theglobeandmail .com/report-on-business/careers/careers-leadership/intuit-founder-scott-cook-keeping-the-books-on-innovation/article7562453/**.

7. This retelling is based on the author's experience as well as discussions with Brad Smith in 2022.
8. Based on data on business formations from the US Census Bureau.
9. Andrea Hsu, "New Businesses Soared to Record Highs in 2021. Here's a Taste of One of Them," NPR, January 12, 2022, **https://www.npr.org/2022/01/12/1072057249/new-business-applications-record-high-great-resignation-pandemic-entrepreneur**.
10. Based on discussions with Brad Smith in 2022.
11. "Intuit Works for Business: QuickBooks 2008 Now Available," press release, Intuit, September 24, 2007, **https://investors.intuit.com/news/news-details/2007/Intuit-Works-for-Business-QuickBooks-2008-Now-Available/default.aspx**.
12. "Intuit QuickBooks 2009 Hits Milestone with Fifth Consecutive PC Magazine Editors' Choice Award: Review Concludes QuickBooks Is 'Superior' to Competitors," *PR News,* November 6, 2008, **https://www.prweb.com/releases/pc_magazine/intuit_QuickBooks/prweb1580194.htm**.
13. "Free for Small Teams to Achieve Big Dreams,"Atlassian, 2023, **https://www.atlassian.com/software/free**.
14. Erick Schonfeld, "Evernote Stats: One Million Registered Users, 360,000 Active, 13,755 Paid," *Tech Crunch,* May 21, 2009, **https://techcrunch.com/2009/05/21/evernote-stats-one-million-registered-users-360000-active-13500-paid/**.
15. Alex Hern, "Evernote Users Vent Anger after It Cuts Free Tier and Raises Prices," *The Guardian,* June 30, 2016, **https://www.theguardian.com/technology/2016/jun/30/evernote-users-vent-anger-after-it-cuts-free-tier-and-raises-prices**.
16. Stephen Shankland, "How Evernote Raised Prices – and Still More of Us Signed Up," *CNET,* October 11, 2017, **https://www.cnet.com/tech/services-and-software/evernote-raised-prices-got-more-of-us-to-sign-up/**.
17. Ina Fried, "Microsoft Killing Off Office Accounting Product," *CNET*, October 30, 2009, **https://www.cnet.com/culture/microsoft-killing-off-office-accounting-product/**.

Chapter 20

1. Frans de Waal, "Moral Behavior in Primates," YouTube, **https://www.ted.com/talks/frans_de_waal_moral_behavior_in_animals?language=en**.
2. Sally Blount, "Whoever Said Markets Were Fair?," *Negotiation Journal* 16 (2000): 237–252.
3. Sarah Maxwell, *The Price Is Wrong* (Hoboken, NJ: John Wiley & Sons, 2008).

4. "Amazon Pricing Flap," *CNN Money*, September 28, 2000, **https://money .cnn.com/2000/09/28/technology/amazon/**.

5. Joseph Turow, Lauren Feldman, and Kimberly Meltzer, "Open to Exploitation: America's Shoppers Online and Offline," *A Report from the Annenberg Public Policy Center of the University of Pennsylvania*, **https://repository .upenn.edu/cgi/viewcontent.cgi?article=1035&context=asc_papers**.

6. Ibid.

7. Ibid.

8. Jagrook Dawra, Kanupriya Katyal, and Vipin Gupta, "'Can You Do Something About the Price?' – Exploring the Indian Deal and Bargaining-Prone Customer," *Journal of Consumer Marketing* 32, no. 5 (August 2015): 356–366, **https://www.researchgate.net/publication/281164118_Can_you_do_ something_about_the_price_-_Exploring_the_Indian_deal_and_ bargaining-prone_customer**.

9. Lothar Katz, "Negotiating International Business – Germany," in *Negotiating International Business – The Negotiator's Reference Guide to 50 Countries Around the World,* (CreateSpace, 2017), **http://www.leadershipcrossroads .com/mat/cou/Germany.pdf**.

10. Jerod Coker and Jean-Manuel Izaret, "Progressive Pricing: The Ethical Case for Price Personalization," *Journal of Business Ethics* 173 (2021): 387–398, **https://doi.org/10.1007/s10551-020-04545-x**.

11. Juan M. Elegido, "The Just Price as the Price Obtainable in an Open Market," *Journal of Business Ethics* 130, no. 3 (2015): 557–572.

12. James Gordley, "The Just Price: The Aristotelian Tradition and John Rawls," *European Review of Contract Law*, October 9, 2015, **https://www.degruyter .com/document/doi/10.1515/ercl-2015-0013/pdf**.

13. Milton Friedman, *Price Theory* (Routledge, 2017), Kindle edition, 17. Originally published by Taylor and Francis, 1962.

14. "Roundtable on 'Price Discrimination,'" Organisation for Economic Co-operation and Development, November 21, 2016, DAF/COMP/WD(2016)69, **https://one.oecd.org/document/DAF/COMP/WD(2016)69/en/pdf**.

15. Ronald J. Baker, *Implementing Value Pricing: A Radical Business Model for Professional Firms* (Hoboken, NJ: John Wiley & Sons), Kindle edition, 102.

16. Ian Ayres, "Fair Driving: Gender and Race Discrimination in Retail Car Negotiations," *Harvard Law Review* 104, no. 4 (1991): 817–872.

17. Ian Ayres and P. Siegelman, "Race and Gender Discrimination in Bargaining for a New Car," *American Economic Review* 85, no. 3 (1995): 304–321.

18. Chanjin Chung and Samuel L. Myers, Jr., "Do the Poor Pay More for Food? An Analysis of Grocery Store Availability and Food Price Disparities," *Journal of Consumer Affairs* 33, no. 3 (1999): 276–296.

19. Douglas Heller and Michelle Styczynski, "Major Auto Insurers Raise Rates Based on Economic Factors: Low- and Moderate-Income Drivers

Charged Higher Premiums," Consumer Federation of America, June 2016, **https://consumerfed.org/wp-content/uploads/2016/06/6-27-16-Auto-Insurance-and-Economic-Status_Report.pdf**.

20. Walid F. Gellad, Niteesh K. Choudhry, Mark W. Friedberg, M. Alan Brookhart, Jennifer S. Haas, and William H. Shrank, "Variation in Drug Prices at Pharmacies: Are Prices Higher in Poorer Areas?," *Health Services Research* 44, no. 2 Part 1 (2009): 606–617.
21. Blount, "Whoever Said Markets Were Fair?"
22. Maxwell, *The Price Is Wrong*.
23. Jean-Manuel Izaret and Just Schürmann, "Why Progressive Pricing Is Becoming a Competitive Necessity," Boston Consulting Group, January 17, 2019, **https://www.bcg.com/publications/2019/why-progressive-pricing-becoming-competitive-necessity**.

Chapter 21

1. "Business and Industry Sector Ratings," Gallup, August 23, 2022, **https://news.gallup.com/poll/12748/business-industry-sector-ratings.aspx**.
2. Francesca Bruce, "New German Law Tightens Volume Agreements & Links Prices to Wastage," *Pharma Intelligence*, November 16, 2022, **https://pink.pharmaintelligence.informa.com/PS147324/New-German-Law-Tightens-Volume-Agreements--Links-Prices-To-Wastage**.
3. Anindya Ghose, *Tap: Unlocking the Mobile Economy* (Cambridge, MA: MIT Press, 2017), Kindle edition.
4. Diane Bartz, "Congress to Hold Hearing on Ticketmaster Problems after Taylor Swift Debacle," Reuters, November 22, 2022, **https://www.reuters.com/technology/us-congress-hold-hearing-ticketing-industry-ticketmaster-problems-selling-taylor-2022-11-22/**.

Chapter 22

1. 5th Annual Global Health Economics Colloquium held at the University of California, San Francisco, Institute for Global Health Sciences, February 9, 2018, **https://globalhealthsciences.ucsf.edu/event/5th-annual-global-health-economics-colloquium**.
2. "Hepatitis C," fact sheet, World Health Organization, June 24, 2022, **https://www.who.int/news-room/fact-sheets/detail/hepatitis-c**.
3. "HIV," The Global Health Observatory, World Health Organization, 2023, **https://www.who.int/data/gho/data/themes/hiv-aids**.

4. Ashley Welch, "The Most Deadly Infectious Disease in America Today," *CBS News*, May 4, 2016, **https://www.cbsnews.com/news/hepatitis-c-the-most-deadly-infectious-disease-in-america/**.

5. David L. Thomas, "State of the Hepatitis C Virus Care Cascade," *Clinical Liver Disease: A Multimedia Review Journal* 16, no. 1 (July 21, 2020), **https://www.ncbi.nlm.nih.gov/pmc/articles/PMC7373772/**.

6. Rich Hutchinson, Pedro Valencia, Shana Topp, and Thomas Eisenhart, "Hepatitis C: Common, Deadly, and Curable," Boston Consulting Group, September 18, 2017, **https://www.bcg.com/publications/2017/health-care-payers-providers-hepatitis-c-common-deadly-curable**.

7. Kohtaro Ooka, James J. Connolly, and Joseph K. Lim. "Medicaid Reimbursement for Oral Direct Antiviral Agents for the Treatment of Chronic Hepatitis C." *American Journal of Gastroenterology* 112, no. 6 (2017).

8. Allison D. Marshall et al., "Restrictions for Reimbursement of Interferon-Free Direct-Acting Antiviral Drugs for HCV Infection in Europe," *The Lancet Gastroenterology & Hepatology* 3, no. 2 (February 2018): P125–133.

9. 5th Annual Global Health Economics Colloquium.

10. Ibid.

11. Ibid.

12. David W. Matthews, Samantha Coleman, Homie Razavi, and Jean-Manuel Izaret, "The Payer License Agreement, or 'Netflix Model,' for Hepatitis C Virus Therapies Enables Universal Treatment Access, Lowers Costs and Incentivizes Innovation and Competition," *Liver International*, March 15, 2022, **https://doi.org/10.1111/liv.15245**.

13. Jean-Manuel Izaret, Dave Matthews, and Mark Lubkeman, "Aligning Economic Incentives to Eradicate Diseases," Boston Consulting Group, January 7, 2019, **https://www.bcg.com/publications/2019/aligning-economic-incentives-to-eradicate-diseases**.

14. Matthews et al., "The Payer License Agreement, or 'Netflix model.'"

15. "Finn Partners National Survey Reveals How Fragmented Health System Places Greater Burden On Patients," *PR Newswire*, February 9, 2016, **https://www.prnewswire.com/news-releases/finn-partners-national-survey-reveals-how-fragmented-health-system-places-greater-burden-on-patients-300217167.html**.

16. Keith Alcorn, "Australia Shows an Alternative to Rationing Hepatitis C Treatment," Aidsmap, June 6, 2016, **https://www.aidsmap.com/news/jun-2016/australia-shows-alternative-rationing-hepatitis-c-treatment**.

17. Suerie Moon and Elise Erickson, "Universal Medicine Access through Lump-Sum Remuneration – Australia's Approach to Hepatitis C," *New England Journal of Medicine* 380, no. 7 (February 14, 2019).

18. Jisoo A. Kwon, Gregory J. Dore, Behzad Hajarizadeh, Maryam Alavi, Heather Valerio, Jason Grebely, Rebecca Guy, and Richard T. Gray, "Australia Could Miss the WHO Hepatitis C Virus Elimination Targets Due to Declining Treatment Uptake and Ongoing Burden of Advanced Liver Disease Complications,"

PLoS ONE 16, no. 9 (2021): e0257369, **https://www.ncbi.nlm.nih.gov/pmc/
articles/PMC8445464/**

19. Moon and Erickson, "Universal Medicine Access through Lump-Sum Remu-
    neration."
20. Nicholas Florko, "With a Promising New Plan to Pay for Pricey Cures, Two
    States Set Out to Eliminate Hepatitis C. But Cost Hasn't Been the Biggest Prob-
    lem," *STAT*, September 13, 2022, **https://www.statnews.com/2022/09/13/
    louisiana-washington-hep-c-investigation/?utm_source=STAT+
    Newsletters&utm_campaign=f559d53bf7-Daily_Recap&utm_medium
    =email&utm_term=0_8cab1d7961-f559d53bf7-151693221.**
21. Ibid.
22. Ibid.
23. Ibid.
24. Jennifer Abassi, "Former NIH Director Francis S. Collins on the New White
    House Plan to Eliminate Hepatitis C," *JAMA*, 329, no. 15 (March 9, 2023): 1246–
    1247, **https://jamanetwork.com/journals/jama/fullarticle/2802535**.

Chapter 23

1. Bill Gates, "The One Thing I Hope People Take Away from My Climate Book,"
   GatesNotes (blog), February 14, 2021, **https://www.gatesnotes.com/
   Lowering-Green-Premiums**.
2. Randi Kronthal-Sacco and Tensie Whelan, "Sustainable Market Share Index:
   2021 Report," NYU Stern Center for Sustainable Business, April 2022, **https://
   www.stern.nyu.edu/sites/default/files/assets/documents/FINAL%
   202021%20CSB%20Practice%20Forum%20website_0.pdf**.
3. Compare Models, Tesla, 2023, **https://www.tesla.com/compare**.
4. Ford, 2023, **https://www.ford.com/**.
5. Kronthal-Sacco and Whelan, "Sustainable Market Share Index."
6. "Renault Raises EV Targets, Pledges to Lower Battery Costs," *Automotive
   News Europe*, June 30, 2021, **https://europe.autonews.com/automakers/
   renault-raises-ev-targets-pledges-lower-battery-costs**.

Chapter 24

1. Shell and BCG, "The Voluntary Carbon Market: 2022 Insights and Trends," Shell
   and Boston Consulting Group, 2022, **https://www.shell.com/shellenergy/
   othersolutions/carbonmarketreports/_jcr_content/root/main/section/
   simple_1854223447/simple/call_to_action/links/item0.stream/16783
   04843217/3312c86506af1c43a3eb05e11bfdab50ce388d16/shellbcg-the-
   voluntary-carbon-market-2022-insights-and-trends-eight-march-
   2023.pdf**.

2. Silvia Favasuli and Vandana Sebastian, "Voluntary Carbon Markets: How They Work, How They're Priced and Who's Involved," *S&P Global Commodity Insight*, June 10, 2021, **https://www.spglobal.com/commodityinsights/en/market-insights/blogs/energy-transition/061021-voluntary-carbon-markets-pricing-participants-trading-corsia-credits**.

3. Scope 3 encompasses emissions that are not produced by the company itself, and not the result of activities from assets owned or controlled by them, but by those that it's indirectly responsible for, up and down its value chain.

4. "The Father Of Conjoint Analysis: Paul Green, Professor," *Wharton Magazine*, July 1, 2007, **https://magazine.wharton.upenn.edu/issues/anniversary-issue/the-father-of-conjoint-analysis-paul-green-professor/**.

5. Additionality is a key concept in the quality of a carbon credit. It refers to the idea that a carbon reduction project should be additional to what would have occurred in the absence of the project. In other words, the project should result in emissions reductions that would not have happened otherwise.

6. Analogous simplified version of the Carbon Credit Quality Initiative (CCQI) scoring system, **https://carboncreditquality.org/**. CCQI, founded by EDF, World Wildlife Fund-US, and Oeko-Institut, provides transparent information on the quality of carbon credits.

7. The Science-Based Targets initiative is a global initiative that encourages and supports businesses in setting ambitious greenhouse gas reduction targets that are grounded in scientific evidence. The SBTi provides guidance, tools, and resources for companies to develop and validate their targets, and helps them align with the Paris Agreement's goal of limiting global warming to well below 2 degrees Celsius above pre-industrial levels. The initiative is a collaboration between CDP, the United Nations Global Compact (UNGC), the World Resources Institute (WRI), and the WWF (World Wide Fund for Nature).

Chapter 25

1. "Become a Girl Scout," Girl Scouts of the United States of America, 2022, **https://www.girlscouts.org/en/get-involved/become-a-girl-scout.html**.

2. "Financial Empowerment and Entrepreneurship," Girl Scouts of America/FINRA Investor Education Foundation, 2022, **https://www.girlscouts.org/content/dam/gsusa/forms-and-documents/cookies/resources/Girl-Scouts-Financial-Empowerment-and-Entrepreneurship-Program.pdf**.

3. "Where Cookie Money Goes," Girl Scouts of Minnesota and Wisconsin River Valleys, 2023, **https://www.girlscoutsrv.org/en/cookies/about-girl-scout-cookies/where-cookie-money-goes.html**.

4. "Who We Are," Out of the Closet Thrift Stores, 2023, **https://outofthecloset .org/**.

5. "The Maji Solutions," *Project Maji,* 2023, **https://www.projectmaji.org/ the-maji-solution**.

6. Richard Thaler, "Toward a Positive Theory of Consumer Choice," *Journal of Economic Behavior & Organization* 1, no. 1 (March 1980): 39–60, **https:// www.sciencedirect.com/science/article/pii/0167268180900517**.

7. Hal R. Arkes and Catherine Blumer, "The Psychology of Sunk Cost," *Organizational Behavior and Human Decision Processes* 35, no. 1 (February 1985): 124–140, **https://www.sciencedirect.com/science/article/abs/ pii/0749597885900494**.

8. "The Price Is Wrong: Charging Small Fees Dramatically Reduces Access to Important Products for the Poor," *Bulletin*, Abdul Latif Jameel Poverty Action Lab, April 2011, **https://poverty-action.org/sites/default/files/ publications/the_price_is_wrong_policy_briefcase.pdf**.

9. "Madagascar," The World Bank, March 2023, **https://data.worldbank.org/ country/MG**.

10. Alison B. Comfort and Paul J. Krezanoski, "The Effect of Price on Demand for and Use of Bednets: Evidence from a Randomized Experiment in Madagascar," *Health Policy and Planning* 32, no. 2 (August 23, 2016): 178–193, **https:// academic.oup.com/heapol/article/32/2/178/2555424**.

11. Jim Finkle, "Nonprofit Group Hikes Price of '$100 Laptop,'" Reuters, September 14, 2007, **https://www.reuters.com/article/us-laptop-children/ nonprofit-group-hikes-price-of-100-laptop-idUSN1427617320070915**.

12. John McMillan and David Hanley, "Grameen Bank," Stanford Graduate School of Business, Case No. SM116, 2003, **https://www.gsb.stanford.edu/ faculty-research/case-studies/grameen-bank**.

13. "Evolution of Microfinance," Kompanion Financial Group, Yale School of Management, Yale Case #J11-01 (October 4, 2017), **https://vol11.cases .som.yale.edu/kompanion-financial-group/microfinance/evolution- microfinance**.

14. Stephen C. Smith, *Case Studies in Economic Development*, third ed. (George Washington University, 2003).

15. Hari Srinivas, "MICRO-FACTS: Data Snapshots on Microfinance," GDRC Research Output. Kobe, Japan: Global Development Research Center, accessed March 23, 2023, **https://www.gdrc.org/icm/data/d-snapshot.html**.

16. "About Grameen Bank (GB)," Grameen Bank, **https://grameenbank.org/ about/introduction**.

17. "FAQ About Playworks' Service Options," Playworks, AmeriCorps, 2023, **https://www.playworks.org/services/faq/**.

Epilogue

1. Stan Choe, "As CEO Pay Grows Even Bigger, So Does Its Complexity," *AP News*, May 26, 2022, **https://apnews.com/article/how-are-ceos-paid-772bbf85 88097eb1cbe2d9435a795b77**.

2. "Executives Are Rewarded Handsomely," *The Economist,* February 22, 2020, **https://www.economist.com/business/2020/02/20/executives-are-rewarded-handsomely**.

3. "Minimum Wages in Times of Rising Inflation," OECD, December 2022, **https://www.oecd.org/employment/Minimum-wages-in-times-of-rising-inflation.pdf**.

4. Drew DeSilver, "The U.S. Differs from Most Other Countries in How It Sets Its Minimum Wage," Pew Research Center, May 20, 2021, **https://www.pewresearch.org/fact-tank/2021/05/20/the-u-s-differs-from-most-other-countries-in-how-it-sets-its-minimum-wage/**.

Acknowledgments

Stepping back and thinking about all the individuals who have contributed to the development of this book is humbling. Decades of client engagements and discussions are the source of our inspiration and experience with pricing, value creation, and growth. Thousands of colleagues have shared insights and contributed ideas to our practice and started the process of crystallizing the ideas in this book. It is impossible to thank them all individually, but we want them to know we are grateful for their diverse and numerous contributions.

When we started this project, we sometimes conceptualized it as the unified theory of pricing. Let's start by recognizing some of the seminal thinkers of pricing as a management discipline. They have established a rich foundation of theoretical frameworks and practical case studies that educated and inspired us. Without being exhaustive, we want to recognize some pioneers such as Thomas Nagle, Hermann Simon, Kent Monroe, and Ron Baker and thank them for the clarity of their thinking and the evangelization of the discipline. We have been lucky to cross paths with a number of pricing authors and experts. Wasim Azhar, Reed and Catherine Holden, Rafi Mohammed, Eric Mitchell, Ron Wilcox, Rob Docters, Oded Koenigsberg . . . we have learned a lot from our rich, sometimes long, conversations, and we thank you. It was a pleasure to collaborate on our Netflix model with Homie Razavi and Samantha Coleman from the Center for Disease Analysis; their expertise on health care pricing and modeling is impressive.

We received very valuable support from the Boston Consulting Group (BCG) senior management team over the years. CEOs Hans Paul Buerkner, Rich Lesser, and Christoph Schweizer provided continuous encouragement for both the development of our pricing practice and this book. Martin Reeves and François Candelon supported the research programs with the BCG Henderson Institute (BHI). Intellectual giants like George Stalk and Phillip Evans have deeply shaped the way we think about business strategy. Miki Tsusaka, the seminal leader of the Marketing, Sales, and Pricing practice, has been a personal mentor and unflinching supporter.

Mark Kistulinec, Sylvain Duranton, and Just Schürmann were part of the initial team that started to focus on pricing, and their ideas have thoroughly shaped our thinking. We are in debt to Rich Hutchinson, who was also a pioneer of the BCG pricing practice, for more ways than we could enumerate. His support ranges from persistent advocacy for the topic to serving as an inspiring thought partner for the intellectual agenda of this book.

Finally, this book is also the result of practical contributions of many colleagues who have worked tirelessly to bring it to the world.

First in this group must be Frank Luby, who has been an indispensable and tireless catalyst to formalize the ideas and commit them to paper. The depth of his pricing experience has been critical to mature the ideas in this book and to push us to differentiate them from conventional pricing orthodoxy. Over several years of writing together, we also have benefited immensely from his ability to clearly articulate in prose what only existed as PowerPoint concepts.

Many of our colleagues, with whom we have built the pricing practice, have dedicated their professional lives to pricing. They have shaped our thinking over many years and contributed most of the stories in this book. They are recognized as co-authors in almost all the chapters, and have made enormous contributions, both intellectually and with their friendship and encouragement. Stephan Liozu, Ekkehard Stadie, and Marco Bertini, who are all deep pricing experts, have shared ideas along the development of this project and provided detailed and valuable feedback, particularly to Part I.

Four colleagues led the research with BHI and helped shape the ideas in Part IV about the societal impact of strategic pricing. Dave Matthews led all the work related to pricing in health care, notably our study of the Netflix pricing model. Christian Haakonsen and John Pineda, both passionate about climate change, led the work on the green premium and voluntary carbon markets. Jerod Coker led the research on pricing fairness, progressive pricing, and all the ethical issues related to pricing. He also deserves credit for the Hexagon, which he formalized one morning by connecting two triangles. The intellectual stimulation that came from working with all of you was the joy of a professional lifetime. We are lucky to count you as friends.

We also want to thank the team that has worked directly on the book over the past few months. Ricard Vila and Marie Costa de Beauregard have been intellectual thought partners and orchestrators of all the contributors to the book. Manal El Mehdi, Ery Zhu, Ana Upyr, and Diego Pedrayes helped with the documentation and research. Ezra Blocker helped proofread the manuscript. Sara Santoro, Mallorie Eurton, and Lauren Warr from our Design Studio team helped with the illustrations. Mike Lear, Alanna Minor, Paa Coss, and Ruby Yang from BrightHouse designed the book cover and visual and branding architecture. We thank you for all your creativity, patience, and conscientiousness. You made this fun.

We also give thanks to the broader BCG community, including current colleagues, alumni, clients, and partners. It is our honor to work with you to continue unlocking the potential of those who advance the world.

About the Authors

Jean-Manuel Izaret (JMI)

JMI is a senior partner and global leader of the marketing, sales, and pricing practice at the Boston Consulting Group (BCG). Before that, he led the pricing practice for more than a decade.

JMI has devoted his entire career to helping companies grow and has been involved with pricing from the beginning. Before joining BCG, he received a PhD and an engineering degree from École Centrale in Paris and a master's in economics and finance from Institut d'Études Politiques in Paris (Sciences Po). His first pricing experience came with gasoline when he worked for Shell in France. He used analytical tools to run promotions and optimize prices station by station. This gave him a taste of the complexity and potential impact of pricing as a discipline. That taste never soured. After joining BCG, he had the opportunity to work consistently around the globe and across industries on pricing and growth projects.

After moving to San Francisco, he focused on the technology sector, where pricing model questions are a fundamental part of a company's business model. In 2016, he became a fellow at BCG's Bruce Henderson Institute (BHI) and conducted research on pricing model innovation in sectors as varied as biopharma, media, industrials, financial services, and consumer services. He also started to work on whether new pricing and economic models could help solve broader societal issues such as climate change or education.

JMI lives in Berkeley with his wife Christine and is the proud father of two young men, Axel and Ernest.

Arnab Sinha

Arnab is a senior partner and managing director at BCG. He leads the pricing practice in the consumer space and in North America.

Arnab focuses on helping companies transform their pricing capabilities to deliver sustained impact and achieve competitive advantages. Prior to BCG, Arnab received a PhD from the Massachusetts Institute of Technology. He has also worked at Intel, where he was a lithography engineer, and at Comcast, where he worked in marketing analytics. Arnab was drawn to pricing at BCG because of its unique combination of strategic insight blended with precise analytical rigor. At BCG, he has worked on pricing across many sectors and on all the continents (except Antarctica).

Arnab moved to Philadelphia after living in Mumbai, Boston, Portland, and Washington, DC. He continues to serve clients in industries such as airlines, automobiles, beverages, food, luxury, restaurants, and biopharma. He has co-developed BCG's intellectual property and software for AI-driven price and promotion optimization, working with a team of BCG's finest data scientists and engineers.

Arnab lives in Center City, Philadelphia, with his wife Varsha and is the proud father of two boys, Arjun and Saahil.

Index

Page numbers followed by *f* refer to figures.